§ 2254 PRO SE GUIDE TO WINNING FEDERAL RELIEF

BY: RAYMOND E. LUMSDEN

"Men are not prisoners of fate, but only prisoners of their own minds."
– Former U.S. President Franklin D. Roosevelt, Pan American Day Address (1937)

Freebird Publishers
www.FreebirdPublishers.com

Freebird Publishers
221 Pearl St., Ste. 541, North Dighton, MA 02764
Info@FreebirdPublishers.com
www.FreebirdPublishers.com

§ 2254 Pro Se Guide to Winning Federal Relief
By Raymond E. Lumsden

All Freebird Publishers titles, imprints, and distributed lines are available at special quantity discounts for bulk purchases for sales promotions, premiums, fundraising, educational, or institutional use.

ISBN-978-1-952159-31-2

Printed in the United States of America

DEDICATION ★★★

To Anthony, Alyssa, Joshua, and Rylee … my children: It is my endless desire to return to you that compels me to fight forward in proving my innocence. May your hearts always show you the truth, and may you always feel my love and pride for you.

To my educators and counselors, who have worked tirelessly to manage the endless "red-tape" and rules of incarceration in an effort to facilitate my correspondence curriculums: My respect and appreciation is endless, and my accomplishments belong to you.

To Betty and Joe Ellis, for your friendship and generosity: I am glad that I have been able to achieve much overdue relief in your legal pursuits and wish you both nothing less than everything.

To Rhonda Lee, for your spirit, love, and endless loyalty. I love you, Rhodelia! Ride-or-Die; RL Inc.

Finally, to all who have purchased my books and written to tell me about your results, experiences, etc., I truly enjoy reading all of your success stories. I hope that you will share your lessons and experiences with others around you who are seeking direction and assistance. Your letters have proven to me that there indeed is a particular and necessary need for my writing, which only compels me to press forward in those endeavors.

– R.

"Men are not prisoners of fate, but only prisoners of their own minds."

– Former U.S. President Franklin D. Roosevelt, Pan American Day Address (1937)

FOREWORD ★★★

There is a common misconception in American society that those charged with a criminal offense are provided every possible act of protection and defense against wrongful conviction. Further, wrongful convictions and mistaken judgments are rare. Those perceptions are very misplaced indeed since such a system exists only in theory. In practice, human nature, frailties, and inadequacies derail the system's design.

Even after thousands of Actual Innocence and Wrongful Conviction cases have been won throughout the United States, society is still blind, prejudiced, and quick to misjudge. Prosecutors who have withheld evidence, lied, manipulated, and falsified evidence and testimony have done so without oversight or accountability. Still, none of this compares to the level of indifference and prejudice imposed by the United States Appellate Courts, which stand as the last resort to correct these injustices.

Indifference and prejudice you will face in your § 2254 action. On the other hand, inmates share an immense amount of responsibility for that inherent prejudice and indifference due to all of the bad, non-meritorious, vague, and flat-out atrocious legal pleadings and writs being filed. This was the sole purpose of establishing the AEDPA and PLRA in 1996: *to stop these ridiculous filings*.

Of the most delusional filings is that of "Sovereignty" that inmates pursue when all other hope is gone. For the life of me I will never understand how any person with common sense could ever believe such a ridiculous notion as Sovereignty. It simply *does not exist*. It is also illegal, an abuse-of-writ to file such pleadings, and the courts in every state, as well as the Federal courts, can cite you, take away good time credit, and charge you. See: *Jones v. Caruso*, 569 F.3d at 261 (6th Cir. 2009); *Monroe v. Beard*, 536 F.3d at 208 n. 11 (3d Cir. 2008). This is also why prisons can and do forbid UCC materials, books, and writings. Again, Sovereignty does not exist, so stop filing these ridiculous pleadings that only destroy any chance you have at filing any real and meritorious claim.

More so, stop allowing the prison "writ writers" to take advantage of you and your commissary account by convincing you and giving you false hope that you are "Sovereign" or could be released from prison. *It has never happened and will never happen*. My efforts to help inmates and to offer a path to obtaining relief are becoming more difficult every day due to the enormous volume of trash being filed in courts across America. These untrained, unqualified "writ writers" are only seeking a quick payday from those they are able to con into allowing them to "handle" their legal acts.

And no, I'm not just talking about "Sovereignty" filings, I am also talking about the horrendously written, outlined, spelled, and composed motions, pleadings, and habeas corpus writs, etc. If the so-called "writ writers" don't stop, it will effectively kill all possibilities for those who have meritorious and valid claims to raise. The Courts simply will not read future motions and writs from an inmate, period, if it continues. It is getting bad, and the Courts are effectively sick of it. And to be truthful, so am I. I am truly working hard to help as many as I can to obtain relief … *and I am qualified, certified, and trained.*

Frequenting a prison Law Library does not make you qualified to write someone else's legal pleadings, nor does completing a second-rate Paralegal Course.

Here, the § 2254 habeas corpus is likely the last chance for most. Once the U.S. district court has denied your petition and likely your Certificate of Appealability (C.O.A.), you have less than a one percent chance of obtaining relief from your circuit court unless they've granted a C.O.A. themselves.

Therefore, it is likely *the most* important of any motion, legal pleading, or writ you will ever file in relationship to your conviction and sentence.

The § 2254 itself is a gambit like no other, with zero exceptions. Even the Federal § 2255 fails to meet the extensive requirements and expectations of the § 2254. Hence its nickname: "The Great Writ." This is likely due to the *millions* of more state convictions than federal convictions every year. And so naturally, there will be far more state post-conviction appeals filed than federal, thus requiring far more rules, procedures, and expectations, which I will attempt to address throughout this book.

It is important that you have a very firm grasp of these rules and expectations *before* you file your petition in the Court. You certainly will not receive any mercy or assistance from the court or the State Attorney General's Office, who will be fighting you all the way … and aggressively so. If not, you can expect a very quick end to your § 2254 action.

You absolutely can obtain relief in the federal court if you have sound and meritorious claims to present there. In fact, just yesterday, I assisted a fellow inmate in obtaining relief in a § 2254 related to parole issues. When he approached me in the chow hall with a shit-eating grin on his face and an envelope, I knew we had prevailed. The federal court ordered his parole be reinstated, and he will be heading home to his family soon. What is important about that case is that he had previously been denied by the same court after another inmate (writ writer) had filed another § 2254 petition on his behalf … incorrectly.

After reviewing the case, I requested permission to file an S.O.S. (Secondary Petition) from the court, which they granted based on his medical history, mental incapacities, etc. And so, as you can see, you absolutely can achieve success in the Federal courts if you do so correctly. This story is only one of dozens about which I can tell you.

Due to the delicate nature of his situation, I will refrain from sharing his name or case results here. I am quite certain that he would not care and would probably insist that I share his story; I feel that doing so may carry negative consequences that I wish to prevent for him … consequences that he himself may not understand as possible. The important part for all of you is that relief can be achieved in § 2254 if you do so correctly.

But again, it will not be an easy task, especially for those who have absolutely no understanding of legal procedures at the federal level. My hope is that this book will assist you in that regard.

Fighting your conviction and sentence is a way for you to push back against any injustice, and you should do so aggressively and accurately. Far too many simply file the petition itself along with a couple of motions and then wait for the inevitable denial, which is certain to come in that situation. Those people are usually the "writ writers" or the guilty, who are simply "throwing shit at the wall," so to speak.

Those of us who truly want justice and have credible and meritorious claims to advance fight with everything we have – and we never, ever, give up. This begins with learning the steps, researching every day until we are capable of advancing those claims and learning the rules and process. We contact every resource available, documents, records, evidence, and other proof to back up our claims. We take an active role in what has happened to us, and we fight, fight, fight. We are usually the innocent and unjustly treated ones.

By "wrongfully convicted and innocent," I am addressing those who:

1. Were convicted of crimes they did not commit,
2. Were overcharged: Guilty of lesser offenses,
3. Were ineffectively represented at trial

4. Were given an illegal sentence, etc.

In closing, I want to state that in no way should this book, or any other books, be substituted for legal counsel where possible. If you have the means to hire an attorney to handle your § 2254, you should not hesitate to do so immediately. You stand a far better chance of obtaining relief through hired counsel. If that is not an option for you, and you are forced to take on the responsibility for yourself … I recommend that you purchase my book, *The Pro Se Guide to Legal Research & Writing*, prior to your filing the petition for writ of habeas corpus §2254. It will teach you fundamental and critical legal research and writing techniques needed to advance a proper and effective § 2254.

Since the Texas Department of Criminal Justice does not allow us to obtain or possess the legal pleadings of other inmates we are not assisting, I am unable to provide actual documents in this book. Instead, I have chosen out of necessity to show examples of the forms, motions, and pleadings you will need.

I cannot overemphasize the use of common sense and caution when you are preparing the § 2254 petition, motions, and pleadings. You should never allow your emotions or moods to show in your writings and pleadings. And, as I have continually preached in all my books, *keep it simple*.

Here again, I assure you that if you follow the contents of this book, your chances of success in your § 2254 endeavors will increase dramatically. Since my first book went to press, I have received literally hundreds of letters, JPay emails, and other communications from *pro se* users and purchasers who have expressed their thanks and appreciation after obtaining the relief they were hoping for or other successes. *You can do this too.*

I am always thankful to receive such communications and feedback, as this has always been my sole purpose in writing these books: to assist those who truly need the help most … *pro se* inmates. I don't care if you are guilty or not since that is not my business. Everyone is entitled to a defense and a fair trial, as well as equal treatment under the laws of this country. If my books have helped obtain that justice and relief, then obviously, there were issues with those cases in the first place. It is, therefore, the system itself that is to blame, and not anything I have presented in my books – even if those who are guilty obtain relief.

As always, I wish you luck, and more so…relief.

3/16/2021

Legal Notice: This book is written and/or published by a prisoner and concerned American citizens. The law prohibits us from providing any legal advice to prisoners. This information is not intended as legal advice or representation, nor should you consider or rely upon it as such. Neither the organization of these people nor any information contained herein is intended to or shall constitute a contract between us and the readers; furthermore, we do not guarantee the accuracy of the court recordings contained in any court. Additionally, your use of this publication should not be construed as creating any relationship with anyone involved with us or anyone whose name may or may not appear in these court filings. Finally, while all provided information was up to date at the time of publication, we cannot guarantee that all information is still current at the time you read this.

★★★ TABLE OF CONTENTS ★★★

INTRODUCTION

§2254, AKA, "*The Big Writ*" as it's known throughout the legal system. In my opinion, the most important Writ that an inmate can or will file in attempting to obtain relief of a State Conviction or Sentence.

In 98% all cases, the decision of the United States District Court in a §2254, is upheld by the Circuit Appeals Courts, or any following appeal, etc.

In this book, I have attempted to provide you as much necessary and pending information as I could, without actually *doing* the writ for you. For that part, you are on your own.

I have attempted to include all of the appropriate Motions, letters, and examples as possible, where listing them all would be far too encompassing, etc.

In a system designed for failure for a pro se applicant, I have done my best to give you every possible "weapon" in seeking relief. I pray, I have served you well in that endeavor.

Lastly, and again, if you can hire a lawyer...*do so*! If not, then this book should assist you in obtaining the relief you seek and deserve.

Good Luck!

CHAPTER 1
THE RULES OF § 2254

The federal writ of habeas corpus, also called "the Great Writ," has traditionally been a very important part of American history. The United States Constitution states: "The Privilege of the Writ of Habeas Corpus shall not be suspended, unless when in Cases of Rebellion or Invasion the public Safety may require it" *U.S. Constitution, Article 1, Section 9, clause 2.*

Historically, however, the Federal Writ of Habeas Corpus § 2254 has been a fundamental avenue in vindicating and protecting federal constitutional rights and has, on more than one occasion, literally saved a defendant's life. See, *e.g.*, *Kyles v. Whitley*, _____ U.S.____, 115 S. Ct. 1555 (1995). Although the scope of federal habeas corpus has been greatly diminished since the days of the Warren Court, it remains a potent and effective tool that can be used by anyone in obtaining relief from a conviction or sentence in state courts, as well as parole issues in certain states.

The right to federal habeas corpus review of state convictions is governed and codified at 28 U.S.C. Sec. 2241, which is the general grant of power to federal courts to issue writs of habeas corpus, and, more specifically, at 28 U.S.C. Sec. 2254.

Where a person is held in custody pursuant to the judgment of a state court, as is the case with this author, federal review of that case is limited to claims "that he is in custody in violation of the Constitution or laws or treaties of the United States" 28 U.S.C. Sec. 2254(a). (For the purposes of this book, the "he" pronoun is being used as a matter of convenience instead of having to use both he/she randomly. I am simply trying to make it simple and in no way offend anyone of either sex.) State law violations and claims are not cognizable in a federal habeas corpus § 2254 petition.

Thus, after all potential habeas claims have been exhausted in a state habeas corpus proceeding, a prisoner still seeking relief from a conviction and sentence must bring the merits of their claims to the federal court under § 2254. Although the chances of success on habeas corpus are never very good in practice, the federal courts typically provide more careful consideration of habeas corpus petitions than the state courts, especially here in Texas, where a petitioner has already lost at trial and on direct appeal and state habeas corpus proceedings.

However, before the federal courts will reach the merits of a federal habeas corpus petition, the petitioner must (1) meet the traditional requirements for habeas corpus imposed prior to the Antiterrorism and Effective Death Penalty Act (AEDPA) of 1996 and (2) satisfy the new requirements imposed by AEDPA.

This is a substantial burden to meet in all regards.

Briefly, the AEDPA was signed into law by President Bill Clinton in 1996 after passing Congress with an affirmative vote by current President Joe Biden, who was then a Senator for Delaware. It reformed the scope of habeas corpus and included, among other provisions, limits on both the procedural and substantive scope of the writ.

Procedurally, it bans the successive filing of petitions by the same person and requires that defendants put all of their claims into one single appeal. Substantively, it narrows the grounds on which successful habeas claims can be made, allowing claims only to succeed when the convictions are contrary to "clearly established federal law" or an "unreasonable determination of the facts in light of the evidence" 28 U.S.C. § 2254.

For your convenience, I have included the *Rules Governing § 2254 Federal Habeas Corpus* here at the end of the Chapter, followed by the *Federal Rules of Civil Procedure.*

Notes:

Rules Governing Section 2254 Cases in the United States District Courts

Rule 1. Scope

(a) Cases Involving a Petition under 28 U.S.C. § 2254. These rules govern a petition for a writ of habeas corpus filed in a United States district court under 28 U.S.C. § 2254 by:
  (1) a person in custody under a state-court judgment who seeks a determination that the custody violates the Constitution, laws, or treaties of the United States; and
  (2) a person in custody under a state-court or federal-court judgment who seeks a determination that future custody under a state-court judgment would violate the Constitution, laws, or treaties of the United States.

(b) Other Cases. The district court may apply any or all of these rules to a habeas corpus petition not covered by Rule 1(a).

Rule 2. The Petition

(a) Current Custody; Naming the Respondent. If the petitioner is currently in custody under a state-court judgment, the petition must name as respondent the state officer who has custody.

(b) Future Custody; Naming the Respondents and Specifying the Judgment. If the petitioner is not yet in custody – but may be subject to future custody – under the state-court judgment being contested, the petition must name as respondents both the officer who has current custody and the attorney general of the state where the judgment was entered. The petition must ask for relief from the state-court judgment being contested.

(c) Form. The petition must:
  (1) specify all the grounds for relief available to the petitioner;
  (2) state the facts supporting each ground;
  (3) state the relief requested;
  (4) be printed, typewritten, or legibly handwritten; and
  (5) be signed under penalty of perjury by the petitioner or by a person authorized to sign it for the petitioner under 28 U.S.C. § 2242.

(d) Standard Form. The petition must substantially follow either the form appended to these rules or a form prescribed by a local district court rule. The clerk must make forms available to petitioners without charge.

(e) Separate Petitions for Judgments of Separate Courts. A petitioner who seeks relief from judgments of more than one state court must file a separate petition covering the judgment or judgments of each court.

Rule 3. Filing the Petition; Inmate Filing

(a) Where to File; Copies; Filing Fee. An original and two copies of the petition must be filed with the clerk and must be accompanied by:
  (1) the applicable filing fee, or
  (2) a motion for leave to proceed *in forma pauperis*, the affidavit required by 28 U.S.C. § 1915, and a certificate from the warden or other appropriate officer of the place of confinement showing the amount of money or securities that the petitioner has in any account in the institution.

(b) Filing. The clerk must file the petition and enter it on the docket.

(c) Time to File. The time for filing a petition is governed by 28 U.S.C. § 2244(d).

(d) Inmate Filing. A paper filed by an inmate confined in an institution is timely if deposited in the institution's internal mailing system on or before the last day for filing. If an institution has a system designed for legal mail, the inmate must use that system to receive the benefit of this rule. Timely filing may be shown by a declaration in compliance with 28 U.S.C. § 1746 or by a notarized statement, either of which must set forth the date of deposit and state that first-class postage has been prepaid.

Rule 4. Preliminary Review; Serving the Petition and Order

The clerk must promptly forward the petition to a judge under the court's assignment procedure, and the judge must promptly examine it. If it plainly appears from the petition and any attached exhibits that the petitioner is not entitled to relief in the district court, the judge must dismiss the petition and direct the clerk to notify the petitioner. If the petition is not dismissed, the judge must order the respondent to file an answer, motion, or other response within a fixed time or to take other action the judge may order. In every case, the clerk must serve a copy of the petition and any order on the respondent and on the attorney general or other appropriate officer of the state involved.

Rule 5. The Answer and the Reply

(a) When required. The respondent is not required to answer the petition unless a judge orders.
(b) Contents: Addressing the Allegations; Stating a Bar. The answer must address the allegations in the petition. In addition, it must state whether any claim in the petition is barred by a failure to exhaust state remedies, a procedural bar, non-retroactivity, or a statute of limitations.
(c) Contents: Transcripts. The answer must also indicate what transcripts (of pretrial, trial, sentencing, or post-conviction proceedings) are available, when they can be furnished and what proceedings have been recorded but not transcribed. The respondent must attach to the answer parts of the transcript that the respondent considers relevant. The judge may order that the respondent furnish other parts of existing transcripts or that parts of untranscribed recordings be transcribed and furnished. If a transcript cannot be obtained, the respondent may submit a narrative summary of the evidence.
(d) Contents: Briefs on Appeal and Opinions. The respondent must also file with the answer a copy of:
 (1) any brief that the petitioner submitted in an appellate court contesting the conviction or sentence or contesting an adverse judgment or order in a post-conviction proceeding;
 (2) any brief that the prosecution submitted in an appellate court relating to the conviction or sentence; and
 (3) the opinions and dispositive orders of the appellate court relating to the conviction or the sentence.
(e) Reply. The petitioner may submit a reply to the respondent's answer or other pleading within a time fixed by the judge.

Rule 6. Discovery

(a) Leave of Court Required. A judge may, for good cause, authorize a party to conduct discovery under the Federal Rules of Civil Procedure and may limit the extent of discovery. If necessary for effective discovery, the judge must appoint an attorney for a petitioner who qualifies to have counsel appointed under 18 U.S.C. § 3006A.
(b) Requesting Discovery. A party requesting discovery must provide reasons for the request. The request must also include any proposed interrogatories and requests for admission and must specify any requested documents.
(c) Deposition Expenses. If the respondent is granted leave to take a deposition, the judge may require

the respondent to pay the travel expenses, subsistence expenses, and fees of the petitioner's attorney to attend the deposition.

Rule 7. Expanding the Record

(a) In General. If the petition is not dismissed, the judge may direct the parties to expand the record by submitting additional materials relating to the petition. The judge may require that these materials be authenticated.
(b) Types of Materials. The materials that may be required include letters predating the filing of the petition, documents, exhibits, and answers under oath to written interrogatories propounded by the judge. Affidavits may also be submitted and considered as part of the record.
(c) Review by the Opposing Party. The judge must give the party against whom the additional materials are offered an opportunity to admit or deny their correctness.

Rule 8. Evidentiary Hearing

(a) Determining Whether to Hold a Hearing. If the petition is not dismissed, the judge must review the answer, any transcripts and records of state-court proceedings, and any materials submitted under Rule 7 to determine whether an evidentiary hearing is warranted.
(b) Reference to a Magistrate Judge. A judge may, under 28 U.S.C. § 636(b), refer the petition to a magistrate judge to conduct hearings and to file proposed findings of fact and recommendations for disposition. When they are filed, the clerk must promptly serve copies of the proposed findings and recommendations to all parties. Within 14 days after being served, a party may file objections as provided by local court rules. The judge must determine de novo any proposed finding or recommendation to which an objection is made. The judge may accept, reject, or modify any proposed finding or recommendation.
(c) Appointing Counsel; Time of Hearing. If an evidentiary hearing is warranted, the judge must appoint an attorney to represent a petitioner who qualifies to have counsel appointed under 18 U.S.C. § 3006A. The judge must conduct the hearing as soon as practicable after giving the attorneys adequate time to investigate and prepare. These rules do not limit the appointment of counsel under Sec. 3006A at any stage of the proceeding.

Rule 9. Second or Successive Petitions

Before presenting a second or successive petition, the petitioner must obtain an order from the appropriate court of appeals authorizing the district court to consider the petition as required by 28 U.S.C. § 2244(b) (3) and (4).

Rule 10. Powers of a Magistrate Judge

A magistrate judge may perform the duties of a district judge under these rules, as authorized under 28 U.S.C. § 636.

Rule 11. Certificate of Appealability; Time to Appeal

(a) Certificate of Appealability. The district court must issue or deny a certificate of appealability when it enters a final order adverse to the applicant. Before entering the final order, the court may direct the parties to submit arguments on whether a certificate should issue. If the court issues a certificate, the court must state the specific issue or issues that satisfy the showing required by 28 U.S.C. § 2253(c) (2). If the court denies a certificate, the parties may not appeal the denial but may seek a certificate from the court of appeals under Federal Rule of Appellate Procedure 22. A motion to reconsider a denial does not extend the time to appeal.

(b) Time to Appeal. Federal Rule of Appellate Procedure 4(a) governs the time to appeal an order entered under these rules. A timely notice of appeal must be filed even if the district court issues a certificate of appealability.

Rule 12. Applicability of the Federal Rules of Civil Procedure

The Federal Rules of Civil Procedure, to the extent that they are not inconsistent with any statutory provisions or these rules, may be applied to a proceeding under these rules.

FEDERAL RULES OF CIVIL PROCEDURE

Rule 1. Scope and Purpose

These rules govern the procedure in all civil actions and proceedings in the United States district courts, except as stated in Rule 81. They should be construed and administered to secure the just, speedy, and inexpensive determination of

Rule 2. One Form of Action

There is one form of action – the civil action.

Rule 3. Commencing an Action

A civil action is commenced by filing a complaint with the court.

Rule 4. Summons

(a) New Contents; Amendments.
(1) *Contents*. A summons must:
(A) name the court and the parties;
(B) be directed to the defendant;
(C) state the name and address of the plaintiff's attorney or – if unrepresented – of the plaintiff;
(D) state the time within which the defendant must appear and defend;
(E) notify the defendant that a failure to appear and defend will result in a default judgment against the defendant for the relief demanded in the complaint;
(F) be signed by the clerk; and
(G) bear the court's seal.
(2) *Amendments*. The court may permit a summons to be amended.

(b) Issuance. On or after filing the complaint, the plaintiff may present a summons to the clerk for signature and seal. If the summons is properly completed, the clerk must sign, seal, and issue it to the plaintiff for service on the defendant. A summons – or a copy of a summons that is addressed to multiple defendants – must be issued for each defendant to be served.

(c) Service.
(1) *In General*. A summons must be served with a copy of the complaint. The plaintiff is responsible for having the summons and complaint served within the time allowed by Rule 4(m) and must furnish the necessary copies to the person who makes service.
(2) *By Whom*. Any person who is at least 18 years old and not a party may serve a summons and complaint.
(3) *By a Marshal or Someone Specially Appointed*. At the plaintiff's request, the court may order that service be made by a United States marshal or deputy marshal or by a person specially appointed by the court. The court must so order if the plaintiff is authorized to proceed *in forma pauperis* under 28 U.S.C. § 1915 or as a seaman under 28 U.S.C. § 1916.

(d) Waiving Service.
(1) *Requesting a Waiver*. An individual, corporation, or association that is subject to service under Rule 4(e), (f), or (h) has a duty to avoid unnecessary expenses of serving the summons. The plaintiff may notify such a defendant that an action has been commenced and request the defendant waives service of a summons. The notice and request must:
(A) be in writing and be addressed:
(i) to the individual defendant; or

(ii) for a defendant subject to service under Rule 4(h), to an officer, a managing or general agent, or any other agent authorized by appointment or by law to receive service of process;
(B) name the court where the complaint was filed;
(C) be accompanied by a copy of the complaint, two copies of a waiver form, and a prepaid means for returning the form;
(D) inform the defendant, using text prescribed in Form 5, of the consequences of waiving or not waiving service;
(E) state the date when the request is sent;
(F) give the defendant a reasonable time of at least 30 days after the request was sent – or at least 60 days if sent to the defendant outside any judicial district of the United States – to return the waiver; and
(G) be sent by first-class mail or other reliable means.

(2) *Failure to Waive*. If a defendant located within the United States fails, without good cause, to sign and return a waiver requested by a plaintiff located within the United States, the court must impose on the defendant:
(A) the expenses later incurred in making service and
(B) the reasonable expenses, including attorney's fees, of any motion required to collect those service expenses.

(3) *Time to Answer After a Waiver*. A defendant who, before being served with process, timely returns a waiver need not serve an answer to the complaint until 60 days after the request was sent – or until 90 days after it was sent to the defendant outside any judicial district of the United States.

(4) *Results of Filing a Waiver*. When the plaintiff files a waiver, proof of service is not required, and these rules apply as if a summons and complaint had been served at the time of filing the waiver.

(5) *Jurisdiction and Venue Not Waived*. Waiving service of a summons does not waive any objection to personal jurisdiction or to venue.

(e) Serving an Individual Within a Judicial District of the United States. Unless federal law provides otherwise, an individual – other than a minor, incompetent person, or a person whose waiver has been filed may be served in a judicial district in the United States by:
(1) following state law for serving a summons in an action brought in courts of general jurisdiction in the state where the district court is located or where service is made; or
(2) doing any of the following:
(A) delivering a copy of the summons and of the complaint to the individual personally;
(B) leaving a copy of each at the individual's dwelling or usual place of abode with someone of suitable age and discretion who resides there; or
(C) delivering a copy of each to an agent authorized by appointment or by law to receive service of process.

(f) Serving an Individual in a Foreign Country. Unless federal law provides otherwise, an individual – other than a minor, an incompetent person, or a person whose waiver has been filed – may be served at a place not within any judicial district of the United States:
(1) by any internationally agreed means of service that is reasonably calculated to give notice, such as those authorized by the Hague Convention on the Service Abroad of Judicial and Extrajudicial Documents;
(2) if there is no internationally agreed means, or if an international agreement allows but does not specify other means, by a method that is reasonably calculated to give notice:

(A) as prescribed by the foreign country's law for service in that country in an action in its courts of general jurisdiction;
(B) as the foreign authority directs in response to a letter rogatory or letter of request; or
(C) unless prohibited by the foreign country's law, by:
(i) delivering a copy of the summons and of the complaint to the individual personally; or
(ii) using any form of mail that the clerk addresses and sends to the individual and that requires a signed receipt; or
(3) by other means not prohibited by international agreement, as the court orders.

(g) Serving a Minor or an Incompetent Person. A minor or an incompetent person in a judicial district of the United States must be served by following state law for serving a summons or like process on such a defendant in an action brought in the courts of general jurisdiction of the state where service is made. A minor or an incompetent person who is not within any judicial district of the United States must be served in the manner prescribed by Rule 4(f) (2) (A), (2) (B), or (f) (3).

(h) Serving a Corporation, Partnership, or Association. Unless federal law provides otherwise or the defendant's waiver has been filed, a domestic or foreign corporation, or a partnership or other unincorporated association that is subject to suit under a common name must be served:
(1) in a judicial district of the United States:
(A) in the manner prescribed by Rule 4(e) (1) for serving an individual; or
(B) by delivering a copy of the summons and of the complaint to an officer, a managing or general agent, or any other agent authorized by appointment or by law to receive service of process and – if the agent is one authorized by statute and the statute so requires – by also mailing a copy of each to the defendant; or
(2) at a place not within any judicial district of the United States, in any manner prescribed by Rule 4(f) for serving an individual, except personal delivery under (f) (2) (C) (i).

(i) Serving the United States and Its Agencies, Corporations, Officers, or Employees.
(1) *United States.* To serve the United States, a party must:
(A)
(i) deliver a copy of the summons and of the complaint to the United States attorney for the district where the action is brought – or to an assistant United States attorney or clerical employee whom the United States attorney designates in a writing filed with the court clerk – or
(ii) send a copy of each by registered or certified mail to the civil-process clerk at the United States attorney's office;
(B) send a copy of each by registered or certified mail to the attorney general of the United States at Washington, D.C.; and
(C) if the action challenges an order of a nonparty agency or officer of the United States, send a copy of each by registered or certified mail to the agency or officer.
(2) *Agency; Corporation: Officer or Employee Sued in an Official Capacity*. To serve a United States agency or corporation, or a United States officer or employee sued only in an official capacity, a party must serve the United States and also send a copy of the summons and of the complaint by registered or certified mail to the agency, corporation, officer, or employee.
(3) *Officer or Employee Sued Individually*. To serve a United States officer or employee sued in an official capacity for an act or omission occurring in connection with duties performed on the United States' behalf (whether or not the officer or employee is also sued in an official capacity), a party must serve the United States and also serve the officer or employee under Rule 4(e), (f), or (g).

(4) *Extending Time.* The court must allow a party the reasonable time to cure its failure to:
(A) serve a person required to be served under Rule 4(i) (2), if the party has served either the United States attorney or the attorney general of the United States; or
(B) serve the United States under Rule 4(i) (3), if the party has served the United States officer or employee.

(j) Serving a Foreign, State, or Local Government.
(1) *Foreign State.* A foreign state or its political subdivision, agency, or instrumentality must be served in accordance with 28 U.S.C. § 1608.
(2) *State or Local Government.* A state, a municipal corporation, or any other state-created governmental organization that is subject to suit must be served by:
(A) delivering a copy of the summons and of the complaint to its chief executive officer; or
(B) serving a copy of each in the manner prescribed by that state's law for serving a summons or like process on such a defendant.

(k) Territorial Limits of Effective Service.
(1) *In General.* Serving a summons or filing a waiver of service establishes personal jurisdiction offer a defendant:
(A) who is subject to the jurisdiction of a court of general jurisdiction in the state where the district court is located;
(B) who is a party joined under Rule 14 or 19 and is served within a judicial district of the United States and not more than 100 miles from where the summons was issued; or
(C) when authorized by a federal statute.
(2) *Federal Claim Outside State-Court Jurisdiction.* For a claim that arises under federal law, serving a summons or filing a waiver of service establishes personal jurisdiction over a defendant if:
(A) the defendant is not subject to jurisdiction in any state's courts of general jurisdiction; and
(B) exercising jurisdiction is consistent with the United States Constitution and laws.

(l) Proving Service.
(1) *Affidavit Required.* Unless service is waived, proof of service must be made to the court. Except for service by a United States marshal or deputy marshal, proof must be by the server's affidavit.
(2) *Service Outside the United States.* Service not within any judicial district of the United States must be proved as follows:
(A) if made under Rule 4(f) (1), as provided in the applicable treaty or convention: or
(B) if made under Rule 4(f) (2) or (f) (3), by a receipt signed by the addressee, or by other evidence satisfying the court that the summons and complaint were delivered to the addressee.
(3) *Validity of Service; Amending Proof.* Failure to prove service does not affect the validity of service. The court may permit proof of service to be amended.

(m) Time Limit For Service, if a defendant is not served within 120 days after complaint is filed, the court – on motion or on its own after notice to the plaintiff – must dismiss the action without prejudice against the defendant or order that service be made within a specified time. But if the plaintiff shows good cause for the failure, the court must extend the time for service for an appropriate period. This subdivision (m) does not apply to service in a foreign country under Rule 4(f) or 4(j) (l).

(n) Assuring Jurisdiction over Property or Assets.
(1) *Federal law.* The court may assert jurisdiction over property if authorized by a federal statute. Notice to claimants of the property must be given as provided in the statute or by serving a

summons under this rule.

(2) *State law.* On a showing that personal jurisdiction over a defendant cannot be obtained in the district where the action is brought by reasonable efforts to serve a summons under this rule, the court may assert jurisdiction over the defendant's assets found in the district. Jurisdiction is acquired by seizing the assets under the circumstances and in the manner provided by state law in that district.

Rule 4.1. Serving Other Process

(a) **In General**. Process – other than a summons under Rule 4 or a subpoena under Rule 45 – must be served by a United States marshal or deputy marshal or by a person specially appointed for that purpose. It may be served anywhere within the territorial limits of the state where the district court is located and, if authorized by a federal statute, beyond those limits. Proof of service must be made under Rule 4(1).

(b) **Enforcing Orders: Committing for Civil Contempt**. An order committing a person for civil contempt of a decree or injunction issued to enforce federal law may be served and enforced in any district. Any other order in a civil-contempt proceeding may be served only in the state where the issuing court is located or elsewhere in the United States within 100 miles from where the order was issued.

Rule 5. Serving and Filing Pleadings and Other Papers

(a) Service: When Required.

(1) *In General.* Unless these rules provide otherwise, each of the following papers must be served on every party:

(A) an order stating that service is required;

(B) a pleading filed after the original complaint, unless the court orders otherwise under Rule 5(c) because there are numerous defendants;

(C) a discovery paper required to be served on a party, unless the court orders otherwise;

(D) a written motion, except on that may be heard *ex parte*; and

(E) a written notice, appearance, demand, or offer of judgment, or any similar paper.

(2) *If a Party Fails to Appear.* No service is required on a party who is in default for failing to appear. But a pleading that asserts a new claim for relief against such a party must be served on that party under Rule 4.

(3) *Seizing Property.* If an action is begun by seizing property and no person is or need be named as a defendant, any service required before the filing of an appearance, answer, or claim must be made on the person who had custody or possession of the property when it was seized.

(b) Service: How Made.

(1) *Serving an Attorney.* If a party is represented by an attorney, service under this rule must be made on the attorney unless the court orders service on the party.

(2) *Service in General.* A paper is served under this rule by:

(A) handing it to the person;

(B) leaving it:

(i) at the person's office with a clerk or other person in charge or, if no one is in charge, in a conspicuous place in the office; or

(ii) if the person has no office or if the office is closed, at the person's dwelling or usual place of abode with someone of suitable age and discretion who resides there;

(C) mailing it to the person's last known address – in which event service is complete upon mailing;

(D) leaving it with the court clerk if the person has no known address;

(E) sending it to a registered user by filing it with the court's electronic filing system or sending it by other electronic means that the person consented to in writing – in either of which events service is complete upon filing or sending, but is not effective if the filer or sender learns that it did not reach the person to be served; or

(F) delivering it by any other means that the person consented to in writing – in which event service is complete when the person making service delivers it to the agency designated to make delivery.

(3) *Using Court Facilities.* If a local rule so authorizes, a party may use the court's transmission facilities to make service under Rule 5(b) (2) (E).

(c) Serving Numerous Defendants.

(1) *In General.* If an action involves an unusually large number of defendants, the court may, on motion or on its own, order that:

(A) defendants' pleadings and replies to them need not he served on other defendants;

(B) any crossclaim, counterclaim, avoidance, or affirmative defense in those pleadings and replies to them will be treated as denied or avoided by all other parties; and

(C) filing any such pleading and serving it on the plaintiff constitutes notice of the pleading to all parties.

(2) *Notifying Parties.* A copy of every such order must he served on the parties as the court directs.

(d) Filing.

(1) Required Filings; Certificate of Service.

(A) *Papers after the Complaint.* Any paper after the complaint that is required to be served must be filed no later than a reasonable time after service. But disclosures under Rule 26(a) (1) or (2) and the following discovery requests and responses must not be filed until they are used in the proceeding or the court orders filing: depositions, interrogatories, requests for documents or tangible things or to permit entry onto land, and requests for admission.

(B) *Certificate of Service.* No certificate of service is required when a paper is served by filing it with the court's electronic-filing system. When a paper that is required to be served is served by other means:

(i) if the paper is filed, a certificate of service must be filed with it or within a reasonable time after service; and

(ii) if the paper is not filed, a certificate of service need not be filed unless filing is required by court order or by local rule.

(2) *Nonelectronic Filing.* A paper not filed electronically is filed by delivering it:

(A) to the clerk; or

(B) to a judge who agrees to accept it for filing, and who must then note the filing date on the paper and promptly send it to the clerk.

(3) Electronic Filing and Signing.

(A) *By a Represented Person – Generally Required; Exceptions.* A person represented by an attorney must file electronically, unless nonelectronic filing is allowed by the court for good cause or is allowed or required by local rule.

(B) By an Unrepresented Person – When Allowed or Required. A person not represented by an attorney:

(i) may file electronically only if allowed by court order or by local rule; and

(ii) may be required to file electronically only by court order, or by a local rule that includes

reasonable exceptions.
(C) *Signing.* A filing made through a person's electronic filing account and authorized by that person, together with that person's name on a signature block, constitutes the person's signature.
(D) *Same as a Written Paper.* A paper filed electronically is a written paper for purposes of these rules.
(4) *Acceptance by the Clerk.* The clerk must not refuse to file a paper solely because it is not in the form prescribed by these rules or by a local rule or practice.

Rule 5.1. Constitutional Challenge to a Statute – Notice, Certification, and Intervention

(a) **Notice by a Party**. A party that files a pleading, written motion, or other paper drawing into question the constitutionality of a federal or state statute must promptly:
(1) file a notice of constitutional question stating the question and identifying the paper that raises it, if:
(A) a federal statute is questioned, and the parties do not include the United States, one of its agencies, or one of its officers or employees in an official capacity; or
(B) a state statute is questioned, and the parties do not include the state, one of its agencies, or one of its officers or employees in an official capacity; and
(2) serve the notice and paper on the attorney general of the United States if a federal statute is questioned – or on the state attorney general if a state statute is questioned – either by certified or registered mail or by sending it to an electronic address designated by the attorney general for this purpose.
(b) **Certification by the Court**. The court must, under 28 U.S.C. § 2403, certify to the appropriate attorney general that a statute has been questioned.
(c) **Intervention; Final Decision on the Merits**. Unless the court sets a later time, the attorney general may intervene within 60 days after the notice is filed or after the court certifies the challenge, whichever is earlier. Before the time to intervene expires, the court may reject the constitutional challenge, but may not enter a final judgment holding the statue unconstitutional.
(d) **No forfeiture**. A party's failure to file and serve the notice, or the court's failure to certify, does not forfeit a constitutional claim or defense that is otherwise timely asserted.

Rule 5.2. Privacy Protection for Filings Made with the Court

(a) **Redacted Filings**. Unless the court orders otherwise, in an electronic or paper filing with the court that contains an individual's social security number, taxpayer-identification number, or birth date, the name of an individual known to be a minor, or a financial-account number, a party or nonparty making the filing may include only:
(1) the last four digits of the social-security number and taxpayer-identification number;
(2) the year of the individual's birth;
(3) the minor's initials; and
(4) the last four digits of the financial-account number.
(b) **Exemptions from the Redaction Requirement**. The redaction requirement does not apply to the following:
(1) a financial account number that identifies the property allegedly subject to forfeiture in a forfeiture proceeding;
(2) the record of an administrative or agency proceeding;
(3) the official record of a state court proceeding;

(4) the record of a court or tribunal, if that record was not subject to the redaction requirement when originally filed;
(5) a filing covered by Rule 5.2(c) or (d); and
(6) a *pro se* filing in an action brought under 28 U.S.C. §§ 2241, 2254, cr 2255.

(c) **Limitations on Remote Access to Electronic Files; Social-Security Appeals and Immigration Cases.** Unless the court orders otherwise, in an action for benefits under the Social Security Act, and in an action or proceeding relating to an order of removal, to relief from removal, or to immigration benefits or detention, access to an electronic file is authorized as follows:
(1) the parties and their attorneys may have remote electronic access to any part of the case file, including the administrative record;
(2) any other person may have electronic access to the full record at the courthouse, but may have remote access only to:
(A) the docket maintained by the court; and
(B) an opinion, order, judgment, or other disposition of the court, but not any other part of the case file or the administrative record.

(d) **Filings Made Under Seal.** The court may order that a filing he made under seal without redaction. The court may later unseal the filing or order the person who made the filing to file a redacted version for the public record.

(e) **Protective Orders.** For good cause, the court may by order in a case:
(1) require redaction of additional information; or
(2) limit or prohibit a nonparty's remote electronic access to a document filed with the court.

(f) **Option for Additional Unredacted Filing Under Seal**. A person making a redacted filing may also file an unredacted copy under seal. The court must retain the unredacted copy as part of the record.

(g) **Option for Filing a Reference List**. A filing that contains information may be filed together with a reference list that identifies each item of redacted information and specifies an appropriate identifier that uniquely corresponds to each item listed. The list must be filed under seal and may be amended as of right. Any reference in the case to a listed identifier will be construed to refer to the corresponding item of information.

(h) **Waiver of Protection of Identifiers**. A person waives the protection of Rule 5.2(a) as to the person's own information by filing it without redaction and

not under seal.

Rule 6. Computing and Extending Time; Time for Motion Papers

(a) **Computing Time**. The following rules apply in computing any time period specified in these rules, in any local rule or court order, or in any statute that does not specify a method of computing time.
(1) *Period Stated in Days or a Longer Unit.* When the period is stated in days or a longer unit of time:
(A) exclude the day of the event that triggers the period;
(B) count every day, including intermediate Saturdays, Sundays, and legal holidays; and
(C) include the last day of the period, but if the last day is a Saturday, Sunday, or legal holiday, the period continues to run until the end of the next day that is not a Saturday, Sunday, or legal holiday.
(2) *Period Stated in Hours.* When the period is stated in hours:
(A) begin counting immediately on the occurrence of the event that triggers the period;
(B) count every hour, including hours on intermediate Saturdays, Sundays, and legal holidays;

and

(C) if the period would end on a Saturday, Sunday, or legal holiday, the period continues to run until the same time on the next day that is not a Saturday, Sunday, or legal holiday.

(3) *Inaccessibility of the Clerk's Office.* Unless the court orders otherwise, if the clerk's office is inaccessible:

(A) on the last day for filing under Rule 6(a) (1), then the time for filing is extended to the first day that is not a Saturday, Sunday, or legal holiday; or

(B) during the last hour of filing under Rule 6(a) (2), then the time for filing is extended to the same time on the first accessible day that is not a Saturday, Sunday, cr legal holiday.

(4) **"Last Day" Defined.** Unless a different time is set by a statute, local rule, or court order, the last day ends:

(A) for electronic filing, at midnight in the court's time zone; and

(B) for filing by other means, when the clerk's office is scheduled to close.

(5) *"Next Day" Defined.* The "next day" is determined by continuing to count forward when the period is measured after an event and backward when measured before an event.

(6) "Legal holiday" Defined. "Legal holiday" means:

(A) the day set aside by statute for observing New Year's Day, Martin Luther King Jr.'s Birthday, Washington's Birthday, Memorial Day, Independence Day, Labor Day, Columbus Day, Veterans' Day, Thanksgiving Day, or Christmas Day;

(B) any day declared a holiday by the President or Congress; and

(C) for periods that are measured after an event, any other day declared a holiday by the state where the district court is located.

(b) **Extending Time.**

(1) *In General.* When an act may or must be done within a specified time, the court may, for good cause, extend the time:

(A) with or without motion or notice if the court acts, or if a request is made, before the original time or its extension expires; or

(B) on motion made after the time has expired if the party failed to act because of excusable neglect.

(2) *Exceptions.* A court must not extend the time to act under Rules 50(b) and (d), 52(b), 59(b), (d), and (e), and 60(b).

(c) **Motions, Notices of Hearing, and Affidavits.**

(1) *In General.* A written motion and notice of the hearing must be served at least 14 days before the time specified for the hearing, with the following exceptions:

(A) when the motion may be heard *ex parte*;

(B) when these rules set a different time; or

(C) when a court order – which a party may, for good cause, apply for *ex parte* – sets a different time.

(2) *Supporting Affidavit.* Any affidavit supporting a motion must be served with the motion. Except as Rule 59(c) provides otherwise, any opposing affidavit must be served at least 7 days before the hearing, unless the court permits service at another time.

(d) **Additional Time After Certain Kinds of Service.** When a party may or must act within a specified time after being served and service is made under Rule 5(b) (2) (C) (mail), (D) (leaving with the clerk), or (F) (other means consented to), 3 days are added after the period would otherwise expire under Rule 6(a).

Rule 7. Pleadings Allowed, Form of Motions and Other Papers

(a) **Pleadings.** Only these pleadings are allowed:
- (1) a complaint;
- (2) an answer to a complaint;
- (3) an answer to a counterclaim designated as a counterclaim;
- (4) an answer to a crossclaim;
- (5) a third-party complaint;
- (6) an answer to a third-party complaint; and
- (7) if the court orders one, a reply to an answer.

(b) Motions and Other Papers.
- (1) *In General.* A request for a court order must be made by motion. The motion must:
  - (A) be in writing unless made during a hearing or trial;
  - (B) state with particularity the grounds for seeking the order; and
  - (C) state the relief sought.
- (2) *Form.* The rules governing captions and other matters of form in pleadings apply to motions and other papers.

Rule 7.1. Disclosure Statement

(a) **Who Must File: Contents.** A nongovernmental corporate party must file 2 copies of a disclosure statement that:
- (1) identifies any parent corporation and any publicly held corporation owning 10% or more of its stock; or
- (2) states that there is no such corporation.

(b) **Time to File: Supplemental Filing.** A party must:
- (1) file the disclosure statement with its first appearance, pleading, petition, motion, response, or other request addressed to the court; and
- (2) promptly file a supplemental statement if any required information changes.

Rule 8. General Rules of Pleading

(a) **Claim for Relief**. A pleading that states a claim for relief must contain:
- (1) a short and plain statement of the grounds for the court's jurisdiction, unless the court already has jurisdiction and the claim needs no new jurisdictional support;
- (2) a short and plain statement of the claim needs showing that the pleader is entitled to relief; and
- (3) a demand for the relief sought, which may Include relief in the alternative or different types of relief.

(b) **Defenses;** Admissions and Denials.
- (1) *In General.* In responding to a pleading, a party must:
  - (A) state in short and plain terms its defenses to each claim asserted against it; and
  - (B) admit or deny the allegations asserts against it by an opposing party.
- (2) *Denials – Responding to the Substance.* A denial must fairly respond to the substance of the allegation.
- (3) *General and Specific Denials.* A party that intends in good faith to deny all the allegations must either specifically deny designated allegations generally deny all except those specifically admitted.
- (4) *Denying Part of an Allegation.* A party that intends in good faith to deny only part of an allega-

tion must admit the part that is true and deny the rest.

(5) *Lacking Knowledge or Information.* A party that lacks knowledge or information sufficient to form a belief about the truth of an allegation must so state, and the statement has the effect of a denial.

(6) *Effect of Failing to Deny.* An allegation – other than one relating to the amount of damages – is admitted if a responsive pleading is required and the allegation is not denied. If a responsive pleading is not required, an allegation is considered denied or avoided.

(c) **Affirmative Defenses.**

(1) *In General.* In responding to a pleading, a party must affirmatively state any avoidance or affirmative defense, including:

- accord and satisfaction;
- arbitration and award;
- assumption of risk;
- contributory negligence;
- duress;
- estoppel;
- failure of consideration;
- fraud;
- illegality;
- injury by fellow servant;
- laches;
- license;
- payment;
- release;
- res judicata;
- statute of frauds;
- statute of limitations; and
- waiver.

(2) *Mistaken Designation.* If a party mistakenly designates a defense as a counterclaim or a counterclaim as a defense, the court must, if justice requires, treat the pleading as though it was correctly designated and may impose terms for doing so.

(d) **Pleading to Be Concise and Direct; Alternative Statements; Inconsistency.**

(1) *In General.* Each allegation must be simple, concise, and direct. No technical form is required.

(2) *Alternative Statements of a Claim or Defense.* A party may set out two or more statements of a claim or defense alternatively or hypothetically, either in a single count or defense or in separate ones. If a party makes alternative statements, the pleading is sufficient if any one of them is sufficient.

(3) *Inconsistent Claims or Defenses.* A party may state as many separate claims or defenses as it has, regardless of consistency.

(e) **Construing Pleadings.** Pleadings must be construed so as to do justice.

Rule 9. Pleading Special Matters

(a) **Capacity or authority to Sue; Legal Existence.**

(1) *In General.* Except when required to show that the court has jurisdiction, a pleading need not allege:

(A) a party's capacity to sue or be sued;

(B) a party's authority to sue or be sued in a representative capacity; or

(C) the legal existence of an organized association of persons that is made a party.

(2) *Raising Those Issues.* To raise any of those issues, a party must do so by a specific denial, which must state any supporting facts that are peculiarly within the party's knowledge.

(b) **Fraud or Mistake; Conditions of Mind.** In alleging fraud or mistake, a party must state with particularity the circumstances constituting fraud or mistake. Malice, intent, knowledge, and other conditions of a person's mind may be alleged generally.

(c) **Conditions Precedent.** In pleading conditions precedent, it suffices to allege generally that all conditions precedent has occurred or been performed. But when denying that a condition precedent has occurred or been performed, a party must do so with particularity.

(d) **Official Document or Act**. In pleading an official document or official act, it suffices to allege that the document was legally issued or the act legally done.

(e) **Judgment.** In pleading a judgment or decision of a domestic or foreign court, a judicial or quasi-judicial tribunal, or a board or officer, it suffices to plead the judgment or decision without showing jurisdiction to render it.

(f) **Time and Place**. An allegation of time or place is material when testing the sufficiency of a pleading.

(g) **Special Damages**. If an item of special damage is claimed, it must be specifically stated.

(h) **Admiralty or Maritime Claim.**

(1) *How Designated.* If a claim for relief is within the admiralty or maritime jurisdiction and also within the court's subject-matter jurisdiction on some other ground, the pleading may designate the claim as an admiralty or maritime claim for purposes of Rules 14(c), 38(e), and 82 and the Supplemental Rules for Admiralty and Maritime Claims and Asset Forfeiture Actions. A claim cognizable only in the admiralty or maritime jurisdiction is an admiralty or maritime claim for those purposes, whether or not so designated.

(2) *Designation for Appeal.* A case that includes an admiralty or maritime claim within this subdivision (h) is an admiralty case within 28 U.S.C. § 1292(a) (3).

Rule 10. Form of Pleadings

(a) **Caption; Names of Parties.** Every pleading must have a caption with the court's name, a title, a file number, and a Rule 7(a) designation. The title of the complaint must name all the parties; the title of other pleadings, after naming the first party on each side, may/refer generality to other parties.

(b) **Paragraphs; Separate Statements**. A party must state its claims or defenses in numbered paragraphs, each limited as far as practicable to a single set of circumstances. A later pleading may refer by number to a paragraph in an earlier pleading. If doing so would promote clarity, each claim founded on a separate transaction or occurrence – and each defense other than a denial – must be stated in a separate count or defense.

(c) **Adoption by Reference; Exhibits**. A statement in a pleading may be adopted by reference elsewhere in the same pleading or in any other pleading or motion. A copy of a written instrument that is an exhibit to a pleading is a part of the pleading for all purposes.

Rule 11. Signing Pleadings, Motions, and Other Papers; Representations to the Court; Sanctions

(1) **Signature**. Every pleading, written motion, and other paper must be signed by at least one attorney of record in the attorney's name or by a party personally if the party is unrepresented. The paper must state the signer's address, e-mail address, and telephone number. Unless a rule or statute specifically states otherwise, a pleading need not be verified or accompanied by an affidavit. The court must strike an unsigned paper unless the omission is promptly corrected after being called to the attorney's or party's attention.

(2) Representations to the Court. By presenting to the court a pleading, written motion, or other paper – whether by signing, filing, submitting, or later advocating it – an attorney or unrepresented party certifies that to the best of the person's knowledge, information, and belief, formed after an inquiry reasonable under the circumstances:

(3) it is not being presented for any improper purpose, such as to harass, cause unnecessary delay, or needlessly increase the cost of litigation;

(4) the claims, defenses, and other legal contentions are warranted by existing law or by a non-frivolous argument for extending, modifying, or reversing existing law or for establishing new law;

(5) the factual contentions have evidentiary support or, if specifically so identified, will likely have evidentiary support after a reasonable opportunity for further investigation or discovery; and

(6) the denials of factual contentions are warranted on the evidence or, if specifically so identified, are reasonably based on belief or a lack of information.

(7) Sanctions.

(8) *In General*. If, after notice and a reasonable opportunity to respond, the court determines that Rule 11(b) has been violated, the court may impose an appropriate sanction on any attorney, law firm, or party that violated the rule or is responsible for the violation. Absent exceptional circumstances, a law firm must be held jointly responsible for a violation committed by its partner, associate, or employee.

(9) *Motion for Sanctions*. A motion for sanctions must be made separately from any other motion and must describe the specific conduct that violates Rule 11(b). The motion must be served under Rule 5, but it must not be filed or be presented to the court if the challenged paper, claim, defense, contention, or denial is withdrawn or appropriately corrected within 21 days after service or within another time the court sets. If warranted, the court may award to the prevailing party the reasonable expenses, including attorney's fees, incurred for the motion.

(10) *On the Court's Initiative*. On its own, the court may order an attorney, law firm, or party to show cause why conduct specifically described in the order has not violated Rule 11(b).

(11) *Nature of a Sanction*. A sanction imposed under this rule must be limited to what suffices to deter repetition of the conduct or comparable conduct by others similarly situated. The sanction may include nonmonetary directives; an order to pay a penalty into court; or, if imposed on motion and warranted for effective deterrence, an order directing payment to the movant of part or all of the reasonable attorney's fees and other expenses directly resulting from the violation.

(12) *Limitations on Monetary Sanctions*. The court must not impose a monetary sanction:

(13) against a represented party for violating Rule 11(b) (2); or

(14) on its own, unless it issued the show-cause order under Rule 11(c) (3) before voluntary dismissal or settlement of the claims made by or against the party that is, or whose attorneys are, to be sanctioned.

(15) *Requirements for an Order*. An order imposing a sanction must describe the sanctioned

conduct and explain the basis for the sanction.

(16) **Inapplicability to Discovery.** This rule does not apply to disclosures and discovery requests, responses, objections, and motions under Rules 26 through 37.

Rule 12. Defenses and Objections: When and How Presented; Motion for Judgment on the Pleadings; Consolidating Motions; Waiving Defenses; Pretrial Hearing

(a) **Time to Serve a Responsive Pleading.**

(1) *In General.* Unless another time is specified by this rule or a federal statute, the time for serving a responsive pleading is as follows:

(A) A defendant must serve an answer:

(i) within 21 days after being served with the summons and complaint; or

(ii) if it has timely waived service under Rule 4(d), within 60 days after the request for a waiver was sent to the defendant outside any judicial district of the United States.

(B) A party must serve an answer to a counterclaim or crossclaim within 21 days after being served with the pleading that states the counterclaim or crossclaim.

(C) A party must serve a reply to an answer within 21 days after being served with an order to reply, unless the order specifies a different time.

(2) *United States and Its Agencies, Officers, or Employees Sued in an Official Capacity.* The United States, a United States agency, or a United States officer or employee sued only in an official capacity must serve an answer to a complaint, counterclaim, or crossclaim within 60 days after service on the United States attorney.

(3) *United States Officers or Employees Sued in an Individual Capacity.* A United States officer or employee sued in an individual capacity for an act or omission occurring in connection with duties performed on the United States' behalf must serve an answer to a complaint, counterclaim, or crossclaim within 60 days after service on the officer or employee or service on the United States attorney, whichever is later.

(4) *Effect of a Motion.* Unless the court sets a different time, serving a motion under this rule alters these periods as follows:

(A) if the court denies the motion or postpones its disposition until trial, the responsive pleading must be served within 14 days after notice of the court's action; or

(B) if the court grants a motion for a more definite statement, the responsive pleading must be served within 14 days after the more definite statement is served.

(b) **How to Present Defenses**. Every defense to a claim of relief in any pleading must be asserted in the responsive pleading if one is required. But a party may assert the following defenses by motion:

(1) lack of subject-matter jurisdiction;

(2) lack of personal jurisdiction;

(3) improper venue;

(4) insufficient process;

(5) insufficient service of process;

(6) failure to state a claim upon which relief can be granted; and

(7) failure to join a party under Rule 19.

(17) A motion asserting any of these defenses must be made before pleading if a responsive pleading is allowed. If a pleading sets out a claim for relief that does not require a responsive pleading, an opposing party may assert at trial any defense to that claim. No defense or objection is waived by joining it with one or more other defenses or objections in a responsive pleading or in a motion.

(c) **Motion for Judgment on the Pleadings**. After the pleadings are closed – but early enough not to delay a trial – a party may move for judgment of the pleadings.
(d) **Result of Presenting Matters Outside the Pleadings**. If, on a motion under Rule 12(b) (6) or 12(c), matters outside the pleadings are presented to and not excluded by the court, the motion must be treated as one for summary judgment under Rule 56. All parties must be given a reasonable opportunity to present all the material that is pertinent to the motion.
(e) **Motion for a More Definite Statement**. A party may move for a more definite statement of a pleading to which a responsive pleading is allowed but which is so vague or ambiguous that the party cannot reasonably prepare a response. The motion must be made before filing a responsive pleading and it must point out the defects complained of and the details desired. If the court orders a more definite statement and the order is not obeyed within 14 days after notice of the order or within the time the court sets, the court may strike the pleading or issue any other appropriate order.
(f) **Motion to Strike.** The court may strike from a pleading an insufficient defense or any redundant, immaterial, impertinent, or scandalous matter. The court may act:
  (1) on its own; or
  (2) on motion made by a party either before responding to the pleading or, if a response is not allowed, within 21 days after being served with the pleading.
(g) **Joining Motions.**
  (1) *Right to Join.* A motion under this rule may be joined with any other motion allowed by this rule.
  (2) *Limitations on Further Motions*. Except as provided in Rule 12(h) (2) or (3), a party that makes a motion under this rule must not make another motion under this rule raising a defense or objection that was available to the party but omitted from its earlier motion.
(h) **Waiving and Preserving Certain Defenses.**
  (1) *When Some Are Waived.* A party waives any defense listed in Rule 12(b) (2)-(5) by:
    (A) omitting it from a motion in the circumstances described in Rule 12(g) (2); or
    (B) failing to either:
      (i) make it by motion under this rule; or
      (ii) include it in a responsive pleading or in an amendment allowed by Rule 15(a) (1) as a matter of course.
  (2) *When to Raise Others*. Failure to state a claim upon which relief can be granted, to join a person required by Rule 19(b), or to state a legal defense to a claim may be raised:
    (A) in any pleading allowed or ordered under Rule 7(a);
    (B) by a motion under Rule 12(c); or
    (C) at trial.
  (3) *Lack of Subject-Matter Jurisdiction.* If the court determines at any time that it lacks subject-matter jurisdiction, the court must dismiss the action.
(i) **Hearing Before Trial**. If a party so moves, any defense listed under Rule 12(b) (l) -(7) – whether made in a pleading or by motion – and a motion under Rule 12(c) must be heard and decided before trial unless the court orders a deferral until trial.

Rule 13. Counterclaim and Crossclaim

(a) **Compulsory Counterclaim.**
  (1) *In General.* A pleading must state as a counterclaim any claim that – at the time of its service – the pleader has against the opposing party if the claim:
    (A) arises out of the transaction or occurrence that is the subject matter of the opposing party's

claim; and
(B) does not require adding another party over whom the court cannot acquire jurisdiction.
(2) *Exceptions.* The pleader need not state the claim if, when the action was commenced, the claim was the subject of another pending action; or the opposing party sued on its claim by attachment or other process that did not establish personal jurisdiction over the pleader in that claim, and the pleader does not assert any counterclaims under this rule.

(b) **Permissive Counterclaim**. A pleading may state as a counterclaim against an opposing party any claim that is not compulsory.

(c) **Relief Sought in a Counterclaim**. A counterclaim need not diminish or defeat the recovery sought by the opposing party. It may request relief that exceeds in amount or differs in kind from the relief sought by the opposing party.

(d) **Counterclaim Against the United States**. These rules do not expand the right to assert a counterclaim – or to claim a credit – against the United States or a United States officer or agency.

(e) **Counterclaim Maturing or Acquired After Pleading**. The court may permit a party to file a supplemental pleading asserting a counterclaim that matured or was acquired by the party after serving an earlier pleading.

(f) **[Abrogated]**

(g) **Crossclaim Against a Coparty**. A pleading may state as a crossclaim any claim by one party against a co-party if the claim arises out of the transaction or occurrence that is the subject matter of the original action or of a counterclaim or if the claim relates to any property that is the subject matter of the original action. The crossclaim may include a claim that the co-party is or may be liable to the cross-claimant for all or part of a claim asserted in action against the cross-claimant.

(h) **Joining Additional Parties**. Rules 19 and 20 govern the addition of a person as a party to a counterclaim or crossclaim.

(i) **Separate Trials; Separate Judgments**. If the court orders separate trials under Rule 42(b), it may enter judgment on a counterclaim or crossclaim under Rule 54(b) when it has jurisdiction to do so, even if the opposing party's claims have been dismissed or otherwise resolved.

Rule 14. Third-Party Practice

(18) When a Defending Party May Bring in a Third Party.

(19) *Timing of the Summons and Complaint.* A defending party may, as third – party plaintiff, serve a summons and complaint on a nonparty who is or may be liable to it for all or part of the claim against it. But the third-party plaintiff must, by motion, obtain the court's leave if it files the third–party complaint more than 14 days after receiving its original answer.

(20) *Third-party Defendant's Claims and Defenses.* The person served with the summons and third-party complaint – the "third-party-defendant":

(21) must assert any defense against the third-party plaintiff's claim under rule 12.

(22) must assert any counterclaim against the third-party plaintiff under Rule 13(a), and may assert any counterclaim against the third-party plaintiff under Rule 13(b) or any crossclaim against another third-party defendant under Rule 13(g);

(23) may assert against the plaintiff any defense that the third-party plaintiff has to the plaintiff's claim; and

(24) may also assert against the plaintiff any claim arising out of the transaction or occurrence that is the subject matter of the plaintiff's claim against the third-party plaintiff.

(25) *Plaintiff's Claims Against a Third-Party Defendant.* The plaintiff may assert against the third-party defendant any claim arising out of the transition or occurrence that is the subject

matter of the plaintiff's claim against the third-party plaintiff. The third-party defendant must then assert any defense under Rule 12 and any counterclaim under Rule 13(a) and may assert any counterclaim under Rule 13(b) or any crossclaim under Rule 13(g).

(26) *Motion to Strike, Server, or Try Separately*. Any party may move to strike the third-party claim, to serve it, or to try it separately.

(27) *Third-Party Defendant's Claim Against a Nonparty*. A third-party defendant may proceed under this rule against a defendant who is or may be liable and may proceed under this rule against a defendant who is or may be liable to the third-party defendant for all or part of any claim against it.

(28) *Third-Party Claim in Rem*. If it is within the admiralty or maritime jurisdiction, a third-party claim may be in rem. In that event, a reference in this rule to the "summons" includes the warrant of arrest, and a reference in this rule to the "summons" includes the warrant of arrest, and a reference to the defendant or third-party plaintiff includes, when appropriate, a person who asserts a right under Supplemental Rule C(6) (a) (i) in the property arrested.

(29) **When a Plaintiff May Bring in a Third Party**. When a claim is asserted against a plaintiff, the plaintiff may bring in a third party if this rule would allow a defendant to do so.

(30) Admiralty or Maritime Claim.

(31) *Scope of Impleader*. If a plaintiff asserts an admiralty or maritime claim under Rule 9(h), the defendant or a person who asserts a right under Supplemental Rule C(96) (a) (i) may, as a third-party plaintiff, bring in a third-party defendant who may be wholly or partly liable – either to the plaintiff or to the third-party plaintiff – for remedy over, contribution, or otherwise on account of the same transaction, occurrence, or series of transactions or occurrences.

(32) *Defending Against a Demand for Judgment for the Plaintiff*. The third-party plaintiff may demand judgment in the plaintiff's favor against the third-party defendant. In that event, the third-party defendant must defend under Rule 12 against the plaintiff's claim as well as the third-party plaintiff's claim; and the action proceeds as if the plaintiff had sued both the third-party defendant and the third-party plaintiff.

Rule 15. Amended and Supplemental Pleadings

(b) **Amendments Before Trial.**

(1) *Amending as a Matter of Course*. A party may amend its pleading once as a matter of course within:

(A) 21 days after serving it, or

(B) if the pleading is one to which a responsive pleading is required, 21 days after service of a responsive pleading or 21 days after service of a motion under Rule 12(b), (e), or (f), whichever is earlier.

(2) Other Amendments. In all other cases, a party may amend its pleading only with the opposing party's written consent or the court's leave. The court should freely give leave when justice so requires.

(3) Time to Respond. Unless the court orders otherwise, any required response to an amended pleading must be made within the time remaining to respond to the original pleading or within 14 days after service of the amended pleading, whichever is later.

(c) **Amendments During and After Trial.**

(1) *Based on an Objection at Trial*. If, at trial, a party objects that evidence is not within the issues raised in the pleadings, the court may permit the pleadings to be amended. The court should freely permit an amendment when doing so will aid in presenting the merits and the objecting party fails to satisfy the court that the evidence would prejudice that party's action or defense on the merits. The court may grant a continuance to enable the objecting party to meet the evidence.

(2) *For Issues Tried by Consent.* When an issue not raised by the pleadings is tried by the parties' express or implied consent, it must be treated in all respects as if raised in the pleadings. A party may move – at any time, even after judgment – to amend the pleadings to conform them to the evidence and to raise an unpleaded issue. But failure to amend does not affect the result of the trial of that issue.

(d) **Relation Back of Amendments.**

(1) When an Amendment Relates Back. An amendment to a proceeding relates back to the date of the original proceeding when:

(A) the law that provides the applicable statute of limitations allows relation back;

(B) the amendment asserts a claim or defense that arose out of the conduct, transaction, or occurrence set out – or attempted to be set out – in the original pleading; or

(C) the amendment changes the party or naming of the party against whom a claim is asserted, if Rule 15(c) (1) (B) is satisfied and if, within the period provided by Rule 4(m) for serving the summons and complaint, the party to be brought in by amendment:

(i) received such notice of the action that it will not be prejudiced in defending on the merits; and

(ii) knew or should have known that the action would have been brought against it, but for a mistake concerning the proper party's identity.

(2) *Notice to the United States.* When the United States or a United States officer or agency is added as a defendant by amendment, the notice requirements of Rule 15(c) (l) (C) (i) and (ii) are satisfied if, during the stated period, process was delivered or mailed to the United States attorney or the United States attorney's designee, to the attorney general of the United States, or to the officer or agency.

(e) **Supplemental Pleadings**. On motion and reasonable notice, the court may, on just terms, permit a party to serve a supplemental pleading setting out any transaction, occurrence, or event that happened after the date of the pleading to be supplemented. The court may permit supplementation even though the original pleading is defective in stating a claim or defense. The court may order that the opposing party plead to the supplemental pleading within a specified time.

Rule 16. Pretrial Conferences; Scheduling; Management

(a) **Purpose of a Pretrial Conference**. In any action, the court may order the attorneys and any unrepresented parties to appear for one or more pretrial conferences for such purposes as:

(1) expediting disposition of the action;

(2) establishing early and continuing control so that the case will not be protracted because of lack of management;

(3) discouraging wasteful pretrial activities;

(4) improving the quality of the trial through more thorough preparation; and

(5) facilitating settlement.

(b) **Scheduling.**

(1) *Scheduling Order*. Except in categories of actions exempted by local rule, the district judge, a magistrate judge or I, when authorized by local rule – must issue a scheduling order:

(A) after receiving the parties' report under Rule 26(f); or

(B) after consulting with the parties' attorneys and any unrepresented parties at a scheduling conference or by telephone, mail, or other means.

(2) *Time to Issue*. The judge must issue the scheduling order as soon as practicable, but in any event, within the earlier of 120 days after any defendant has been served with the complaint or 90 days after any defendant has appeared.

(3) Contents of the Order.

(A) *Required Contents*. The scheduling order must limit the time to join other parties, amend the pleadings, complete discovery, and file motions.

(B) *Permitted Contents*. The scheduling order may:

(i) modify the timing of disclosure under Rules 26(a) and 26(e) (1);

(ii) modify the extent of discovery;

(iii) provide for disclosure or discovery of electronically stored information;

(iv) include any agreements the parties reach for asserting claims of privilege or of protection as trial-preparation material after the information is produced;

(v) set dates for pretrial conferences and for trial; and

(vi) include other appropriate matters.

(4) Modifying a Schedule. A schedule may be modified only for good cause and with the judge's consent.

(c) **Attendance and Matters for Consideration at a Pretrial Conference.**

(1) *Attendance*. A represented party must authorize at least one of its attorneys to make stipulations and admissions about all matters that can reasonably be anticipated for discussion at a pretrial conference. If appropriate, the court may require that a party or its representative be present or reasonably available by other means to consider possible settlement.

(2) *Matters for Consideration*. At any pretrial conference, the court may consider and take appropriate action on the following matters:

(A) formulating and simplifying the issues, and eliminating frivolous claims or defenses;

(B) amending the pleadings if necessary or desirable;

(C) obtaining admissions and stipulations about facts and documents to avoid unnecessary proof, and ruling in advance on the admissibility of evidence;

(D) avoiding unnecessary proof and cumulative evidence, and limiting the use of testimony under Federal Rule of Evidence 702;

(E) determining the appropriateness and timing of summary adjudication under Rule 56;

(F) controlling and scheduling discovery, including orders affecting disclosures and discovery under Rule 26 and Rules 29 through 37;

(G) identifying witnesses and documents, scheduling the filing and exchange of any pretrial briefs, and setting dates for further conferences and for trial;

(H) referring matters to a magistrate judge or master;

(I) setting the case and using special procedures to assist in resolving the dispute when authorized by statute or local rule;

(J) determining the form and content of the pretrial order;

(K) disposing of pending motions;

(L) adopting special procedures for managing potentially difficult or protracted actions that may involve complex issues, multiple parties, difficult legal questions, or unusual proof problems;

(M) ordering a separate trial under Rule 42(b) of a claim, counterclaim, crossclaim, third-party claim, or particular issue;

(N) ordering the presentation of evidence early in the trial on a manageable issue that might, on the evidence, be the basis for a judgment as a matter of law under Rule 50(a) or a judgment on partial findings under Rule 52(c);

(O) establishing a reasonable limit on the time allowed to present evidence; and

(P) facilitating in other ways the just, speedy, and inexpensive disposition of the action.

(d) **Pretrial Orders**. After any conference under this rule, the court should order an issue reciting the action taken. This order controls the course of the action unless the court modifies it.

(e) **Final Pretrial Conference and Orders**. The court may hold a final pretrial conference to formulate a trial plan, including a plan to facilitate the admission of evidence. The conference must he held as close as possible to the start of trial as reasonable and must be attended by at least one attorney who will conduct the trial for each party and by an unrepresented party. The court may modify an order issued after a final pretrial conference only to prevent manifest injustice.

(f) **Sanctions.**

(1) *In General*. On motion or on its own, the court may |Issue any just orders, including those authorized by Rule 37(b) (2) (A) (ii)-(vii), if a party or its attorney:

(A) fails to appear at a scheduling or other pretrial conference;

(B) is substantially unprepared to participate or does not participate in good faith – in the conference; or

(C) fails to obey a scheduling or other pretrial order.

(2) *Imposing Fees and Costs*. Instead of or in addition to any other sanction, the court must order the party, its attorney, or both to pay the reasonable expenses including attorney's fees – incurred because of any noncompliance with this rule, unless the noncompliance was substantially justified, or other circumstances make an award of expenses unjust.

Rule 17. Plaintiff and Defendant; Capacity; Public Officers

(a) **Real Party in Interest**.

(1) *Designation in General*. An action must be prosecuted in the name of the real party in interest. The following may sue in their own names without joining the person for whose benefit the action is brought:

(A) an executor;

(B) an administrator;

(C) a guardian;

(D) a bailee;

(E) a trustee of an express trust;

(F) a party with whom or in whose name a contract has been made for another's benefit; and

(G) a party authorized by statute.

(2) *Action in the Name of the United States for Another's Use or Benefit*. When a federal statute so provides, an action for another's use or benefit must be brought in the name of the United States.

(3) *Joinder of the Real Party in Interest*. The court may not dismiss an action for failure to prosecute in the name of the real party in interest until, after an objection, a reasonable time has been allowed for the real party in interest to ratify, join, or be substituted into the action. After ratification, joinder, or substitution, the action proceeds as if it had been originally commenced by the real party in interest.

(b) **Capacity to Sue or Be Sued**. Capacity to sue or be sued is determined as follows:

(1) for an individual who is not acting in a representative capacity by the law of the individual's domicile;

(2) for a corporation, by the law under which it was organized; and

(3) for all other parties, by the law of the state where the court is located, except that:
  (A) a partnership or other unincorporated association with no such capacity under that state's law may sue or be sued in its common name to enforce a substantive right existing under the United States Constitution or laws; and
  (B) 28 U.S.C. §§ 754 and 959(a) govern the capacity of a receiver appointed by a United States court to sue or be sued in a United States court.

(c) **Minor or Incompetent Person.**
  (1) *With a Representative.* The following representatives may sue or defend on behalf of a minor or an incompetent person:
    (A) a general guardian;
    (B) a committee;
    (C) a conservator; or
    (D) a like fiduciary.
  (2) *Without a Representative.* A minor or incompetent person who does not have a duly appointed representative may sue by a next friend or guardian ad litem. The court must appoint guardian ad litem – or issue another appropriate order – to protect a minor or incompetent person who is unrepresented in an action.

(d) **Public Officer's Title and Name.** A public officer who sues or is sued in an official capacity may be designated by official title rather than by name, but the court may order that the officer's name be added.

Rule 18. Joinder of Claims

(a) *In General.* A party asserting a claim, counterclaim, crossclaim, or third – party claim may join, as independent or alternative claims, as many claims as it has against an opposing party.
(b) *Joinder of Contingent Claims.* A party may join two claims even though one of them is contingent on the disposition of the other; but the court may grant relief only in accordance with the parties' substantive rights. In particular, a plaintiff may state a claim for money and a claim to set aside a conveyance that is fraudulent as to that plaintiff, without first obtaining a judgment for the money.

Rule 19. Required Joinder of Parties

(a) **Persons Required to Be Joined if Feasible.**
  (1) *Required Party.* A person who is subject to service of process and whose joinder will not deprive the court of subject-matter jurisdiction must be joined as a party if:
    (A) in that person's absence, the court cannot accord complete relief among existing parties; or
    (B) that person claims an interest relating to the subject of the action and is so situated that disposing of the action in the person's absence may:
      (i) as a practical matter, impair or impede the person's ability to protect the interest; or
      (ii) leave an existing party subject to a substantial risk of incurring double, multiple, or otherwise inconsistent obligations because of the interest.
  (2) *Joinder by Court Order.* If a person has not been joined as required, the court must order that the person be made a party. A person who refuses to join as a plaintiff may be made either a defendant or, in a proper case, an involuntary plaintiff.
  (3) *Venue.* If a joined party objects to venue, and the joinder would make venue improper, the court must dismiss that party.

(b) **When Joinder Is Not Feasible.** If a person who is required to be joined if feasible cannot be joined, the court must determine whether, in equity and good conscience, the action should proceed among the existing parties or be dismissed. The factors for the court to consider include:
- (1) the extent to which a judgment rendered in the person's absence might prejudice that person or the existing parties;
- (2) the extent to which and prejudice could be lessened or avoided by:
  - (A) protective provisions in the judgment;
  - (B) shaping the relief; or
  - (C) other measures;
- (3) whether a judgment rendered in the person's absence would be adequate; and
- (4) whether the plaintiff would have an adequate remedy if the action were dismissed for non-joinder.

(c) **Pleading the Reasons for Nonjoinder**. When asserting a claim for relief, a party must state:
- (1) the name, if known, of any person who is required to be joined if feasible but is not joined; and
- (2) the reasons for not joining that person.

(d) **Exceptions for Class Actions**. This rule is subject to Rule 23.

Rule 20. Permissive Joinder of Parties

(a) **Persons Who May Join or Be Joined.**
- (1) *Plaintiffs*. Persons may join in one action as plaintiffs if:
  - (A) they assert any right to relief jointly, severally, or in the alternative with respect to or arising out of the same transaction, occurrence, or series of transactions or occurrences; and
  - (B) any question of law or fact common to all plaintiffs will arise in the action.
- (2) *Defendants*. Persons – as well as a vessel, cargo, or other property subject to admiralty process in rem – may be joined in one action as defendants if:
  - (A) any right to relief is asserted against them jointly, severally, or in the alternative with respect to or arising out of the same transaction, occurrence, or series of transactions or occurrences; and
  - (B) any question of law or fact common to all defendants will arise in the action.
- (3) *Extent of Relief*. Neither a plaintiff nor a defendant need be interested in obtaining or defending against all the relief demanded. The court may grant judgment to one or more plaintiffs according to their rights and against one or more defendants according to their liabilities.

(b) **Protective Measures**. The court may issue orders – including an order for separate trials – to protect a party against embarrassment, delay, expense, or other prejudice that arises from including a person against whom the party asserts no claim and who asserts no claim against the party.

Rule 21. Misjoinder and Nonjoinder of Parties

Misjoinder of parties is not a ground for dismissing an action. On motion or on its own, the court may at any time, on just terms, add or drop a party. The court may also sever any claim against a party.

Rule 22. Interpleader

(a) **Grounds.**

By a Plaintiff. Persons with claims that may expose a plaintiff to double or multiple liability may be joined as defendants and required to interplead. Joinder for interpleader is proper even though:

(A) the claims of several claimants, or the titles on which their claims depend, lack a common origin or are adverse and independent rather than identical; or
(B) the plaintiff denies liability in whole or in part to any or all of the claimants.
(2) *By a Defendant.* A defendant exposed to similar liability may seek interpleader through a crossclaim or counterclaim.
(b) Relation to Other Rules and Statutes. This rule supplements – and does not limit – the joinder of parties allowed by Rule 20. The remedy it provides is in addition to – and does not supersede or limit – the remedy provided by 28 U.S.C. §§ 1335, 1397, and 2361. An action under those statutes must be conducted under those rules.

Rule 23. Class Actions

(a) **Prerequisites.** One or more members of a class may sue or be sued as representative parties on behalf of all members only if:
(1) the class is so numerous that the joinder of all members is impracticable;
(2) there are questions of law or fact common to the class;
(3) the claims or defenses of the representative parties are typical of the claims or defenses of the class; and
(4) the representative parties will fairly and adequately protect the interests of the class.
(b) **Types of Class Actions**. A class action may be maintained if Rule 23(a) is satisfied and if:
(1) prosecuting separate actions by or against individual class members would create a risk of:
(A) inconsistent or varying adjudications with respect to individual class members that would establish incompatible standards of conduct for the party of the opposing class; or
(B) adjudications with respect to individual class members that, as a practical matter, would be dispositive of the interests of the other members not parties to the individual adjudications or would substantially impair or impede their ability to protect their interests;
(2) the party opposing the class has acted or refused to act on grounds that apply generally to the class, so that final injunctive relief or corresponding declaratory relief is appropriate respecting the class as a whole; or
(3) the court finds that the questions of law or fact common to class members predominate over any questions affecting only individual members and that a class action is superior to other available methods for fairly and efficiently adjudicating the controversy. The matters pertinent to these findings include:
(A) the class members' interests in individually controlling the prosecution or defense of separate actions;
(B) the extent and nature of any litigation concerning the controversy already begun by or against class members;
(C) the desirability or undesirability of concentrating the litigation of the claims in the particular forum; and
(D) the likely difficulties in managing a class action.
(c) **Certification Order; Notice to Class Members; Judgment; Issues Classes; Subclasses.**
(1) Certification Order.
(A) *Time to Issue.* At an early practicable time after a person sues or is sued as a class representative, the court must determine by order whether to certify the action as a class action.
(B) *Defining the Class; Appointing Class Counsel.* An order that certifies a class action must define the class and the class claims, issues, or defenses and must appoint class counsel under Rule 23(g).
(C) *Altering or Amending the Order.* An order that grants or denies class certification may be

altered or amended before final judgment.

(2) Notice.

(A) *For (b) (1) or (b) (2) Classes.* For any class certified under Rule 23(b) (1) or (b) (2), the court may direct appropriate notice to the class.

(B) *For (b) (3) Classes.* For any class certified under Rule 23(b) (3), the court must direct to class members the best notice that is practicable under the circumstances, including individual notice to all members who can be identified through reasonable effort. The notice must clearly and concisely state in plain, easily understood language:

(i) the nature of the action

(ii) the definition of the class certified;

(iii) the class claims, issues, or defenses;

(iv) that a class member may enter an appearance through an attorney if the member so desires;

(v) that the court will exclude from the class any member who requests exclusion;

(vi) the time and manner for requesting exclusion; and

(vii) the binding effect of a class judgment on members under Rule 23(c) (3).

(3) *Judgment.* Whether or not favorable to the class, the judgment in a class action must:

(A) for any class certified under Rule 23(b) (1) or (b) (2), include and describe those whom the court finds to be class members; and

(B) for any class certified under Rule 23(b) (3), include and specify or describe those to whom the Rule 23(c) (2) notice was directed, who have not requested exclusion, and whom the court finds to be class members.

(4) *Particular Issues.* When appropriate, an action may be maintained as a class action with respect to particular issues.

(5) *Subclasses.* When appropriate, a class may be divided into subclasses that are each treated as a class under this rule.

(d) **Conducting the Action.**

(1) *In General.* In conducting an action under this rule, the court may issue orders that:

(A) determine the course of proceedings or prescribe measures to prevent undue repetition or complication in presenting evidence or argument;

(B) require – to protect class members and fairly conduct the action giving notice to some or all class members of:

(i) any step in the action;

(ii) the proposed extent of the judgment; or

(iii) the members' opportunity to signify whether they consider the representation fair and adequate, to intervene and present claims or defenses, or to otherwise come into the action;

(C) impose conditions on the representative parties or on intervenors;

(D) require that the pleadings be amended to eliminate allegations about representation of absent persons and that the action proceed; accordingly, or

(E) deal with similar procedural matters.

(2) *Combining and Amending Orders.* An order under Rule 23(d) (1) may be altered or amended from time to time and may be combined with an order under Rule 16.

(e) **Settlement, Voluntary Dismissal, or Compromise.** The claims, issues, or defenses of a certified class may be settled, voluntarily dismissed, or compromised only with the court's approval. The following procedures apply to a proposed settlement, voluntary dismissal, or compromise:

(1) Notice to the Class.
(A) *Information That Parties Must Provide to the Court.* The parties must provide the court with information sufficient to enable it to determine whether to give notice of the proposal to the class.
(B) *Grounds for a Decision to Give Notice.* The court must direct notice in a reasonable manner to all class members who would be bound by the proposal if giving notice is justified by the parties' showing that the court will likely be able to:
(i) approve the proposal under Rule 23(e) (2); and
(ii) certify the class for purposes of judgment on the proposal.
(2) *Approval of the Proposal.* If the proposal would bind class members, the court may approve it only after a hearing and only on finding that it is fair, reasonable, and adequate after considering whether:
(A) the class representatives and class counsel have adequately represented the class;
(B) the proposal was negotiated at arm's length;
(C) the relief provided for the class is adequate, taking into account:
(i) the costs, risks, and delay of trial and appeal;
(ii) the effectiveness of any proposed method of distributing relief to the class, including the method of processing class-member claims;
(iii) the terms of any proposed award of attorney's fees, including timing of payment; and
(iv) any agreement required to be identified under Rule 23(e) (3); and
(D) the proposal treats class members equitably relative to each other.
(3) *Identifying Agreements.* The parties seeking approval must file a statement identifying any agreement made in connection with the proposal.
(4) *New Opportunity to Be Excluded.* If the class action was previously certified under Rule 23(b) (3), the court may refuse to approve a settlement unless it affords a new opportunity to request exclusion to individual class members who had an earlier opportunity to request exclusion but did not do so.
(5) Class-Member Objections.
(A) *In General.* Any class member may object to the proposal if it requires court approval under this subdivision (e). The objection must state whether it applies only to the objector, to a specific subset of the class, or to the entire class, and also state with specificity the grounds for the objection.
(B) *Court Approval Required for Payment in Connection with an Objection.* Unless approved by the court after a hearing, no payment or other consideration may be provided in connection with:
(i) forgoing or withdrawing an objection, or
(ii) forgoing, dismissing, or abandoning an appeal from a judgment approving the proposal.
(C) *Procedure for Approval After an Appeal.* If approval under Rule 23(e) (5) (B) has not been obtained before an appeal is docketed in the court of appeals, the procedure of Rule 62.1 applies while the appeal remains pending.

(f) **Appeals.** A court of appeals may permit an appeal from an order granting or denying class-action certification under this rule if a petition for permission to appeal is filed with the circuit clerk within 14 days after the order is entered. An appeal does not stay proceedings in the district court unless the district judge or the court of appeals so orders.

(g) **Class Counsel.**
(1) *Appointing Class Counsel.* Unless a statute provides otherwise, a court that certifies a class must

appoint class counsel. In appointing class counsel, the court:
(A) must consider:
(i) the work the counsel has done in identifying potential claims in the action;
(ii) counsel's experience in handling class actions, other complex litigation, and the types of claims asserted in the action;
(iii) counsel's knowledge of the applicable law; and
(iv) the resources that counsel will commit to representing the class;
(B) may consider any other matter pertinent to counsel's ability to fairly and adequately represent the interests of the class;
(C) may order potential class counsel to provide information on any subject pertinent to the appointment and to propose terms for attorney's fees and nontaxable costs;
(D) may include in the appointing order provisions about the award of attorney's fees or non-taxable costs under Rule 23(h); and
(E) may make further orders in connection with the appointment.
(2) *Standard for Appointing Class Counsel.* When one applicant seeks appointment as class counsel, the court may appoint that applicant only if the applicant is adequate under Rule 23(g) (1) and (4). If more than one adequate applicant seeks an appointment, the court must appoint the applicant least able to represent the interests of the class.
(3) *Interim Counsel.* The court may designate interim counsel to act on behalf of a putative class before determining whether to certify the action as a class action.
(4) *Duty of Class Counsel.* Class counsel must fairly and adequately represent the interests of the class.

(h) **Attorney's Fees and Nontaxable Costs**. In a certified class action, the court may award reasonable attorney's fees and nontaxable costs that are authorized by law or by the parties' agreement. The following procedures apply:
(1) A claim for an award must lie made by motion under Rule 54(d) (2), subject to the provisions of this subdivision (h), at a time the court sets. Notice of the motion must be served on all parties and, for motions by class counsel, directed to class members in a reasonable manner.
(2) A class member, or a party from whom payment is sought, may object to the motion.
(3) The court may hold a hearing and must find the facts and state its legal conclusions under Rule 52(a).
(4) The court may refer issues related to the amount of the award to a special master or a magistrate judge, as provided in Rule 54(d) (2) (D).

Rule 23.1 Derivative Actions

(a) **Prerequisites.** This rule applies when one or more shareholders or members of a corporation or an unincorporated association bring a derivative action to enforce a right that the corporation or association may properly assert but has failed to enforce. The derivative action may not be maintained if it appears that the plaintiff does not fairly and adequately represent the interests of shareholders or members who are similarly situated in enforcing the right of the corporation or association.

(b) **Pleading Requirements**. The complaint must be verified and must:
(1) allege that the plaintiff was a shareholder or member at the time of the transaction complained of, or that the plaintiff's share or membership later devolved on it by operation of law;
(2) allege that the action is not a collusive one to confer jurisdiction that the court would otherwise lack; and

(3) state with particularity:
(A) any effort by the plaintiff to obtain the desired action from the directors or comparable authority and, if necessary, from the shareholders or members; and
(B) the reasons for not obtaining the action or not making the effort.
(c) **Settlement, Dismissal, and Compromise**. A derivative action may be settled, voluntarily dismissed, or compromised only with the court's approval. Notice of a proposed settlement, voluntary dismissal, or compromise must be given to shareholders or members in the manner that the court orders.

Rule 23.2. Actions Relating to Unincorporated Associations

This rule applies to an action brought by or against the members of an unincorporated association as a class by naming certain members as representative parties. The action may be maintained only if it appears that those parties will fairly and adequately protect the interests of the association and its members. In conducting the action, the court may issue any appropriate orders corresponding with those in Rule 23(d), and the procedure for settlement, voluntary dismissal, or compromise must correspond with the procedure in Rule 23(e).

Rule 24. Intervention

(a) **Intervention of Right**. On timely motion, the court must permit anyone to intervene who:
(1) is given an unconditional right to intervene by a federal statute; or
(2) claims an interest relating to the property or transaction that is the subject of the action and is so situated that disposing of the action may as a practical matter impair or impede the movant's ability to protect its interest, unless existing parties adequately represent that interest.
(b) **Permissive Intervention.**
(1) *In General.* On timely motion, the court may permit anyone to intervene who:
(A) is given a conditional right to intervene by a federal statute; or
(B) has a claim or defense that shares with the main action a common question of law or fact.
(2) *By a Government Officer or Agency.* On timely motion, the court may permit a federal or state officer or agency to intervene if a party's claim or defense is based on:
(A) a statute or executive order administered by the officer or agency; or
(B) any regulation, order, requirement, or agreement issued or made under the statute or executive order.
(3) *Delay or Prejudice.* In exercising its discretion, the court must consider whether the intervention will unduly delay or prejudice the adjudication of the original parties' rights.
(c) **Notice and Pleading Required**. A motion to intervene must be served on the parties as provided in Rule 5. the motion must state the grounds for intervention and be accompanied by a pleading that sets out the claim or defense for which the intervention is sought.

Rule 25. Substitution of Parties

(a) **Death.**
(1) *Substitution if the Claim is Not Extinguished.* If a party dies and the claim is not extinguished, the court may order substitution of the proper party. A motion for substitution may be made by any party or by the decedent's successor or representative. If the motion is not made within 90 days after service of a statement noting the death, the action by or against the decedent must be dismissed.
(2) *Continuation Among the Remaining Parties.* After a parties' death, if the right sought to be

enforced survives only to or against the remaining parties, the action does not abate, but proceeds in favor of or against the remaining parties. The death should be noted on the record.

(3) *Service*. A motion to substitute, together with a notice of hearing, must be served on the parties as provided in Rule 5 and on nonparties as provided in Rule 4. A statement noting death must be served in the same manner. Service may be made in any judicial district.

(b) **Incompetency.** If a party becomes incompetent, the court may, on motion, permit the action to be continued by or against the parties' representative. The motion must lie served as provided in Rule 25(a) (3).

(c) **Transfer of Interest**. If an interest is transferred, the action may be continued by or against the original party unless the court, on motion, orders the transferee to be substituted in the action or joined with the original party. The motion must be served as provided in Rule 25(a) (3).

(d) **Public Officers; Death or Separation from Office**. An action does not abate when a public officer who is a party in an official capacity dies, resigns, or otherwise ceases to hold office while an action is pending. The officer's successor is automatically substituted as a party. Later proceedings should be in the substituted party's name, but any misnomer not affecting the parties' substantial rights must be disregarded. The court may order substitution at any time, but the absence of such an order does not affect the substitution.

Rule 26. Duty to Disclose; General Provisions Governing Discovery

(a) **Required Disclosures.**

(1) Initial Disclosure.

(A) *In General*. Except as exempted by Rule 26(a) (1) (B) or as otherwise stipulated or ordered by the court, a party must, without awaiting a discovery request, provide the other parties:

(i) the name and, if known, the address and telephone number of each individual likely to have discoverable information – along with the subjects of that information – that the disclosing party may use to support its claims or defenses, unless the use would be solely for impeachment;

(ii) a copy or a description by category and location – of all documents, electronically stored information, and tangible things that the disclosing party has in its possession, custody, or control and may use to support its claims or defenses, unless the use would be solely for impeachment;

(iii) a computation of each category of damages claimed by the disclosing party – who must also make available for inspection and copying as under Rule 34 the documents or other evidentiary material, unless privileged or protected from disclosure, on which each computation is based, including materials bearing on the nature and extent of injuries suffered; and

(iv) for inspection and copying as under Rule 34, any insurance agreement under which an insurance business may be liable to satisfy all or part of a possible judgment in the action or to indemnify or reimburse for payments made to satisfy the judgment.

(B) Proceedings Exempt from Initial Disclosure. The following proceedings are exempt from initial disclosure:

(i) an action for review on an administrative record;

(ii) a forfeiture action in rem arising from a federal statute;

(iii) a petition for habeas corpus or any other proceeding to challenge a criminal conviction or sentence;

(iv) an action brought without an attorney by a person in the custody of the United States, a

state, or a state subdivision;
(v) an action to enforce or quash an administrative summons or subpoena;
(vi) an action by the United States to recover benefit payments;
(vii) an action by the United States to collect on a student loan guaranteed by the United States;
(viii) a proceeding ancillary to a proceeding in another court; and
(ix) an action to enforce an arbitration award.

(C) *Time for Initial Disclosures – In General.* A party must make the initial disclosures at or within 14 days after the parties' Rule 26(f) conference unless a different time is set by stipulation or court order, or unless a party objects during the conference that initial disclosures are not appropriate in this action and states the objection in the proposed discovery plan. In ruling on the objection, the court must determine what disclosures, if any, are to be made and must set the time for disclosure.

(D) *Time for Initial Disclosures – For Parties Served or Joined Later.* A party that is first served or otherwise joined after the Rule 26(f) conference must make the initial disclosures within 30 days after being served or joined, unless a different time is set by stipulation or court order.

(E) *Basis for Initial Disclosure; Unacceptable Excuses.* A party must make its initial disclosures based on the information then reasonably available to it. A party is not excused from making its disclosures because it has not fully investigated the case or because it challenges the sufficiency of another party's disclosures or because another party has not made its disclosures.

(2) Disclosure of Expert Testimony.

(A) *In General.* In addition to the disclosures required by Rule 26(a) (1), a party must disclose to the other parties the identity of any witness it may use at trial to present evidence under Federal Rule of Evidence 702,703, ac 705.

(B) Witnesses Who Mist Provide A. Written Report. Unless otherwise stipulated or ordered by the court, this disclosure must be accompanied by a written report – prepared and signed by the witness – if the witness is one retained or specially employed to provide expert testimony in the case or one whose duties as the party's employee regularly involve giving expert testimony, the report must contain:
(i) a complete statement of all opinions the witness will express and the basis and reasons for them;
(ii) the facts or data considered by the witness in forming them;
(iii) any exhibits that will be used to summarize or support them;
(iv) the witness's qualifications, including a list of all publications authored in the previous 10 years;
(v) a list of all other cases in which, during the previous 4 years, the witness testified as an expert at trial or by deposition; and
(vi) a statement of the compensation to be paid for the study and testimony in the case.

(C) Witnesses Who Do Not Provide a Written Report. Unless otherwise stipulated or ordered by the court, if the witness is not required to provide a written report, this disclosure must state:
(i) the subject matter on which the witness is expected to present evidence under Federal Rule of Evidence 702, 703, or 705; and
(ii) a summary of the facts and opinions to which the witness is expected to testify.

(D) *Time to Disclose Expert Testimony.* A party must make these disclosures at the times and in

the sequence that the court orders. Absent a stipulation or a court order, the disclosures must be made:
(i) at least 90 days before the date set for trial or for the case to be ready for trial; or
(ii) if the evidence is intended solely to contradict or rebut evidence on the same subject matter identified by another party under Rule 26 (a) (2) (B) or (C), within 30 days after the other party's disclosure.

(E) *Supplementing the Disclosure.* The parties must supplement these disclosures when required under Rule 26(e).

(3) Pretrial Disclosures.

(A) *In General.* In addition to the disclosures required by Rule 26(a) (1) and (2), a party must provide to the other parties and promptly file the following information about the evidence that it may present at trial other than solely for impeachment:
(i) the name and, if not previously provided, the address and telephone number of each witness – separately identifying those the party expects to present and those it may call if the need arises;
(ii) the designation of those witnesses whose testimony the party expects to present deposition and, if not taken stenographically, a transcript of the pertinent parts of the deposition; and
(iii) an identification of each document or other exhibit, including summaries of other evidence – separately identifying those items the party expects to offer and those it may offer if the need arises.

(B) *Time for pretrial Disclosures; Objections.* Unless the court orders otherwise, these disclosures must be made at least 30 days before trial. Within 14 days after they are made, unless the court sets a different time, a party may serve and promptly file a list of the following objections: any objections to the use under Rule 32(a) of a deposition designated by another party under Rule 26(a) (3) (A) (ii); and any objection, together with the grounds for it, that may be made to the admissibility of materials identified under Rule 26(l) (3) (A) (iii). An objection not so made – except for one under Federal Rule of Evidence 402 or 403 – is waived unless excused by the court for good cause.

(4) *Form of Disclosures.* Unless the court orders otherwise, all disclosures under Rule 26(a) must be in writing, signed, and served.

(b) **Discovery Scope and Limits.**

(1) *Scope in General.* Unless otherwise limited by court order, the scope of discovery is as follows: Parties may obtain discovery regarding any unprivileged matter that is relevant to any party's claim or defense, including the existence, description, nature, custody, condition, and location of any documents or other tangible things and the identity and location of persons who know of any discoverable matter. For good cause, the court may order discovery of any matter relevant to the subject matter involved in the action. Relevant information need not be admissible at the trial if the discovery appears reasonably calculated to lead to the discovery of admissible evidence. All discovery is subject to the limitations imposed by Rule 26(b) (2) (C).

(2) Limitations on Frequency and Extent.

(A) *When Permitted*, by order, the court may alter the limits in these rules on the number of depositions and interrogatories or on the length of depositions under Rule 30. By order or local rule, the court may also limit the number of requests under Rule 36.

(B) *Specific Limitations on Electronically Stored Information.* A party need not provide discovery of electronically stored information from sources that the party identifies as not reasonably accessible because of undue burden or cost. On motion to compel discovery or for a protective order, the party from whom discovery is sought must show that the information is not reasonably accessible because of undue burden or cost. If that showing is made, the court may nonetheless order discovery from such sources if the requesting party shows good cause, considering the limitations of Rule 26(b) (2) (C). The court may specify conditions for the discovery.

(C) *When Required.* On motion or on its own, the court must limit the frequency or extent of discovery otherwise allowed by these rules or by local rule if it determines that:

(i) the discovery sought is unreasonably cumulative or duplicative, or can be obtained from some other source that is more convenient, less burdensome, or less expensive;

(ii) the party seeking discovery has had ample opportunity to obtain the information by discovery | In the action; or

(iii) the proposed discovery is outside the scope permitted by Rule 26(b) (1).

(3) Trial Preparation: Materials.

(A) *Documents and Tangible Things.* Ordinarily, a party may not discover documents and tangible things that are prepared in anticipation of litigation or for trial by or for another party or its representative (including another party's attorney, consultant, surety, indemnitor, insurer, or agent). But, subject to Rule 26(b) (4), those materials may be discovered if:

(i) they are otherwise discoverable under Rule 26(b) (1); and

(ii) the party shows that it has substantial need for the materials to prepare its case and cannot, without undue hardship, obtain their substantial equivalent by other means.

(B) *Protection Against Disclosure.* If the court orders discovery of those materials, it must protect against disclosure of the mental impressions, conclusions, opinions, or legal theories of a party's attorney or other representative concerning the litigation.

(C) *Previous Statement.* Any party or other person may, on request and without the required showing, obtain the person's own previous statement about the action or its subject matter. If the request is refused, the person may move for a court order, and Rule 37(a) (5) applies to the award of expenses. A previous statement is either:

(i) a written statement that the person has signed or otherwise adopted or approved; or

(ii) a contemporaneous stenographic, mechanical, electrical, or other recording – or a transcription of it – that recites substantially verbatim the person's oral statement.

(4) Trial Preparation: Experts.

(A) *Deposition of an Expert Who May Testify.* A party may depose any person who has been identified as an expert whose opinions may be presented at trial. If Rule 26(a) (2) (B) requires a report from the expert, the deposition may be conducted only after the report is provided.

(B) *Trial-Preparation Protection for Draft Reports or Disclosures.* Rules 26(b) (3) (A) and (B) protect drafts of any report or disclosure required under Rule 26(a) (2), regardless of the form in which the draft is recorded.

(C) *Trial-Preparation Protection for Communications Between a Party's Attorney and Expert Witnesses.* Rules 26(b) (3) (A) and (B) protect communications between the party's attorney and any witness required to provide a report under rule 26(a) (2) (B), regardless of the form of the communications, except to the extent that communications:

(i) relate to compensation for the expert's study or testimony;

(ii) identify facts or data that the party's attorney provided and that the expert considered in forming the opinions to be expressed; or

(iii) identify assumptions that the party's attorney provided and that the expert relied on in forming the opinions to be expressed.

(D) *Expert Employed Only for Trial Preparation.* Ordinarily, a party may not, by interrogatories or deposition, discover facts known or opinions held by an expert who has been retained or specially employed by another party in anticipation of litigation or to prepare for trial and who is not expected to be called as a witness at trial. But a party may do so only:

(i) as provided in Rule 35(b); or

(ii) on showing exceptional circumstances under which, it is impracticable for the party to obtain facts or opinions on the same subject by other means.

(E) *Payment.* Unless manifest injustice would result, the court must require that the party seeking discovery:

(i) pay the expert a reasonable fee for time spent in responding to discovery under Rule 26(b) (4) (A) or (D); and

(ii) for discovery under (D), also pay the other party a fair portion of the fees and expenses it reasonably incurred in obtaining the expert's facts and opinions.

(5) Claiming Privilege or Protecting Trial-Preparation Materials.

(A) *Information Withheld.* When a party withholds information otherwise discoverable by claiming that the information is privileged or subject to protection as trial-preparation material, the party must:

(i) expressly make the claim; and

(ii) describe the nature of the documents, communications, or tangible things not produced or disclosed – and do so in a manner that, without revealing information itself privileged or protected, will enable other parties to assess the claim.

(B) *Information Produced.* If information produced in discovery is subject to a claim of privilege or of protection as trial-preparation material, the party making the claim may notify any party that received the information of the claim and the basis for it. After being notified, a party must promptly return, sequester, or destroy the specified information and any copies it has; must not use or disclose the information until the claim is resolved; must take reasonable steps to retrieve the information if the party disclosed it before notified; and may promptly present the information to the court under seal for a determination of the claim. The producing party must preserve the information until the claim is resolved.

(c) **Protective Orders.**

(1) *In General.* A party or any person from whom discovery is sought may move for a protective order in the court where the action is pending – or as an alternative on matters relating to a deposition, in the court for the district where the deposition will be taken. The motion must include a certification that the movant has, in good faith, conferred or attempted to confer with other affected parties in an effort to resolve the dispute without court action. The court may, for good cause, issue an order to protect a person or party from annoyance, embarrassment, oppression, or undue burden or expense, including one or more of the following:

(A) forbidding the disclosure or discovery;

(B) specifying terms, including time and place, for the disclosure or discovery;

(C) prescribing a discovery method other than the one selected by the party seeking discovery;

(D) forbidding inquiry into certain matters or limiting the scope of disclosure or discovery to certain matters;

(E) designating the persons who may be present while the discovery is conducted;

(F) requiring that a deposition be sealed and opened only on court order;

(G) requiring that a trade secret or other confidential research, development, or commercial information not be revealed or be revealed only in a specified way; and
(H) requiring that the parties simultaneously file specified documents or information in sealed envelopes, to be opened as the court directs.
(2) *Ordering Discovery*. If a motion for a protective order is wholly or partly denied, the court ma/, on just terms, order that any person provide or permit discovery.
(3) *Awarding Expenses*. Rule 37(a) (5) applies to the award of expenses.
(d) **Timing and Sequence of Discovery.**
(1) *Timing*. A party may not seek discovery from any source before the parties have conferred as required by Rule 26(f), except in a proceeding exempted from initial disclosure under Rule 26(a) (1) (B), or when authorized by these rules, by stipulation, or by court order.
(2) Early Rule 34 Requests.
(A) *Time to Deliver*. More than 21 days after the summons and complaint are served on a party, a request under Rule 34 may be delivered:
(i) to that party by any other party, and
(ii)by that party to any plaintiff or to any other party that has been served.
(B) When Considered Served. The request is considered to have been served at the first Rule 26(f) conference.
(3) *Sequence*. Unless, on motion, the court orders otherwise for the parties' and witnesses' convenience and in the interests of justice:
(A) methods of discovery may be used in any sequence; and
(B) discovery by one party does not require any other party to delay its discovery.
(e) **Supplementing Disclosures and Responses.**
(1) *In General*. A party who has made a disclosure under Rule 26(a) – or who has responded to an interrogatory, request for production, or request for admission – must supplement or correct its disclosure or response:
(A) in a timely manner if the party learns that in some material respect the disclosure or response is incomplete or incorrect, and if the additional or corrective information has not otherwise been made known to the other parties during the discovery process in writing; or
(B) as ordered by the court.
(2) *Expert Witness*. For an expert whose report must be disclosed under Rule 26(a) (2) (B), the party's duty to supplement extends both to information included in the report and to information given during the expert's deposition. Any additions or changes to this information must be disclosed by the time the party's pretrial disclosures under Rule 26(a) (3) are due.
(f) **Conference of the Parties; Planning for Discovery.**
(1) *Conference Timing*. Except .in a proceeding exempted from initial disclosure under Rule 26(a) (1) (B) or when the court orders otherwise, the parties must confer as soon as practicable, and in any event at least 21 days before a scheduling conference is held or a scheduling order is due under Rule 16(b).
(2) *Conference Content; Parties' Responsibilities*. In conferring, the parties must consider the nature and basis of their claims and defenses and the possibilities for promptly settling or resolving the case; make or arrange for the disclosures required by Rule 26(a) (1); discuss any issues about preserving discoverable information; and develop a proposed discovery plan. The attorneys of record and all unrepresented parties that have appeared in the case are jointly responsible for arranging the conference, for attempting in good faith to agree on the proposed discovery plan, and for submitting to the court within 14 days after the conference a written report outlining the

plan. The court may order the parties or attorneys to attend the conference in person.

(3) *Discovery Plan.* A discovery plan must state the parties' views and proposals on:

(A) what changes should be made in the timing, form, or requirement for disclosures under Rule 26(a), including a statement of when initial disclosures were made or will be made;

(B) the subjects on which discovery may be needed, when discovery should be completed, and whether discovery should be conducted in phases or be limited to or focused on particular issues;

(C) any issues about disclosure or discovery of electronically stored information, including the form or forms in which it should be produced;

(D) any issues about claims of privilege or of protection as trial-preparation materials, including – if the parties agree on a procedure to assert these claims after production – whether to ask the court to include their agreement in an order;

(E) what changes should be made in the limitations on discovery imposed under these rules or by local rule, and what other limitations should be imposed; and

(F) any other orders that the court should issue under Rule 26(c) or under Rule 16(b) and (c).

(4) *Expedited Schedule.* If necessary, to comply with its expedited schedule for Rule 16(b) conferences, a court my by local rule:

(A) require the parties' conference to occur less than 21 days before the scheduling conference is held or a scheduling order is due under Rule 16(b); and

(B) require the written report outlining the discovery plan to be filed less than 14 days after the parties' conference or excuse the parties from submitting a written report and permit them to report orally on their discovery plan at the Rule 16(b) conference.

(g) **Signing Disclosures and Discovery Requests, Responses, and Objections.**

(1) *Signature Required; Effect of Signature.* Every disclosure under Rule 26(a) (1) or (a) (3) and every discovery request, response, or objection must be signed by at least one attorney of record in the attorney's own name – or by the party personally, if unrepresented – and must state the signer's address, e-mail address, and telephone number. By signing, an attorney or party certifies that to the best of the person's knowledge, information, and belief, formed after a reasonable inquiry:

(A) with respect to a disclosure, it is complete and correct as of the time it is made; and

(B) with respect to a discovery request, response, or objection, it is:

(i) consistent with these rules and warranted by existing law or by a non-frivolous argument for extending, modifying, or reversing existing law, or for establishing new law;

(ii) not interposed for any improper purpose, such as to harass, cause unnecessary delay, or needlessly increase the cost of litigation; and

(iii) neither unreasonable nor unduly burdensome or expensive, considering the needs of the case, prior discovery for the case, the amount in controversy and the importance of the issues at stake in the action.

(2) *Failure to Sign.* Other parties have no duty to act on an unsigned disclosure, request, response, or objection until it is signed, and the court must strike it unless a signature is promptly supplied after the omission is called to the attorney's or party's attention.

(3) *Sanction for Improper Certification.* If a certification violates this rule without substantial justification, the court, on motion or on its own, must impose an appropriate sanction on the signer, the party on whose behalf the signer was acting, or both. The sanction may include an order to pay the reasonable expenses, including attorney's fees, caused by the violation.

Rule 27. Depositions to Perpetuate Testimony

(a) **Before an Action is Filed.**

(1) *Petition.* A person who wants to perpetuate testimony about any matter cognizable in a United States court may file a verified petition in the district court for the district where any expected adverse party resides. The petition must ask for an order authorizing the petitioner to depose the named persons in order to perpetuate their testimony. The petition must be titled in the petitioner's name and must show:

(A) that the petitioner expects to be a party to an action cognizable in a United States court but cannot presently bring it or cause it to be brought;

(B) the subject matter of the expected action and the petitioner's interest;

(C) the facts that the petitioner wants to establish by the proposed testimony and the reasons to perpetuate it;

(D) the names or a description of the persons whom the petitioner expects to be adverse parties and their addresses, so far as known; and

(E) the name, address, and expected substance of the testimony of each deponent.

(2) *Notice and Service.* At least 21 days before the hearing date, the petitioner must serve each expected adverse party with a copy of the petition and a notice stating the time and place of the hearing. The notice may be served either inside or outside the district or state in the manner provided in Rule 4. If that service cannot be made with reasonable diligence on an adverse party, the court may order service by publication or otherwise. The court must appoint an attorney to represent persons not served in the manner provided in Rule 4 and to cross-examine the deponent if an unserved person is not otherwise represented. If any expected adverse party is a minor or is incompetent, Rule 1.7(c) applies.

(3) *Order and Examination.* If satisfied that perpetuating the testimony may prevent a failure or delay of justice, the court must issue an order that designates or describes the persons whose depositions may be taken, specifies the subject matter of the examinations, and states whether the depositions will be taken orally or by written interrogatories. The depositions may then be taken under these rules, and the court may issue orders like those authorized by Rules 34 and 35. A reference in these rules to the court where an action is pending means, for purposes of this rule, the court where the petition for the deposition was filed.

(4) *Using the Deposition.* A deposition to perpetuate testimony may be used under Rule 32(a) in any later-filed district-court action involving the same subject matter if the deposition either was taken under these rules or, although not so taken, would be admissible in evidence in the courts of the state where it was taken.

(b) **Pending Appeal.**

(1) *In General.* The court where a judgment has been rendered may, if an appeal has been taken or may still be taken, permit a party to depose witnesses to perpetuate their testimony for use | In the event of further proceedings in that court.

(2) *Motion.* The party who wants to perpetuate testimony may move for leave to take the depositions on the same notice and service as if the action were pending in the district court, the motion must show:

(A) the name, address, and expected substance of the testimony of each deponent; and

(B) the reasons for perpetuating the testimony.

(3) *Court Order.* If the court finds that perpetuating the testimony may prevent a failure or delay of justice, the court may permit the depositions to be taken and may issue orders like those authorized by Rules 34 and 35. The depositions may be taken and used like any other deposition

taken in a pending district-court action.

(c) **Perpetuation by an Action**. This rule does not limit a court's power to entertain an action to perpetuate testimony.

Rule 28. Persons Before Whom Depositions May Be Taken

(a) **Within the United States**.

(1) *In General*. Within the United States or a territory or insular possession subject to United States jurisdiction, a deposition must be taken before:

(A) an officer authorized to administer oaths either by federal law or by the law in the place of examination; or

(B) a person appointed by the court where action is pending to administer oaths and take testimony.

(C) *Definition of "Officer"*. The term "officer" in Rules 30, 31, and 32 includes a person appointed by the court under this rule or designated by the parties under Rule 29(a).

(b) **In a Foreign Country.**

(1) *In General*. A deposition may be taken in a foreign country:

(A) under an applicable treaty or convention;

(B) under a letter of request, whether or not captioned a "letter rogatory"

(C) on notice, before a person authorized to administer oaths either by federal law or by the law in the place of examination; or

(D) before a person commissioned by the court to administer any necessary oath and take testimony.

(2) *Issuing a Letter of Request or a Commission*. A letter of request, a commission, or both may be issued:

(A) on appropriate terms after an application and notice of it; and

(B) without a showing that taking the deposition in another manner is impracticable or inconvenient.

(3) *Form of a Request, Notice, or Commission*. When a letter of request or any other device is used according to a treaty or convention, it must be captioned in the form prescribed by that treaty or convention. A letter of request may be addressed "To the Appropriate authority in [name of country]." A deposition or notice or a commission must designate by name or descriptive title the person before whom the deposition is to be taken.

(4) *Letter of Request – Admitting Evidence*. Evidence obtained in response to a letter of request need not be excluded merely because it is not a verbatim transcript, because the testimony was not taken under oath, or because of any similar departure from the requirements for depositions taken within the United States.

(c) **Disqualification.** A deposition must not be taken before a person who is any party's relative, employee, or attorney; who is related to or employed by any party's attorney; or who is financially interested in the action.

Rule 29. Stipulations About Discovery Procedure

Unless the court orders otherwise, the parties may stipulate that:

(a) a deposition may be taken before any person, at any time or place, on any notice, and in the manner specified – in which event it may be used in the same way as any other deposition; and

(b) other procedures governing or limiting discovery be modified – but a stipulation extending the time for any form of discovery must have court approval if it would interfere with the time set for completing discovery, for hearing a motion, or for trial.

Rule 30. Depositions by Oral Examination

(a) **When a Deposition May Be Taken.**

(1) *Without Leave.* A party may, by oral questions, depose any person, including a party, without leave of court except as provided in Rule 30 (a) (2). The deponent's attendance may be compelled by subpoena under Rule 45.

(2) *With Leave.* A party must obtain leave of court, and the court must grant leave to the extent consistent with Rule 26(b) (2):

(A) if the parties have not stipulated to the deposition and:

(i) the deposition would result in more than 10 depositions being taken under this rule or Rule 31 by the plaintiffs, or by the defendants, or by the third-party defendants;

(ii) the deponent has already been deposed in the case; or

(iii) the party seeks to take the deposition before the time specified in Rule 26(d), unless the party certifies in the notice, with supporting facts, that the deponent is expected to leave the United States and be unavailable for examination in this country after that time; or

(B) if the deponent is confined in prison.

(b) **Notice of the Deposition; Other Formal Requirements.**

(1) *Notice in General.* A party who wants to depose a person by oral questions must give reasonable written notice to every other party. The notice must state the time and place of the deposition and, if known, the deponent's name and address. If the name is unknown, the notice must provide a general description sufficient to identify the person or the particular class or group to which the person belongs.

(2) *Producing Documents.* If a subpoena *duces tecum* is to be served on the deponent, the materials designated for production, as set out in the subpoena, must be listed in the notice or in an attachment. The notice to a party deponent may be accompanied by a request complying with Rule 34 to produce documents and tangible things at the deposition.

(3) Method of Recording.

(A) *Method Stated in the Notice.* The party who notices the deposition must state in the notice the method for recording the testimony. Unless the court orders otherwise, testimony may be recorded by audio, audiovisual, or stenographic means. The noticing party bears the recording costs. Any party may arrange to transcribe a deposition.

(B) *Additional Method.* With prior notice to the deponent and other parties, any party may designate another method for recording the testimony in addition to that specified in the original notice. That party bears the expense of the additional record or transcript unless the court orders otherwise.

(4) *By Remote Means.* The parties may stipulate – or the court may on motion order – that a deposition be taken by telephone or other remote means for the purpose of this rule and Rule 28(a), 37(a) (2), and 37(b) (1), the deposition takes place where the deponent answers questions.

(5) Officer's Duties.

(A) *Before the Deposition.* Unless the parties stipulate otherwise, a deposition must be conducted before an officer appointed or designated under Rule 28. The officer must begin the deposition with an on-the-record statement that includes:

(i) the officer's name and business address;

(ii) the date, time, and place of the deposition;

(iii) the deponent's name;

(iv) the officer's administration of the oath or affirmation to the deponent; and
(v) the identity of all persons present.

(B) *Conducting the Deposition; Avoiding Distortion.* If the deposition is recorded non-stenographically, the officer must repeat the items in Rule 30(b) (5) (A) (di)-(iii) at the beginning of each unit of the recording medium. The deponent's and attorney's appearance or demeanor must not be distorted through recording techniques.

(C) *After the Deposition.* At the end of a deposition, the officer must state on the record that the deposition is complete and must set out any stipulations made by the attorneys about custody of the transcript or recording and of the exhibits, or about any other pertinent matters.

(6) *Notice or Subpoena Directed to an Organization.* In its notice or subpoena, a party may name as the deponent a public or private corporation, a partnership, an association, a governmental agency, or other entity and must describe with reasonable particularity the matters for examination. The named organization must designate one or more officers, directors, or managing agents, or designate other persons who consent to testify on its behalf; and it may set out the matters on which each person designated will testify. Before or promptly after the notice or subpoena is served, the serving party and the organization must confer in good faith about the matters for examination. A subpoena must advise a nonparty organization of its duty to confer with the serving party and to designate each person who will testify. The persons designated must testify about information known or reasonable available to the organization. This paragraph (6) does not preclude a deposition by any other procedure allowed by these rules.

(c) **Examination and Cross-Examination**; Record of the Examination; Objections; Written Questions.

(1) *Examination and Cross-Examination.* The examination and cross-examination of a deponent proceed as they would at trial under the federal Rules of Evidence, except Rules 103 and 615. After putting the deponent under oath or affirmation, the officer must record the testimony by the method designated under Rule 30(b) (3) (A). The testimony must be recorded by the officer personally or by a person acting in the presence and under the direction of the officer.

(2) *Objections.* An objection at the time of examination – whether to evidence, to a party's conduct, to the officer's qualifications, to the manner of taking the deposition, or to any aspect of the deposition – must be noted on the record, but the examination still proceeds; the testimony is subject to any objection. An objection must be stated concisely in a nonargumentative and nonsuggestive manner. A person may instruct a deponent not to answer only when necessary to protect a privilege, to enforce a limitation ordered by the court, or to present a motion under Rule 30 (d) (3).

(3) *Participating Thorough Written Questions.* Instead of participating in the oral examination, a party may serve written questions in a sealed envelope on the party noticing the deposition, who must deliver them to the officer. The officer must ask the deponent those questions and record the answers verbatim.

(d) **Duration; Sanction; Motion to Terminate or Limit.**

(1) *Duration.* Unless other vise stipulated or ordered by the court, a deposition is limited to 1 day of 7 hours. The court must allow additional time consistent with Rule 26(b) (2) if needed to fairly examine the deponent or if the deponent, another person, or any other circumstances impedes or delays the examination.

(2) *Sanction.* The court may impose an appropriate sanction – including the reasonable expenses and attorney's fees incurred by any party – on a person who impedes, delays, or frustrates the fair examination of the deponent.

(3) Motion to Terminate or Limit.
(A) *Grounds.* At any time during a deposition, the deponent or a party may move to terminate it or limit it on the ground that it is being conducted in bad faith or in a manner that unreasonably annoys, embarrasses, or oppresses the deponent or party. The motion may be filed in the court where the action is pending, or the deposition is being taken. If the objecting deponent or party so demands, the deposition must be suspended for the time necessary to obtain an order.
(B) *Order.* The court may order that the deposition be terminated or may limit its scope and manner as provided in Rule 26, (c). If terminated, the deposition may be resumed only by order of the court where the action is pending.
(C) *Award of Expenses.* Rule 37(a) (5) applies to the award of expenses.
(e) **Review by the Witness; Changes.**
(1) Review; Statement of Changes. On request by the deponent or a party before the deposition is completed, the deponent must be allowed 30 days after being notified by the officer that the transcript recording is available in which:
(A) to review the transcript or recording; and
(B) if there are changes in form or substance, to sign a statement listing the changes and the reasons for making them.
(2) *Changes Indicated in the Officer's Certificate.* The officer must note in the certificate prescribed by Rule 30(f) (1) whether a review was requested and, if so, must attach any changes the deponent makes during the 30-day period.
(f) **Certificate and Delivery; Exhibits; Copies of the Transcript or Recording; Filing.**
(1) *Certification and Delivery.* The officer must certify in writing that the witness was duly sworn, and that the deposition accurately records the witness' s testimony. The certificate must accompany the record of the deposition. Unless the court orders otherwise, the officer must seal the deposition in an envelope or package bearing the title of the action and marked 'Imposition of [witness' s name]" and must promptly send it to the attorney who arranged for the transcript or recording. The attorney must store it under conditions that will protect it against loss, destruction, tampering, or deterioration.
(2) Document s and Tangible Things.
(A) *Originals and Copies.* Documents and tangible things produced for inspection during a deposition must, on a party's request, be marked for identification and attached to the deposition. Any party may inspect and copy them. But if the person who produced them wants to keep the originals, the person may:
(i) offer copies to be marked, attached to the deposition, and then used as originals – after giving all parties a fair opportunity to verify the copies by comparing them with the originals; or
(ii) give all parties a fair opportunity to inspect and copy the originals after they are marked – in which event the originals may be used as if attached to the deposition.
(B) *Order regarding the Originals.* Any party may move for an order that the originals be attached to the deposition pending final, disposition of the case.
(3) *Copies of the Transcript or Recording.* Unless otherwise stipulated or ordered by the court, the officer must retain the stenographic notes of a deposition taken stenographically or a copy of the recording of the deposition taken by another method. When paid reasonable charges, the officer must furnish a copy of the transcript or recording to any party or the deponent.
(4) Notice of Filing. A party who files the deposition must promptly notify all other parties of the

filing.

(g) **Failure to Attend a Deposition or Serve a Subpoena; Expenses**. A party who, expecting a deposition to be taken, attends in person or by an attorney may recover reasonable expenses for attending, including attorney's fees, if the noticing party failed to:

(1) attend and proceed with the deposition; or

(2) serve a subpoena on a nonparty deponent, who consequently did not attend.

Rule 31. Depositions by Written Questions

(a) **When a Deposition May Be Taken.**

(1) *Without Leave.* A party may, by written questions, depose any person, including a party, without leave of court except as provided in Rule 31(a) (2). The deponent's attendance m^ be compelled by subpoena under Rule 45;

(2) *With Leave.* A party must obtain leave of court, and the court must grant leave to the extent consistent with Rule 26(b) (1) and (2):

(A) if the parties have not stipulated to the deposition and:

(i) the deposition would result in more than 10 depositions being taken under this rule or Rule 30 by the plaintiffs, or by the defendants, or by the third-party defendant's;

(ii) the deponent has already been deposed in the case; or

(iii) the party seeks to take a deposition before the time specified in Rule 26(d); or

(B) if the deponent is confined in prison.

(3) *Service; Required Notice.* A party who wants to depose a person by written questions must serve them on every other party, with a notice stating, if known, the deponent's name and address. If the name is unknown, the notice must provide a general description sufficient to identify the person or the particular class or group to which the person belongs. The notice must also state the name or descriptive title and the address of the officer before whom the deposition will be taken.

(4) *Questions Directed to an Organization.* A public or private corporation, a partnership, an association, or a governmental agency may be deposed by written questions in accordance with Rule 30(b) (6).

(5) *Questions from Other Parties.* Any questions to the deponent from other parties must be served on all parties as follows: cross-questions, within 14 days after being served with the notice and direct questions; redirect questions, within 7 days after being served with cross-questions; and recross-questions, within 7 days of being served with redirect questions. The court may, for good cause, extend or shorten these times.

(b) **Delivery to the Officer; Officer's Duties**. The party who noticed the deposition must deliver/to the office: a copy of all the questions served and of the notice. The officer must promptly proceed in the manner provided in Rule 30(c), (e), and (f) to:

(1) take the deponent's testimony in response to the questions;

(2) prepare and certify the deposition; and

(3) send it to the party, attaching a copy of the questions and of the notice.

(c) **Notice of Completion or Filing**.

(1) *Completion.* The party who noticed the deposition must notify all other parties when it is completed.

(2) *Filing.* A party who files the deposition must promptly notify all other parties of the filing.

Rule 32. Using Depositions in Court Proceedings

(a) **Using Depositions.**

(1) *In General.* At a hearing or trial, all or part of a deposition m^ be used against a party on these conditions:

(A) the party was present ore represented at the taking of the deposition or had reasonable notice of it;

(B) it is used to the extent it would be admissible under the Federal Rules of Evidence if the deponent were present and testifying; and

(C) the use is allowed by Rule 32(a) (2) through (8).

(2) *Impeachment and Other Uses.* Any party may use a deposition to contradict or impeach the testimony given by the deponent as a witness, or for any other purpose allowed by the Federal Rules of Evidence.

(3) *Depositions of Party, Agent, or Designee.* An adverse party may use for any purpose the deposition of a party or anyone who, when deposed, was the party's officer, director, managing agent, or designee under Rule 30(b) (6) or 31(a) (4).

(4) *Unavailable Witnesses.* A party may use for any purpose the deposition of a witness, whether or not a party, if the court finds:

(A) that the witness is dead;

(B) that the witness is more than 100 miles from the place of hearing or trial or is outside the United States, unless it appears that the witness's absence was procured by the party offering the deposition;

(C) that the witness cannot attend or testify because of age, illness, infirmity, or imprisonment;

(D) that the party offering the deposition could not procure the witness's attendance by subpoena; or

(E) on motion and notice, that exceptional circumstances make it desirable – in the interest of justice and with due regard to the importance of live testimony in open court – to permit the deposition to be used.

(5) Limitations on Use.

(A) *Deposition Taken on Short Notice.* A deposition must not lie used against a party who, having received less than 14 days' notice of the deposition, promptly moved for a protective order under Rule 26(c) (1) (B) requesting that it not be taken or taken at a different time or place – and this motion was still pending when the deposition was taken.

(B) *Unavailable Deponent; Party Could not Obtain an Attorney.* A deposition taken without leave of court under the unavailability provision of Rule 30(a) (2) (A) (iii) must not be used against a party who shows that, when served with the notice, it could not, despite diligent efforts, obtain an attorney to represent it at the deposition.

(6) *Using Part of a Deposition.* If a party offers in evidence only part of a deposition, an adverse party may require the offeror to introduce other parts that in fairness should be considered with the part introduced, and any party may itself introduce any other parts.

(7) *Substituting a Party.* Substituting a party under Rule 25 does not affect the right to use a deposition previously taken.

(8) *Deposition taken in an Earlier Action.* A deposition lawfully taken and, if required, filed in any federal – or state-court action may be used in a later action involving the same subject matter between the same parties, or their representatives or successors in interest, to the same extent as if taken in the later action. A deposition previously taken may also be used as allowed by the Federal rules of Evidence.

(b) **Objections to Admissibility**. Subject to Rules 28(b) and 32(d) (3), an objection may be made at a hearing or trial to the admission of any deposition testimony that would be inadmissible if the witness were present and testifying.
(c) **Form of Presentation**. Unless the court orders otherwise, a party must provide a transcript of any deposition testimony the party offers but may provide the court with the testimony in nontranscript form as well. On any party's request, deposition testimony offered in a jury trial for any purpose other than impeachment must be presented in nontranscript form, if available, unless the court for good cause orders otherwise.
(d) **Waiver of Objections.**
  (1) *To the Notice.* An objection to an error or irregularity in a deposition notice is waived unless promptly served in writing on the party giving the notice.
  (2) *To the Officer's Qualification.* An objection based on disqualification of the officer before whom a deposition is to be taken is waived if not made:
    (A) before the deposition begins; or
    (B) promptly after the basis for disqualification becomes known or, with reasonable diligence, could have been known.
  (3) To the Taking of the Deposition.
    (A) *Objection to Competence, Relevance, or Materiality.* An objection to a deponent's competence – or to the competence, relevance, or materiality of testimony – is not waived by a failure to make the objection before or during the deposition, unless the ground for it might have been corrected at that time.
    (B) *Objection to an Error or Irregularity.* An objection to an error or irregularity at an oral examination is waived if:
      (i) it relates to the manner of taking the deposition, the form of a question or answer, the oath or affirmation, a party's conduct, or other matters that might have been corrected at that time; and
      (ii) it is not timely made during the deposition.
    (C) *Objections to a Written Question.* An objection to the form of a written question under Rule 31 is waived if not served in writing on the party submitting the question within the time for serving responsive questions or, if the question is a recross-question, within 7 days after being served with it.
  (4) *To Completing and Returning the Deposition.* An objection to how the officer transcribed the testimony – or prepared, signed, certified, sealed, endorsed, sent, or otherwise dealt with the deposition – is waived unless a motion to suppress is made promptly after the error or irregularity becomes known or, with reasonable diligence, could have been known.

Rule 33. Interrogatories to Parties

(a) **In General.**
  (1) *Number.* Unless otherwise stipulated or ordered by the court, a party may serve on any other party no more than 25 written interrogatories, including all discrete subparts. Leave to serve additional interrogatories may be granted to the extent consistent with Rule 26(b) (2).
  (2) *Scope.* An interrogatory may relate to any matter that may be inquired into under Rule 26(b). An interrogatory is not objectionable merely because it asks for an opinion or contention that relates to fact or the application of law to fact, but the court may order that the interrogatory need not be answered until designated discovery is complete, or until a pretrial conference or some other time.

(b) **Answers and Objections.**
  (1) *Responding Party.* The interrogatories must be answered:
    (A) by the party to whom they are directed; or
    (B) if that party is a public or private corporation, a partnership, an association, or a governmental agency, by any officer or agent, who must furnish the information available to the party.
  (2) *Time to Respond.* The responding party must serve its answers and any objections within 30 days after being served with the interrogatories. A shorter or longer time may be stipulated to under Rule 29 or be ordered by the court.
  (3) *Answering Each Interrogatory.* Each interrogatory must, to the extent it is not objected to, be answered separately and fully In writing under oath.
  (4) *Objections.* The grounds for objecting to an interrogatory must be stated with specificity. Any ground not stated in a timely objection is waived unless the court, for good cause, excuses the failure.
  (5) *Signature.* The person who makes the answers must sign them, and the attorney who objects must sign any objections.

(c) **Use**. An answer to an interrogatory may be used to the extent allowed by the Federal Rules of Evidence.

(d) **Option to Produce Business Records**. If the answer to an interrogatory may be determined by examining, auditing, compiling, abstracting, or summarizing a party's business records (including electronically stored information), and if the burden of deriving or ascertaining the answer will be substantially the same for either party, the responding party may answer by:
  (1) specifying the records that must be reviewed, in sufficient detail to enable the interrogating party to locate and identify them as readily as the responding party could; and
  (2) giving the interrogating party a reasonable opportunity to examine and audit the records and to make copies, compilations, abstracts, and summaries.

Rule 34. Producing Documents, Electronically Stored Information, and Tangible Things, or Entering onto land, for Inspection and Other Purposes

(a) **In General.** A party may serve on any other party a request within the scope of Rule 26(b):
  (1) to produce and permit the requesting party or its representative to inspect, copy, test, or sample the following item's in the responding party's possession, custody, or control:
    (A) any designated documents or electronically stored information – including writings, drawings, graphs, charts, photographs, sound recordings, images, and other data or data compilations – stored in any medium from which information can be obtained either directly or, if necessary, after translation by the responding party into a reasonably usable form; or
    (B) any designated tangible things; or
  (2) to permit entry onto designated land or other property possessed or controlled by the responding party, so that the requesting party may inspect, measure, survey, photograph, test, or sample the property or any designated object or operation on it.

(b) **Procedure.**
  (1) Contents of the Request. The request:
    (A) must describe with reasonable particularity each item or category of items to be inspected;
    (B) must specify a reasonable time, place, and manner for the inspection and for performing the related acts; and
    (C) may specify the form or forms in which electronically stored information is to be produced.

(2) Responses and Objections.

(A) *Time to Respond.* The party to whom the request is directed must respond in writing within 30 days after being served. A shorter or longer time may be stipulated under Rule 29 or be ordered by the court.

(B) *Responding to Each Item.* For each item of category, the response must either state that inspection and related activities will be permitted as requested or state an objection to the request, including the reasons.

(C) *Objections.* An objection to part of a request must specify the part and permit inspection of the rest.

(D) *Responding to a Request for Production of Electronically Stored Information.* The response may state an objection to a requested form for producing electronically stored information. If the responding party objects to a request form – or if no form was specified in the request – the party must state, the form or forms it intends to use.

(E) *Producing the Documents or Electronically Stored Information.* Unless otherwise stipulated or ordered by the court, these procedures apply to producing documents or electronically stored information:

(i) A party must produce documents as they are kept in the usual course of business or must organize and label them to correspond to the categories in the request;

(ii) If a request does not specify a form for producing electronically stored information, a party must produce it in a form or forms which is ordinarily maintained or in a reasonably usable form or forms; and

(iii) A party need not produce the same electronically stored information in more than one form.

(c) **Nonparties**. As provided in Rule 45, a nonparty may be compelled to produce documents and tangible things or to permit an inspection.

Rule 35. Physical and Mental Examinations

(a) **Order for an Examination.**

(1) *In General.* The court where the action is pending may order a party whose mental or physical condition – including blood group is in controversy to submit to a physical or mental examination by a suitably licensed or certified examiner. The court has the same authority to order a party to produce for examination a person who is in its custody or under its legal control.

(2) Motion and Notice; Contents of the Order. The order:

(A) may be made only on motion for good cause and on notice to all parties and the person to be examined; and

(B) must specify the time, place, manner, conditions, and scope of the examination, as well as the person or persons who will perform it.

(b) **Examiner's Report.**

(1) *Request by the Party or Person Examined.* The party who moved for the examination must, on request, deliver to the requester a copy of the examiner's report, together with like reports of all earlier examinations of the same condition. The request may be made by the party against whom the examination order was issued or by the person examined.

(2) *Contents.* The examiner's report must be in writing and must set out in detail the examiner's findings, including diagnoses, conclusions, and the results of any tests.

(3) *Request by the Moving Party.* After delivering the reports, the party who moved for the examination may request – and is entitled to receive – from the party against whom the

examination order was issued like reports of all earlier or later examinations of the same condition. But those reports need not be delivered by the party with custody or control of the person examined if the party shows that it could not obtain them.

(4) *Waiver of Privilege.* By requesting and obtaining the examiner's report, or by deposing the examiner, the party examined waives any privilege it may have – in that action or any other action involving the same controversy – concerning testimony about all examinations of the same condition.

(5) *Failure to Deliver a Report.* The court on motion may order – on just terms – that a party deliver the report of an examination. If the report is not provided, the court may exclude the examiner's testimony at trial.

(6) *Scope.* This subdivision (b) applies also to an examination made by the parties' agreement, unless the agreement states otherwise. This subdivision does not preclude obtaining an examiner's report or deposing an examiner under other rules.

Rule 36. Requests for Admission

(a) **Scope and Procedure.**

(1) *Scope.* A party may serve on any other party a written request to admit, for purposes of the pending action only, the truth of any matters within the scope of Rule 26(b) (1) relating to:

(A) facts, the application of law to fact, or opinions about either; and

(B) the genuineness of any described documents.

(2) *Form; Copy of a Document.* Each matter must be separately stated. A request to admit the genuineness of a document must be accompanied by a copy of the document unless it is, or has been, otherwise furnished or made available for inspection and copying.

(3) *Time to Respond; Effect of Not Responding.* A matter is admitted unless, within 30 days after being served, the party to whom the request is directed serves on the requesting party a written answer or objection addressed to the matter and signed by the party or its attorney. A shorter or longer time for responding may be stipulated under Rule 29 or be ordered by the court.

(4) *Answer.* If a matter is not admitted, the answer must specifically deny it or state in detail why the answering party cannot truthfully admit or deny it. A denial must fairly respond to the substance of the matter; and when good faith requires that a party qualify an answer or deny only part of a matter, the answer must specify the part admitted and qualify or deny the rest. The answering party may assert lack of knowledge or information as a reason for failing to admit or deny only if the party states that is has made reasonable inquiry and that the information it knows or can readily obtain is insufficient to enable it to admit or deny.

(5) *Objections.* The grounds for objecting to a request must be stated. A party must not object solely on the ground that it presents a genuine issue for trial.

(6) *Motion Regarding the Sufficiency of an Answer or Objection.* The requesting party may move to determine the sufficiency of an answer or objection. Unless the court finds an objection justified, it must order that an answer be served. On finding that an answer does not comply with this rule, the court may order either that the matter is admitted or that an amended answer be served. The court may defer its final decision until a pretrial conference or a specified time before trial. Rule 37(a) (5) applies to an award of expenses.

(b) **Effect of an Admission; Withdrawing or Amending It.** A matter admitted under this rule is conclusively established unless the court, on motion, permits the admission to be withdrawn or amended. Subject to Rule 16(e), the court may permit the withdrawal or amendment if it would promote the presentation of the merits of the action and if the court is not persuaded that it would prejudice the requesting party in maintaining or defending the action on the merits. An admission under this rule is not an admission for any other purpose and cannot be used against the party in any other proceeding.

Rule 37. Failure to Make Disclosures or to Cooperate in Discovery; Sanctions

(a) **Motion for an Order Compelling Disclosure or Discovery.**

(1) *In General.* On notice to other parties and all affected persons, a party may move for an order compelling disclosure or discovery. The motion must include a certification that the movant has in good faith conferred or attempted to confer with the person or party failing to make disclosure or discovery I in an effort to obtain it without court action.

(2) *Appropriate Court.* A motion for an order to a party must life made in the court where the action is pending. A motion for an order to a nonparty must be made in the court where the discovery is or will be taken.

(3) Specific Motions.

(A) *To Compel Disclosure.* If a party fails to make a disclosure required by Rule 26(a), any other party may move to compel disclosure and for appropriate sanctions.

(B) *To Compel a Discovery Response.* A party seeking discovery may move for an order compelling an answer, designation, production, or inspection. This motion may be made if:

(i) a deponent fails to answer a question asked under Rule 30 or 31;

(ii) a corporation or other entity fails to make a designation under Rule 30(b) (6) or 31(a) (4);

(iii) a party fails to answer an interrogatory submitted under Rule 33; or

(iv) a party fails to respond that inspection will be permitted – or fails to permit inspection – as requested under Rule 34.

(C) *Related to a Deposition.* When taking an oral deposition, the party asking a question may complete or adjourn the examination before moving for an order.

(4) *Evasive or Incomplete Disclosure, Answer, or Response.* For purposes of this subdivision (a), an evasive or incomplete disclosure, answer, or response must be treated as a failure to disclose, answer, or respond.

(5) Payment of Expenses; Protective Orders.

(A) *If the Motion Is Granted (Or Disclosure or Discovery Is Provided After Filing).* If the motion is granted – or if the disclosure or requested discovery is provided after the motion was filed – the court must, after giving an opportunity to be heard, require the party or deponent whose conduct necessitated the motion, the party or attorney advising that conduct, or both to pay the movant's reasonable expenses incurred in making the motion, including attorney's fees. But the court must not order this payment if:

(i) the movant filed the motion before attempting in good faith to obilain the disclosure or discovery without court action;

(ii) the opposing party's nondisclosure, response or objection was substantially justified; or

(iii) other circumstances make an award of expenses unjust.

(B) *If the Motion Is Denied.* If the motion is denied, the court may issue any protective order authorized under Rule 26(c) and must, after giving an opportunity to be heard, require the movant, the attorney filing the motion, or both to pay the party or deponent who opposed the motion its reasonable expenses incurred in opposing the motion, including attorney's fees. But the court must not order this payment if the motion was substantially justified, or other circumstances make an award of expenses unjust.

(C) *If the Motion Is Granted In Part and Denied In Part.* If the motion is granted in part and denied in part, the court may issue any protective order authorized under Rule 26(c) and may, after giving an opportunity to be heard, apportion the reasonable expenses for the motion.

(b) **Failure to Comply with a Court Order.**

(1) *Sanctions Sought in the District Where the Deposition is Taken.* If the court where the discovery is taken orders a deponent to be sworn or to answer a question and the deponent fails to obey, the failure may be treated as contempt of court. If a deposition-related motion is transferred to the court where the action is pending, and that court orders a deponent to be sworn or to answer a question and the deponent fails to obey, the failure may be treated as contempt of either the court where the discovery is taken or the court where the action is pending.

(2) Sanctions Sought in the District Where the Action is Pending.

(A) *For Not Obeying a Discovery Order.* If a party or a party's officer, director, or managing agent – or a witness designated under Rule 30(b) (6) or 31(a) (4) – fails to obey an order to provide or permit discovery, including an order under Rule 26(f), 35, or 37(a), the court where the action is pending, may issue further just orders. They may include the following:

(i) directing those matters embraced in the order or other designated facts be taken as established for purposes of the action, as the prevailing party claims;

(ii) prohibiting the disobedient party from supporting or opposing designated claims or defenses, or from introducing designated miters in evidence;

(iii) striking pleadings in whole or in part;

(iv) staying further proceedings until the order is obeyed;

(v) dismissing the action or proceeding in whole or in part;

(vi) rendering a default judgment against the disobedient party; or

(vii) treating as contempt of court the failure to obey any order except an order to submit to a physical or mental examination.

(B) *For not producing a Person for Examination.* If a party fails to comply with an order under Rule 35(a) requiring it to produce another person for examination, the court may I Issue any of the orders listed in Rule 37(b) (2) (A) (i)-(vi), unless the disobedient party shows that it cannot produce the other person.

(C) *Payment of Expenses.* Instead of or in addition to the orders listed above, the court must order the disobedient party, the attorney advising that party, or both to pay the reasonable expenses, including attorney's fees, caused by the failure, unless the failure was substantially justified or other circumstances make an award of expenses unjust.

(c) **Failure to Disclose, to Supplement an Earlier Response, or to Admit.**

(1) *Failure to Disclose or Supplement.* If a party fails to provide information or identify a witness as required by Rule 26(a) or (e), the party is not allowed to use that information or witness to supply evidence on a motion, at a hearing, or at a trial, unless the failure was substantially justified or is harmless. In addition to or instead of this sanction, the court, on motion and after giving an opportunity to be heard:

(A) may order payment of the reasonable expenses, including attorney's fees, caused by the failure;

(B) may inform the jury of the party's failure; and

(C) may impose other appropriate sanctions, including any of the orders listed in Rule 37(b) (2) (A) (i)-(vi).

(2) *Failure to Admit.* If a party fails to admit what is requested under Rule 36 and if the requesting party later proves a document to be genuine or the matter true, the requesting party may move

that the party who failed to admit pay the reasonable expenses, including attorney's fees, incurred in making that proof. The court must so order unless:

(A) the request was held objectionable under Rule 36(a);
(B) the admission sought was of no substantial importance;
(C) the party failing to admit had a reasonable ground to believe that it might prevail on the matter; or
(D) there was other good reason for the failure to admit.

(d) **Party's Failure to Attend Its Own Deposition, Serve Answers to Interrogatories or Respond to a Request for Inspection.**

(1) In General.

(A) *Motion; Grounds for Sanctions*. The court where the action is pending may, on motion, order sanctions if:

(i) a party or party's officer, director, or managing agent – or a person designated under Rule 30(b) (6) or 31(a) (4) – fail§, after being served with proper notice, to appear for that person's deposition; or

(ii) a party, after being properly served with interrogatories under Rule 33 or a request for inspection under Rule 34, fails to serve its answers, objections, or written response.

(B) *Certification*. A motion for sanctions for failing to answer or respond must include a certification that the movant has in good faith conferred or attempted to confer with the party failing to act in an effort to obtain the answer or response without court action.

(2) *Unacceptable Excuse for Failing to Act*. A failure described in Rule 37(d) (1) (A) is not excused on the ground that the discovery sought was objectionable, unless the party failing to act has a pending motion for a protective order under Rule 26(c).

(3) *Types of Sanctions*. Sanctions may include any of the orders listed in Rule 37(b) (2) (A) (i)-(vi). Instead of or in addition to these sanctions, the court must require the party failing to act, the attorney advising that party, or both to pay the reasonable expenses, including attorney's fees, caused by the failure, unless the failure was substantially justified, or other circumstances make an award of expenses unjust.

(e) **Failure to Provide Electronically Stored Information**. If electronically stored information that should have been preserved in the anticipation or conduct of litigation is lost because a party failed to take reasonable steps to preserve it, and it cannot be restored or replaced through additional discovery, the court:

(1) upon finding prejudice to another party from loss of the information, may order measures no greater than necessary to cure the prejudice; or

(2) only upon finding that the party acted with the intent to deprive another party of the information's use in the litigation may:

(A) presume that the lost information was unfavorable to the party;
(B) instruct the jury that it may or must presume the information was unfavorable to the party; or
(C) dismiss the action or enter a default judgment.

(f) **Failure to Participate in Framing a Discovery Plan**. If a party or its attorney fails to participate in good faith in developing and submitting a proposed discovery plan as required by Rule 26(f), the court may, after giving an opportunity to be heard, require that party or attorney to pay to any other party the reasonable expenses, including attorney's fees, caused by the failure.

Rule 38. Right to a Jury Trial; Demand

(a) **Right Preserved**. The right of trial by jury as declared by the Seventh Amendment to the Constitution – or as provided by a federal statute – is preserved to the parties inviolate.
(b) **Demand**. On any issue triable of right by a jury, a party may demand a jury trial by:
  (1) serving the other parties with a written demand – which may be included in a pleading – no later than 14 days after the last pleading directed to the issue is served; and
  (2) filing the demand in accordance with Rule 5(d).
(c) **Specifying Issues**. In its demand, a party may specify the issues that it wishes to have tried by a jury; otherwise, it is considered to have demanded a jury trial on all the issues so triable. If the party has demanded a jury trial on only some issues, any other party may-within 14 days after being served with the demand or within a shorter time ordered by the court – serve a demand for a jury trial on any other or all factual issues triable by jury.
(d) **Waiver; Withdrawal**. A party waives a jury trial unless its demand is properly served and filed. A proper demand may be withdrawn only if the parties consent.
(e) **Admiralty and Maritime Claims**. These rules do not create a right to a jury trial on issues in a claim designated as an admiralty or maritime claim under Rule 9(h).

Rule 39. Trial by Jury or by the Court

(a) **When a Demand Is Made**. When a jury trial has been demanded under Rule 38, the action must be designated on the docket as a jury action. The trial on all issues so demanded must be by jury unless:
  (1) the parties or their attorneys file a stipulation to a nonjury trial or so stipulate on the record; or
  (2) the court, on motion or on its own, finds that on some or all of those issues there is no federal right to a jury trial.
(b) **When No Demand Is Made**. Issues on which a jury trial is not properly demanded are to be tried by the court. But the court may, on motion, order a jury trial on any issue for which a jury might have been demanded.
(c) **Advisory Jury; Jury Trial by Consent**. In an action not triable by a jury, the court, on motion or on its own:
  (1) may try any Issue with an advisory jury; or
  (2) may, with the parties' consent, try any issue by a jury whose verdict has the same effect as if a jury trial had been a matter of right, unless the action is against the United States and a federal statute provides for a nonjury trial.

Rule 40. Scheduling Cases for Trial

Each court may provide by rule for scheduling trials. The court must give priority to actions entitled to priority by a federal statute.

Rule 41. Dismissal of Actions

(a) **Voluntary Dismissal.**
  (1) By the Plaintiff.
    (A) *Without a Court Order*. Subject to Rules 23(e), 23.1(c), 23.2, and 66 and any applicable federal statute, the plaintiff may dismiss as action without a court order by filing:
      (i) a notice of dismissal before the opposing party serves either an answer or a motion for summary judgment; or
      (ii) a stipulation of dismissal signed by all parties who have appeared.

(B) *Effect*. Unless the notice or stipulation states otherwise, the dismissal is without prejudice. But if the plaintiff previously dismissed any federal – or state-court action based on or including the same claim, a notice of dismissal operates as an adjudication on the merits.

(2) *By Court Order; Effect*. Except as provided in Rule 41(a) (1), an action may be dismissed at the plaintiff's request only by court order on terms that the court considers proper. If a defendant has pleaded a counterclaim before being served with the plaintiff's motion to dismiss, the action may be dismissed over the defendant's objection only if the counterclaim can remain pending for independent adjudication. Unless the order states otherwise, a dismissal under this paragraph (2) is without prejudice.

(b) **Involuntary Dismissal; Effect**, if the plaintiff fails to prosecute or comply with these rules or a court order, a defendant may move to dismiss the action or any claim against it. Unless the dismissal order states otherwise, a dismissal under this subdivision (b) and any dismissal not under this rule – except one for lack of jurisdiction, improper venue, or failure to join a party under Rule 19 – operates as an adjudication on the merits.

(c) **Dismissing a Counterclaim, Crossclaim, or Third-Party Claim**. This rule applies to a dismissal of any counterclaim, crossclaim, or third-party claim. A claimant's voluntary dismissal under Rule 4(l) (a) (l) (A) (i) must be made:
(1) before a responsive pleading is served; or
(2) if there is no responsive pleading, before evidence is introduced at a hearing or trial.

(d) **Costs of a Previously Dismissed Action**. If a plaintiff who previously dismissed an action in any court files an action based on or including the same claim against the same defendant, the court:
(1) may order the plaintiff to pay all or part of the costs of that previous action; and
(2) may stay the proceedings until the plaintiff has complied.

Rule 42. Consolidation; Separate Trials

(a) **Consolidation**. If actions before the court involve a common question of law or fact, the court may:
(1) join for hearing or trial any or all matters at issue in the actions;
(2) consolidate the actions; or
(3) issue any other orders to avoid unnecessary cost or delay.

(b) **Separate Trials**. For convenience, to avoid prejudice, or to expedite and economize, the court may order a separate trial of one or more separate issues, claims, crossclaims, counterclaims, or third-party claims. When ordering a separate trial, the court must preserve any federal right to a jury trial.

Rule 43. Taking Testimony

(a) **In Open Court.** At trial, the witnesses' testimony must be taken in open court unless a federal statute, the Federal Rules of Evidence, these rules, or other rules adopted by the Supreme Court provide otherwise. For good cause in compelling circumstances and with appropriate safeguards, the court may permit testimony in open court by contemporaneous transmission from a different location.

(b) **Affirmation Instead of an Oath**. When these rules require an oath, a solemn affirmation suffices.

(c) **Evidence on a Motion**. When a motion relies on facts outside the record, the court may hear the matter on affidavits or may hear it wholly or partly on oral testimony or on deposition.

(d) **Interpreter.** The court may appoint an interpreter of its choosing; fix reasonable compensation to be paid from funds provided by law or by one or more parties; and tax the compensation as costs.

Rule 44. Proving an Official Record

(a) **Means of Proving.**
  (1) *Domestic Record.* Each of the following evidence is an official record – or an entry in it – that is otherwise admissible and is kept within the United States, any state, district, or commonwealth, or any territory subject to the administrative or judicial jurisdiction of the United States:
    (A) an official publication of the record; or
    (B) a copy attested by the officer with legal custody of the record – or by the officer's deputy – and accompanied by a certificate that the officer has custody. The certificate must be made under seal:
      (i) by a judge of a court of record in the district or political subdivision where the record is kept; or
      (ii) by any public officer with a seal of office and with official duties in the district or political subdivision where the record is kept.
  (2) Foreign Record.
    (A) *In General.* Each of the following evidence a foreign official record – or an entry in it – that is otherwise admissible:
      (i) an official publication of the record; or
      (ii) the record – or a copy – that is attested by an authorized person and is accompanied either by a final certification of genuineness or by a certification under a treaty or convention to which the United States and the country where the record id located are parties.
    (B) *Final Certification of Genuineness.* A final certification must certify the genuineness of the signature and official position of the attester or of any foreign official whose certificate of genuineness relates to the attestation or is in a chain of certificates of genuineness relating to the attestation. A final certification may be made by a secretary of a United States embassy or legation, by a consul general, vice consul, or consular agent of the United States, or by a diplomatic or consular official of the foreign country assigned or accredited to the United States.
    (C) *Other Means of Proof.* If all parties have had a reasonable opportunity to investigate a foreign record's authenticity and accuracy, the court may, for good cause, either:
      (i) admit an attested copy without final certification; or
      (ii) permit the record to be evidenced by an attested summary with or without a final certification.

(b) **Lack of a Record**. A written statement that a diligent search of designated records revealed no record or entry of a specified tenor is admissible as evidence that the records contain no such record or entry. For domestic records, the statement must be authenticated under Rule 44(a) (1). For foreign records, the statement must comply with (a) (2) (C) (ii).

(c) **Other Proof**. A party may prove an official record – or an entry or lack thereof on it – by any other method authorized by law.

Rule 44.1. Determining Foreign law

A party who intends to raise an issue about a foreign country's law must give notice by a pleading or in other writing. In determining foreign law, the court may consider any relevant material or course, including testimony, whether or not submitted by a party or admissible under the Federal Rules of Evidence. The court's determination must be treated as a ruling on a question of law.

Rule 45. Subpoena

(a) **In General.**

(1) Forms and Contents.

(A) Requirements – In General. Every subpoena must:

(i) state the court from which it issued;

(ii) state the title of the action and its civil action number;

(iii) command each person to whom it is directed to do the following at a specified time and place: attend and testify; produce designated documents, electronically stored information, or tangible things in that person's possession, custody, or control; or permit the inspection of premises; and

(iv) set out the text of Rule 45(d) and (e).

(B) *Command to Attend a Deposition – Notice of the Recording Method.* A subpoena commanding attendance at a deposition must state the method for recording the testimony.

(C) *Combining or Separating a Command to Produce or Permit Inspection; Specifying the Form for Electronically Stored Information.* A command to produce documents, electronically stored information, or tangible things or to permit the inspection of premises may be included in a subpoena commanding attendance at a deposition, hearing or trial, or may be set out in a separate subpoena. A subpoena may specify the form or forms in which electronically stored information is to be produced.

(D) *Command to Produce; Included Obligations.* A command in a subpoena to produce documents, electronically stored information, or tangible things requires the responding party to permit inspection, copying, testing, or sampling of the materials.

(2) *Issuing Court.* A subpoena must issue from the court where the action is pending.

(3) *Issued by Whom.* The clerk must issue a subpoena, signed but otherwise in blank, to a party who requests it. That party must complete it before service. An attorney also may issue and sign a subpoena if the attorney is authorized to practice in the issuing court.

(4) *Notice to Other Parties before Service.* If the subpoena commands the production of documents, electronically stored information, or tangible things or the inspection of premises before trial, then before it is served on the person to whom it is directed, a notice and a copy of the subpoena must be served on each party.

(b) **Service.**

(1) *By Whom and How; Tendering Fees.* Any person who is at least 18 years old and not a party may serve a subpoena. Serving a subpoena requires delivering a copy to the named person and, if the subpoena requires that person's attendance, tendering the fees for 1 day's attendance and mileage allowed by law. Fees and mileage need not be tendered when the subpoena issues on behalf of the United States or any of its officers or agencies.

(2) *Service in the United States.* A subpoena may be served at any place in the United States.

(3) *Service in a Foreign Country.* 28 U.S.C. § 1783 governs issuing and serving a subpoena directed to a United States national or resident who is in a foreign country.

(4) *Proof of Service.* Proving service, when necessary, requires filing with the issuing court a statement showing the date and manner of service and the names of the persons served. The statement must be certified by the server.

(c) **Place of Compliance.**

(1) *For a Trial, Hearing, or Deposition.* A subpoena may command a person to attend a trial, hearing, or deposition only as follows:

(A) within 100 miles of where the person resides, is employed, or regularly transacts business in

person; or
(B) within the state where the person resides, is employed, or regularly transacts business in person if the person
(i) is a party or a party's officer; or
(ii) is commanded to attend a trial and would not incur substantial expense.
(2) *For Other Discovery.* A subpoena may command:
(A) production of documents, electronically stored information, or tangible things at a place within 100 miles of where the person resides, is employed, or regularly transacts business in person; and
(B) inspection of premises at the premises to be inspected.
(d) **Protecting a Person Subject to a Subpoena; Enforcement.**
(1) *Avoiding Undue Burden or Expense; Sanctions.* A party or attorney responsible for issuing and serving a subpoena must take reasonable steps to avoid imposing undue burden or expense on a person subject to the subpoena. The court for the district where compliance is required must enforce this duty and impose an appropriate sanction – which may include lost earnings and reasonable attorney's fees on a party or attorney who fails to comply.
(2) Command to Produce Materials or Permit Inspection.
(A) *Appearance Not Required.* A person commanded to produce documents, electronically stored information, or tangible things, or to permit the inspection of premises, need not appear in person at the place of production or inspection unless also commanded to appear for a deposition, hearing, or trial.
(B) *Objections.* A person commanded to produce documents or tangible things or to permit inspection may serve on the party or attorney designated in the subpoena a written objection to inspecting, copying, testing, or sampling any or all of the materials or to inspecting the premises – or to producing electronically stored information in the form or forms requested. The objection must be served before the earlier of the time specified for compliance or 14 days after the subpoena is served. If an objection is made, the following rules apply:
(i) At any time, on notice to the commanded person, the serving party may move the court for the district where compliance is required for an order compelling production or inspection.
(ii) These acts may be required only as directed in the order, and the order must protect a person who is neither a party nor a party's officer from significant expense resulting from compliance.
(3) Quashing or Modifying a Subpoena.
(A) *When Required.* On timely motion, the court for the district where compliance is required must quash or modify a subpoena that:
(i) fails to allow a reasonable time to comply;
(ii) requires a person to comply beyond the geographical limits specified in Rule 45(c);
(iii) requires disclosure of privileged or other protected matter, if no exception or waiver applies; or
(iv) subjects a person to undue burden.
(B) *When permitted.* To protect a person subject to or affected by a subpoena, the court for the district where compliance is required may, on motion, quash or modify the subpoena if it requires:
(i) disclosing a trade secret or other confidential research, development, or commercial information; or

(ii) disclosing an unrestrained expert's opinion or information that does not describe specific occurrences in dispute and results from the expert's study that was not requested by a party.

(C) *Specifying Conditions as an Alternative*. In the circumstances described in Rule 45(d) (3) (B), the court may, instead of quashing or modifying a subpoena, order appearance or production under specified conditions if the serving party:

(i) shows a substantial need for the testimony or material that cannot be otherwise met without undue hardship; and

(ii) ensures that the subpoenaed person will be reasonably compensated.

(e) **Duties in Responding to a Subpoena.**

(1) *Producing Documents or Electronically Stored Information*. These procedures apply to producing documents or electronically stored information.

(A) *Documents*. A person responding to a subpoena to produce documents must produce them as they are kept in the ordinary course of business or must organize and label them to correspond to the categories in demand.

(B) *Form for Producing Electronically Stored Information Not Specified*. If a subpoena does not specify a form for producing electronically stored information, the person responding must produce it in a form or forms in which it is ordinarily maintained or in a reasonably usable form or forms.

(C) *Electronically Stored Information Produced in Only One Form*. The person responding need not produce the same electronically stored information in more than one form.

(D) *Inaccessible Electronically Stored Information*. The person responding need not provide discovery of electronically stored information from sources that the person identifies as not reasonably accessible because of undue burden or cost. On motion to compel discovery or for a protective order, the person responding must show that the information is not reasonably accessible because of undue burden or cost. If that showing is made, the court may nonetheless order discovery from such sources if the requesting party shows good cause, considering the limitations of Rule 26(b) (2) (C). The court may specify conditions for the discovery.

(2) Claiming Privilege or Protection.

(A) Information Withheld. A person withholding subpoenaed information under a claim that it is privileged or subject to protection as trial-preparation material must:

(i) expressly make the claim; and

(ii) describe the nature of the withheld documents, communications, or tangible things in a manner that, without revealing information itself privileged or protected, will enable the parties to assess the claim.

(B) *Information Produced*. If information produced in response to a subpoena is subject to a claim of privilege or of protection as trial–preparation material, the person making the claim may notify any party that received the information of the claim and the basis for it. After being notified, a party must promptly return, sequester, or destroy the specified information and any copies it has; must not use or disclose the information until the claim is resolved; must take reasonable steps to retrieve the information if the party disclosed it before being notified; and may promptly present the information under seal to the court for the district where compliance is required for a determination of the claim. The person who produced the information must preserve the information until the claim is resolved.

(f) **Transferring a Subpoena-Related Motion**. When the court where compliance is required did not issue the subpoena, it may transfer a motion under this rule to the issuing court if the person subject to the subpoena consents or if the court finds exceptional circumstances. Then, if the attorney for a person subject to a subpoena is authorized to practice in the court where the motion was made, the attorney may file papers and appear on the motion as an officer of the issuing court. To enforce its order, the issuing court may transfer the order to the court where the motion was made.

(g) **Contempt.** The court for the district where compliance is required and also, after a motion is transferred, the issuing court may hold in contempt a person who, having been served, fails without adequate excuse to obey the subpoena or an order related to it.

Rule 46. Objecting to a Ruling or Order

A formal exception to a ruling or order is unnecessary. When the ruling or order is requested or made, a party need only state the action that it wants the court to take or objects to, along with the grounds for the request or objection. Failing to object does not prejudice a party who had no opportunity to do so when the ruling or order was made.

Rule 47. Selecting Jurors

(a) **Examining Jurors**. The court may permit the parties or their attorneys to examine prospective jurors or may I Itself do so. If the court examines the jurors, it must permit the parties or their attorneys to make any further inquiry it considers proper or must itself ask any of their-additional questions it considers proper.

(b) **Peremptory Challenges**. The court must allow the number of peremptory challenges provided by 28 U.S.C. § 1870.

(c) Excusing a Juror. During trial or deliberation, the court may excuse a juror for good cause.

Rule 48 Number of Jurors; Verdict; Polling

(a) **Number of Jurors**. A jury must begin with at least 6 and no more than 12 members, and each juror must participate in the verdict unless excused under Rule 47(c).

(b) **Verdict.** Unless the parties stipulate otherwise, the verdict must be unanimous and must be returned by a jury of at least 6 members.

(c) **Polling**. After a verdict is returned but before the jury is discharged, the court must, on a party's request, or may on its own, poll the jurors individually. If the poll reveals a lack of unanimity or lack of assent by the number of jurors that the parties stipulated to, the court may direct the jury to deliberate further or may order a new trial.

Rule 49. Special Verdict; General Verdict and Questions

(a) **Special Verdict.**

(1) *In General.* The court may require a jury to return only a special verdict in the form of a written finding on each issue of fact. The court may do so by:

(A) submitting written questions susceptible of a categorical or other brief answer;

(B) submitting written forms of the special findings that might properly be made under the pleadings and evidence; or

(C) using any other method that the courts consider appropriate.

(2) *Instructions.* The court must give the instructions and explanations necessary to enable the jury to make its findings on each submitted issue.

(3) *Issues Not Submitted.* A party waives the right to a jury trial on any issue of fact raised by the pleadings or evidence but not submitted to the jury unless, before the jury retires, the party

demands its submission to the jury. If the party does not demand submission, the court may make a finding on the issue. If the court makes no finding, it is considered to have made a finding consistent with its judgment on the special verdict.

(b) **General Verdict with Answers to Written Questions.**
  (1) *In General.* The court may submit to the jury forms for a general verdict, together with written questions on one or more issues of fact that the jury must decide, the court must give the instructions and explanations necessary to enable the jury to render a general verdict and answer the questions in writing and must direct the jury to do both.
  (2) *Verdict and Answers Consistent.* When the general verdict and the answers are consistent, the court must approve, for entry under Rule 58, an appropriate judgment on the verdict and answers.
  (3) *Answers Inconsistent with the Verdict.* When the answers are consistent with each other but one or more is inconsistent with the general verdict, the court may:
    (A) approve, for entry under Rule 58, an appropriate judgment according to the answers, notwithstanding the general verdict;
    (B) direct the jury to further consider its answers and verdict; or
    (C) order a new trial.
  (4) *Answers Inconsistent with Each Other and the Verdict.* When the answers are inconsistent with each other, and one or more is also inconsistent with the general verdict, judgment must not be entered; instead, the court must direct the jury to further consider its answers and verdict or must order a new trial.

Rule 50. Judgment as a Matter of Law in a Jury Trial; Related Motion for a New Trial; Conditional Ruling

(a) **Judgment as a Matter of law.**
  (1) *In General.* If a party has been fully heard on an issue during a jury trial and the court finds that a reasonable jury would not have a legally sufficient evidentiary basis to find for the party on that issue, the court may:
    (A) resolve the issue against the party; and
    (B) grant a motion for judgment as a matter of law against the party on a claim or defense that, under the controlling law, can be maintained or defeated only with a favorable finding on that issue.
    (C) *Motion.* A motion for judgment as a matter of law may be made at any time before the case is submitted to the jury. The motion must specify the judgment sought and the law and facts that entitle the movant to the judgment.

(b) **Renewing the Motion After Trial; Alternative Motion for a New Trial.** If the court does not grant a motion for judgment as a matter of law made under Rule 50(a), the court is considered to have submitted the action to the jury subject to the court's later deciding the legal questions raised by the motion. No later than 28 days after the entry of judgment – or if the motion addresses a jury issue not decided by a verdict, no later than 28 days after the jury was discharged – the movant may file a renewed motion for judgment as a matter of law and may I Include an alternative or joint request for a new trial under Rule 59. In ruling on the renewed motion, the court may:
  (1) allow judgment on the verdict, if the jury returned a verdict;
  (2) order a new trial; or
  (3) direct the entry of judgment as a matter of law.

(c) **Granting the Renewed Motion; Conditional Ruling on a Motion for a New Trial.**

(1) *In General.* If the court grants a renewed motion for judgment as a matter of law, it must also conditionally rule on any motion for a new trial by determining whether a new trial should be granted if the judgment is later vacated or reversed. The court must state the grounds for conditionally granting or denying the motion for a new trial.

(2) *Effect of a Conditional Ruling.* Conditionally granting the motion for a new trial does not affect the judgment's finality; if the judgment is reversed, the new trial must proceed unless the appellate court orders otherwise. If the motion for a new trial is conditionally denied, the appellee may assert error in that denial; if the judgment is reversed, the case must proceed as the appellate court orders.

(d) **Time for a Losing Party's New Trial Motion**. Any motion for a new trial under Rule 59 by a party against whom judgment as a matter of law is rendered must be filed no later than 28 days after the entry of the judgment.

(e) **Denying the Motion for Judgment as a Matter of Law; Reversal on Appeal.** If the court denies the motion for judgment as a matter of law, the prevailing party may, as appellee, assert grounds entitling it to a new trial should the appellate court conclude that the trial court erred in denying the motion. If the appellate court reverses the judgment, it may order a new trial, direct the trial court to determine whether a new trial should be granted, or direct the entry of judgment.

Rule 51. Instructions to the Jury; Objections; Preserving a Claim of Error

(a) **Requests.**

(1) *Before the Close of the Evidence.* At the close of the evidence or at any earlier reasonable time that the court orders, a party may file and furnish to every other party written requests for the jury instructions it wants the court to give.

(2) *After the Close of Evidence.* After the close of evidence, a party may:

(A) file requests for instructions on issues that could not reasonably have been anticipated by an earlier time that the court set for requests; and

(B) with the court's permission, file untimely requests for instructions on any issue.

(b) **Instructions. The court:**

(1) must inform the parties of its proposed instructions and proposed action on the requests before instructing the jury and before final jury arguments;

(2) must give the parties an opportunity to object on the record and out of the jury's hearing before the instructions and arguments are delivered; and

(3) may instruct the jury at any time before the jury is discharged.

(c) **Objections.**

(1) *How to Make.* A party who objects to an instruction or the failure to give an instruction must do so on the record, stating distinctly the matter objected to and the grounds for the objection.

(2) *When to Make.* An objection is timely if:

(A) a party objects at the opportunity provided under Rule 51(b) (2); or

(B) a party was not informed of an instruction or action on a request before that opportunity to object, and the party objects promptly after learning that the instruction or request will be, or has been, given or refused.

(d) **Assigning Error; Plain Error.**

(1) *Assigning Error.* A party may assign as error:

(A) an error in an instruction actually given, if that party properly objected; or

(B) a failure to give an instruction, if that party properly requested it and – unless the court rejected the request in a definitive ruling on the record – also properly objected.

(2) *Plain Error*. A court may consider a plain error in the instructions that has not been preserved as required by Rule 51(d) (1) if the error affects substantial rights.

Rule 52. Findings and Conclusions by the Court; Judgment on Partial Findings

(a) **Findings and Conclusions.**
(1) *In General*. In an action tried on the facts without a jury or an advisory jury, the court must find the facts specially and state its conclusions of law separately. The findings and conclusions may be stated on the record after the close of the evidence or may appear in an opinion or memorandum of decision filed by the court. Judgment must be entered under Rule 58.
(2) *For an Interlocutory Injunction*. In granting or refusing an interlocutory injunction, the court must similarly state the findings and conclusions that support its action.
(3) *For a Motion*. The court is not required to state findings or conclusions when ruling on a motion under Rule 12 or 56 or, unless these rules provide otherwise, on any other motion.
(4) *Effect of a Master's Findings*. A master's findings, to the extent adopted by the court, must be considered the court's findings.
(5) *Questioning the Evidentiary Support*. A party may later question the sufficiency of the evidence supporting the findings, whether or not the party requested findings, objected to them, moved to amend them, or moved for partial findings.
(6) *Setting Aside the Findings*. Findings of fact, whether based on oral or other evidence, must not be set aside unless clearly erroneous, and the reviewing court must give due regard to the trial court's opportunity to judge the witnesses' credibility.

(b) **Amended or Additional Findings**. On a party's motion filed no later than 28 days after the entry of judgment, the court may amend its findings – or make additional findings – and may amend the judgment accordingly. The motion may accompany a motion for a new trial under Rule 59.

(c) **Judgment on Partial: Findings**. If a party has been fully heard on an issue during a nonjury trial and the court finds against the party on that issue, the court may enter judgment against the party on a claim or defense that, under the controlling law, can be maintained or defeated only with a favorable ruling on that issue. The court may, however, decline to render any judgment until the close of evidence. A judgment on partial findings must be supported by findings of fact and conclusions of law as required by Rule 52(a).

Rule 53. Masters

(a) **Appointment.**
(1) *Scope*. Unless a statute provides otherwise, a court may appoint a master only to:
(A) perform duties consented to by the parties;
(B) hold trial proceedings and make or recommend findings of fact on issues to be decided without a jury if appointment is warranted by:
(i) some exceptional condition; or
(ii) the need to perform an accounting or resolve a difficult computation of damages; or
(C) address pretrial and post-trial matters that cannot be effectively and timely addressed by an available district judge or magistrate judge of the district.
(2) *Disqualification*. A master must not have a relationship to the parties, attorneys, action, or court that would require disqualification of a judge under 28 U.S.C. § 455, unless the parties, with the court's approval, consent to the appointment after the master discloses any potential grounds for disqualification.
(3) *Possible Expense or Delay*. In appointing a master, the court must consider the fairness of

imposing the likely expenses on the parties and must protect against unreasonable expense or delay.

(b) **Order Appointing a Master.**
- (1) *Notice.* Before appointing a master, the court must give the parties notice and an opportunity to be heard. Any party may suggest candidates for appointment.
- (2) *Contents.* The appointing order must direct the master to proceed with all reasonable diligence and must state:
  - (A) the master's duties, including any investigation or enforcement duties, and any limits on the master's authority under Rule 53(c);
  - (B) the circumstances, if any, in which the master may communicate *ex parte* with the court or a party;
  - (C) the nature of the materials to be preserved and filed as the record of the master's activities;
  - (D) the time limits, method of filing the record, other procedures, and standards for reviewing the master's orders, findings, and recommendations; and
  - (E) the basis, terms, and procedure for fixing the master's compensation under Rule 53(g).
- (3) *Issuing.* The court may issue the order only after:
  - (A) the master files an affidavit disclosing whether there are any grounds for disqualification under 28 U.S.C. § 455; and
  - (B) if a ground is disclosed, the parties, with the court's approval, waive the disqualification.
- (4) *Amending.* The order may be amended at any time after notice to the parties and an opportunity to be heard.

(c) **Master's authority.**
- (1) *In General.* Unless the appointing order directs otherwise, a master may:
  - (A) regulate all proceedings;
  - (B) take all appropriate measured to perform the assigned duties fairly and efficiently; and
  - (C) if conducting an evidentiary hearing, exercise the appointing court's power to compel, take, and record evidence.
- (2) *Sanctions.* The master may by order impose on a party any noncontempt sanction provided by Rule 37 or 45 and may recommend a contempt sanction against a party and sanctions against a nonparty.

(d) **Master's Orders**. A master who issues an order must file it and promptly serve a copy on each party; the clerk must enter the order on the docket.

(e) **Master's Reports**. A master must report to the court as required by the appointing order. The master must file the report and promptly serve a copy on each party, unless the court orders otherwise.

(f) **Action on the Master's Order, Report, or Recommendations.**
- (1) *Opportunity for a Hearing; Action in General.* In acting on a master's order, report, or recommendations, the court must give the parties notice and an opportunity to be heard; may receive evidence; and may adopt or affirm, modify, wholly or partly reject or reverse, or resubmit to the master with instructions.
- (2) *Time to Object or Move to Adopt or Modify.* A party may file objections to – or a motion to adopt or modify – the master's order, report, or recommendations no later than 21 days after a copy is served, unless the court sets a different time.
- (3) *Reviewing Factual Findings.* The court must decide de novo all objections to findings of fact made or recommended by a master, unless the parties, with the court's approval, stipulate that:
  - (A) the findings will be reviewed for clear error; or

(B) the findings of a master appointed under Rule 53(a) (1) (A) or (C) will be final.

(4) *Reviewing Legal Conclusions*. The court must decide the novo all objections to conclusions of law made or recommended by a master.

(5) *Reviewing Procedural Matters*. Unless the appointing order establishes a different standard of review, the court may set aside a master's ruling on a procedural matter only for an abuse of discretion.

(g) **Compensation.**

(1) *Fixing Compensation*. Before or after judgment, the court must fix the master's compensation on the basis and terms stated in the appointing order, but the court may set a new basis and terms after giving notice and an opportunity to be heard.

(2) *Payment*. The compensation must be paid either:

(A) by a party or parties; or

(B) from a fund or subject matter of the action within the court's control.

(3) *Allocating Payment*. The court must allocate payment among the parties after considering the nature and amount of the controversy, the parties' means, and the extent to which any party is more responsible than other parties for the reference to a master. An interim allocation may be amended to reflect a decision on the merits.

(h) **Appointing a Magistrate Judge**. A magistrate judge is subject to this rule only when the order referring a matter to the magistrate judge states that the reference is made under this rule.

Rule 54. Judgments; Costs

(a) **Definition**; Form. "Judgment" as used in these rules includes a decree and any order from which an appeal lies. A judgment must not include recitals of pleadings, a master's report, or a record of prior proceedings.

(b) **Judgment on Multiple Claims or Involving Multiple Parties**. When an action presents more than one claim for relief – whether as a claim, counterclaim, crossclaim, or third-party claim – or when multiple parties are involved, the court may direct entry of a final judgment as to one or more, but fewer than all, claims or parties only if the court expressly determines that there is no just reason for delay. Otherwise, any order or other decision, however, designated, that adjudicates fewer than all the claims or the rights and liabilities of fewer than all the parties does not end the action as to any of the claims or parties and may be revised at any time before the entry of a judgment adjudicating all the claims and all the parties rights and liabilities.

(c) **Demand for Judgment; Relief to be Granted**. A default judgment must not differ in kind from, or exceed in amount, what is demanded in the pleadings. Every other final judgment should grant the relief to which each party is entitled, even if the party has not demanded that relief in its pleadings.

(d) **Costs; Attorney's Fees.**

(1) *Costs Other Than Attorney's Fees*. Unless a federal statute, these rules, or a court order provides otherwise, costs – other than attorney's fees – should be allowed to the prevailing party. But costs against the United States, its officers, and its agencies may be imposed only to the extent allowed by law. the clerk may tax costs on 14 days' notice. On motion served within the next 7 days, the court may review the clerk's action.

(2) Attorney's Fees.

(A) *Claim to Be by Motion*. A claim for attorney's fees and related nontaxable expenses must be made by motion unless the substantive law requires those fees be proved at trial as an element of damages.

(B) *Timing and Contents of the Motion*. Unless a statute or a court order provides otherwise, the motion must:

(i) be filed no later than 14 days after the entry of judgment;

(ii) specify the judgment and the statute, rule, or other grounds entitling the movant to the award;

(iii) state the amount sought or provide a fair estimate of it; and

(iv) disclose, if the court so orders, the terms of any agreement about fees for the services for which claim is made.

(C) *Proceedings*. Subject to Rule 23(h), the court must, on a party's request, give an opportunity for adversary submissions on the motion in accordance with Rule 43(c) or 78. The court may decide issues of liability for fees before receiving submissions on the value of services. The court must find the facts and state its conclusions of law as provided in Rule 52(a).

(D) *Special Procedures by Local Rule; Reference to a Master or Magistrate Judge*. By local rule, the court may establish special procedures to resolve fee-related issues without extensive evidentiary hearings. Also, the court may refer issues concerning the value of services to a special master under Rule 53(a) (1) and may refer a motion for attorney's fees to a magistrate judge under Rule 72(b) as if it were a dispositive pretrial matter.

(E) *Exceptions*. Subparagraphs (A)-(D) do not apply to claims for fees and expenses as sanctions for violating these rules or as sanctions under 28 U.S.C. § 1927.

Rule 55. Default; Default Judgment

(a) **Entering a Default**. When a party against whom a judgment for affirmative relief is sought has failed to plead or otherwise defend, and that failure is shown by affidavit or otherwise, the clerk must enter the party's default.

(b) **Entering a Default Judgment.**

(1) *By the Clerk.* If the plaintiff's claim is for a sum certain or a sum that can be made certain by computation, the clerk – on the plaintiff's request, with an affidavit showing the amount due – must enter judgment for that amount and costs against a defendant who has been defaulted for not appearing and who is neither a minor nor an incompetent person.

(2) *By the Court.* In all other cases, the party must apply to the court for a default judgment. A default judgment may be entered against a minor or incompetent person only if represented by a general guardian, conservator, or other like fiduciary who has appeared. If the party against whom a default judgment is sought has appeared personally or by a representative, that party or its representative must be served with written notice of the application at least 7 days before the hearing. The court may conduct hearings or make referrals – preserving any federal statutory right to a jury trial – when, to enter or effectuate judgment, it needs to:

(A) conduct an accounting;

(B) determine the amount of damages;

(C) establish the truth of any allegation by evidence; or

(D) investigate any other matter.

(c) **Setting Aside a Default or Default Judgment**. The court may set aside an entry of default for good cause, and it may set aside a default judgment under Rule 60(b).

(d) **Judgment Against the United States**. A default judgment may be entered against the United States, its officers, or its agencies only if the claimant establishes a claim or right to relief by evidence that satisfies the court.

Rule 56. Summary Judgment

(a) **Motion for Summary Judgment or Partial Summary Judgment**. A party may move for summary judgment, identifying each claim or defense – or the part of each claim or defense – on which summary judgment is sought. The court shall grant summary judgment if the movant shows that there is no genuine dispute as to any material fact and the movant is entitled to judgment as a matter of law. The court should state on the record the reasons for granting or denying the motion.

(b) **Time to File a Motion**. Unless a different time is set by local rule or the court orders otherwise, a party may file a motion for summary judgment at any time until 30 days after the close of all discovery.

(c) **Procedures.**

(1) *Supporting Factual Positions*. A party asserting that a fact cannot be or is genuinely disputed must support the assertion by:

(A) citing to particular parts of materials in the record, including depositions, documents, electronically stored information, affidavits or declarations, stipulations (including those made for purposes of the motion only), admissions, interrogatory answers, or other materials; or

(B) showing that the materials cited do not establish the absence or presence of a genuine dispute, or that an adverse party cannot produce admissible evidence to support the fact.

(2) *Objection That a Fact Is Not Supported by Admissible Evidence*. A party may object that the material cited to support or dispute a fact cannot be presented in a form that would be admissible in evidence.

(3) *Materials not Cited*. The court need consider only the cited materials, but it may consider other materials in the record.

(4) *Affidavits or Declarations*. An affidavit or declaration used to support or oppose a motion must be made on personal knowledge, set out facts that would be admissible in evidence, and show that the affiant or declarant is competent to testify on the matters stated.

(d) **When Facts Are Unavailable to the Nonmovant**. If a nonmovant shows by affidavit or declaration that, for specified reasons, it cannot present facts essential to justify its opposition, the court may:

(1) defer considering the motion or deny it;

(2) allow time to obtain affidavits or declarations or to take discovery; or

(3) issue any other appropriate order.

(e) **Failing to Properly Support or Address a Fact**. If a party fails to properly support an assertion of fact or fails to properly address another party's assertion of fact as required by Rule 56(c), the court may:

(1) give an opportunity to properly support or address the fact;

(2) consider the fact undisputed for purposes of the motion;

(3) grant summary judgment if the motion and supporting materials – including the facts considered undisputed – show that the movant is entitled to it; or

(4) issue any other appropriate order.

(f) **Judgment Independent of the Motion.** After giving notice and a reasonable time to respond, the court may:

(1) grant summary judgment for a nonmovant;

(2) grant the motion on grounds not raised by a party; or

(3) consider summary judgment on its own after identifying for the parties material facts that may not be genuinely in dispute.

(g) **Failing to Grant All the Requested Relief**. If the court does not grant all the relief requested by the motion, it may enter an order stating any material fact – including an item of damages or other relief – that is not genuinely in dispute and treating the fact as established in the case.

(h) **Affidavit or Declaration Submitted in Bad Faith**. If satisfied that an affidavit or declaration under this rule is submitted in bad faith or solely for delay, the court – after notice and a reasonable time to respond – may order the submitting party to pay the other party the reasonable expenses, including attorney's fees, it incurred as a result. An offending party or attorney may also be held in contempt or subjected to other sanctions.

Rule 57. Declaratory Judgment

These rules govern the procedure for obtaining a declaratory judgment under 28 U.S.C. § 2201. Rules 38 and 39 govern a demand for a jury trial. The existence of another adequate remedy does not preclude a declaratory judgment that is otherwise appropriate. The court may order a speedy hearing of a declaratory – judgment action.

Rule 58. Entering Judgment

(a) **Separate Document**. Every judgment and amended judgment must be set out in a separate document, but a separate document is not required for an order disposing of a motion:
  (1) for judgment under Rule 50(b);
  (2) to amend or make additional findings of fact under Rule 52(b);
  (3) for attorney's fees under Rule 54;
  (4) for a new trial, or to alter or amend the judgment, under Rule 59; or
  (5) for relief under Rule 60.

(b) **Entering Judgment.**
  (1) *Without the Court's Direction*. Subject to Rule 54(b) and unless the court orders otherwise, the clerk must, without awaiting the court's direction, promptly prepare, sign, and enter the judgment when:
    (A) the jury returns a general verdict;
    (B) the court awards only costs or a sum certain; or
    (C) the court denies all relief.
  (2) *Court's Approval Required*. Subject to Rule 54(b), the court must promptly approve the form of judgment, which the clerk must promptly enter, when:
    (A) the jury returns a special verdict or a general verdict with answers to written questions; or
    (B) the court grants other relief not described in this subdivision (b).

(c) **Time of Entry**. For purposes of these rules, judgment is entered at the following times:
  (1) if a separate document is not required, when the judgment is entered on the civil docket under Rule 79(a); or
  (2) if a separate document is required, when the judgment is entered in the civil docket under Rule 79(a) and the earlier of these events occurs:
    (A) it is set out in a separate document; or
    (B) 150 days have run from the entry in the civil docket.

(d) **Request for Entry**. A party may request that judgment be set out in a separate document as required by Rule 58(a).

(e) **Cost or Fee Awards**. Ordinarily, the entry of judgment may not be delayed, nor the time for appeal extended, in order to tax costs or award fees. But if a timely motion for attorney's fees is made under Rule 54(d) (2), the court may act before a notice of appeal has been filed and become effective to order that the motion have the same effect under Federal Rule of Appellate Procedure

4(a) (4) as a timely motion under Rule

Rule 59. New Trial; Altering or Amending a Judgment

(a) **In General.**
  (1) *Grounds for New Trial.* The court may, on motion, grant a new trial on all or some of the issues – and to any party – as follows:
    (A) after a jury trial, for any reason for which a new trial has heretofore been granted in an action at law in federal court; or
    (B) after a nonjury trial, for any reason for which a rehearing has heretofore been granted in a suit in equity in federal court.
  (2) *Further Action After a Nonjury Trial.* After a nonjury trial, the court may, on motion for a new trial, open the judgment if one has been entered, take additional testimony, amend findings of fact and conclusions of law or make new ones, and direct the entry of a new judgment.
(b) **Time to File a Motion for a New Trial.** A motion for a new trial must be filed no later than 28 days after the entry of the judgment.
(c) **Time to Serve Affidavits.** When a motion for a new trial is based on affidavits, they must be filed with the motion. The opposing party has 14 days after being served to file opposing affidavits. The court may permit reply to affidavits.
(d) **New Trial on the Court's Initiative or for Reasons Not in the Motion**. No later than 28 days after the entry of the judgment, the court, on its own, may order a new trial for any reason that would justify granting one on a party's motion. After giving the parties notice and an opportunity to be heard, the court may grant a timely motion for a new trial for a reason not stated in the motion. In either event, the court must specify the reasons in the order.
(e) **Motion to Alter or Amend a Judgment.** A motion to alter or amend a judgment must be filed no later than 28 days after the entry of the judgment.

Rule 60. Relief from a Judgment or Order

(a) **Corrections Based on Clerical Mistakes; Oversights and Omissions**. The court may correct a clerical mistake or a mistake arising from an oversight or omission whenever one is found in a judgment, order, or other part of the record. The court may do so on motion or on its own, with or without notice. But after an appeal has been docketed in the appellate court and while it is still pending, such a mistake may be corrected only with the appellate court's leave.
(b) **Grounds for Relief from a Final Judgment, Order, or Proceeding**. On motion and just terms, the court may relieve a party or its legal representative from a final judgment, order, or proceeding for the following reasons:
  (1) mistake, inadvertence, surprise, or excusable neglect;
  (2) newly discovered evidence that, with reasonable diligence, could not have been discovered in time to move for a new trial under Rule 59(b);
  (3) fraud (whether previously called intrinsic or extrinsic), misrepresentation, or misconduct by an opposing party;
  (4) the judgment is void;
  (5) the judgment has been satisfied, released, or discharged; it is based on an earlier judgment that has been reversed or vacated; or applying it prospectively is no longer equitable; or
  (6) any other reason that justifies relief.
(c) **Timing and Effect of the Motion.**
  (1) *Timing.* A motion under Rule 60(b) must be made within a reasonable time – and for reasons (1),

(2), and (3) no more than a year after the entry of the judgment or order or the date of the proceeding.

(2) *Effect on Finality*. The motion does not affect the judgment's finality or suspend its operation.

(d) **Other Powers to Grant Relief**. This rule does not limit a court's power to:

(1) Entertain an independent action to relive a party from a judgment, order, or proceeding;

(2) grant relief under 28 USC § 1655 to a defendant who was not personally notified of the action; or

(3) set aside a judgment for fraud on the court.

(e) **Bills and Writs Abolished**. The following are abolished: bills of review, bills in the nature of bills of review, and writs of *coram nobis*, *coram vobis*, and *audita querela*.

Rule 61. Harmless Error

Unless justice requires otherwise, no error in admitting or excluding evidence – or any other error by the court or a party – is ground for granting a new trial, for setting aside a verdict, or for vacating, modifying, or otherwise disturbing a judgment or order. At every stage of the proceeding, the court must disregard all errors and defects that do not affect any party's substantial rights.

Rule 62. Stay of Proceedings to Enforce a Judgment

(a) **Automatic Stay**. Except as provided in Rule 62(c) and (d), execution on a judgment and proceedings to enforce it are stayed for 30 days after its entry, unless the court orders otherwise.

(b) **Stay by Bond or Other Security**. At any time after judgment is entered, a party may obtain a stay by providing a bond or other security. The stay takes effect when the court approves the bond or other security and remains in effect for the time specified in the bond or other security.

(c) **Stay of an Injunction, Receivership, or Patent Accounting Order.** Unless the court orders otherwise, the following are not stayed after being entered, even if an appeal is taken:

(1) an interlocutory or final judgment in an action for an injunction or receivership; or

(2) a judgment or order that directs an accounting in an action for patent infringement.

(d) **Injunction Pending an Appeal**. While an appeal is pending from an interlocutory order or final judgment that grants, dissolves, or denies an injunction, the court may suspend, modify, restore, or grant an injunction on terms for bond or other terms that secure the opposing party's rights. If the judgment appealed from is rendered by a statutory three-judge district court, the order must be made either:

(1) by that court sitting in open session; or

(2) by the assent of all its judges, as evidenced by their signatures.

(e) **Stay Without Bond on an Appeal by the United States, Its Officers, or Its Agencies**. The court must not require a bond, obligation, or other security from the appellant when granting a stay on an appeal by the United States, its officers, or its agencies or on an appeal directed by a department of the federal government.

(f) **Stay in Favor of a Judgment Debtor Under State Law**. If a judgment is a lien on the judgment debtor's property under the law of the state where the court is located, the judgment debtor is entitled to the same stay of execution the state court would give.

(g) **Appellate Court's Power Not Limited**. This rule does not limit the power of the appellate court or one of its judges or justices:

(1) to stay proceedings – or suspend, modify, restore, or grant an injunction – while an appeal is pending; or

(2) to issue an order to preserve the status quo or the effectiveness of the judgment to be entered.

(h) **Stay with Multiple Claims or Parties**. A court may stay the enforcement of a final judgment entered under Rule 54(b) until it enters a later judgment or judgments and may prescribe terms necessary to secure the benefit of the stayed judgment for the party in whose favor it was entered.

Rule 62.1. Indicative Ruling on a Motion for Relief That is Barred By a Pending Appeal

(a) **Relief Pending Appeal**. If a timely motion is made for relief that the court lacks authority to grant because of an appeal that has been docketed and is pending, the court may:
  (1) defer considering the motion;
  (2) deny the motion; or
  (3) state either that it would grant the motion if the court of appeals remands for that purpose or that the motion raises a substantial issue.
(b) **Notice to the Court of Appeals**. The movant must promptly notify the circuit clerk under Federal Rule of Appellate Procedure 12.1 if the district court states that it would grant the motion or that the motion raises a substantial issue.
(c) **Remand**. the district court may decide the motion if the court of appeals remands for that purpose.

Rule 63. Judge's Inability to Proceed

If a judge conducting a hearing or trial is unable to proceed, any other judge may proceed upon certifying familiarity with the record and determining that the case may be completed without prejudice to the parties. In a hearing or a nonjury trial, the successor judge must, at a party's request, recall any witness whose testimony is material and disputed and who is available to testify again without undue burden. The successor judge may also recall any other witness.

Rule 64. Seizing a Person or Property

(a) **Remedies Under State Law – In General**. At the commencement of and throughout an action, every remedy is available that, under the law of the state where the court is located, provides for seizing a person or property to secure satisfaction of the potential judgment. But a federal statute governs to the extent it applies.
(b) **Specific Kinds of Remedies**. The remedies available under this rule include the following – however, designated and regardless of whether state procedure requires an independent action:

- arrest;
- attachment;
- garnishment;
- replevin;
- sequestration; and
- other corresponding or equivalent remedies.

Rule 65. Injunctions and Restraining Orders

(a) **Preliminary Injunction.**
  (1) *Notice.* The court may issue a preliminary injunction only on notice to the adverse party.
  (2) *Consolidating the Hearing with the Trial on the Merits.* Before or after beginning a hearing on a motion for a preliminary injunction, the court may advance the trial on the merits and consolidate it with the hearing. Even when consolidation is not ordered, evidence that is received

on the motion and that would be admissible at trial becomes part of the trial record and need not be repeated at trial. But the court must preserve any party's right to a jury trial.

(b) **Temporary Restraining Order.**

(1) *Issuing Without Notice.* The court may issue a temporary restraining order without written or oral notice to the adverse party or its attorney only if:

(A) specific facts in an affidavit or a verified complaint clearly show that immediate and irreparable injury, loss, or damage will result to the movant before the adverse party can be heard in opposition; and

(B) the movant's attorney certifies in writing any efforts made to give notice and the reasons why it should not be required.

(2) *Contents; Expiration.* Every temporary restraining order issued without notice must state the date and hour it was issued; describe the injury and state why it was irreparable; state why the order was issued without notice; and be promptly filed in the clerk's office and entered in the record. The order expires at the time after entry not to exceed 14 days – that the court sets, unless before that time the court, for good cause, extends it for a like period or the adverse party consents to a longer extension. The reasons for an extension must be entered in the record.

(3) *Expediting the Preliminary-Injunction Hearing.* If the order is issued without notice, the motion for a preliminary injunction must be set for hearing at the earliest possible time, taking precedence over all other matters except hearings on older matters of the same character. At the hearing, the party who obtained the order must proceed with the motion; if the party does not, the court must dissolve the order.

(4) *Motion to Dissolve.* On 2 days' notice to the party who obtained the order without notice – or on shorter notice set by the court – adverse party may appear and move to dissolve or modify the order, the court must then hear and decide the motion as promptly as justice requires.

(c) **Security**. The court may issue a preliminary injunction or a temporary restraining order only if the movant gives security in an amount that the court considers proper to pay the costs and damages sustained by any party found to have been wrongfully enjoined or restrained. The United States, its officers, and its agencies are not required to give security.

(d) **Contents and Scope of Every Injunction and Restraining Order.**

(1) *Contents.* Every order granting an injunction and every restraining order must:

(A) state the reasons why it was issued;

(B) state the terms specifically; and

(C) describe in reasonable detail – and not by referring to the complaint or other document – the act or acts restrained or required.

(2) *Persons Bound.* The order binds only the following who receive actual notice of it by personal service or otherwise:

(A) the parties;

(B) the parties' officers, agents, servants, employees, and attorneys; and

(C) other persons who are in active concert or participation with anyone described in Rule 62(d) (2) (A) or (B).

(e) **Other Laws Not Modified**. These rules do not modify the following:

(1) any federal statute relating to temporary restraining orders or preliminary injunctions in actions affecting employer and employee;

(2) 28 U.S.C. § 2361, which relates to preliminary injunctions in actions of interpleader or in the nature of interpleader;

(3) 28 U.S.C. § 2284, which relates to actions that must be heard and decided by a three-judge

district court.

(f) **Copyright Impoundment**. This rule applies to copyright–impoundment proceedings.

Rule 65.1. Proceedings Against a Security Provider

Whenever these rules (including the Supplemental Rules for Admiralty or Maritime Claims and Asset Forfeiture Actions) require or allow a party to give security, and security is given with one or more security providers, each provider submits to the court's jurisdiction and irrevocably appoints the court clerk as its agent for receiving service of any papers that affect its liability on the security. The security provider's liability may be enforced on motion without an independent action. The motion and any notice that the court orders may be served on the court clerk, who must promptly send a copy of each to every security provider whose address is known.

Rule 66. Receivers

These rules govern an action in which the appointment of a receiver is sought, or a receiver sues or is sued. But the practice in administering an estate by a receiver or a similar court-appointed officer must accord with the historical practice in federal courts or with a local rule. An action in which a receiver has been appointed may be dismissed only by court order.

Rule 67. Deposit into Court

(a) **Depositing Property**. If any part of the relief sought is a money judgment or the disposition of a sum of money or some other deliverable thing, a party on notice to every other party and by leave of court – may deposit with the court all or part of the money or thing, whether or not that party claims any of it. The depositing party must deliver to the clerk a copy of the order permitting deposit.

(b) **Investing and Withdrawing Funds**. Money paid into court under this rule must be deposited and withdrawn in accordance with 28 U.S.C. §§ 2041 and 2042 and any like statute. The money must be deposited in an interest-bearing account or invested in a court-approved, interest-bearing instrument.

Rule 68. Offer of Judgment

(a) **Making an Offer; Judgment on an Accepted Offer**. At least 14 days before the date set for trial, a party defending against a claim may serve on an opposing party an offer to allow judgment on specified terms, with the costs then accrued. If, within 14 days after being served, the opposing party serves written notice accepting the offer, either party may then file the offer and notice of acceptance, plus proof of service. The clerk must then enter judgment.

(b) **Unaccepted Offer.** An unaccepted offer is considered withdrawn but does not preclude a later offer. Evidence of an unaccepted offer is not admissible except in a proceeding to determine costs.

(c) **Offer After Liability is Determined**. When one party's liability to another has been determined but the extent of liability remains to be determined by further proceedings, the party held liable may make an offer of judgment. It must be served within a reasonable time – but at least 14 days – before the date set for a hearing to determine the extent of liability.

(d) **Paying Costs After an Unaccepted Offer.** If the judgment that the offeree finally obtains is not more favorable than the unaccepted offer, the offeree must pay the costs incurred after the offer was made.

Rule 69. Execution

(a) **In General.**

(1) *Money Judgment; Applicable Procedure.* A money judgment is enforced by a writ of execution,

unless the court directs otherwise. The procedure on execution – and in proceedings supplementary to and in aid of judgment or execution must accord with the procedure of the state where the court is located, but a federal statute governs to the extent it applies.

(2) *Obtaining Discovery*. In aid of the judgment or execution, the judgment creditor or a successor in interest whose interest appears of record may obtain discovery from any person – including the judgment debtor as provided in these rules or by the procedure of the state where the court is located.

(b) **Against Certain Public Officers.** When a judgment has been entered against a revenue officer in the circumstances stated in 28 U.S.C. § 2006, or against an officer of Congress in the circumstances stated in 2 U.S.C. § 118, the judgment must be satisfied as those statutes provide.

Rule 70. Enforcing a Judgment for a Specified Act

(a) **Party's Failure to Act; Ordering Another to Act.** If a judgment requires a party to convey land, to deliver a deed or other document, or to perform any other specific act and the party fails to comply within the time specified, the court may order the act to be done – at the disobedient party's expense – by another person appointed by the court. When done, the act has the same effect as if done by the party.

(b) **Vesting Title**. If the real or personal property is within the district, the court – instead of ordering a conveyance – may enter a judgment divesting any party's title and vesting it in others. That judgment has the effect of a legally executed conveyance.

(c) **Obtaining a Writ of Attachment or Sequestration**. On application by a party entitled to performance of an act, the clerk must issue a writ of attachment or sequestration against the disobedient party's property to compel obedience.

(d) **Obtaining a Writ of Execution or Assistance**. On application by a party who obtains a judgment or order for possession, the clerk must issue a writ of execution or assistance.

(e) **Holding in Contempt**. The court may also hold the disobedient party in contempt.

Rule 71. Enforcing Relief for or Against a Nonparty.

Mien an order grants relief for a nom party or may be enforced against a nonparty, the procedure for enforcing the order is the same as for a party.

Rule 71.1. Condemning Real or Personal Property

(a) **Applicability of Other Rules**. These rules govern proceedings to condemn real and personal property by eminent domain, except as this rule provides otherwise.

(b) **Joinder of Properties**. The plaintiff may join separate pieces of property in a single action, no matter whether they are owned by the same persons or sought for the same use.

(c) **Complaint.**

(1) *Caption.* The complaint must contain a caption as provided in Rule 1.0(a). The plaintiff must, however, name as defendants both the property-designated generally by kind, quantity, and location – and at least one owner of some part of or interest in the property.

(2) *Contents.* The complaint must contain a short and plain statement of the following:

(A) the authority for the taking;

(B) the uses for which the property is to be taken;

(C) a description sufficient to identify the property;

(D) the interests to be acquired; and

(E) for each piece of property, a designation of each. defendant who has been joined as an owner or owner of an interest in it.

(3) *Parties.* When the action commences, the plaintiff needs to join as defendants only those persons who have or claim an interest in the property and whose names are then known. But before any hearing on compensation, the plaintiff must add as defendants all those persons who have or claim an interest and whose names have become known or can be found by a reasonably diligent search of the records, considering both the property's character and value and the interests to be acquired. All others may be made defendants under the designation "Unknown Owners".

(4) *Procedure.* Notice must be served on all defendants as provided in Rule 71.1(d), whether they were named as defendants when the action commenced or were added later. A defendant may answer as provided in Rule 71.1(e). The court, meanwhile, may order any distribution of a deposit that the facts warrant.

(5) *Filing; Additional Copies.* In addition to filing the complaint, the plaintiff must give the clerk at least one copy for the defendant's use and additional copies at the request of the clerk or a defendant.

(d) **Process.**

(1) *Delivering Notice to the Clerk.* On filing a complaint, the plaintiff must promptly deliver to the clerk a joint or several notices directed to the named defendants. When adding defendants, the plaintiff must deliver to the clerk additional notices directed to the new defendants.

(2) Contents of the Notice.

(A) *Main Contents.* Each notice must name the court, the title of the action, and the defendant to whom it is directed. It must describe the property sufficiently to identify it but need not describe any property other than that to be taken from the named defendant. The notice must also state:

(i) that the action is to condemn property;

(ii) the interest to be taken;

(iii) the authority for the taking;

(iv) the uses for which the property is to be taken;

(v) that the defendant may serve an answer on the plaintiff's attorney within 21 days after being served with the notice;

(vi) that the failure to so serve an answer constitutes consent to the taking and to the court's authority to proceed with the action and fix the compensation; and

(vii) that a defendant who does not serve an answer may file a notice of appearance.

(B) *Conclusion.* The notice must conclude with the name, telephone number, and e-mail address of the plaintiff's attorney and an address within the district in which the action is brought where the attorney may be served.

(3) Serving the Notice.

(A) *Personal Service.* When a defendant whose address is known resides within the United States or a territory subject to the administrative or judicial jurisdiction of the United States, personal service of the notice (without a copy of the complaint) must be made in accordance with Rule 4.

(B) Service by Publication.

(i) A defendant may be served by publication only when the plaintiff's attorney files a certificate stating that the attorney believes the defendant cannot be personally served, because after diligent inquiry within the state where the complaint is filed, the defendant's place of residence is still unknown or, if known, that it is beyond the territorial limits of personal service. Service is then made by publishing the notice – once a week for at least three successive weeks – in a newspaper published in the county where the property is located or, if there is no such newspaper, in a newspaper with general circulation where the property is located. Before the last publication, a copy of the notice must also be mailed to every defendant who cannot be personally served but whose place of residence is then known. Unknown owners may be served by publication in the same manner by a notice addressed to "Unknown Owners".

(ii) Service by publication is complete on the date of the last publication. The plaintiff's attorney must prove publication and mailing by a certificate, attach a printed copy of the published notice, and mark on the copy the newspaper's name and the dates of publication.

(4) *Effect of Delivery and Service.* Delivering the notice to the clerk and serving it have the same effect as serving a summons under Rule 4.

(5) *Amending the Notice; Proof of Service and Amending the Proof.* Rule 4(a) (2) governs amending the notice. Rule 4(1) governs proof of service and amending it.

(e) **Appearance or Answer.**

(1) *Notice of Appearance.* A defendant that has no objection or defense to the taking of his property may serve a notice of appearance designating the property in which it claims an interest. The defendant must then be given notice of all later proceedings affecting the defendant.

(2) *Answer.* A defendant that has an objection or defense to the taking must serve an answer within 21 days after being served with the notice. The answer must:

(A) identify the property in which defendant claims an interest;

(B) state the nature and extent of the interest; and

(C) state all the defendant's objections and defenses to the taking.

(3) *Waiver of Other Objections and Defenses; Evidence on Compensation.* A defendant waives all objections and defenses not stated in its answer. No other pleading or motion asserting an additional objection or defense is allowed. But at the trial on compensation, a defendant – whether or not it has previously appeared or answered – may present evidence on the amount of compensation to be paid and may share in the award.

(f) **Amending Pleadings**. Without leave of court, the plaintiff may – as often as it wants – amend the complaint at any time before the trial on compensation. But no amendment may be made if it would result in a dismissal inconsistent with Rule 71.1(i) (l) or (2). The plaintiff need not serve a copy of an amendment, but must serve notice of the filing, as provided in Rule 5(b), on every affected party who has appeared and as provided in Rule 71.1(d), on every affected party who has not appeared. In addition, the plaintiff must give the clerk at least one copy of each amendment for the defendants' use, and additional copies at the request of the clerk or a defendant. A defendant may appear or answer in the time and manner and with the same effect as provided in Rule 71.1(e).

(g) **Substituting Parties**. If a defendant dies, becomes incompetent, or transfers an interest after being joined, the court may, on motion and notice of hearing, order that the proper party be substituted. Service of the motion and notice on a nonparty must be made as provided in Rule 71.1(d) (3).

(h) **Trial of the Issues.**

(1) *Issues Other Than Compensation; Compensation.* In an action involving eminent domain under federal law, the court tries all issues, including compensation, except when compensation must be determined:

(A) by any tribunal specially constituted by a federal statute to determine compensation; or

(B) if there is no such tribunal, by a jury when a party demands one within the time to answer or within any additional time the court sets, unless the court appoints a commission.

(2) Appointing a Commission; Commission's Powers and Report.

(A) Reasons for Appointing, if a party has demanded a jury, the court may instead appoint a three-person commission to determine compensation because of the character, location, or quantity of the property to be condemned or for other just reasons.

(B) *Alternate Commissioners.* The court may appoint up to two additional persons to serve as alternate commissioners to hear the case and replace commissioners who, before a decision is filed, the court finds unable or disqualified to perform their duties. Once the commission renders its final decision, the court must discharge any alternate who has not replaced a commissioner.

(C) *Examining the Prospective Commissioners.* Before making its appointments, the court must advise the parties of the identity and qualifications of each prospective commissioner and alternate and may permit the parties to examine them. The parties may not suggest appointees, but for good cause may object to a prospective commissioner or alternate.

(D) *Commission's Power and Report.* A commission has the powers of a master under Rule 53(c). Its action and report are determined by a majority. Rule 53(d), (e), and (f) apply to its action and report.

(i) **Dismissal of the Action or a Defendant.**

(1) Dismissing the Action.

(A) *By the Plaintiff.* If no compensation hearing on a piece of property has begun, and if the plaintiff has not acquired title or a lesser interest or taken possession, the plaintiff may, without a court order, dismiss the action as to that property by filing a notice of dismissal briefly describing the property.

(B) *By Stipulation.* Before a judgment is entered vesting the plaintiff with title or a lesser interest in or possession of the property, the plaintiff and affected defendants may, without a court order, dismiss the action in whole or in ||art by filing a stipulation of dismissal. And if the parties so stipulate, the court may vacate a judgment already entered.

(C) *By Court Order.* At any time before compensation has been determined and paid, the court may, after a motion and hearing, dismiss the action as to a piece of property. But if the plaintiff has already taken title, a lesser interest, or possession as to any part of it, the court must award compensation for title, lesser interest, or possession taken.

(2) *Dismissing a Defendant.* The court may at any time dismiss a defendant who was unnecessarily or improperly joined.

(3) *Effect.* A dismissal is without prejudice unless otherwise stated in the notice, stipulation, or court order.

(j) **Deposit and Its Distribution.**

(1) *Deposit.* The plaintiff must deposit with the court any money required by law as a condition to the exercise of eminent domain and may make a deposit when allowed by statute.

(2) *Distribution; Adjusting Distribution.* After a deposit, the court and attorneys must expedite the proceedings so as to distribute the deposit and to determine and pay compensation. If the compensation finally awarded to a defendant is less than the amount distributed to that defendant, the court must enter judgment against that defendant for the overpayment.

(k) **Condemnation Under a State's Power of Eminent Domain**. This rule governs an action involving eminent domain under state law. But if gate law provides for trying an issue by jury – or for trying the issue of compensation by jury or commission or both – that law governs.

(l) **Costs.** Costs are not subject to Rule 54(d).

Rule 72. Magistrate Judges: Pretrial Order

(a) **Nondispositive Matters**. When a pretrial matter not dispositive of a party's claim or defense is referred to a magistrate judge to hear and decide, the magistrate judge must promptly conduct the required proceedings and, when appropriate, issue a written order stating the decision. A party may serve and file objections to the order within 14 days after being served with a copy. A party may not assign as error a defect in the order not timely objected to. The district judge in the case must consider timely objections and modify or set aside any part of the order that is clearly erroneous or is contrary to law.

(b) **Dispositive Motions and Prisoner Petitions.**

(1) *Findings and Recommendations*. A magistrate judge must promptly conduct the required proceedings when assigned, without the parties' consent, to hear a pretrial matter dispositive of a claim or defense or a prisoner petition challenging the conditions of confinement. A record must be made of all evidentiary proceedings and may, at the magistrate judge's discretion, be made of any other proceedings. The magistrate judge must enter a recommended disposition, including, if appropriate, proposed findings of fact. The clerk must mail a copy to each party.

(2) *Objections*. Within 14 days after being served with a copy of the recommended disposition, a party may serve and file specific written objections to the proposed findings and recommendations. A party may respond to another party's objections within 14 days after being served with a copy. Unless the district judge orders otherwise, the objecting party must promptly arrange for transcribing the record, or whatever portions of it the parties agree to, or the magistrate judge considers sufficient.

(3) *Resolving Objections*. The district judge must determine de novo any part of the magistrate judge's disposition that has been properly objected to. The district judge may accept, reject, or modify the recommended disposition; receive further evidence; or return the matter to the magistrate judge with instructions.

Rule 73. Magistrate Judges: Trial by Consent; Appeal

(a) **Trial by Consent**. When authorized under 28 U.S.C. § 636(c), a magistrate judge may, if all parties consent, conduct a civil action or proceeding, including a jury or nonjury trial. A record must be made in accordance with 28 U.S.C. § 636(c) (5).

(b) **Consent Procedure.**

(1) *In General.* When a magistrate judge has been designated to conduct civil actions or proceedings, the clerk must give the parties written notice of their opportunity to consent under 28 U.S.C. § 636(c). To signify their consent, the parties must jointly or separately file a statement consenting to the referral. A district judge or magistrate judge may be informed of a party's response to the clerk's notice only if all parties have consented to the referral.

(2) *Reminding the Parties About Consenting.* A district judge, magistrate judge, or other court official may remind the parties of the magistrate judge's availability but must also advise them that they are free to withhold consent without adverse substantive consequences.

(3) *Vacating a Referral.* On its own for good cause – or when a party shows extraordinary circumstances – the district judge may vacate a referral to a magistrate judge under this rule.

(c) **Appealing a Judgment**. In accordance with 28 U.S.C. § 636(c) (3), an appeal from a judgment entered at a magistrate judge's direction may be taken to the court of appeals as would any other appeal from a district-court judgment.

Rule 74. – 76 [Abrogated]

Rule 77. Conducting Business; Clerk's authority; Notice of an Order or Judgment

(a) **When Court Is Open**. Every district court is considered always open for filing any paper, issuing and returning process, making a motion, or entering an order.

(b) **Place for Trial and Other Proceedings**. Every trial on the merits must be conducted in open court and, so far as convenient, in a regular courtroom. Any other act or proceeding may be done or conducted by a judge in chambers, without the attendance of the clerk or other court official, and anywhere inside or outside the district. But no hearing – other than one *ex parte* – may be conducted outside the district unless all parties consent.

(c) **Clerk's Office Hours; Clerk's Orders.**

(1) *Hours*. The clerk's office – with a clerk or deputy on duty – must be open during business hours every day except Saturdays, Sundays, and legal holidays. But a court may, by local rule or order, require that the office be open for specified hours on Saturday or a particular legal holiday other than one listed in Rule 6(a) (6) (A).

(2) *Orders*. Subject to the court's power to suspend, alter, or rescind the clerk's action for good cause, the clerk may:

(A) issue process;

(B) enter a default;

(C) enter a default judgment under Rule 55(b) (1); and

(D) act on any other matter that does not require the court's attention.

(d) **Serving Notice of an Order or Judgment.**

(1) *Service*. Immediately after entering an order or judgment, the clerk must serve notice of the entry, as provided in Rule 5(b), on each party who is not in default for failure to appear. The clerk must record the service on the docket. A party also may serve notice of the entry as provided in Rule 5(b).

(2) *Time to Appeal Not Affected by Lack of Notice*. Lack of notice of the entry does not affect the time for appeal or relieve – or authorize the court to relieve a party for failing to appeal within the time allowed, except as allowed by Federal Rule of Appellate Procedure (4) (a).

Rule 78. Hearing Motions; Submissions on Briefs

(a) **Providing a Regular Schedule for Oral Hearings**. A court may establish regular times and places for oral hearings on motions.

(b) **Providing for Submissions on Briefs**. By rule or order, the court may provide for submitting and determining motions on briefs, without oral hearings.

Rule 79. Records Kept by the Clerk

(a) **Civil Docket.**

(1) *In General*. The clerk must keep a record known as the "civil docket" in the form and manner prescribed by the Director of the Administrative Office of the United States Courts with the approval of the Judicial Conference of the United States. The clerk must enter each civil action in the docket. Actions must be assigned consecutive file numbers, which must be noted in the docket where the first entry of the action is made.

(2) *Items to be Entered*. The following items must be marked with the file number and entered chronologically in the docket:

(A) papers filed with the clerk;

(B) process issued, and proofs of service or other returns showing execution; and
(C) appearances, orders, verdicts, and judgments.

(3) *Contents of Entries; Jury Trial Demanded.* Each entry must briefly show the nature of the paper filed or writ issued, the substance of each proof of service or other return, and the substance and date of entry of each order and judgment. When a jury trial has been properly demanded or ordered, the clerk must enter the word "jury" in the docket.

(b) **Civil Judgments and Orders**. The clerk must keep a copy of every final judgment and appealable order; of every order affecting title to or a lien on real or personal property; and of any other order that the court directs to be kept. The clerk must keep these in the form and manner prescribed by the Director of the Administrative Office of the United States Courts with the approval of the Judicial Conference of the United States.

(c) **Indexes; Calendars**. Under the court's direction, the clerk must:
(1) keep indexes of the docket and of the judgments and orders described in Rule 79(b); and
(2) prepare calendars of all actions ready for trial, distinguishing jury trials from nonjury trials.

(d) **Other Records**. The clerk must keep any other records required by the Director of the Administrative Office of the United States Courts with the approval of the Judicial Conference of the United States.

Rule 80. Stenographic Transcript as Evidence

If stenographically reported testimony at a hearing or trial is admissible in evidence at a later trial, the testimony may be proved by a transcript certified by the person who recorded it.

Rule 81. Applicability of the Rules in General; Removed Actions

(a) **Applicability to Particular Proceedings.**

(1) *Prize Proceedings.* These rules do not apply to prize proceedings in admiralty governed by 10 U.S.C. §§ 7651-7681.

(2) *Bankruptcy.* These rules apply to bankruptcy proceedings to the extent provided by the Federal Rules of bankruptcy Procedure.

(3) *Citizenship.* These rules apply to proceedings for admission to citizenship to the extent that the practice in those proceedings is not specified in federal statutes and has previously conformed to the practice in civil actions. The provisions of 8 U.S.C. § 1451 for service by publication and for answers apply in proceedings to cancel citizenship certificates.

(4) *Special Writs.* These rules apply to proceedings for habeas corpus and for quo warrantor to the extent that the practice in those proceedings:
(A) is not specified in a federal statute, the Rules Governing Section 2254 Cases and the Rules Governing Section 2255 Cases; and
(B) has previously conformed to the practice in civil actions.

(5) *Proceedings Involving a Subpoena.* These rules apply to proceedings to compel testimony or the production of documents through subpoena issued by a United States officer or agency under a federal statute, except as otherwise provided by statute, by local rule, or by court order in the proceedings.

(6) *Other Proceedings.* These rules, to the extent applicable, govern proceedings under the following laws, except as these laws provide other procedures:
(A) 7 U.S.C. §§ 292, 499 g (c), for reviewing an order of the Secretary of Agriculture;
(B) 9 U.S.C., relating to arbitration;
(C) 15 U.S.C. § 522, for reviewing an order of the Secretary of the Interior;

(D) 15 U.S.C. § 715d(c), for reviewing an order denying a certificate of clearance;
(E) 29 U.S.C. §§ 159, 160, for enforcing an order of the National Labor Relations Board;
(F) 33 U.S.C. §§ 918, 921, for enforcing or reviewing a compensation order under the Longshore and Harbor Worker's Compensation Act; and
(G) 45 U.S.C. § 159, for reviewing an arbitration award in a railway-labor dispute.

(b) **Scire Facias and Mandixnus.** The writs of *scire facias* and mandamus are abolished. Relief previously available through them may be obtained by appropriate action or motion under these rules.

(c) **Removed Actions.**

(1) *Applicability.* These rules apply to a civil action after it is removed from a state court.
(2) *Further Pleading.* After removal, repleading is unnecessary unless the court orders it. A defendant who did not answer before removal must answer or present other defenses or objections under these rules within the longest of these periods:
(A) 21 days after receiving – through service or otherwise – a copy of the initial pleading stating the claim for relief;
(B) 21 days after being served with the summons for an initial pleading on file at the time of service; or
(C) 7 days after the notice of removal is filed.
(3) Demand for a Jury Trial.
(A) *As Affected by State Law.* A party who, before removal, expressly demanded a jury trial in accordance with state law need not renew the demand after removal. If the state law did not require an express demand for a jury trial, a party need not make one after removal unless the court orders the parties to do so within a specified time. The court must so order at a party's request and may so order on its own. A party who fails to make a demand when so ordered waives a jury trial.
(B) *Under Rule 38.* If all necessary pleadings have been served at the time of removal, a party entitled to a jury trial under Rule 38 must be given one if the party serves a demand within 14 days after:
(i) it files a notice of removal; or
(ii) it is served with a notice of removal filed by another party.

(d) **Law Applicable.**

(1) "State law" Defined. When these rules refer to state law, the term "law" includes the state's statutes and the state's judicial decisions.
(2) "State" Defined. The term "state" includes, where appropriate, the District of Columbia and any United States commonwealth or territory.
(3) "Federal Statute" Defined in the District of Columbia. In the United States district court for the District of Columbia, the term "federal statute" includes any Act of Congress that applies locally to the district.

Rule 82. Jurisdiction and Venue Unaffected

These rules do not extend or limit the jurisdiction of the district courts or the venue of actions in those courts. An admiralty or maritime claim under Rule 9(h) is governed by 28 U.S.C. § 1390

Rule 83. Rules by District Courts; Judge's Directives

(a) **Local Rules.**

(1) *In General.* After giving public notice and an opportunity for comment, a district court, acting by

a majority of its district judges, may adopt and amend rules governing its practice. A local rule must be consistent with but not duplicate federal statutes and rules adopted under 28 U.S.C. §§ 2072 and 2075 and must conform to any uniform numbering system prescribed by the Judicial Conference of the United States. A local rule takes effect on the date specified by the district court and remains in effect unless amended by the court or abrogated by the judicial council of the circuit. Copies of rules and amendments must, on their adoption, be furnished to the judicial council and the Administrative Office of the United States Courts and be made available to the public.

(2) *Requirement of Form.* A local rule imposing a requirement of form must not be enforced in a way that causes a party to lose any right because of a non-willful failure to comply.

(b) **Procedures When There is No Controlling Law**. A judge may regulate practice in any manner consistent with federal law, rules adopted under 28 U.S.C.§ 2072 and 2075, and the district's local rules. No sanction or other disadvantage may be imposed for noncompliance with any requirement not in federal law, federal rules, or the local rules unless the alleged violator has been furnished in the particular case with actual notice of the requirement.

Rule 84. [Abrogated]

Rule 85. Title

These rules may be cited as the Federal Rules of Civil Procedure.

Notes:

CHAPTER 2 ★★★

BEFORE FILING THE § 2254 PETITION

Before you file your § 2254 petition for habeas corpus, you need to be fully aware of the numerous procedural hurdles you will have to cross before the federal court will even consider the merits of the claims in the petition.

Your petition for writ of habeas corpus § 2254 will be considered by the court as "filed" on the day you place it in the prison mailbox, or to prison authorities directly, see *Houston v. Lack*, U.S. 266, 270-74, 108 S.Ct. 2379 (1988). It is my advice, that you always send a federal habeas corpus petition, as well as any other writ, brief, or legal pleading, by certified mail to ensure its delivery and to defeat any issues as to timeliness, etc.

But prior to that, let's address a few of the procedures and hurdles you need to deal with first.

"In Custody" Requirement

First, before doing anything, you must be "in custody" as a result of the state court judgment, see 28 U.S.C. Sec. 2241(c) and 2254(a). Custody includes not only physical imprisonment, but also any significant restraints on personal liberty and freedoms. A person released on parole is still considered to be "in custody" for the purposes of § 2254, see *Jones v. Cunningham*, 371 U.S. 236, 243 (1963).

Additionally, a habeas petitioners release from custody after he has filed a petition for habeas corpus relief under § 2254 will not "moot" the challenge to his conviction if he will be subjected to adverse collateral consequences from the conviction, such as inability to vote, serve on a jury, etc., see *Carafas v. LaValle*, 391 U.S. 234, 237-39 (1968).

If you are serving consecutive sentences, you are considered to be "in custody" as to a consecutive sentence that has not yet begun, as well as the sentence you are currently serving, see *Maleng v. Cook*, 490 U.S. at 493-94 (1989) (per curium). Effectively, you will be considered "in custody" under all of your consecutive sentences until all are served, see *Garlotte v. Fordice*,____ U.S. ____, 115 S.Ct. 1948, 1952 (1995).

All in all, this requirement is easily met since all prisoners are in custody, usually in one form or fashion.

Exhaustion Requirement

Federal habeas corpus claims cannot be heard unless it has first been properly and fully exhausted in the state's highest court. There are a few exceptions to this rule that I will address more in-depth in the following chapter since it will entail a lot of unknown information to most *pro se* petitioners, etc.

Basically, "exhaustion" simply means that the state courts have had an opportunity first to review claims arising from a state trial, etc. They get the first crack at correcting their mistakes, so to speak. This is found under 28 U.S.C. Sec. 2254 (b) and (c). You will not be found to have exhausted "if you have the right under law of the State to raise, by any available procedure, the claims you are presenting to the federal court."

In essence, be sure to present all of your claims to your state court before you bring them to the federal court in a § 2254 action. If you have a mixed petition containing both exhausted and unexhausted claims, your petition must be dismissed without prejudice before you are able to refile, and then only after you have fully exhausted those claims.

That being said, federal courts may consider habeas petitions containing both exhausted and unexhausted claims and may deny unexhausted claims on their merits, see 28 U.S.C. § 2254 (b) (2) (2012). If a federal court does not consider a petition with both exhausted and unexhausted claims ("mixed petition"), a state prisoner may either (1) return to state court to litigate the unexhausted claims so they can be then presented together in a single petition, or (2) amend the habeas corpus petition to present only the exhausted claims to the federal district court, see *Rhines v. Weber*, 544 U.S.L. 269, 278 (2005).

In most states, fully exhausted means one "full round," which is when you have presented the claim to an appeals court and then in a state habeas corpus/post-conviction review to that state's highest court. If your claim is barred on state procedural grounds, it will be procedurally defaulted in federal court, so be sure to fully and timely exhaust all of your state remedies in state court while you can, and when you can, prior to filing the § 2254 petition.

Procedural default/procedural bar

Where a state court declines to reach the merits of a claim due to failure to comply with state procedural requirements (*e.g.*, where you fail to make a contemporaneous objection at trial), federal habeas corpus review of the claim may be barred because the procedural default constitutes "adequate and independent state grounds" for denial of relief. See *Harris v. Reed*, 489 U.S. 255, 262 (1989).

You can, however, overcome the procedural bar only if you fully demonstrate either (1) cause for the procedural default and actual prejudice as a result of the alleged violation of federal law or (2) that failure to review the claim will "result in a fundamental miscarriage of justice." See *Coleman v. Thompson*, 501 U.S. 722, 750 (1991); *Murray v. Carrier*, 477 U.S. 478, 485 (1986).

Briefly, you should know that the Coleman Court established that the cause and prejudice standard will be applied "[in] all cases in which a state prisoner has defaulted their federal claims in state court pursuant to an independent and adequate state procedural rule," Id at 750.

Establishing Prejudice

At this stage of the game, in a Federal Habeas Corpus proceeding, there is no room or temperance for nit-picking errors or attempting to "throw shit at the wall," so to speak. The judge will not be kind to you if you choose this route, I assure you. To the contrary, at this stage of the "game," you are trying to raise the strongest of your claims: major violations and denials of your constitutional rights, as well as your fundamental rights. Such claims might then include:

- Actual innocence (you are not guilty of the offense)
- You are only guilty of a lesser crime
- Your conviction, plea, or sentence was obtained because of procedural violations, which denied your Due Process rights under the Constitution.

In short, simply citing the mistakes that were made at your trial or witnesses who lied will never obtain relief in the federal courts. Then, you'll have to prove how that Constitutional violation prejudiced you. By prejudice, I mean that it had such a powerful effect on your conviction or sentence that if the error hadn't been made, it is reasonably likely that the results would have favored you. "Federal Constitutional error and resulting prejudice" is what you need to cite and prove if you want relief in a U.S. district court.

New Rule Doctrine (Teague Rule)

In 1989, the Supreme Court drastically changed the face of habeas corpus litigation when it held in *Teague v. Lane*, 489 U.S. 288 (1989) that, henceforward, "[u]nless they fall within an exception to the general rule, new constitutional rules of criminal procedure will not be applicable to those cases which have become final before the new rules are announced." Basically, and in layman terms, it means that you cannot benefit from a favorable change in the law that has occurred after the time that the conviction became "final" on your direct appeal.

You are essentially stuck with the law as it was on your direct appeal. But there are two extremely narrow exceptions to this *Teague* rule. First, new rules that are found to be "substantive" rather than procedural are not covered by *Teague* in the first place, so if a rule is found to be "substantive," it can be applied retroactively. However, the definition of "substantive" as it applies to *Teague* is extremely, extremely, extremely narrow. A substantive rule is one which either "decriminalizes" conduct that was previously illegal: or which prohibits the imposition of punishment on a particular class of persons who were previously subjected to that punishment.

Yep, it is probably never going to happen anywhere! That is because the Supreme Court usually does not declare previously illegal conduct to be legal (state legislatures do that), all new rules declared in the 20 years since *Teague* have been found to be procedural rather than substantive.

The second Teague exception applies to when a new procedural rule is found to be such a blockbuster – so important that it is indispensable to our justice system – that it can fairly be seen as a huge change in the law. So, if the Supreme Court feels it is of "blockbuster/watershed status," it is applied to prisoners retroactively relying on the claim in a habeas corpus § 2254 petition. This, however, is so rare that it has only been applied to the right to counsel under *Gideon v. Wainwright.*

Bottom line, you are probably stuck with the laws that were in effect at the time your direct appeal was affirmed.

Law and Evidence

A federal habeas corpus petitioner must advance and rely upon the very same habeas corpus law and the same evidence that was considered in denying that habeas corpus claim in state court.

This is not easy to do at all, but it is also not impossible. Because a state court can never ignore or deny a prisoner's federal constitutional rights, a federal court not only has the power, but it has the duty to grant habeas corpus on a claim that the state court's denial violated the U.S. Constitution.

Notes:

CHAPTER 3 ★★★

FILING YOUR PETITION

If you haven't been completely discouraged by the minefield of obstacles in the previous chapter, which are capable of destroying your chances at winning your habeas claims, then you are ready to begin the fight. You are ready to file the petition.

A Petition for Relief from a Conviction or Sentence by a Person in State Custody (Form) is usually available in your prison law library or from the district clerk upon request. A petition for a writ of habeas corpus must be filed in the district court having jurisdiction over cases from the county where your sentence took place. Here in Texas, there are many different U.S. district courts due to the sheer size of the state and the massive number of people in prison. Vermont, however, only has one U.S. district court in the entire state.

The rules require that the petition be "typewritten or legibly handwritten and shall be signed under penalty of perjury by the petitioner." Further, it must "allege facts concerning the petitioner's commitment or detention, the name of the person who has custody over him and by virtue of what claim or authority, if known."

The petition must also specify all the grounds for relief which are available to the petitioner and of which he has or by the exercise of reasonable diligence, should have knowledge and shall set forth in summary form the facts supporting each of the grounds. It also must state the relief you are requesting.

The petition requires a filing fee of five dollars ($5) unless you apply for and are granted leave to proceed *in forma pauperis* (as a poor person) by the court. If you are pursuing this IFP status, your petition must include a six-month account statement from your prison commissary account, which you must request from either the warden or some other appropriate person who handles that for your unit or prison. The court requires this in order to proceed *in forma pauperis*.

A look at the example filings at the end of this chapter should provide you with enough guidance to effectively file the petition, as well as the application to proceed *in forma pauperis*. It is just, more or less, answering the questions and filling in the blanks at this stage. After that, it gets quite difficult, but you can do it.

Breathe in … breathe out. Repeat five times.

Now, let's get down to business.

Once you have filled out your petition for habeas corpus § 2254 form and the application to proceed in forma pauperis (and, if you needed to, waived the $5 dollar filing fee), you are ready to move onto the next steps, first of which is the "Civil Cover Sheet."

Civil Cover Sheet

When filling out the Civil Cover Sheet, be sure to observe the following:

- The prisoner/you are the "Petitioner." Provide your legal name and prisoner number.
- The "Respondent" is the warden or superintendent of the prison where you are serving your

sentence.

- The "Real Party in Interest" is the attorney general of the state in which you are confined.
- The nature of the action is: "Petition for Writ of Habeas Corpus by a State Prisoner." The legal authority is 28 U.S.C. § 2254.
- Where you are asked to check a box for the type of action, indicate "General" under "Prisoner Cases."

Note: Some district courts do not require a Civil Cover Sheet. If you are uncertain, you can write to the district court and ask them if they require it. Be sure to request they send you one if they do. It is also advised that you request a copy of their rules.

Memorandum of Points and Authorities

This is just a fancy name for a legal brief that provides the supporting case law for your claims. Since you don't necessarily want to "tip your hand" to the opposing party early in the game, the initial memorandum should be very brief. Once the state files a response, you will have the opportunity to file your "traverse," where you can then pound your attack. (A traverse is a response.)

The Memorandum will need to include the following sections:

- Statement of the Case (summarizing key events in the development of the case through the state courts and on to federal court);
- A Statement of Facts (detailing the facts in support of the petition, with citations to the record wherever possible);
- Argument section (listing each ground and the facts and law in support thereof);
- Conclusion (asking for relief sought, namely an evidentiary hearing and the granting of the petition).

If you do file a Memorandum of Points and Authorities, you should be certain to follow the court's rules on page count or ask the court for leave to exceed the page limit when you file. Again, I prefer to be as brief as possible initially, and then unload with everything in the traverse to the state's response.

Exhibits

Any exhibits to the petition need to be submitted as a separate document, entitled "Exhibits to Petition for Writ of Habeas Corpus," and should include an index. An "Index of Exhibits" should be included on the first or second page.

Where appropriate, the "Facts" section of the attachment to the petition should refer to the exhibits listed in the index. When you are setting out the facts in the petition, refer to the exhibits by the number you have given them in the Exhibits Table.

If you are under the gun to file the petition due to "tolling" issues, you should file the petition first and the exhibits a few days later, after you have composed them and the petition has been given a case number by the court.

Once the petition and supporting documents are received, they will be screened by the court to determine if it should be dismissed, which is very rare if you have followed the basic rules. This will all happen within a few days or weeks after you have filed the petition, but there is no time limit. You must be patient and not harass the court with requests for "updates," etc. Once the petition is accepted, the court will order the attorney general to respond.

Then the "ball" is in the attorney general's court.

Discovery

Though extremely rare to most *pro se* litigants due to the very complications related to it, discovery is available to a petitioner under the Federal Rules of Civil Procedure, but only "if, and to the extent that, the judge in the exercise of his discretion and for good cause shown grants leave to do so, but not otherwise," Sec. § 2254 Cases, Rule 6(a).

"[W]here specific allegations before the Court show reason to believe that the petitioner may if the facts are fully developed, be able to demonstrate that he is illegally confined and is therefore entitled to relief, it is the duty of the Court to provide the very necessary facilities and procedures for) an adequate inquiry." See Rules Sec. §2254, Commentary to Rule 6, quoting *Harris v. Nelson*, 394 U.S. 286, 300 (1969).

Thus, "[W]hile the district court generally has discretion to grant or deny discovery requests under Rule 6, a courts blanket denial of discovery is an abuse of discretion if discovery is indispensable to a fair, rounded, development of the material facts," see *East v. Scott*, 55 F.3d 996, 1001 (5th Cir. 1995).

I have filed dozens of federal § 2254 petitions over the past five years, and I have only been granted discovery in a handful of those cases. This is because those cases weren't those in which discovery was "crucial" or "indispensable" to the outcome, though I attempted to argue that they were.

If you are going to request discovery, be sure to file the proper motion, listing the type of discovery you are seeking, as well as the documents you are requesting and why you need them. That should be filed at the same time you file your petition.

Again, discovery is extremely rare under the AEDPA, and the case that governs discovery is more than 20 years old: *Bracy v. Gramley*, 520 U.S. 899 (1997). *Bracy* emphasizes that "good cause" cannot be shown unless there are "specific allegations before the Court [to] show reason to believe that the petitioner may if the facts are fully developed, be able to demonstrate that he is entitled to relief."

In short, if you want discovery, you are going to have to pull a rabbit out of your ass, so to speak, to convince the judge to order discovery in your case. You will need to be very specific and insistent as to what you want and why you need it. That said, if you think you can get it accomplished, you should absolutely file the motion requesting discovery in your case. As for the motion, it should include the following:

- Proposed Discovery Request: You must list the proposed discovery you want the court to order in one of the following forms that are commonly used in civil cases.
    - Interrogatories: Written questions the other side must answer under oath.
    - Depositions: A request to place a certain witness under oath and ask them questions. This is never granted to *pro se* inmates
    - Requests for Admissions: Statements for the state to admit or deny, under oath, as to facts postulated by you.

Expansion of the Record

Under Rule 7, "the judge may direct that the record be expanded by the parties through the inclusion of additional materials relevant to the determination of the petition's merits." These materials "may include, without limitation, letter predating the filing of the petition in the district court, documents, exhibits, and answers under oath, if so directed, to written interrogatories propounded by the judge" Rule 7 (a).

As a practical matter, Rule 7 rarely comes into play because it is unusual for documents to surface for the first time within a short interval between the completion of exhaustion in state court and the filing for federal habeas corpus. Nevertheless, if you have exercised "due diligence" in state court to obtain certain relevant materials and have been unsuccessful, and if those materials have since become available, you can ask the court to add them to the record under rule 7, see *Cooper-Smith v. Palmateer*, 397 F.3d 1236, 1241 (9th Cir. 2005).

That said, you should be prepared for and expect the attorney general to oppose your discovery request to the fullest extent and on the ground that it was not "exhausted" by presenting it first to the state court. This is a Catch-22 objection, because most state courts prohibit any discovery in state habeas, so the attorney general is arguing that you were prohibited from doing the very thing they are saying you failed to do in the first place.

Expect the objection and overcome it by requesting discovery in your state habeas proceedings (which will be denied) if you are still in that proceeding.

You can almost be guaranteed that the attorney general will argue the Supreme Court decision in *Cullen v. Pinholster*, 563 U.S. 170 (2011), which requires that unreasonableness under AEDPA be shown exclusively by reliance upon state court records, now prohibits any discovery on federal habeas corpus, regardless of whether or not good cause can be shown. There hasn't been much of any litigation on this issue, and the best I could find was from the District of New York, which reasoned that such an interpretation of *Pinholster* would render Habeas Rule 6 a nullity, and since Congress hasn't done so, discovery is still available after *Pinholster*, see *Quezada v. Brown*, 08-CV-5088 (EDNY) (KAM).

If the attorney general argues *Pinholster*, you should rebut it with the citing in *Quezada, supra*:

"Even if the Court were to deem the respondents' motion as timely, it would still fail on the merits. First, *Pinholster* is not controlling law regarding discovery in habeas corpus cases. While *Pinholster* addresses the question of whether a district court can consider new evidence when assessing whether a state court's decision was 'contrary to, involved an unreasonable application of clearly and established Federal law' under 28 U.S.C. § 2254 (d) (1), it does not mention discovery in the context of a habeas corpus petition nor does it reference *Bracy v. Gramley*, 520 U.S. 899 (1997) or Rule 6, upon which the court relied in reaching its original decision to grant petitioners discovery request motion. See *E.G., Conway v. Houk*, No. 07-cv-947, 2011 U.S. Dist. LEXIS 57228, at *9-10 (S.D. Ohio May 26, 2011)."

"Indeed, if this Court were to adopt the respondent's reading of *Pinholster*, it would effectively render completely and utterly meaningless Rule 6 and require the court to determine that *Bracy v. Gramley* is no longer applicable to discovery determinations."

If you quote that exactly as I have written it, you should be able to overcome the attorney general's opposition where they are advancing *Pinholster*. It has worked for me, and it should work for you if you do so effectively.

Stay and Abeyance

This procedure, essentially "freezes time" so that you are not tolled out (out of time) in filing your federal habeas corpus if the court determines that there are unexhausted claims in your habeas petition.

Federal laws under the AEDPA have established a Catch-22 scenario for the Court, which you can benefit from if you do so correctly. The opportunity and need for a Stay and Abeyance arise when you file a petition that contains one or more claims which, for some good reason, was unable to exhaust within the time permitted by the AEDPA's one-year statute of limitations. A federal court cannot entertain on the merits any habeas petition that has not been completely and thoroughly exhausted, as I've explained previously.

Thus, the district court judge has only two options:

1) Formally notify you of the problem and allow you to permanently remove the unexhausted claims and go forward with just the exhausted claims. But this option is worthless to someone who believes the unexhausted claims are as strong or stronger than the exhausted ones and therefore does not want to throw them away.

2) Dismiss the entire petition "without prejudice," which theoretically allows the petitioner to re-file the petition in federal court after the petitioner has then returned to state court to complete exhaustion.

Do you see the Catch-22 here? Because: (a) AEDPA imposes a one-year statute of limitations on federal habeas corpus petitions; (b) The one-year period continues to run out after a dismissal without prejudice, and (c) It will very likely take more than whatever time remains of that one-year to go back and exhaust in state court. This would violate the AEDPA.

In fact, this was recognized by the United States Supreme Court in *Rhines v. Weber*, 544 U.S. 269 (2005). There, the Court held that federal courts have the discretion to grant Stay and Abeyance, but only in "limited circumstances." Specifically, the U.S. District Court can only grant Stay and Abeyance where the petitioner (1) has good cause for his failure to exhaust; (2) has unexhausted claims that are not "plainly meritless."

Since any claim worthy of being brought in a habeas petition has merit, generally, this will satisfy the first requirement. As to the second requirement, the U.S. Supreme Court has been relatively quiet on the matter. Some reasons to consider in showing good cause are ineffective assistance of counsel, failure of appellate counsel to properly explain the AEDPA tolling requirement, investigation, lack of funds to hire a habeas attorney, lack of access to legal supplies if you are indigent, prison lockdowns, health-related illness, etc.

And so, if you are up against the cloak, so to speak, you should try to seek a Stay and Abeyance from the District Court, which will provide you with the time to accomplish the exhaustion and file your petition for habeas corpus § 2254.

If, however, you are already tolled out (time-barred) under the AEDPA, I will show you how to get around that in a future chapter dedicated solely to that issue. I can tell you here, though, you are not alone. Ninety percent of the inmate cases I am aware of fall under this issue for one reason or another.

Evidentiary Hearing

After the pleadings have been filed in the court and the attorney general has had an opportunity to respond to the petition, the federal court must determine whether an evidentiary hearing is now required under Rule 8(a).

This is because the United States Supreme Court in *Townsend v. Sain*, 372 U.S. 293 (1963), held that an evidentiary hearing is *mandatory* if the petitioner had alleged facts which, if true, justified the granting of relief and one of six other circumstances are present: (1) the merits of the dispute were not resolved at a state hearing; (2) the state determination was not fairly supported by the record; (3) the fact-finding procedure was inadequate; (4) there was substantial allegation of newly discovered evidence; (5) the material facts were not adequately developed; or (6) the petitioner was not afforded a full and fair hearing, *Id.* at 312-13.

To the contrary, and where a habeas petitioner has failed to fully develop the factual bases of his claims in state court, he is then precluded from further factual development in federal court unless (1) his claims rely on a new rule of constitutional law or factual predicate previously undiscoverable through the exercise of due diligence, and (2) he establishes by clear and convincing evidence that, but for-constitutional error, no reasonable fact finder would have found him guilty. 28 U.S.C. § 2254(e) (2).

A failure to meet this standard of "diligence" will bar a federal evidentiary hearing in the absence of a convincing claim of actual innocence that can be established by newly discovered evidence, only, see *Williams v. Taylor*, 529 U.S. 420, 436 (2000). But even then, the federal court can still deny a hearing if sufficient facts exist to make an informed decision on the merits, see *Schriro v. Landrigan*, 550 U.S. 465, 474-75 (2007); 28 U.S.C. § 2254(e) (2) (A) (i). ("It follows that if the record refutes the petitioners' factual allegations or otherwise precludes habeas relief, a district court is not required to hold an evidentiary hearing."); see *Clark v. Johnson*, 227 F.3d 273, 284-85 (2000).

And so, if the federal court determines that there are factual issues not resolved by the record, a hearing may be ordered. At that hearing, both parties will call witnesses, typically attorneys who represented the inmate during the trial or on appeal, the state prosecutors, witnesses who were not called at the original hearing or trial, and forensic and psychological experts. The hearing is always held before either the federal district judge or the court magistrate judge; there is no jury. And sometimes, in place of an evidentiary hearing, the judge will order depositions. Here, both parties have a chance to ask questions of the witnesses just as they would at the hearing, the only difference being that no judge is present there. It's all on record, only.

The Decision

After the district court has received both the petition and the state's answer from the attorney general, transcripts, and any of the materials expanded by the record, and after it has held any evidentiary hearing, it is then faced with its most difficult task: making the actual decision. In performing this task, however, the district court is bound by a number of decisional rules and other principles.

First and foremost, the federal district court, sitting in habeas, generally gives the presumption of correctness to the written factual findings of a state court, see 28 U.S.C. Sec. 2254 (d). However, the federal habeas court need not apply the presumption of correctness if it finds that one of eight exceptions codified in 28 U.S.C. Sec. 2254 (d) is applicable. Moreover, the presumption of correctness does not apply to questions of law or to mixed questions of law and facts, see *Miller v. Fenton*, 474 U.S. 104, 110-116 (1985).

Second, even if the court finds a constitutional error, it may only grant habeas relief if it finds that the error "had a substantial and injurious effect or influence in determining the jury's verdict," see *Brecht v. Abrahamson*, ____ U.S. ____, 113 S.Ct. 1710, 1714 (1993). (On the other hand, a "structural defect in the trial mechanism … requires automatic reversal because [it] infect[s] the entire trial process;" *Id.* at 1717, quoting and citing *Arizona v. Fulminante*, 499 U.S. 279, 111 S.Ct. 1246, 1254 (1991).

If, however, "a federal judge in a habeas proceeding is in grave doubt about whether trial error of federal law had 'substantial and injurious effect or influence in determining the jury's verdict,' that error is not harmless [a]nd, the petitioner must win," see *O'Neal v. McAninch*, ____ U.S. ____ 115 S.Ct. 992, 994 (1995). And additionally, the federal courts are split on the question of whether the federal habeas court should apply the *Brecht* "substantial and injurious effect" standard as opposed to the "harmless beyond a reasonable doubt" standard in *Chapman v. California*, 386 U.S. 18 (1967), where the state courts have not made the *Chapman* "harmless beyond a reasonable doubt" analysis in the first instance. See *Orndorff v. Lockhart*, 998 F.2d 1426, 1429-30 (8th Cir. 1993), cert. denied, ____ U.S. ____ 114 S.Ct. 1631 (1994).

If the petition is referred to a magistrate judge for an evidentiary hearing and/or recommendation for disposition, which is permitted under both statute and rule, the magistrate judge will submit for filing with the district court proposed findings of fact and the recommendations for disposition. See 28 U.S.C. Sec. 636 (b) (1) (B); Rules Sec. 2254 Cases, Rule 8 (b) (1).

Once you receive this proposed finding of fact and recommendation from the court, you have only ten days (10) to object to it in a written format. This is very important since many circuit courts of appeal have opined that a failure to object to a magistrate's report will preclude you from challenging the magistrate's report and factual findings on appeal, except on the grounds of plain error or manifest injustice. See *Carter v. Collins*, 918 F.2d 1198, 1203 (5th Cir. 1990).

Thus, it is critical to file timely objections to the magistrate's report. The district court "shall make a de novo review of those portions of the report or specified proposed findings to which you are objecting," Rule 8(b) (4).

Keep in mind that there is no time limit for the court to make a decision following the filing of a federal habeas corpus petition, traverse, and supporting brief, and it's common for several months, if not more, to pass without hearing anything from the court. And, although there is no way to force the court to act, *you shouldn't do so even if there were*, lest you want to piss off the judge.

Objecting to the Magistrate's Report and Recommendations

Before it ever comes to this, as most attorneys will also tell you, it's recommended that you *not* stipulate to or agree to a Magistrate Judge deciding the case. In district courts that have magistrates, they act as a kind of "junior varsity" judge who assists the court judge. Shortly after you file your petition, you will be asked by the court if you will agree to have a magistrate handle your case.

If you agree, you will forfeit any ability to object to the magistrate's findings of facts and recommendations. They will be free to make the decision on the case. I do not recommend this. You do not want to lose that extra bite at the apple, plus the additional time you will get by refusing the offer.

Note, however, that even if you refuse to stipulate/agree to have a Magistrate Judge rule on the case, they will still make some preliminary decisions and submit recommendations to the District Judge that are almost always followed.

Notes:

PETITION FOR WRIT OF HABEAS CORPUS: 28 USC §2254 (Rev. 9/10)
ADOPTED BY ALL FEDERAL COURTS IN TEXAS

IN THE UNITED STATES DISTRICT COURT

FOR THE NORTHERN DISTRICT OF TEXAS

SHERMAN DIVISION

PETITION FOR A WRIT OF HABEAS CORPUS BY
A PERSON IN STATE CUSTODY

JOHN B. DOE	HUGHES UNIT
PETITIONER (Full name of Petitioner)	CURRENT PLACE OF CONFINEMENT
vs.	
	PRISONER ID NUMBER
MARY POPPINS	
RESPONDENT (Name of TDCJ Director, Warden, Jailor, or authorized person having custody of Petitioner)	CASE NUMBER (Supplied by the District Court Clerk)

INSTRUCTIONS - READ CAREFULLY

1. The petition must be legibly handwritten or typewritten and signed and dated by the petitioner, under penalty of perjury. Any false statement of an important fact may lead to prosecution for perjury. Answer all questions in the proper space on the form.

2. Additional pages are not allowed except in answer to questions 11 and 20. Do not cite legal authorities. Any additional arguments or facts you want to present must be in a separate memorandum. The petition, including attachments, may not exceed 20 pages.

3. Receipt of the $5.00 filing fee or a grant of permission to proceed *in forma pauperis* must occur before the court will consider your petition.

4. If you do not have the necessary filing fee, you may ask permission to proceed *in forma pauperis*. To proceed *in forma pauperis*, (1) you must sign the declaration provided with this petition to show that you cannot prepay the fees and costs, and (2) if you are confined in TDCJ-CID, you must send in a certified *In Forma Pauperis* Data Sheet form from the institution in which you are confined. If you are in an institution other than TDCJ-CID, you must send in a certificate completed by an authorized officer at your institution certifying the amount of money you have on deposit at that institution. If you have access or have had access to enough funds to pay the filing fee, then you must pay the filing fee.

5. Only judgments entered by one court may be challenged in a single petition. A separate petition must be filed to challenge a judgment entered by a different state court.

6. Include all of your grounds for relief and all of the facts that support each ground for relief in this petition.

7. Mail the completed petition and one copy to the U. S. District Clerk. The "Venue List" in your unit law library lists all of the federal courts in Texas, their divisions, and the addresses for the clerk's offices. The proper court will be the federal court in the division and district in which you were convicted (for example, a Dallas County conviction is in the Northern District of Texas, Dallas Division) or where you are now in custody (for example, the Huntsville units are in the Southern District of Texas, Houston Division).

8. Failure to notify the court of your change of address could result in the dismissal of your case.

PETITION

What are you challenging? (Check all that apply)

- ☒ A judgment of conviction or sentence, probation or deferred-adjudication probation. (Answer Questions 1-4, 5-12 & 20-25)
- ☐ A parole revocation proceeding. (Answer Questions 1-4, 13-14 & 20-25)
- ☐ A disciplinary proceeding. (Answer Questions 1-4, 15-19 & 20-25)
- ☐ Other:_________________ (Answer Questions 1-4, 10-11 & 20-25)

All petitioners must answer questions 1-4:
Note: In answering questions 1-4, you must give information about the conviction for the sentence you are presently serving, even if you are challenging a prison disciplinary action. (Note: If you are challenging a prison disciplinary action, do not answer questions 1-4 with information about the disciplinary case. Answer these questions about the conviction for the sentence you are presently serving.) Failure to follow this instruction may result in a delay in processing your case.

1. Name and location of the court (district and county) that entered the judgment of conviction and sentence that you are presently serving or that is under attack: 100th Judicial District Court, Dallas County, Texas

2. Date of judgment of conviction: January 1, 2021

3. Length of sentence: 50 Years

4. Identify the docket numbers (if known) and all crimes of which you were convicted that you wish to challenge in this habeas action: F20-11-1111CR

Judgment of Conviction or Sentence, Probation or Deferred-Adjudication Probation:

5. What was your plea? (Check one) ☒ Not Guilty ☐ Guilty ☐ Nolo Contendere

6. Kind of trial: (Check one) ☒ Jury ☐ Judge Only

7. Did you testify at trial? ☐ Yes ☒ No

8. Did you appeal the judgment of conviction? ☒ Yes ☐ No

9. If you did appeal, in what appellate court did you file your direct appeal? 5th Court of Appeals of Dallas Cause Number (if known): CR123456

   What was the result of your direct appeal (affirmed, modified or reversed)? Affirmed

   What was the date of that decision? March 1, 2021

   If you filed a petition for discretionary review after the decision of the court of appeals, answer the following:

   Grounds raised: None Filed

   ____

   Result: ____________________

   Date of result: ____________ Cause Number (if known): ____________

   If you filed a petition for a *writ of certiorari* with the United States Supreme Court, answer the following:

   Result: Denied

   Date of result: March 10, 2021

10. Other than a direct appeal, have you filed any petitions, applications or motions from this judgment in any court, state or federal? This includes any state applications for a writ of habeas corpus that you may have filed. ☐ Yes ☐ No

11. If your answer to 10 is "Yes," give the following information:

    Name of court: 100th Judicial District Court

    Nature of proceeding: Application for Writ of Habeas Corpus 11.07

    Cause number (if known): WR-2000000

Date (month, day and year) you filed the petition, application or motion as shown by a file-stamped date from the particular court: March 20, 2021

Grounds raised: Ineffective Assistance of Counsel; Prosecutorial Misconduct

Date of final decision: March 25, 2021

What was the decision? Denied Without Written Order

Name of court that issued the final decision: Court of Criminal Appeals of Texas

As to any second petition, application or motion, give the same information:

Name of court: ______

Nature of proceeding: ______

Cause number (if known): ______

Date (month, day and year) you filed the petition, application or motion as shown by a file-stamped date from the particular court:

______

Grounds raised: ______

______

Date of final decision: ______

What was the decision? ______

Name of court that issued the final decision: ______

If you have filed more than two petitions, applications or motions, please attach an additional sheet of paper and give the same information about each petition, application or motion.

12. Do you have any future sentence to serve after you finish serving the sentence you are attacking in this petition? ☐ Yes ☒ No

(a) If your answer is "Yes," give the name and location of the court that imposed the sentence to be served in the future: ______

______

(b) Give the date and length of the sentence to be served in the future: ______

______

(c) Have you filed, or do you intend to file, any petition attacking the judgment for the sentence you must serve in the future? ☐ Yes ☒ No

Parole Revocation:

13. Date and location of your parole revocation: ______________________

14. Have you filed any petitions, applications or motions in any state or federal court challenging your parole revocation? ☐ Yes ☐ No

If your answer is "Yes," complete Question 11 above regarding your parole revocation.

Disciplinary Proceedings:

15. For your original conviction, was there a finding that you used or exhibited a deadly weapon? ☐ Yes ☐ No

16. Are you eligible for release on mandatory supervision? ☐ Yes ☐ No

17. Name and location of the TDCJ Unit where you were found guilty of the disciplinary violation:
____

Disciplinary case number: ______________________

What was the nature of the disciplinary charge against you? ______________________

18. Date you were found guilty of the disciplinary violation: ______________________

Did you lose previously earned good-time days? ☐Yes ☐ No

If your answer is "Yes," provide the exact number of previously earned good-time days that were forfeited by the disciplinary hearing officer as a result of your disciplinary hearing:
____

Identify all other punishment imposed, including the length of any punishment, if applicable, and any changes in custody status:

____

____

____

19. Did you appeal the finding of guilty through the prison or TDCJ grievance procedure? ☐ Yes ☐ No

If your answer to Question 19 is "Yes," answer the following:

Step 1 Result: ______________________

Date of Result: ______________________________

Step 2 Result: ______________________________

Date of Result: ______________________________

All petitioners must answer the remaining questions:

20. For this petition, state every ground on which you claim that you are being held in violation of the Constitution, laws, or treaties of the United States. Summarize briefly the facts supporting each ground. If necessary, you may attach pages stating additional grounds and facts supporting them.

CAUTION: To proceed in the federal court, you must ordinarily first exhaust your available state-court remedies on each ground on which you request action by the federal court. Also, if you fail to set forth all the grounds in this petition, you may be barred from presenting additional grounds at a later date.

A. **GROUND ONE:** Trial Counsel provided ineffective assistance of counsel for failing to investigate mitigating evidence.

Supporting facts (Do not argue or cite law. Just state the specific facts that support your claim.):

Prior to trial, counsel failed to investigate and obtain critical mitigation evidence related to applicant's childhood hardships. Had he done so, he would have readily uncovered extensive evidence of childhood physical abuse, sexual abuse, and homelessness. This evidence would have been explosive.

B. **GROUND TWO:** Trial Counsel provided ineffective assistance at trial when he failed to object to known false testimony.

Supporting facts (Do not argue or cite law. Just state the specific facts that support your claim.):

During the guilt phase of trial, the state introduced testimony that the victim was killed with a knife, when in fact, the victim was after being hit by a car. Trial counsel, did not object.
died
This prejudiced the applicant, and violated his right to Due Process and a fair trial.

C. **GROUND THREE:** etc...

Supporting facts (Do not argue or cite law. Just state the specific facts that support your claim.):

Etc......

D. **GROUND FOUR:** etc....

Supporting facts (Do not argue or cite law. Just state the specific facts that support your claim.):

Etc.....

21. Relief sought in this petition: Applicant prays this Court hold an Evidentiary Hearing, and then reverse and remand the case for a new trial.

22. Have you previously filed a federal habeas petition attacking the same conviction, parole revocation or disciplinary proceeding that you are attacking in this petition? ☐ Yes ☒ No
If your answer is "Yes," give the date on which each petition was filed and the federal court in which it was filed. Also state whether the petition was (a) dismissed without prejudice, (b) dismissed with prejudice, or (c) denied.

____

____

If you previously filed a federal petition attacking the same conviction and such petition was denied or dismissed with prejudice, did you receive permission from the Fifth Circuit to file a second petition, as required by 28 U.S.C. § 2244(b)(3) and (4)? ☐ Yes ☒ No

23. Are any of the grounds listed in question 20 above presented for the first time in this petition?
☐ Yes ☒ No

If your answer is "Yes," state briefly what grounds are presented for the first time and give your reasons for not presenting them to any other court, either state or federal.

____

____

____

24. Do you have any petition or appeal now pending (filed and not yet decided) in any court, either state or federal, for the judgment you are challenging? ☐ Yes ☒ No

If "Yes," identify each type of proceeding that is pending (i.e., direct appeal, art. 11.07 application, or federal habeas petition), the court in which each proceeding is pending, and the date each proceeding was filed. ____

____

25. Give the name and address, if you know, of each attorney who represented you in the following stages of the judgment you are challenging:

(a) At preliminary hearing: John Johnson

(b) At arraignment and plea: John Johnson

(c) At trial: David Anderson

(d) At sentencing: David Anderson

(e) On appeal: Steve Smith

(f) In any post-conviction proceeding: ________________________________

(g) On appeal from any ruling against you in a post-conviction proceeding: ____________

____

Timeliness of Petition:

26. If your judgment of conviction, parole revocation or disciplinary proceeding became final over one year ago, you must explain why the one-year statute of limitations contained in 28 U.S.C. § 2244(d) does not bar your petition.[1]

____

____

____

____

____

[1] The Antiterrorism and Effective Death Penalty Act of 1996 ("AEDPA"), as contained in 28 U.S.C. § 2244(d), provides in part that:

(1) A one-year period of limitation shall apply to an application for a writ of habeas corpus by a person in custody pursuant to the judgment of a State court. The limitation period shall run from the latest of -

(A) the date on which the judgment became final by the conclusion of direct review or the expiration of the time for seeking such review;

(B) the date on which the impediment to filing an application created by State action in violation of the Constitution or laws of the United States is removed, if the applicant was prevented from filing by such State action;

(C) the date on which the constitutional right asserted was initially recognized by the Supreme Court, if the right has been newly recognized by the Supreme Court and made retroactively applicable to cases on collateral review; or

(D) the date on which the factual predicate of the claim or claims presented could have been discovered through the exercise of due diligence.

(2) The time during which a properly filed application for State post-conviction or other collateral review with respect to the pertinent judgment or claim is pending shall not be counted toward any period of limitation under this subsection.

Wherefore, petitioner prays that the Court grant him the relief to which he may be entitled.

____
Signature of Attorney (if any)

____

I declare (or certify, verify, or state) under penalty of perjury that the foregoing is true and correct and that this Petition for a Writ of Habeas Corpus was placed in the prison mailing system on

March 25, 2021 (month, day, year).

Executed (signed) on March 25, 2021 (date).

____
Signature of Petitioner (required)

Petitioner's current address: 12345 Main St. Gatesville, Texas 777777

____

IN THE UNITED STATES DISTRICT COURT
FOR THE ____________ DISTRICT OF TEXAS
____________ DIVISION

____
Plaintiff's name and ID Number

____
Place of Confinement

CASE NO.______________________
(Clerk will assign the number)

V.

APPLICATION TO PROCEED IN FORMA PAUPERIS

____
Defendant's name and address

I, ______________________, declare, depose, and say I am the Plaintiff in the above entitled case. In support of my motion to proceed without being required to prepay fees, costs, or give security therefor, I state because of my poverty, I am unable to pay in advance the filing fee for said proceedings or to give security for the filing fee. I believe I am entitled to relief.

I, further declare the responses which I have made to the questions and instructions below are true.

1. Have you received, within the last 12 months, any money from any of the following sources?

   a. Business, profession or from self-employment? Yes ☐ No ☐
   b. Rent payments, interest or dividends? Yes ☐ No ☐
   c. Pensions, annuities or life insurance payments? Yes ☐ No ☐
   d. Gifts or inheritances? Yes ☐ No ☐
   e. Family or friends? Yes ☐ No ☐
   f. Any other sources? Yes ☐ No ☐

   If you answered **YES** to any of the questions above, describe each source of money and state the amount received from each during the past 12 months.

   ____
   ____

2. Do you own cash, or do you have money in a checking or savings account, including any funds in prison accounts?

   Yes ☐ No ☐

   If you answered **YES** to any of the questions above, state the total value of the items owned.

   ____
   ____

3. Do you own real estate, stocks, bonds, note, automobiles, or other valuable property, excluding ordinary household furnishings and clothing?

Yes ☐ No ☐

If you answered **YES**, describe the property and state its approximate value.

____

____

I understand a false statement in answer to any question in this affidavit will subject me to penalties for perjury. I declare (certify, verify, or state) under penalty of perjury that the foregoing is true and correct (28 U.S.C. §1746).

Signed this the ____________ day of ____________________, 20 ____.

____

Signature of Plaintiff ID Number

YOU <u>MUST</u> ATTACH A CURRENT SIX (6) MONTH HISTORY OF YOUR INMATE TRUST ACCOUNT. YOU CAN ACQUIRE THE APPROPRIATE INMATE ACCOUNT CERTIFICATE FROM THE LAW LIBRARY AT YOUR PRISON UNIT.

CHAPTER 4

NOW – IT'S THEIR TURN! (THE STATE'S RESPONSE)

One thing I can guarantee at this stage, as happens in almost all cases, is that the attorney general will respond with a Motion to Dismiss your case. And for numerous reasons, they believe are true. Rarely, however, if you have successfully done your homework and have left no holes for them to see, they will respond with a formal Answer to your petition without seeking to dismiss.

If, you receive a Motion to Dismiss from the attorney general, it means that they are attempting to have your entire petition thrown out without addressing any of your claims. Usually, they will raise arguments such as:

- Time Barred under the AEDPA
- Failure to Exhaust in state court
- State procedural default
- Improper petition

Once you receive a Motion to Dismiss, you will have to fight it immediately by filing an "Opposition to Respondents Motion to Dismiss." After you have done so, the attorney general will get yet another chance to respond, and then the Court will make a decision as to whether or not your petition will be dismissed.

Now, let's address any and all angles the attorney general's office is likely to pursue in having your petition dismissed so that you can be prepared to attack it.

Time Barred (Untimeliness)

Here, the attorney general will detail the history of the case in attempting to show the court that, even allowing for the one-year tolling, you have exceeded the allowed time frame of 365 days between the date your direct appeal was denied and the filing of your § 2254 petition.

To defeat this claim by the attorney general, you will either have to show the court that you are entitled to additional time or that "equitable tolling" (additional tolling) should be allowed for any filing delays caused by some external forces that were not your fault.

Some of these external forces might include medical conditions, lack of law library access, prison lockdowns, transfers, ineffective assistance of counsel, abandonment by an attorney, etc., see *Maples v. Thomas*, 565 U.S. 266 (2012).

Failure to Exhaust

As I pointed out to you in an earlier chapter, you must have fully exhausted every single claim in state court prior to having raised them in a federal habeas corpus petition. If you haven't, the attorney general will see it and will get your petition dismissed quickly.

If you are facing a Motion to Dismiss because you have failed to exhaust, you must do one of the following:

- File an Opposition to the Motion proving that you have in fact, fully exhausted, if this is true;
- File a First Amended Petition that dismisses the unexhausted claim(s);
- Dismiss the entire petition without prejudice and then refile it completely without the unexhausted claims.

Dismissing the petition without prejudice is an easy process and only requires that you write a one-page letter or form notifying the court that you are dismissing the action "without prejudice." But keep in mind that the clock will begin to tick again, and the one-year tolling will come back into play. You might get time-barred before you have the opportunity to refile the petition.

State Procedural Default

There are many state procedural defaults that you need to try and avoid and anticipate before you file the petition for habeas corpus or overcome them in state court. If not, the attorney general will move to have your petition dismissed.

There is a two-part test for State Procedural Default.

If, under the rules, a state court denies your state habeas corpus application based on a state procedural default, the federal court cannot touch that decision and must respect it. They do this by asking first (1) whether state courts acted fairly and evenhandedly with the petitioner (you) in imposing the state procedural default, and if so, (2) whether the petitioner (you) can demonstrate a valid "excuse or reason" for the default under federal law. If the court can answer "yes" to both of these questions, which you will attempt to accomplish by filing an Opposition to Respondents Motion to Dismiss, then the federal court can survive the state procedural default, and your petition will not be dismissed on this basis.

In determining whether a state court acted fairly in determining and finding a state procedural default, the federal court is supposed to apply the "independent and adequate state ground" doctrine. No, I did not just make that up. In order for a state procedural default to prevent you from being heard in federal court, it must be shown first that the state procedural default rule in question was then sufficiently well-established and regularly and consistently followed by the state court. That it is fair to expect that you knew about it and were expected to follow it.

That principle is called the "independent and adequate state ground" doctrine. You should familiarize yourself with that prior to filing your petition, if possible. It essentially provides that a state procedural default is sufficient to bar federal relief where a state carries the burden of showing that the state-law ruling is both "independent" of federal law and "adequate" to hold the petitioner (you) responsible for violating it.

Let's take a close look at the difference between "independent" and "adequate" rulings so that you are less confused by them.

a. *Independent*: is when a state court actually denies a claim on the basis of the state procedural rule rather than on the merits of the claim. For example, a state court denial exclusively on the grounds that the claim was one that could have been raised on appeal but was not would be independent.

b. *Adequate*: is if a state's procedural ground is based on a rule that is firmly established and strictly, regularly, and uniformly followed by the state.

You, the petitioner, are responsible for showing that a procedural default is not independent or adequate. But once that has been done successfully, the state then bears the burden of actually proving, based on court decisions etc., that the rule in question is, in fact, independent and adequate.

Last Reasoned Decision

Typically, you will have already filed a state habeas corpus in your state court (trial court), the state court of appeal, and the state supreme court in some states. Thus, there will be three different orders denying the claim(s).

What the federal court will now do is apply something called the "look through" principle in determining what basis a state court used in denying a petition. This rule requires that the federal court look back through the "last reasoned decision" by the state courts and assume that any subsequent "silent" denials – for example, the common, one-word "denied" that 99% of all prisoners will receive. Here in Texas, it is simply "denied without written order."

If you can convince the district court that what the attorney general is claiming to be a state procedural default was not an independent or adequate determination, then the alleged default will be disregarded, and the case can proceed on the merits. If not, you will have to fight to be "excused" from the default.

Now, I will teach you how to get around these minefields that are designed to frustrate you and effectively get your petition dismissed completely. That will take a whole new chapter.

Notes:

CHAPTER 5
DEFEATING FEDERAL PROCEDURAL DEFAULT AND TIME-BAR

If I had a dollar for every time an inmate told me he was "time barred" from filing his § 2254, or that he was procedurally barred, I'd be a quadrillionaire by now. It's simply untrue in most cases.

And even more so if you followed my advice in my state habeas corpus book, *The Habeas Corpus Manual*, which I will prove in just a few more minutes. Let's just jump right in, shall we?

Defeating State Procedural Default

There are two bases on which the federal court can excuse a state procedural default that has been found to be adequate and independent: *Cause and Prejudice* and *Miscarriage of Justice*. Let's look at them separately to ensure you are able to understand these very different approaches.

Cause and Prejudice:

State procedural defaults can be excused if you, the petitioner, can establish a sufficiently good reason for suffering a procedural default ("Cause") and show that the default related to an issue or evidence important enough to have made a difference in the outcome ("Prejudice").

"Cause" can be established by showing that the default was the result of an "external" force beyond your control. Most often, as I pounded extensively in *The Habeas Corpus Manual*," this will be done by showing facts that amount to ineffective assistance of counsel. For example, if your direct appeal attorney failed to raise a particular claim or failed to file your appeal on time, this can be the "cause" for those procedural violations.

Additionally, if you filed a timely habeas corpus and gave it to prison officials to mail, but it didn't get mailed on time, you have then proven "cause" for an untimely petition under the law.

"Prejudice" is shown by demonstrating that the default involved something so important that it likely affected the outcome of the proceedings in the lower courts. You are required to show that the claim in question actually had a reasonable chance of being granted had it been considered on the merits.

And so here, you can show prejudice by proving up the merits of your claims in the same way you would have done if the claim had not been procedurally barred. Additionally, if cause has been thus established, and if you have stated facts which, if true, would support the granting of the habeas corpus, you should be able to then demonstrate prejudice enough to overcome a procedural default.

Does that make sense? Is it starting to? If not, read it again until it does, because it is very important in your habeas corpus.

Previously, ineffective assistance of counsel couldn't be relied upon to establish cause and prejudice enough to overcome default, since there wasn't any right to counsel on habeas corpus. But that all changed in *Martinez v. Ryan*, 566 U.S. 1, 132 S.Ct. 1309 (2012).

The Martinez Effect

Though it is nearly 9 years old now, most people (including high-dollar post-conviction attorneys) are unfamiliar with *Martinez,* which is simply unacceptable. In this colossal decision, the United States Supreme Court opened the door to ineffective assistance -of-trial-counsel claims. Ninety-nine percent of the claims being reversed by federal courts were ineffective assistance claims arising from trial errors.

Remember, this does not include appellate counsel or post-conviction counsel, only trial counsel. But there, of course, are some ways around that, which I will show and explain as we go further along.

Does it work? Well … I recently filed a petition for habeas corpus § 2254 for an inmate who was nearly 9-years' time barred from doing so. After arguing the Order to Show Cause issued by the court and establishing the exhibits to support the claims, the district court allowed the petition, and it is currently pending there.

Did you hear me? *Nearly 9 years!*

And so, don't tell me you are "time barred."

Due process requires the effective assistance of trial counsel under *Strickland v. Washington*, 466 U.S. 668, 80 L.Ed. 2d 674, 104 S.Ct. 2052. So naturally, the *Martinez* court addressed a state prisoner's failure to raise ineffective assistance -of-trial-counsel in only proceeding with initial collateral review in which the state allowed such claims not to bar federal habeas corpus court from hearing those claims; if the prisoner had no, or ineffective, counsel in the proceeding.

I encourage you to read the entire *Martinez* Supreme Court opinion that I have included at the end of this chapter. And after you have read that case, you can read the next important one.

The Trevino Effect

Only a year after *Martinez*, in 2013, the United States Supreme Court again addressed and opined that procedural default was not a bar to federal habeas corpus courts from hearing substantial claims of ineffective assistance of counsel at trial, where state procedural framework typically made meaningful opportunity to raise ineffective assistance claims on direct appeal highly unlikely.

For instance, here in Texas, as was the focus of the United States Supreme Court in *Trevino*, it is effectively and utterly impossible to raise a claim of ineffective assistance of counsel on direct appeal. Because of this, the Supreme Court of the United States (SCOTUS) in *Trevino*, vacated and remanded the case against Texas's intense arguments.

I have also included this Supreme Court decision at the end of this chapter, and you should read it until you can basically recite it because it is that important to your habeas corpus petition.

And after you read those cases, you should familiarize yourself with these other circuit court decisions related to the issues decided in both *Martinez* and *Trevino*:

- *Trevino v. Davis*, 829 F.3d 328, 348-49 (5th Cir. 2016)
- *Sullivan v. Sec'y Fla. Dept. of Corr*, 837 F.3d 1195, 1207 (11th Cir. 2016)
- *Bey v. Superintendent Greene SCI*, 856 F.3d 230, 237-38 (3rd Cir. 2017)
- *Frost v. Gilbert*, 835 F.3d 883 (9th Cir. 2016)

And so, contrary to what you've inaccurately been told by the prison "writ writers," and what you may have concluded yourself, you do have a constitutional right to effective assistance of counsel on a first habeas corpus petition, to include state habeas corpus litigants as well. This encompasses both ineffective claims on appeal as well as at trial.

Actual Innocence (Miscarriage of Justice)

This rule provides that, even if you cannot show cause and prejudice, you can still overcome procedural defaults by proving that you are as a factual matter, "innocent" of the crime in which you were convicted. A new DNA test that clears you from the crime, for instance, would excuse any defaults, etc.

Of course, and naturally so, making a showing strong enough to overcome the "actual innocence" showing is the hardest one to prove in our system, without exception. Indeed, you must show that "it is more than likely than not, that no reasonable juror would have voted for guilt." What is more, "actual innocence" is also "factual innocence," which means that you cannot simply show that the state prosecutor didn't meet the burden of proof in your case. You *must* prove that you are absolutely innocent of the crime. Simply stated, without explosive DNA test results, or a recantation (which also sometimes isn't enough), you will not be able to meet the standard required to prove that you in fact actually innocent.

There are two ways you can advance this claim in your petition: (1) argue for actual innocence in your petition from the start; (2) respond to the state's Motion to Dismiss by filing a First Amended Petition that includes the actual innocence claim. My professional recommendation is that you raise it from the start, and do not wait.

Now let's get down to the nitty-gritty and show you how to fight for your claims, and obtain some relief, shall we?

(Slip Opinion) OCTOBER TERM, 2011

Syllabus

NOTE: Where it is feasible, a syllabus (headnote) will be released, as is being done in connection with this case, at the time the opinion is issued. The syllabus constitutes no part of the opinion of the Court but has been prepared by the Reporter of Decisions for the convenience of the reader. See United States v, Detroit Timber & Lumber Cu., 200 U. S. 321, 337.

SUPREME COURT OF THE UNITED STATES

Syllabus

Martinez v. Ryan, DIRECTOR, ARIZONA DEPARTMENT OF CORRECTIONS

CERTIORARI TO THE UNITED STATES COURT OF APPEALS FOR THE NINTH CIRCUIT

No. 10-1001. Argued October 4, 2011 – Decided March 20, 2012

Arizona prisoners may raise claims of ineffective assistance -of-trial-counsel only in state collateral proceedings, not on direct review. In petitioner Martinez's first state collateral proceeding, his counsel did not raise such a claim. On federal habeas review with new counsel, Martinez argued that he received ineffective assistance both at trial and in his first state collateral proceeding. He also claimed that he had a constitutional right to an effective attorney in the collateral proceeding because it was the first place to raise his claim of ineffective assistance at trial. The District Court denied the petition, finding that Arizona's preclusion rule was an adequate and independent state-law ground barring federal review, and that under *Coleman v. Thompson*, 501 U. S. 722, the attorney's errors in the post-conviction proceeding did not qualify as cause to excuse the procedural default. The Court of Appeals for the Ninth Circuit affirmed.

Held: 1. Where, under state law, ineffective assistance -of-trial-counsel claims must be raised in an initial-review collateral proceeding, a procedural default will not bar a federal habeas court from hearing those claims if in the initial-review collateral proceeding, there was no counselor counsel in that. proceeding was ineffective. Pp.5-14.

(a) Given that the precise question here is whether ineffective assistance in an initial-review collateral proceeding on an ineffective assistance -at-trial claim may provide cause for a procedural default in federal habeas proceeding, this is not the case to resolve the question left open in Coleman: whether a prisoner has a constitutional right to effective counsel in initial-review collateral proceedings. However, to protect prisoners with potentially legitimate ineffective assistance claims, it is necessary to recognize a narrow exception to Coleman's unqualified statement that an attorney's ignorance or inadvertence in a post-conviction proceeding does not qualify as cause to excuse a procedural default, namely, that inadequate assistance of counsel at initial-review collateral proceedings may establish cause. Pp.5-6.

(b) A federal court can hear Martinez's ineffective assistance claim only if he can establish cause to excuse the procedural default and prejudice from a violation of federal law. Coleman held that a post-conviction attorney's negligence "does not qualify as 'cause,' because "the attorney is the prisoner's agent," and "the principal bears the risk of" his agent's negligent conduct, *Maples v. Thomas*, *ante*, at 12. However, in Coleman, counsel's alleged error was on appeal from an initial-review collateral proceeding. Thus, his claims had been addressed by the state habeas trial court. This marks a key difference between initial-review collateral proceedings and other collateral proceedings. Here, where the initial-review collateral proceeding is the first designated proceeding for a prisoner to raise the ineffective assistance claim, the collateral proceeding is the equivalent of a prisoner's direct appeal as to that claim because the state habeas court decides the claim's merits, no other court has addressed the claim, and defendants "are generally ill-equipped to represent themselves" where they have no brief from counsel and no court opinion addressing their claim. *Halbert v. Michigan*, 545 U. S. 605, 617. An attorney's errors during an appeal on direct review may provide cause to excuse a procedural default; for if the attorney appointed by the State is ineffective, the prisoner has been denied fair process and the opportunity to comply with the State's procedures and obtain an adjudication on the merits of his claim. Without adequate representation in an initial review collateral proceeding, a prisoner will have similar difficulties vindicating substantial ineffective assistance at trial claims. The same would be true if the State did not appoint an attorney for the initial-review collateral proceeding. A prisoner's inability to present an ineffective assistance claim is of particular concern because the right to effective trial counsel is a bedrock principle in this Nation's justice system.

Allowing a federal habeas court to hear a claim of ineffective assistance at trial when an attorney's errors (or an attorney's absence) caused a procedural default in an initial-review collateral proceeding acknowledges, as an equitable matter, that a collateral proceeding, if undertaken with no counselor ineffective counsel, may not have been sufficient to ensure that propel' consideration was given to a substantial claim. It thus follows that when a State requires a prisoner to raise a claim of ineffective assistance at trial in a collateral proceeding, a prisoner may establish cause for a procedural default of such claim in two circumstances: where the state courts did not appoint counsel in the initial-review collateral proceeding for an ineffective assistance -at-trial claim; and where appointed counsel in the initial-review collateral proceeding, where that claim should have been raised, was ineffective under *Strickland v. Washington*, 466 U. S. 668. To overcome the default, a prisoner must also demonstrate that the underlying ineffective assistance at trial claim is substantial. Most jurisdictions have procedures to ensure counsel is appointed for substantial ineffective assistance claims. It is likely that such attorneys are qualified to perform, and do perform, according to prevailing professional norms. And where that is so, States may enforce a procedural default in federal habeas proceedings. Pp.6-12.

(c) This limited qualification to *Coleman* does not implicate *stare decisis* concerns. *Coleman*'s holding remains true except as to initial-review collateral proceedings for claims of ineffective assistance at trial. The holding, in this case, should not put a significant strain on state resources. A State facing the question of cause for an apparent default may answer that the ineffective assistance -of-trial-counsel claim is insubstantial. The limited circumstances recognized here also reflect the importance of the right to effective assistance at trial. Other claims may not implicate the same fundamentals of the adversary system. The Antiterrorism and Effective Death Penalty Act of 1996 does not speak to the question presented here, and thus does not bar Martinez from asserting attorney error as cause for a procedural default. Pp. 12-14.

2. Whether Martinez's attorney in his first collateral proceeding was ineffective and whether his ineffective assistance -at-trial claim is substantial, as well as the question of prejudice, are questions that remain open for a decision on remand. P. 15.

623 F. 3d 731, reversed and remanded.

KENNEDY, J., delivered the opinion of the Court, in which ROBERTS, C. J., and GINSBURG,

BREYER, ALITO, SOTOMAYOR, and KAGAN, JJ., joined. SCALIA, J., filed a dissenting opinion, in which THOMAS, J., joined.

Cite as: 566 U. S. ___ (2012)

Opinion of the Court

NOTICE: This opinion is subject to formal revision before publication in the preliminary print of the United States Reports. Readers are requested to notify the Reporter of Decisions, Supreme Court of the United States. Washington, D. C. 20543, of any typographical or other formal errors, in order that corrections may be made before the preliminary print goes to press.

SUPREME COURT OF THE UNITED STATES

No. 10-1001

LUIS MARIANO MARTINEZ, PETITIONER v. CHARLES L. RYAN, DIRECTOR, ARIZONA DEPARTMENT OF CORRECTIONS

ON WRIT OF CERTIORARI TO THE UNITED STATES COURT OF APPEALS FOR THE NINTH CIRCUIT

[March 20, 2012]

JUSTICE KENNEDY delivered the opinion of the Court.

The State of Arizona does not permit a convicted person alleging ineffective assistance - of-trial-counsel to raise that claim on direct review. Instead, the prisoner must bring the claim in state collateral proceedings. In the instant case, however, petitioner's post-conviction counsel did not raise the ineffective assistance claim in the first collateral proceeding, and, indeed, filed a statement that, after reviewing the case, she found no meritorious claims helpful to petitioner. On federal habeas review, and with new counsel, petitioner sought to argue he had received ineffective assistance of counsel at trial and in the first phase of his state collateral proceeding. Because the state collateral proceeding was the first place to challenge his conviction on grounds of ineffective assistance, petitioner maintained he had a constitutional right to an effective attorney in the collateral proceeding. While petitioner frames the question in this case as a constitutional one, a narrower, but still dispositive, formulation is whether a federal habeas court may excuse a procedural default of an ineffective assistance claim when the claim was not properly presented in state court due to an attorney's errors in an initial-review collateral proceeding.

I

A jury convicted petitioner, Luis Mariano Martinez, of two counts of sexual conduct with a minor under the age of 15. The prosecution introduced a videotaped forensic interview with the victim, Martinez's 11-year-old stepdaughter. It also put in evidence the victim's nightgown, with traces of Martinez's DNA. As part of his defense, Martinez introduced evidence of the victim's recantations, including testimony from the victim's grandmother and mother and a second videotaped interview in which the victim denied any abuse. The victim also denied any abuse when she testified at trial. App. to Pet. for Cert. 38a-39a. To explain the inconsistencies, a prosecution expert testified that recantations of child-abuse accusations are caused often by reluctance on the part of the victim's mother to lend support to the child's claims. Pet. for Cert. 3. After considering the conflicting evidence, the jury convicted Martinez. He was sentenced to two consecutive terms of life imprisonment with no possibility of parole for 35 years. App. to Pet. for Cert. 39a.

The State appointed a new attorney to represent Martinez in his direct appeal. *Ibid.*; Pet. for Cert. 4. She made numerous arguments on Martinez's behalf, including a claim that the evidence was insufficient and that newly discovered evidence warranted a new trial. App. to Pet. for Cert. 39a. Arizona law, however, did not permit her to argue on direct appeal that trial counsel was ineffective. *State v. Spreitz*, 202 Ariz. 1, 3, 39 P. 3d 525, 527 (2002). Arizona instead requires claims of ineffective assistance at trial to be reserved for state collateral proceedings.

While Martinez's direct appeal was pending, the attorney began a state collateral proceeding by filing a "Notice of Post-Conviction Relief." *Martinez v. Schriro*, 623 F. 3d 731, 733-734 (CA9 2010); Ariz. Rule Crim. Proc. 32.4(a) (2011). Despite initiating this proceeding, counsel made no claim trial counsel was ineffective and later filed a statement asserting she could find no colorable claims at all. 623 F. 3d, at 734. Cf. *State v. Smith*, 184 Ariz. 456, 459, 910 P. 2d 1, 4 (1996).

The state trial court hearing the collateral proceeding gave Martinez 45 days to file a *pro se* petition in support of post-conviction relief and to raise any claims he believed his counsel overlooked. 623 F. 3d, at 734; see *Smith, supra*, at 459, 910 P. 2d, at 4. Martinez did not respond. He later alleged that he was unaware of the ongoing col-lateral proceedings and that counsel failed to advise him of the need to file a *pro se* petition to preserve his rights. The state trial court dismissed the action for post-conviction relief, in effect affirming counsel's determination that Martinez had no meritorious claims. 623 F. 3d, at 734. The Arizona Court of Appeals affirmed Martinez's conviction, and the Arizona Supreme Court denied review. *Id.*, at 733.

About a year and a half later, Martinez, now represented by new counsel, filed a second notice of post-conviction relief in the Arizona trial court. *Id.*, at 734. Martinez claimed his trial counsel had been ineffective for failing to challenge the prosecution's evidence. He argued, for example, that his trial counsel should have objected to the expert testimony explaining the victim's recantations or should have called an expert witness in rebuttal. Martinez also faulted trial counsel for not pursuing an exculpatory explanation for the DNA on the nightgown. App. to Brief in Opposition B-6 to B-12. Martinez's petition was dismissed, in part in reliance on an Arizona Rule barring relief on a claim that could have been raised in a previous collateral proceeding. *Id.*, at B-27; see Ariz. Rule Crim. Proc. 32.2(a)(3). Martinez, the theory went, should have asserted the claims of ineffective assistance -of-trial-counsel in his first notice for post-conviction relief. The Arizona Court of Appeals agreed. It denied Martinez relief because he failed to raise his claims in the first collateral proceeding. 623 F. 3d, at 734. The Arizona Supreme Court declined to review Martinez's appeal.

Martinez then sought relief in the United States District Court for the District of Arizona, where he filed a petition for a writ of habeas corpus, again raising the ineffective assistance -of-trial-counsel claims. Martinez acknowledged the state courts denied his claims by relying on a well-established state procedural rule, which, under the doctrine of procedural default, would prohibit a federal court from reaching the merits of the claims. See, *e.g.*, *Wainwright v. Sykes*, 433 U. S. 72, 84-85, 90-91 (1977). He could overcome this hurdle to federal review, Martinez argued, because he had cause for the default: His first post-conviction counsel was ineffective in failing to raise any claims in the first notice of post-conviction relief and in failing to notify Martinez of her actions. See *id.*, at 84-85.

On the Magistrate Judge's recommendation, the District Court denied the petition, ruling that Arizona's preclusion rule was an adequate and independent state-law ground to bar federal review. App. to Pet. for Cert. 36a. Martinez had not shown cause to excuse the procedural default, the District Court reasoned, because under *Coleman v. Thompson*, 501 U. S. 722, 753-754 (1991), an attorney's errors in a post-conviction proceeding do not qualify as cause for a default. See *id.*, at 754-755.

The Court of Appeals for the Ninth Circuit affirmed. The Court of Appeals relied on general statements in Coleman that, absent a right to counsel in a collateral proceeding, an attorney's errors in the proceeding do not establish cause for a procedural default. Expanding on the District Court's opinion, the Court of Appeals, citing *Coleman*, noted the general rule that there is no constitutional right to counsel in collateral proceedings. 623 F. 3d, at 736. The Court of Appeals recognized that Coleman reserved ruling on whether there is "an exception" to this rule in those cases "where 'state collateral review is the first place a prisoner can present a challenge to his conviction.'" 623 F. 3d, at 736 (quoting *Coleman, supra*, at 755). It concluded, nevertheless, that the controlling cases established no basis for the exception. Certiorari was granted. 563 U. S. ___ (2011).

II

Coleman v. Thompson, supra, left open, and the Court of Appeals in this case addressed a question of constitutional law: whether a prisoner has a right to effective counsel in collateral proceedings which provide the first occasion to raise a claim of ineffective assistance at trial. These proceedings can be called, for purposes of this opinion, "initial-review collateral proceedings." *Coleman* had suggested, though without holding, that the Constitution may require States to provide counsel in initial-review collateral proceedings because "in [these] cases ... state collateral review is the first place a prisoner can present a challenge to his conviction." *Id.*, at 755. As *Coleman* noted, this makes the initial review collateral proceeding a prisoner's "one and only appeal" as to an ineffective assistance claim, *id.*, at 756 (emphasis deleted; internal quotation marks omitted), and this may justify an exception to the constitutional rule that there is no right to counsel in collateral proceedings. See *id.*, at 755; *Douglas v. California*, 372 U. S. 353, 357 (1963) (holding States must appoint counsel on a prisoner's first appeal).

This is not the case, however, to resolve whether that exception exists as a constitutional matter. The precise question here is whether ineffective assistance in an initial-review collateral proceeding on a claim of ineffective assistance at trial may provide cause for a procedural default in federal habeas proceeding. To protect prisoners with a potentially legitimate claim of ineffective assistance of trial counsel, it is necessary to modify the unqualified statement in Coleman that an attorney's ignorance or inadvertence in a post-conviction proceeding does not qualify as cause to excuse a procedural default. This opinion qualifies Coleman by recognizing a narrow exception: Inadequate assistance of counsel at initial-review collateral proceedings may establish cause for a prisoner's procedural default of a claim of ineffective assistance at trial.

A

Federal habeas courts reviewing the constitutionality of a state prisoner's conviction and sentence are guided by rules designed to ensure that state-court judgments are accorded the finality and respect necessary to preserve the integrity of legal proceedings within our system of federalism. These rules include the doctrine of procedural default, under which a federal court will not review the merits of claims, including constitutional claims, that a state court declined to hear because the prisoner failed to abide by a state procedural rule. See, *e.g.*, *Coleman, supra*, at 747-748; *Sykes, supra*, at 84-85. A state court's invocation of a procedural rule to deny a prisoner's claims precludes federal review of the claims if, among other requisites, the state procedural rule is a nonfederal ground adequate to support the judgment and the rule is firmly established and consistently followed. See, *e.g.*, *Walker v. Martin*, 562 U. S. ___, ___ (2011) (slip op., at 7-8); *Beard v. Kindler*, 558 U. S. ___, ___ (2009) (slip op., at 7). The doctrine barring procedurally defaulted claims from being heard is not without exceptions. A prisoner may obtain federal review of a defaulted claim by showing cause for the default and prejudice from a violation of federal law. See *Coleman*, 501 U. S., at 750. There is no dispute that Arizona's procedural bar on successive petitions is an independent and adequate state ground. Thus, a federal court can hear Martinez's ineffective assistance claim only if he can establish cause to excuse the procedural default.

Coleman held that "[n]egligence on the part of a prisoner's post-conviction attorney does not qualify as 'cause.'" *Maples v. Thomas*, 565 U. S ___, ___ (2011) (slip op., at 12). *Coleman* reasoned that "because the attorney is the prisoner's agent ... under 'well-settled principles of agency law,' the principal bears the risk of negligent conduct on the part of his agent." Maples, *supra,* at ___ (slip op., at 12).

Coleman, however, did not present the occasion to apply this principle to determine whether attorney errors in initial-review collateral proceedings may qualify as cause for a procedural default. The alleged failure of counsel in Coleman was on appeal from an initial-review collateral proceeding, and in that proceeding the prisoner's claims had been addressed by the state habeas trial court. See 501 U. S., at 755.

As *Coleman* recognized, this marks a key difference between initial-review collateral proceedings and other kinds of collateral proceedings. When an attorney errs in initial-review collateral proceedings, it is likely that no state court at any level will hear the prisoner's claim. This Court on direct review of the state proceeding could not consider or adjudicate the claim. See, *e.g.*, *Fox Film Corp. v. Mulier*, 296 U. S. 207 (1935); *Murdock v. Memphis*, 20 Wall. 590 (1875); cf. *Coleman, supra*, at 730-731. And if counsel's errors in an initial review collateral proceeding do not establish cause to excuse the procedural default in a federal habeas proceeding, no court will review the prisoner's claims.

The same is not true when counsel errs in other kinds of post-conviction proceedings. While counsel's errors in these proceedings preclude any further review of the prisoner's claim, the claim will have been addressed by one court, whether it be the trial court, the appellate court on direct review, or the trial court in an initial-review collateral proceeding. See, *e.g.*, *Coleman, supra*, at 756.

Where, as here, the initial-review collateral proceeding is the first designated proceeding for a prisoner to raise a claim of ineffective assistance at trial, the collateral proceeding is in many ways the equivalent of a prisoner's direct appeal as to the ineffective assistance claim. This is because the state habeas court "looks to the merits of the clai[m]" of ineffective assistance, no other court has addressed the claim, and "defendants pursuing first-tier review ... are generally ill-equipped to represent themselves" because they do not have a brief from counselor an opinion of the court addressing their claim of error. *Halbert v. Michigan*, 545 U. S. 605, 617 (2005); see *Douglas*, 372 U. S., at 357-358.

As *Coleman* recognized, an attorney's errors during an appeal on direct review may provide cause to excuse a procedural default; for if the attorney appointed by the State to pursue the direct appeal is ineffective, the prisoner has been denied fair process and the opportunity to comply with the State's procedures and obtain an adjudication on the merits of his claims. See 501 U. S., at 754; *Evitts v. Lucey*, 469 U. S. 387, 396 (1985); *Douglas, supra*, at 357-358. Without the help of an adequate attorney, a prisoner will have similar difficulties vindicating a substantial ineffective assistance -of-trial-counsel claim. Claims of ineffective assistance at trial often require investigative work and an understanding of trial strategy. When the issue cannot be raised on direct review, more-over, a prisoner asserting ineffective assistance -of-trial-counsel claim in an initial review collateral proceeding cannot rely on a court opinion or the prior work of an attorney addressing that claim. *Halbert*, 545 U. S., at 619. To present a claim of ineffective assistance at trial in accordance with the State's procedures, then a prisoner likely needs an effective attorney.

The same would be true if the State did not appoint an attorney to assist the prisoner in the initial-review collateral proceeding. The prisoner, unlearned in the law, may not comply with the State's procedural rules or may misapprehend the substantive details of federal constitutional law. Cf., *e.g.*, *id.*, at 620-621 (describing the educational background of the prison population). While confined to prison, the prisoner is in no position to develop the evidentiary basis for a claim of ineffective assistance, which often turns on evidence outside the trial record.

A prisoner's inability to present a claim of trial error is of particular concern when the claim is one of ineffective assistance of counsel. The right to the effective assistance of counsel at trial is a bedrock principle in our justice system. It is deemed as an "obvious truth," the idea that "any person hauled into court, who is too poor to hire a lawyer, cannot be assured a fair trial unless counsel is provided for him." *Gideon v. Wainwright*, 372 U. S. 335, 344 (1963). Indeed, the right to counsel is the foundation for our adversary system. Defense counsel tests the prosecution's case to ensure that the proceedings serve the function of adjudicating guilt or innocence while protecting the rights of the person charged. See, *e.g.*, *Powell v. Alabama*, 287 U. S. 45, 68-69 (1932) ("[The defendant] requires the guiding hand of counsel at every step in the proceedings against him. Without it, though he be not guilty, he faces the danger of conviction because he does not know how to establish his innocence"). Effective trial counsel preserves the claim to be considered on appeal; see, *e.g.*, Fed. Rule Crim. Proc. 52(b), and in federal habeas proceedings, *Edwards v. Carpenter*, 529 U. S. 446 (2000).

This is not to imply the State acted with any impropriety by reserving the claim of ineffective assistance for a collateral proceeding. See *Massaro v. United States*, 538 U. S. 500, 505 (2003). Ineffective assistance claims often depend on evidence outside the trial record. Direct appeals, without evidentiary hearings, may not be as effective as other proceedings for developing the factual basis for the claim. *Ibid.* Abbreviated deadlines to expand the record on direct appeal may not allow adequate time for an attorney to investigate the ineffective assistance claim. See Primus, Structural Reform in Criminal Defense, 92 Cornell L. Rev. 679, 689, and n. 57 (2004) (most rules give between 5 and 30 days from the time of conviction to file a request to expand the record on appeal). Thus, there are sound reasons for deferring consideration of ineffective assistance -of-trial-counsel claims until the collateral-review stage, but this decision is not without consequences for the State's ability to assert a procedural default in later proceedings. By deliberately choosing to move trial-ineffectiveness claims outside of the direct-appeal process, where counsel is constitutionally guaranteed, the State significantly diminishes prisoners' ability to file such claims. It is within the context of this state procedural framework that counsel's ineffectiveness in an initial-review collateral proceeding qualifies as cause for a procedural default.

The rules for when a prisoner may establish cause to excuse a procedural default are elaborated in the exercise of the Court's discretion. *McCleskey v. Zant*, 499 U. S. 467, 490 (1991); see also *Coleman, supra*, at 730-731; *Sykes*, 433 U. S., at 83; *Reed v. Ross*, 468 U. S. 1, 9 (1984); *Fay v. Noia*, 372 U. S. 391, 430 (1963), overruled in part by *Sykes, supra*. These rules reflect an equitable judgment that only where a prisoner is impeded or obstructed in complying with the State's established procedures will a federal habeas court excuse the prisoner from the usual sanction of default. See, *e.g.*, *Strickler v. Greene*, 527 U. S. 263, 289 (1999); *Reed, supra*, at 16. Allowing a federal habeas court to hear a claim of ineffective assistance -of-trial-counsel when an attorney's errors (or the absence of an attorney) caused a procedural default in an initial-review collateral proceeding acknowledges, as an equitable matter, that the initial-review collateral proceeding, if undertaken without counselor with ineffective counsel, may not have been sufficient to ensure that proper consideration was given to a substantial claim. From this, it follows that when a State requires a prisoner to raise an ineffective assistance -of-trial-counsel claim in a collateral proceeding, a prisoner may establish cause for a default of an ineffective assistance claim in two circumstances. The first is where the state courts did not appoint counsel in the initial-review collateral proceeding for a claim of ineffective assistance at trial. The second is where appointed counsel in the initial-review collateral proceeding, where the claim should have been raised, was ineffective under the standards of *Strickland v. Washington*, 466 U. S. 668 (1984). To overcome the default, a prisoner must also demonstrate that the underlying ineffective assistance -of-trial-counsel claim is a substantial one, which is to say that the prisoner must demonstrate that the claim has some merit. Cf. *Miller-El v. Cockrell*, 537 U. S. 322 (2003) (describing standards for certificates of appealability to issue).

Most jurisdictions have in place procedures to ensure counsel is appointed for substantial ineffective assistance claims. Some states, including Arizona, appoint counsel in every first collateral proceeding. See, *e.g.*, Alaska Stat. 18.85.100(c) (2010); Ariz. Rule Crim. Proc. 32.4(c)(2) (2011); Conn. Gen. Stat. §51-296(a) (2011); Me. Rules Crim. Proc. 69, 70(c) (2010); N. C. Gen. Stat. Ann. §7A-451(a)(2) (2009); N. J. Ct. Rule 3:22-6(b) (2012); R. I. Gen. Laws §10-9.1-5 (Lexis 1997); Tenn. Code Ann. §8-14-205 (2011). Some States appoint counsel if the claims require an evidentiary hearing. as claims of ineffective assistance often do. See, *e.g.*, Ky. Rule Crim. Proc. 11.42(5) (2011); La. Code Crim. Proc. Ann., Art. 930.7(C) (West 2008); Mich. Rule Crim. Proc. 6.505(A) (2011); S. C. Rule Civ. Proc. 71.1(d) (2011). Other States appoint counsel if the claims have some merit to them or the state habeas trial court deems the record worthy of further development. See, *e.g.*, Ark. Rule Crim. Proc. 37.3(b) (2011); Colo. Rule Crim. Proc. 35(b) (2011); Del. Super. Ct. Rule Crim. Proc. 61(e)(1) (2011); Indiana Rule Post-Conviction Remedies Proc. 1, §9(a) (rev. 2011); Kan. Stat. Ann. §22-4506 (2007); N. M. Dist. Ct. Rule Crim. Proc. 5-802 (2011); *Hust v. State*, 147 Idaho 682, 683-684, 214 P.3d 668, 669-670 (2009); *Hardin v. Arkansas*, 350 Ark. 299, 301, 86 S. W. 3d 384, 385 (2007) (*per curiam*); *Jensen v. State*, 2004 ND 200, ¶13, 688 N. W. 2d 374, 378; *Wu v. United*

States, 798 A. 2d 1083, 1089 (D. C. 2002); *Kostal v. People*, 167 Colo. 317, 447 P.2d 536 (1968). It is likely that most of the attorneys appointed by the courts are qualified to perform and do perform according to prevailing professional norms, and where that is so, the States may enforce a procedural default in federal habeas proceedings.

B

This limited qualification to Coleman does not implicate the usual concerns with upsetting reliance interests protected by *stare decisis* principles. Cf., *e.g.*, *Montejo v. Louisiana*, 556 U. S. 778, 792-793 (2009). *Coleman* held that an attorney's negligence in a post-conviction proceeding does not establish cause, and this remains true except as to initial-review collateral proceedings for claims of ineffective assistance of counsel at trial. Coleman itself did not involve an occasion when an attorney erred in an initial-review collateral proceeding with respect to a claim of ineffective trial counsel; and in the 20 years since Coleman was decided, we have not held Coleman applies in circumstances like this one.

The holding here ought not to put a significant strain on state resources. When faced with the question whether there is cause for an apparent default, a State may answer that the ineffective assistance -of-trial-counsel claim is insubstantial, *i.e.*, it does not have any merit or that it is wholly without factual support, or that the attorney in the initial-review collateral proceeding did not perform below constitutional standards.

This is but one of the differences between a constitutional ruling and the equitable ruling of this case. A constitutional ruling would provide defendants a free-standing constitutional claim to raise; it would require the appointment of counsel in initial-review collateral proceedings; it would impose the same system of appointing counsel in every State; and it would require a reversal in all state collateral cases on direct review from state courts if the States' system of appointing counsel did not conform to the constitutional rule. An equitable ruling, by contrast, permits States a variety of systems for appointing counsel in initial-review collateral proceedings. And it permits a State to elect between appointing counsel in initial-review collateral proceedings or not asserting a procedural default and raising a defense on the merits in federal habeas proceedings. In addition, state collateral cases on direct review from state courts are unaffected by the ruling in this case.

The rule of *Coleman* governs in all, but the limited circumstances recognized here. The holding in this case does not concern attorney errors in other kinds of proceedings, including appeals from initial-review collateral proceedings, second or successive collateral proceedings, and petitions for discretionary review in a State's appellate courts. See 501 U. S., at 754; *Carrier*, 477 U. S., at 488. It does not extend to attorney errors in any proceeding beyond the first occasion the State allows a prisoner to raise a claim of ineffective assistance at trial, even though that initial-review collateral proceeding may be deficient for other reasons.

In addition, the limited nature of the qualification to Coleman adopted here reflects the importance of the right to the effective assistance of trial counsel and Arizona's decision to bar defendants from raising ineffective assistance claims on direct appeal. Our holding here addresses only the constitutional claims presented in this case, where the State barred the defendant from raising the claims on direct appeal.

Arizona contends that the Antiterrorism and Effective Death Penalty Act of 1996 (AEDPA), 28 U.S.C. §2254, bars Martinez from asserting attorney error as cause for a procedural default. AEDPA refers to attorney error in collateral proceedings, but it does not speak to the question presented in this case. Section 2254(i) provides that "the ineffectiveness or incompetence of counsel during Federal or State collateral post-conviction proceedings shall not be a ground for relief." "Cause," however, is not synonymous with "a ground for relief." A finding of cause and prejudice does not entitle the prisoner to habeas relief. It merely allows a federal court to consider the merits of a claim that otherwise would have been procedurally defaulted. In this case, for example, Martinez's "ground for relief" is his ineffective assistance-of-trial-counsel claim, a claim that AEDPA does not bar. Martinez relies on the ineffectiveness of his post-conviction attorney to excuse his failure to comply with Arizona's procedural rules, not as an independent basis for overturning his conviction. In short, while §2254(i) precludes Martinez from relying on the ineffectiveness of his post-conviction attorney as a "ground for relief," it does not stop Martinez from using it to establish "cause." *Holland v. Florida*, 560 U. S. ___, ___ (2010) (slip op., at 18).

III

Where, under state law, claims of ineffective assistance -of-trial-counsel must be raised in an initial-review collateral proceeding, a procedural default will not bar a federal habeas court from hearing a substantial claim of ineffective assistance at trial if, in the initial-review collateral proceeding, there was no counselor counsel in that proceeding was ineffective.

In this case, Martinez's attorney, in the initial review collateral proceeding, filed a notice akin to an *Anders* brief, in effect conceding that Martinez lacked any meritorious claim, including his claim of ineffective assistance at trial. See *Anders v. California*, 386 U. S. 738 (1967). Martinez argued before the federal habeas court that filing the *Anders* brief constituted ineffective assistance. The Court of Appeals did not decide whether that was so. Rather, it held that because Martinez did not have a right to an attorney in the initial-review collateral proceeding, the attorney's errors in the initial-review collateral proceeding could not establish cause for the failure to comply with the State's rules. Thus, the Court of Appeals did not determine whether Martinez's attorney in his first collateral proceeding was ineffective or whether his claim of ineffective assistance -of-trial-counsel is substantial. The court did not address the question of prejudice. These issues remain open for a decision on remand.

* * *

The judgment of the Court of Appeals is reversed, and the case is remanded for further proceedings consistent with this opinion.

It is so ordered.

Cite as: 566 U. S. ___ (2012)

SCALIA, J., dissenting

SUPREME COURT OF THE UNITED STATES

No. 10-1001

LUIS MARIANO MARTINEZ, PETITIONER *v.* CHARLES L. RYAN, DIRECTOR, ARIZONA DEPARTMENT OF CORRECTIONS

ON WRIT OF CERTIORARI TO THE UNITED STATES COURT OF APPEALS FOR THE NINTH CIRCUIT

[March 20, 2012]

JUSTICE SCALIA, with whom JUSTICE THOMAS joins, dissenting.

I

A

Let me get this straight: Out of concern for the values of federalism; to preserve the ability of our States to provide prompt justice; and in light of our longstanding jurisprudence holding that there is no constitutional right to counsel in state collateral review; the Court, in what it portrays as an admirable exercise of judicial restraint, abstains from holding that there is a constitutional right to counsel in initial-review state habeas. After all, that would have meant, in a case such as the one before us, that failing to provide assistance of counsel, or providing assistance of counsel that falls below the *Strickland* standard, would constitute cause for excusing procedural default. See *Strickland v. Washington*, 466 U. S. 668 (1984). Instead of taking that radical step, the Court holds that, *for equitable reasons*, in a case such as the one before us, failing to provide assistance of counsel, or providing assistance of counsel that falls below the *Strickland* standard, constitutes cause for excusing procedural default. The result, of course, is precisely the same.

Ah, but perhaps the explanation of why the Court's action today amounts to praiseworthy self-restraint is this: It pronounces this excuse from the usual rule of procedural default only in initial-review state habeas raising an ineffective assistance -of-trial-counsel claim. But it could have limited its invention of a new constitutional right to collateral-review counsel in precisely the same fashion and with precisely the same consequences. Moreover, no one really believes that the newly announced "equitable" rule will remain limited to ineffective assistance of trial-counsel cases. There is not a dime's worth of difference in principle between those cases and many other cases in which initial state habeas will be the first opportunity for a particular claim to be raised: claims of "newly discovered" prosecutorial misconduct, for example, see *Brady v. Maryland*, 373 U. S. 83 (1963), claims based on "newly discovered" exculpatory evidence or "newly discovered" impeachment of prosecutorial witnesses, and claims asserting ineffective assistance of appellate counsel. The Court's soothing assertion, *ante*, at 14, that its holding "addresses only the constitutional claims presented in this case," insults the reader's intelligence.[1]

---

[1] The Court also seeks to restrict its holding to cases in which the State has "deliberately cho[sen]" to move the asserted claim "outside of the direct-appeal process," *ante*, at 10. That line lacks any principled basis and will not last. Is there any relevant difference between cases in which the State says that certain claims can only be brought

Moreover, even if today's holding could (against all logic) be restricted to ineffective assistance -of-trial-counsel claims, it would have essentially the same practical consequences as a holding that collateral-review counsel is constitutionally required. Despite the Court's suggestion to the contrary, see *ante*, at 13, the rule it adopts calls into question the common state practice of not appointing counsel in all first collateral proceedings, see *ante*, at 11-12. It does not, to be sure, call into question the *lawfulness* of that practice, only its sanity. For if the prisoner goes through state collateral proceedings without counsel and fails to raise an ineffective assistance -of-trial-counsel claim, which is, because of that failure, defaulted, the default will not preclude federal habeas review of the merits of that claim. And since ineffective assistance -of-trial-counsel is a monotonously standard claim on federal habeas (has a duly convicted defendant ever been effectively represented?), whoever advises the State would himself be guilty of ineffective assistance if he did not counsel the appointment of state-collateral-review counsel in all cases – lest the failure to raise that claim in the state proceedings be excused and the State be propelled into federal habeas review of the adequacy of trial-court representation that occurred many years ago.[2] This is to say that the Court's pretended avoidance of requiring States to appoint collateral-review counsel is a sham.[3]

Of course, even the appointment of state-collateral-review counsel will not guarantee that the State's criminal proceeding can be concluded without years-long federal retrial. Appointment of counsel may, as I have said, avoid federal review of the adequacy of representation that occurred years ago, at the original trial. But since, under today's opinion, the condition for

---

on collateral review and cases in which those claims by their nature can only be brought on collateral review, since they do not manifest themselves until the appellate process is complete? Our cases establish that to constitute cause for failure to raise an issue on direct review, the excuse must be "an objective factor external to the defense." See *infra*, at 7. That the factual basis for a claim was not available until the collateral-review stage is no less such a factor than a State's requiring that a claim be brought on collateral review. See *Murray v. Carrier*, 477 U. S. 478, 488 (1986). The Court's asserted limitation makes sense only if the opinion means that a State has "deliberately chos[en]" to move newly-arisen claims "outside of the direct-appeal process" if it fails to *reopen* the direct-appeal process in order to entertain such claims. Such a radical change in what we require of the States surely ought to be prescribed by language clearer than what today's opinion contains.

[2] The Court says that to establish cause a prisoner must demonstrate that the ineffective assistance -of-trial-counsel claim is "substantial," which apparently means the claim has at least some merit. See *ante*, at 11. The Court does not explain where this substantiality standard comes from, and how it differs from the normal rule that a prisoner must demonstrate actual prejudice to avoid the enforcement of a procedural default, see Coleman v. Thompson, 501 U. S. 722, 750 (1991). But whatever the standard, examination of the adequacy of years-ago representation has been substituted for summary dismissal by reason of procedural default.

[3] The Court also claims, *ante*, at 18, that its "equitable" ruling, unlike a constitutional ruling, will not require "a reversal in all state collateral cases on direct review from state courts" where counsel has not been appointed. Surely the Court does not mean to suggest that an un-constitutional failure to appoint counsel on collateral review, like an unconstitutional failure to appoint counsel at trial, would require the entire conviction to be set aside. That is inconceivable. So either one of two things would happen: Either the reviewing state court would be able to inquire into prejudice (which is an improvement over having the federal habeas court make that inquiry, as the Court's "equitable" solution requires); or else the appellate state court will remand for a collateral proceeding with counsel (which is, as we have said, just what the Court's "equitable" ruling effectively requires anyway). So the Court's "equitable" ruling is no boon to the States.

exclusion of federal habeas is the very same condition that would apply if the appointment of state-collateral-review counsel were constitutionally required, it will remain to be determined in federal habeas review whether the state-appointed counsel was effective. Thus, as a consequence of today's decision, the States will always be forced to litigate in federal habeas for all defaulted ineffective assistance -of-trial-counsel claims (and who knows what other claims), either (1) the validity of the defaulted claim (where collateral-review counsel was not appointed), or (2) the effectiveness of collateral-review counsel (where collateral-review counsel was appointed). The Court notes that many States already provide for the appointment of counsel in first col lateral challenges, though this proves that what the Court forces the States to do today is eminently reasonable. But what the Court fails to point out is that currently, when state-appointed counsel does not raise an ineffective assistance -of-trial-counsel claim, that is the end of the matter: The issue has been procedurally defaulted. By virtue of today's opinion, however, all those cases can (and where capital punishment is at issue assuredly will) proceed to federal habeas on the issue of whether state-appointed counsel was ineffective in failing to raise the ineffective assistance -of-trial-counsel issue. That is the meaning of the Court's (supposedly comforting) statement:

> "It is likely that most of the attorneys appointed by the courts are qualified to perform, and do perform, according to prevailing professional norms; and, *where that is so*, the States may enforce a procedural default in federal habeas proceedings." *Ante*, at 12 (emphasis added).

To be more precise, the Court should have said, "Where that is so, and where federal habeas courts have finally rejected claims that it is not so, the States may enforce a procedural default in federal habeas proceedings."

I cannot possibly imagine the basis for the Court's confidence, *ante*, at 12-13, that all this will not put a significant strain on state resources. The principal escape route from federal habeas – existence of an "adequate and in-dependent state ground" – has been closed.[4] Whether counsel appointed for state collateral review raises the ineffective assistance -of-trial-counsel claim or not, federal habeas review will proceed. In practical effect, that may not make much difference in noncapital cases (except for the squandering of state taxpayers' money): The defendant will stay in prison, continuing to serve his sentence, while federal habeas review grinds on. But in capital cases, it will effectively reduce the sentence, giving the defendant as many more years to live, beyond the lives of the innocent victims whose lives he snuffed out, as the process of federal habeas may consume. I guarantee that an assertion of ineffective assistance -of-trial-counsel will be made in all capital cases from this date on, causing (because of today's holding) execution of the sentence to be deferred until either that claim or the claim that appointed counsel was

[4] See N. King, F. Cheesman, & B. Ostrom, Final Technical Report: Habeas Litigation in U. S. District Courts 45-49 (2007) (documenting the percentage of habeas petitions that included claims dismissed for various procedural reasons); Administrative Office of the United States Courts, Habeas Corpus Petitions Disposed of Procedurally During the 12-Month Period Ending September 30, 2011 (reporting that for appeals in noncapital state-prisoner habeas cases, procedural default accounted for the largest percentage of procedural dispositions, with the exception of the denial of a certificate of appealability) (available in Clerk of Court's case file).

ineffective in failing to make that claim, has worked its way through the federal system.

B

The Court would have us believe that today's holding is no more than a "limited qualification" to *Coleman v. Thompson*, 501 U. S. 722 (1991). *Ante*, at 12. It is much more than that: a repudiation of the longstanding principle governing procedural default, which *Coleman* and other cases consistently applied. *Coleman* itself involved a habeas petitioner's contention that his attorney's failure to file a timely notice of appeal in his state habeas proceeding, which resulted in procedural default of the claims raised in that proceeding, was cause to excuse that default in federal habeas. 501 U. S., at 752. The petitioner in that case contended that whether a violation of his constitutional right to effective counsel had occurred was of no consequence, so long as the attorney's conduct fell short of the effectiveness standard set forth in *Strickland*. See 501 U. S., at 753. Whereas *Coleman* flatly repudiated that claim as being inconsistent with our precedent, see *Ibid.*, today's majority wholeheartedly embraces it, *ante*, at 11.

Rejection of the argument in *Coleman* was compelled by our jurisprudence pertaining to cause for excusing procedural default, and in particular, *Murray v. Carrier*, 477 U. S. 478 (1986). See *Coleman, supra*, at 752-753. *Carrier* involved the failure of a defendant's attorney to raise a claim on direct appeal. 477 U. S., at 482. This failure did not constitute cause, we explained, because it was not an "objective factor *external* to the defense." *Id.*, at 488 (emphasis added). This external-factor requirement reflects the judgment that States should not be forced to undergo federal habeas review of a defaulted claim unless a factor not attributable to the prisoner obstructed his compliance with state procedures. See id., at 487-488.

Although this externality requirement has been the North Star of our excuse-for-cause jurisprudence, today's opinion does not whisper its name – no doubt because it is impossible to say that *Martinez*'s procedural default was caused by a factor external to his defense. Coleman and Carrier set forth in clear terms when it is that attorney error constitute an external factor: Attorney error by itself does not because when an attorney acts (or fails to act) in furtherance of the litigation, he is acting as the petitioner's agent. *Coleman, supra*, at 753; *Carrier, supra*, at 492. Any other rule would be inconsistent with our system of representative litigation, under which "each party is deemed bound by the acts of his lawyer-agent." *Irwin v. Department of Veterans Affairs*, 498 U. S. 89, 92 (1990) (internal quotation marks omitted). But, when attorney error amounts to constitutionally ineffective assistance of counsel, that error is imputed to the State (for the State has failed to comply with the constitutional requirement to provide effective counsel), rendering the error external to the petitioner. *Coleman, supra*, at 754; *Carrier, supra*, at 488. Accordingly, as Martinez himself appears to recognize, see Brief for Petitioner 22, our cases require that absent a determination that Arizona violated the Constitution by failing to provide effective counsel, attorney error cannot provide cause to excuse his procedural default. Rather than apply that rule here, the Court adopts the very approach Coleman explicitly addressed and rejected.

The Court essentially disclaims any need to give full consideration to the principle of stare decisis because Coleman did not involve an initial-review collateral proceeding for a claim of ineffective assistance of trial counsel. See *ante*, at 12. That is rather like saying that *Marbury v. Madison*, 1 Cranch 137 (1803), does not establish our authority to review the constitutionality of a new federal statute because it involved a different enactment. Just as the reasoning of Marbury was categorical, so was the reasoning of Coleman and Carrier: Attorney error is not an external factor constituting cause for excusing default unless the State has a constitutional obligation to provide effective counsel. Had the majority seriously considered the relevant stare decisis factors, see, *e.g.*, *Montejo v. Louisiana*, 556 U. S. 778, 792-793 (2009), it would have had difficulty justifying today's decision. Nor can it escape the demands of stare decisis by saying that our rules regarding the excuse of procedural default reflect an "equitable judgment" that is "elaborated in the exercise of the Court's discretion." *Ante*, at 10. Equity is not lawlessness, and discretion is not a license to cast aside established jurisprudence reaffirmed by this very Term. See *Maples v. Thomas*, 565 U. S. ___, ___ (2012) (slip op., at 12) ("Negligence on the part of a prisoner's post-conviction attorney does not qualify as 'cause'" (quoting *Coleman, supra*, at 753)). "'[C]ourts of equity must be governed by rules and precedents no less than courts of law.'" *Lonchar v. Thomas*, 517 U. S. 314, 323 (1996) (quoting *Missouri v. Jenkins*, 515 U. S. 70, 127 (1995) (THOMAS, J., concurring)).

Noticeably absent from the Court's equitable analysis, moreover, is any consideration of the very reason for a procedural-default rule: the comity and respect that federal courts must accord state-court judgments. See *Edwards v. Carpenter*, 529 U. S. 446, 451 (2000). The procedural-default doctrine reflects the understanding that federal review of defaulted claims may "circumvent the jurisdictional limits of direct review and 'undermine the State's interest in enforcing its laws." *Lee v. Kemna*, 534 U. S. 362, 388 (2002) (KENNEDY, J., dissenting) (quoting *Coleman, supra*, at 731). Unlike today's decision, *Carrier* and *Coleman* took account of the significant costs federal habeas review imposes on States, including the "reduction in the finality of litigation and the frustration of 'both the States' sovereign power to punish offenders and their good-faith attempts to honor constitutional rights." *Carrier, supra*, at 487 (quoting *Engle v. Isaac*, 456 U. S. 107, 128 (1982)). Criminal conviction ought to be final before society has forgotten the crime that justifies it. When a case arrives at federal habeas, the state conviction and sentence at issue (never mind the underlying crime) are already a dim memory, on average more than 6 years old (7 years for capital cases).[5] I would adhere to the precedents that prevent a bad situation from becoming worse.

II

We granted certiorari on, and the parties addressed their arguments to, the following question:

> "Whether a defendant in a state criminal case who is prohibited by state law from raising on direct appeal any claim of ineffective assistance of trial counsel, but who has a state-law right to raise such a claim in a first post-conviction proceeding, has a federal constitutional right to effective assistance of first post-conviction counsel specifically with respect to his ineffective assistance -of-trial-counsel claim." Pet. for Cert. *i*.

While the Court's decision not to answer the question did not avoid the costs a constitutional holding would have imposed on States, it did avoid the Court's need to confront the established rule that there is no right to counsel in collateral proceedings. To avoid his procedural default, Martinez advocates in favor of an exception to this rule where the prisoner seeks the right to counsel in an initial-review collateral proceeding – an argument we have

---

[5] See King, Cheesman, & Ostrom, Final Technical Report, at 21-22 (reporting the average interval between state judgment and federal habeas filing for a sample of federal habeas cases filed in the early-to-mid 2000's).

previously declined to address. See *Coleman*, 501 U. S., at 755.

The argument is quite clearly foreclosed by our precedent. In *Pennsylvania v. Finley*, 481 U. S. 551 (1987), and *Murray v. Giarratano*, 492 U. S. 1 (1989), we stated unequivocally that prisoners do not "have a constitutional right to counsel when mounting collateral attacks upon their convictions." *Finley, supra*, at 555. See also *Giarratano*, 492 U. S., at 10 (plurality opinion) ("[T]he rule of *Pennsylvania v. Finley* should apply no differently in capital cases than in noncapital cases"); id., at 14 (KENNEDY, J., concurring in judgment) (indicating that the Constitution does not categorically require States to provide counsel to death-row inmates seeking state habeas review). Though *Finley* may have involved only claims that could have been raised on direct review, see 481 U. S., at 553; *Giarratano, supra*, at 24 (Stevens, J., dissenting), the Court was no doubt aware that States often limit "the collateral review process [to] issues that have not previously been litigated or argued on the direct appeal." Brief for Respondent in *Finley*, O. T. 1986, No. 85-2099, p. 11, n. 5. And *Giarratano*, which involved a class action filed under 42 U.S.C. §1983, addressed the general assertion that the Constitution requires the appointment of counsel for collateral attacks on capital convictions. See 492 U. S., at 3-4 (plurality opinion). The Court rejected that assertion without qualification. The dissenting opinion, moreover, made the precise argument Martinez now asserts under state law "some claims [including ineffective assistance of trial counsel] ordinarily heard on direct review will be relegated to post-conviction proceedings." *Id.*, at 24 (Stevens, J., dissenting). See also Brief for Respondents in *Giarratano*, O. T. 1988, No. 88-411, p. 29, n. 8 ("In [Virginia capital habeas] proceedings, Death Row inmates seek to assert claims that have not been and could not have been addressed on direct appeal..."). Thus, in announcing a categorical rule in *Finley*, see *Giarratano, supra*, at 12 (plurality opinion), and then reaffirming it in *Giarratano*, the Court knew full well that a collateral proceeding may present the first opportunity for a prisoner to raise a constitutional claim. I would follow that rule in this case and reject Martinez's argument that there is a constitutional right to counsel in initial-review collateral proceedings.

* * *

Far from avoiding the consequences a constitutional holding would have imposed on the States, today's holding as a practical matter requires States to appoint counsel in initial-review collateral proceedings – and, to boot, eliminates the pre-existing assurance of escaping federal habeas review for claims that appointed counsel fails to present. Despite the Court's protestations to the contrary, the decision is a radical alteration of our habeas jurisprudence that will impose considerable economic costs on the States and further impair their ability to provide justice in a timely fashion. The balance it strikes between the finality of criminal judgments and the need to provide for review of defaulted claims of ineffective assistance -of-trial-counsel grossly underestimates both the frequency of such claims in federal habeas, and the incentives to argue (since it is a free pass to federal habeas) that appointed counsel was ineffective in failing to raise such claims. The balance might have been close (though it would disregard our established jurisprudence) if the Court merely held that uncounseled failure to raise ineffective assistance -of-trial-counsel would not constitute default. But in adding to that the rule that counseled failure to raise it may also provide an excuse, the Court creates a monstrosity. For these reasons, I respectfully dissent.

Cite as: 569 U. S. ___ (2013)

SCALIA, J., dissenting

SUPREME COURT OF THE UNITED STATES

No. 11-10189

CARLOS TREVINO, PETITIONER *v.* RICK THALER, DIRECTOR, TEXAS DEPARTMENT OF CRIMINAL JUSTICE, CORRECTIONAL INSTITUTIONS DIVISION

ON WRIT OF CERTIORARI TO THE UNITED STATES COURT OF APPEALS FOR THE FIFTH CIRCUIT

[May 28, 2013]

JUSTICE SCALIA, with whom JUSTICE THOMAS joins, dissenting.

I dissent for the reasons set forth in my dissent in *Martinez v. Ryan*, 566 U. S. 1 (2012). That opinion sought to minimize the impact of its novel holding as follows:

> "Our holding here addresses only the constitutional claims presented in this case, where the State barred the defendant from raising the claims on direct appeal" *Id.*, at ___ (slip op., at 14).

I wrote in my dissent:

> "That line lacks any principled basis and will not last." *Id.*, at ___ (slip op., at 2, n. 1).

The Court says today:

> "Texas law on its face appears to permit (but not require) the defendant to raise the claim on direct appeal. Does this difference matter?" "[W]e can find no significant difference between this case and *Martinez*." *Ante*, at 8, 13 (emphasis removed).

Cite as: 569 U. S. ___ (2013)

ROBERTS, C. J., dissenting

SUPREME COURT OF THE UNITED STATES

No. 11-10189

CARLOS TREVINO, PETITIONER *v.* RICK THALER, DIRECTOR, TEXAS DEPARTMENT OF CRIMINAL JUSTICE, CORRECTIONAL INSTITUTIONS DIVISION

ON WRIT OF CERTIORARI TO THE UNITED STATES COURT OF APPEALS FOR THE FIFTH CIRCUIT

[May 28, 2013]

CHIEF JUSTICE ROBERTS, with whom JUSTICE ALITO joins, dissenting.

In our federal system, the "state courts are the principal forum for asserting constitutional challenges to state convictions." *Harrington v. Richter*, 562 U. S. ___, ___ (2011) (slip op., at 13). "Federal courts sitting in habeas," we have said, "are not an alternative forum for trying...issues which a prisoner made insufficient effort to pursue in state proceedings." *Williams v. Taylor*, 529 U. S. 420, 437 (2000). This basic principle reflects the fact that federal habeas review "'intrudes on state sovereignty to a degree matched by few exercises of federal judicial authority.'" Richter, *supra*, at ___ (slip op., at 13) (quoting *Harris v. Reed*, 489 U. S. 255, 282 (1989) (KENNEDY, J., dissenting)).

In order to prevent circumvention of the state courts and the unjustified intrusion on state sovereignty that results, we have held that "a state prisoner [who] fails to exhaust state remedies...[or] has failed to meet the State's procedural requirements for presenting his federal claims" will not be entitled to federal habeas relief unless he can show "cause" to excuse his default. *Coleman v. Thompson*, 501 U. S. 722, 732, 750 (1991). There is an exception to that rule where "failure to consider the claims will result in a fundamental miscarriage of justice," *Ibid.*; that exception is not at issue here.

Cause comes in different forms, but the one relevant here is attorney error. We recognized in Coleman that "[w]here a [habeas] petitioner defaults a claim as a result of the denial of the right to effective assistance of counsel, the State, which is responsible for the denial as a constitutional matter, must bear the cost of any resulting default." *Id.*, at 754. But we simultaneously recognized that "[a] different allocation of costs is appropriate in those circumstances where the State has no responsibility to ensure that the petitioner was represented by competent counsel." *Ibid.* In that situation, we held, "it is the petitioner who must bear the burden of a failure to follow state procedural rules." *Ibid.* Because the error in *Coleman* occurred during state postconviction proceedings, a point at which the habeas petitioner had no constitutional right to counsel, the petitioner had to bear the cost of his default. *Id.*, at 757.

Last Term, in *Martinez v. Ryan*, we announced a "narrow exception" to Coleman's "unqualified statement...that an attorney's ignorance or inadvertence in a postconviction proceeding does not qualify as cause to excuse a procedural default." 566 U. S. 1, ___ (2012) (slip op., at 6). In Martinez, Arizona law did not allow defendants to raise ineffective assistance of counsel claims on direct appeal; they could only raise such claims in state collateral proceedings. *Id.*, at ___ (slip op., at 2). We held that while Arizona was free to structure its state court procedures in this way, its "decision is not without consequences for the State's ability to assert a procedural default in later proceedings." *Id.*, at ___ (slip op., at 10). "By deliberately choosing to move trial-ineffectiveness claims outside of the direct-appeal process, where counsel is constitutionally guaranteed, the State significantly diminishes prisoners' ability to file such claims." *Ibid.* Thus, "within the context of this state procedural framework," attorney error would qualify as cause to excuse procedural default if it occurred in the first proceeding at which the prisoner was "allow[ed]" to raise his trial ineffectiveness claim. *Id.*, at ___, ___ (slip op., at 10, 13).

We were unusually explicit about the narrowness of our decision: "The holding in this case does not concern attorney errors in other kinds of proceedings," and "does not extend to attorney errors in any proceeding beyond the first occasion the State allows a prisoner to raise a claim of ineffective assistance at trial." *Id.*, at ___-___ (slip op., at 13-14). "Our holding here addresses only the constitutional claims presented in this case, where the State barred the defendant from raising the claims on direct appeal." *Id.*, at ___ (slip op., at 14). In "all but the limited circumstances recognized here," we said, "[t]he rule of Coleman governs." *Id.*, at ___ (slip op., at 13).

This aggressively limiting language was not simply a customary nod to the truism that "we decide only the case before us." *Upjohn Co. v. United States*, 449 U. S. 383, 396 (1981). It was instead an important part of our explanation for why "[t]his limited qualification to Coleman does not implicate the usual concerns with upsetting reliance interests protected by stare decisis principles." *Martinez, supra*, at ___ (slip op., at 12). The fact that the exception was clearly delineated ensured that the Coleman rule would remain administrable. And because States could readily anticipate how such a sharply defined exception would apply to various procedural frameworks, the exception could be reconciled with our concerns for comity and equitable balancing that led to Coleman's baseline rule in the first place. See *Coleman, supra*, at 750-751. The States had a clear choice, which they could make with full knowledge of the consequences: If a State "deliberately cho[se] to move trial-ineffectiveness claims outside of the direct-appeal process" through a "decision to bar defendants from raising" them there, then-and only then-would "counsel's ineffectiveness in an initial-review collateral proceeding qualif[y] as cause for a procedural default." Martinez, 566 U. S., at ___, ___ (slip op., at 10, 14).

Today, with hardly a mention of these concerns, the majority throws over the crisp limit we made so explicit just last Term. We announced in Martinez that the exception applies "where the State barred the defendant from raising the claims on direct appeal." *Id.*, at ___ (slip op., at 14). But today, the Court takes all the starch out of its rule with an assortment of adjectives, adverbs, and modifying clauses: Martinez's "narrow exception" now applies whenever the "state procedural framework, by reason of its design and operation, makes it highly unlikely in a typical case that a defendant will have a meaningful opportunity" to raise his claim on direct appeal. *Ante*, at 14.

The questions raised by this equitable equation are as endless as will be the state-by-state litigation it takes to work them out. We are not told, for example, how meaningful is meaningful enough, how meaningful-ness is to be measured, how unlikely highly unlikely is, how often a procedural framework's "operation" must be reassessed, or what case qualifies as the "typical" case. Take just this last example: The case before us involved a jury trial (hardly typical), a capital conviction (even less typical), and the majority emphasizes a particular species of ineffectiveness claim that depends on the time-consuming investigation of personal background and other mitigating circumstances. *Ante*, at 10. Yet the majority holds it up, apparently, as a case that is typical in the relevant sense, saying that "[t]he present capital case illustrates" the "systematic" working of Texas's procedural framework. *Ibid.*

Given that the standard is so opaque and malleable, the majority cannot describe the exception applied here as narrow and does not do so. Gone are the repeated words of limitation that characterized the *Martinez* opinion. Gone, too, is the clear choice that Martinez gave the States about how to structure their criminal justice systems. Now, the majority offers them a gamble: If a State allows defendants to bring ineffectiveness claims both on direct appeal and in postconviction proceedings, then a prisoner might have to comply with state procedural requirements in order to preserve the availability of federal habeas review if a federal judge decides that the state system gave the defendant (or enough other "typical" defendants) a sufficiently meaningful opportunity to press his claim.

This invitation to litigation will, in precisely the manner that *Coleman* foreclosed, "'frustrate both the States' sovereign power to punish offenders and their good-faith attempts to honor constitutional rights." *Coleman*, 501 U. S., at 748 (quoting *Engle v. Isaac*, 456 U. S. 107, 128 (1982)). In what I suspect (though I cannot know) will be a broad swath of cases, the Court's approach will excuse procedural defaults that, under *Coleman*, should preclude federal review. But even in cases where federal courts ultimately decide that the habeas petitioner cannot establish cause under the new standard, the years of procedural wrangling it takes to reach that decision will themselves undermine the finality of sentences necessary to effective criminal justice. Because that approach is inconsistent with *Coleman*, *Martinez* itself, and the principles of equitable discretion and comity at the heart of both, I respectfully dissent.

(Slip Opinion) OCTOBER TERM, 2012

Syllabus

NOTE: *Where it is feasible, a syllabus (headnote) will be released. as is being done in connection with this case, at the time the opinion is issued. The syllabus constitutes no part of the opinion of the Court but has been prepared by the Reporter of Decisions for the convenience of the reader. See United States v, Detroit Timber & Lumber Cu., 200 U. S. 321, 337.*

SUPREME COURT OF THE UNITED STATES

Syllabus

TREVINO *v*. THALER, DIRECTOR, TEXAS DEPARTMENT OF CRIMINAL JUSTICE, CORRECTIONAL INSTITUTIONS DIVISION

CERTIORARI TO THE UNITED STATES COURT OF APPEALS FOR THE FIFTH CIRCUIT

No. 11-10189. Argued February 25, 2013-Decided May 28, 2013

In *Martinez v. Ryan*, 566 U. S. 1, ___, this Court held that "a procedural default will not bar a federal habeas court from hearing a substantial claim of ineffective assistance at trial if, in the [State's] initial-review collateral proceeding, there was no counselor counsel in. that proceeding was ineffective." Martinez regarded a prisoner from Arizona, where state procedural law required the prisoner to raise the claim during his first state collateral review proceeding. *Ibid.* This case regards a prisoner from Texas, where state procedural law does not require a defendant to raise his ineffective assistance -of-trial-counsel claim on collateral review. Rather, Texas law appears to permit a prisoner to raise such a claim on direct review, but the structure and design of the Texas system make it virtually impossible for a prisoner to do so. The question presented in this case is whether, despite this difference, the rule set out in *Martinez* applies in Texas.

Petitioner Trevino was convicted of capital murder in Texas state court and sentenced to death after the jury found insufficient mitigating circumstances to warrant a life sentence. Neither new counsel appointed for his direct appeal nor new counsel appointed for state collateral review raised the claim that Trevino's trial counsel provided ineffective assistance during the penalty phase by failing to adequately investigate and present mitigating circumstances. When that claim was finally raised in Trevino's federal habeas petition, the District Court stayed the proceedings so Trevino could raise it in state court. The state court found the claim procedurally defaulted because of Trevino's failure to raise it in his initial state postconviction proceedings, and the federal court then concluded that this failure was an independent and adequate state ground barring the federal courts from considering the claim. The Fifth Circuit affirmed. Its decision predated Martinez, but that court has since concluded that Martinez does not apply in Texas because Martinez's good-cause exception applies only where state law says that a defendant must initially raise his ineffective assistance -of-trial-counsel claim in initial state collateral review proceedings, while Texas law appears to permit a defendant to raise that claim on direct appeal.

Held: Where, as here, a State's procedural framework, by reason of its design and operation, makes it highly unlikely in a typical case that a defendant will have a meaningful opportunity to raise an ineffective assistance -of-trial-counsel claim on direct appeal, the exception recognized in Martinez applies. Pp. 5-15.

(a) A finding that a defendant's state law "procedural default" rests on "an independent and adequate state ground" ordinarily prevents a federal habeas court from considering the defendant's federal constitutional claim. *Coleman v. Thompson*, 501 U. S. 722,729-730. However, a "prisoner may obtain federal review of a defaulted claim by showing cause for the default and prejudice from a violation of the federal law." *Martinez, supra*, at ___. In *Martinez*, the Court recognized a "narrow exception" to Coleman's statement "that an attorney's ignorance or inadvertence in a postconviction proceeding does not qualify as cause to excuse a procedural default." 566 U. S., at ___. That exception allows a federal habeas court to find "cause" to excuse such default where (1) the ineffective assistance -of-trial-counsel claim was a "substantial" claim; (2) the "cause" consisted of there being "no counsel" or only "ineffective" counsel during the state collateral review proceeding; (3) the state collateral review proceeding was the "initial" review proceeding in respect to the "ineffective assistance -of-trial-counsel claim"; and (4) state law requires that the claim "be raised in an initial-review collateral proceeding." *Id.*, at ___. Pp.5-8.

(b) The difference between the Texas law in theory, grants permission to bring an ineffective assistance -of-trial-counsel claim on direct appeal but in practice denies a meaningful opportunity to do so and the Arizona law at issue in Martinez – which required the claim to be raised in an initial collateral review proceeding – does not matter in respect to the application of Martinez. Pp.8-14.

(1) This conclusion is supported by two characteristics of Texas' procedures. First, Texas procedures make it nearly impossible for an ineffective assistance -of-trial-counsel claim to be presented on direct review. The nature of an ineffective assistance claim means that the trial record is likely to be insufficient to support the claim. A motion for a new trial to develop the record is usually inadequate because of Texas rules regarding time limits on the filing and the disposal of such motions and the availability of trial transcripts. Thus, a writ of habeas corpus is normally needed to gather the facts necessary for evaluating these claims in Texas. Second, were Martinez not to apply, the Texas procedural system would create significant unfairness because Texas courts, in effect, have directed defendants to raise ineffective assistance -of-trial-counsel claims on collateral, rather than on direct review. Texas can point to only a few cases in which a defendant has used the motion-for-a-new-trial mechanism to expand the record on appeal. Texas suggests that there are other mechanisms by which a prisoner can expand the record on appeal, but these mechanisms seem special and limited in their application and cannot overcome the Texas courts' own well-supported determination that collateral review normally is the preferred procedural route for raising an ineffective assistance -of-trial-counsel claim. Respondent also argues that there is no equitable problem here, where appellate counsel's failure to bring a substantial ineffective assistance claim on direct appeal may constitute cause to excuse the procedural default, but respondent points to no case in which such a failure by appellate counsel has been deemed constitutionally ineffective. Pp. 8-13.

(2) The very factors that led this Court to create a narrow exception to *Coleman* in *Martinez* similarly argue for applying that exception here. The right involved – adequate assistance of trial counsel – is similarly and critically important. In both instances practical considerations – the need for a new lawyer, the need to expand the trial court record, and the need for sufficient time to develop the claim – argue strongly for initial consideration of the claim during collateral, not on direct, review. See *Martinez*, 566 U. S., at ___. In both instances failure to consider a lawyer's "ineffectiveness" during an initial-review collateral proceeding as

a potential "cause" for excusing a procedural default will deprive the defendant of any opportunity for review of an ineffective assistance -of-trial-counsel claim. See *id.*, at ___. Thus, for present purposes, a distinction between (1) a State that denies permission to raise the claim on direct appeal and (2) a State that grants permission but denies a fair, meaningful opportunity to develop the claim is a distinction without a difference. Pp. 13-14.

449 Fed. Appx. 415, vacated and remanded.

BREYER, J., delivered the opinion for the Court, in which KENNEDY, GINSBURG, SOTOMAYOR, and KAGAN, JJ., joined. ROBERTS, C. J., filed a dissenting opinion, in which ALITO, J., joined. SCALIA, J., filed a dissenting opinion, in which THOMAS, J., joined.

Cite as: 569 U. S. ___ (2013)

Opinion of the Court

NOTICE: *This opinion is subject to formal revision before publication in the preliminary print of the United States Reports. Readers are requested to notify the Reporter of Decisions, Supreme Court of the United States, Washington, D. C. 20543, of any typographical or other formal errors, in order that corrections may be made before the preliminary print goes to press.*

SUPREME COURT OF THE UNITED STATES

No. 11-10189

CARLOS TREVINO, PETITIONER *v.* RICK THALER, DIRECTOR, TEXAS DEPARTMENT OF CRIMINAL JUSTICE, CORRECTIONAL INSTITUTIONS DIVISION

ON WRIT OF CERTIORARI TO THE UNITED STATES COURT OF APPEALS FOR THE FIFTH CIRCUIT

[May 28, 2013]

JUSTICE BREYER delivered the opinion of the Court.

In *Martinez v. Ryan*, 566 U. S. 1 (2012), we considered the right of a state prisoner to raise, in a federal habeas corpus proceeding, a claim of ineffective assistance of trial counsel. In that case an Arizona procedural rule required a defendant convicted at trial to raise a claim of ineffective assistance -of-trial-counsel during his first state collateral review proceeding-or lose the claim. The defendant in Martinez did not comply with the state procedural rule. But he argued that the federal habeas court should excuse his state procedural failing, on the ground that he had good "cause" for not raising the claim at the right time, namely that, not only had he lacked effective counsel during trial, but also he lacked effective counsel during his first state collateral review proceeding.

We held that lack of counsel on collateral review might excuse defendant's state law procedural default. We wrote:

> "[A] procedural default will not bar a federal habeas court from hearing a substantial claim of ineffective assistance at trial if, in the [State's] initial-review collateral proceeding, there was no counselor counsel in that proceeding was ineffective." *Id.*, at ___ (slip op., at 15).

At the same time, we qualified our holding. We said that the holding applied where state procedural law said that "claims of ineffective assistance -of-trial-counsel must be raised in an initial-review collateral proceeding." *Ibid.* (emphasis added).

In this case Texas state law does not say "must." It does not on its face require a defendant initially to raise an ineffective assistance -of-trial-counsel claim in a state collateral review proceeding. Rather, that law appears at first glance to permit (but not require) the defendant initially to raise a claim of ineffective assistance -of-trial-counsel on direct appeal. The structure and design of the Texas system in actual operation, however, make it "virtually impossible" for an ineffective assistance claim to be presented on direct review. See *Robinson v. State*, 16 S. W. 3d 808, 810-811 (Tex. Crim. App. 2000). We must now decide whether the Martinez exception applies in this procedural regime. We conclude that it does.

I

A Texas state court jury convicted petitioner Carlos Trevino of capital murder. After a subsequent penalty-phase hearing, the jury found that Trevino "would commit criminal acts of violence in the future which would constitute a continuing threat to society," that he "actually caused the death of Linda Salinas or, if he did not actually cause her death, he intended to kill her or another, or he anticipated a human life would be taken," and that "there were insufficient mitigating circumstances to warrant a sentence of life imprisonment" rather than death. 449 Fed. Appx. 415, 418 (CA5 2011). The judge consequently imposed a sentence of death.

Eight days later, the judge appointed new counsel to handle Trevino's direct appeal. App. 1, 3. Seven months after sentencing, when the trial transcript first became available, that counsel filed an appeal. The Texas Court of Criminal Appeals then considered and rejected Trevino's appellate claims. Trevino's appellate counsel *did not claim that Trevino's trial counsel had been constitutionally ineffective during the penalty phase of the trial court proceedings. Id.*, at 12-24.

About six months after sentencing, the trial judge appointed Trevino a different new counsel to seek state collateral relief. As Texas' procedural rules provide, that third counsel initiated collateral proceedings while Trevino's appeal was still in progress. This new counsel first sought postconviction relief (through collateral review) in the trial court itself. After a hearing, the trial court denied relief, and the Texas Court of Criminal Appeals affirmed that denial. *Id.*, at 25-26, 321-349. Trevino's postconviction claims included a claim that his trial counsel was constitutionally ineffective during the penalty phase of Trevino's trial, but it did not include a claim that the trial counsel's ineffectiveness consisted in part of a failure adequately to investigate and to present mitigating circumstances during the penalty phase of Trevino's trial. *Id.*, at 321-349; see *Wiggins v. Smith*, 539 U. S. 510, 523 (2003) (counsel's failure to investigate and present mitigating circumstances deprived the defendant of effective assistance of counsel).

Trevino then filed a petition in federal court seeking a writ of habeas corpus. The Federal District Court appointed another new counsel to represent him. And that counsel claimed for the first time that Trevino had not received constitutionally effective counsel during the penalty phase of his trial in part because of the trial counsel's failure to adequately investigate and present mitigating circumstances during the penalty phase. App. 438. 456478. Federal habeas counsel pointed out that Trevino's trial counsel had presented only one witness at the sentencing phase, namely Trevino's aunt. The aunt had testified that Trevino had had a difficult upbringing, that his mother had an alcohol problem, that his family was on welfare, and that he had dropped out of high school. She had added that Trevino had a child, that he was good with children, and that he was not violent. *Id.*, at 285-291.

Federal habeas counsel then told the federal court that Trevino's trial counsel should have found and presented at the penalty phase other mitigating matters that his own investigation had brought to light. These included, among other things, that Trevino's mother abused alcohol while she was pregnant with Trevino, that Trevino weighed only four pounds at birth, that throughout his life, Trevino suffered the deleterious effects of Fetal Alcohol Syndrome, that as a child, Trevino had suffered numerous head injuries without receiving adequate medical attention, that Trevino's mother had abused him physically and emotionally, that from an early age, Trevino was exposed to, and abused, alcohol and drugs, that Trevino had attended school irregularly and performed poorly, and that Trevino's cognitive abilities were impaired. *Id.*, at 66-67.

The federal court stayed proceedings to permit Trevino to raise this claim in state court. The state court held that because Trevino had not raised this claim during his initial postconviction proceedings, he had procedurally defaulted the claim, id., at 27-28; and the Federal District Court then denied Trevino's ineffective assistance -of-trial-counsel claim, *id.*, at 78-79. The District Court concluded in relevant part that, despite the fact that "even the most minimal investigation ... would have revealed a wealth of additional mitigating evidence," an independent and adequate state ground (namely Trevino's failure to raise the issue during his state postconviction proceeding) barred the federal habeas court from considering the ineffective assistance -of-trial-counsel claim. *Id.*, at 131132. See *Coleman v. Thompson*, 501 U. S. 722, 729-730 (1991).

Trevino appealed. The Fifth Circuit, without considering the merits of Trevino's claim of ineffective assistance of trial counsel, agreed with the District Court that an independent, adequate state ground —namely, Trevino's procedural default —barred its consideration. 449 Fed. Appx., at 426. Although the Circuit decided Trevino's case before this Court decided *Martinez*, the Fifth Circuit's reasoning in a later case, *Ibarra v. Thaler*, 687 F. 3d 222 (2012), makes clear that the Fifth Circuit would have found that *Martinez* would have made no difference.

That is because in *Ibarra* the Circuit recognized that *Martinez* had said that its good-cause exception applies where state law says that a criminal defendant must initially raise his claim of ineffective assistance -of-trial-counsel in initial state collateral review proceedings. 687 F. 3d, at 225-226. Texas law, the Circuit pointed out, does not say explicitly that the defendant must initially raise the claim in state collateral review proceedings. Rather, Texas law, on its face, appears to permit a criminal defendant to raise such a claim on direct appeal. *Id.*, at 227. And the Circuit held that that fact means that Martinez does not apply in Texas. 687 F. 3d, at 227. Since the Circuit's holding in *Ibarra* (that *Martinez* does not apply in Texas) would similarly govern this case, we granted certiorari here to determine whether *Martinez* applies in Texas.

II

A

We begin with *Martinez*. We there recognized the historic importance of federal habeas corpus proceedings as a method for preventing individuals from being held in custody in violation of federal law. *Martinez*, 566 U. S., at ___ (slip op., at 6-7). See generally *Preiser v. Rodriguez*, 411 U. S. 475, 484-485 (1973). In general, if a convicted state criminal defendant can show a federal habeas court that his conviction rests upon a violation of the Federal Constitution, he may well obtain a writ of habeas corpus that requires a new trial, a new sentence, or release.

We similarly recognized the importance of federal habeas corpus principles designed to prevent federal courts from interfering with a state's application of its own firmly established, consistently followed, constitutionally proper procedural rules. *Martinez, supra*, at ___ (slip op., at 6-7). Those principles have long made clear that a conviction that rests upon a defendant's state law "procedural default" (for example, the defendant's failure to raise a claim of error at the time or in the place that state law requires), normally rests upon "an independent and adequate state ground." *Coleman*, 501 U. S., at 729-730. And where a conviction rests upon such a ground, a federal habeas court normally cannot consider the defendant's federal constitutional claim. *Ibid.*; see *Martinez*, 566 U. S., at ___ (slip op., at 6-7).

At the same time, we pointed out that "[t]he doctrine barring procedurally defaulted claims from being heard is not without exceptions. A prisoner may obtain federal review of a defaulted claim by showing cause for the default and prejudice from a violation of federal law." *Id.*, at ___ (slip op., at 6-7). And we turned to the issue directly before the Court: whether Martinez had shown "cause" to excuse his state procedural failing. *Id.*, at ___ (slip op., at 15).

Martinez argued that his lawyer should have raised, but did not raise, his claim of ineffective assistance -of-trial-counsel during state collateral review proceedings. *Id.*, at ___ (slip op., at 4). He added that this failure, itself amounting to ineffective assistance, was the "cause" of, and ought to excuse, his procedural default. *Id.*, at ___ (slip op., at 4). But this Court had previously held that "[n]egligence on the part of a prisoner's postconviction attorney does not qualify as 'cause," primarily because a "principal" such as the prisoner, "bears the risk of negligent conduct on the part of his agent," the attorney. *Maples v. Thomas*, 565 U. S. ___, ___ (2012) (slip op., at 12) (quoting *Coleman, supra*, at 753-754; emphasis added). Martinez, in effect, argued for an exception to *Coleman*'s broad statement of the law.

We ultimately held that a "narrow exception" should "modify the unqualified statement in Coleman that an attorney's ignorance or inadvertence in a postconviction proceeding does not qualify as cause to excuse a procedural default." *Martinez*, 566 U. S., at ___ (slip op., at 6). We did so for three reasons. First, the "right to the effective assistance of counsel at trial is a bedrock principle in our justice system. ... Indeed, the right to counsel is the foundation for our adversary system." *Id.*, at ___ (slip op., at 9).

Second, ineffective assistance of counsel on *direct appellate review* could amount to "cause," excusing a defendant's failure to raise (and thus procedurally defaulting) a constitutional claim. *Id.*, at ___ (slip op., at 8). But States often have good reasons for initially reviewing claims of ineffective assistance -of-trial-counsel during state collateral proceedings rather than on direct appellate review. *Id.*, at ___ (slip op., at 9-10). That is because review of such a claim normally requires a different attorney, because it often "depend[s] on evidence outside the trial record," and because efforts to expand the record on direct appeal may run afoul of "[a]bbreviated deadlines," depriving the new attorney of "adequate time ... to investigate the ineffective assistance claim." *Id.*, at ___ (slip op., at 10).

Third, where the State consequently channels the initial review of this constitutional claim to collateral proceedings, a lawyer's failure to raise an ineffective assistance of-trial-counsel claim during initial-review collateral proceedings could (were *Coleman* read broadly) deprive a defendant of any review of that claim at all. *Martinez, supra*, at ___ (slip op., at 7).

We consequently read *Coleman* as containing an exception, allowing a federal habeas court to find "cause," thereby excusing a defendant's procedural default, where (1) the claim of "ineffective assistance of trial counsel" was a "substantial" claim; (2) the "cause" consisted of there being "no counsel" or only "ineffective" counsel during the state collateral review proceeding; (3) the state collateral review proceeding was the "initial" review proceeding in respect to the "ineffective assistance -of-trial-counsel claim"; and (4) state law requires that an "ineffective assistance -of-trial-counsel [claim]...be raised in an initial-review collateral proceeding." *Martinez, supra*, at ___ (slip op., at 11, 15).

B

Here state law differs from that in Martinez in respect to the fourth requirement. Unlike Arizona, Texas does not expressly *require* the defendant to raise a claim of ineffective assistance -of-trial-counsel in an initial *collateral* review proceeding. Rather Texas law on its face appears to permit (but not require) the defendant to raise the claim on *direct appeal*. Does this difference matter?

1

Two characteristics of the relevant Texas procedures lead us to conclude that it should *not* make a difference in respect to the application of *Martinez*. First, Texas procedure makes it "virtually impossible for appellate counsel to adequately present an ineffective assistance [of trial counsel] claim" on direct review. *Robinson*, 16 S. W. 3d, at 810-811. As the Texas Court of Criminal Appeals itself has pointed out, "the inherent nature of most ineffective assistance" of trial counsel "claims" means that the trial court record will often fail to "contain[n] the information necessary to substantiate" the claim. *Ex parte Torres*, 943 S. W. 2d 469,475 (1997) (en banc).

As the Court of Criminal Appeals has also noted, a convicted defendant may make a motion in the trial court for a new trial in order to develop the record on appeal. See *Reyes v. State*, 849 S. W. 2d 812, 816 (1993). And, in principle, the trial court could, in connection with that motion, allow the defendant *some* additional time to develop a further record. *Ibid.* But that motion-for-new-trial "vehicle is often inadequate because of time constraints and because the trial record has generally not been transcribed at this point." *Torres, supra*, at 475. See Tex. Rule App. Proc. 21.4 (2013) (motion for a new trial must be made within 30 days of sentencing); Rules 21.8(a), (c) (trial court must dispose of motion within 75 days of sentencing); Rules 35.2(b), 35.3(c) (transcript must be prepared within 120 days of sentencing where a motion for a new trial is filed and this deadline may be extended). Thus, as the Court of Criminal Appeals has concluded, in Texas, "a writ of habeas corpus" issued in state collateral proceedings ordinarily "is essential to gathering the facts necessary to...evaluate...[ineffective assistance -of-trial-counsel] claims." *Torres, supra*, at 475. See *Robinson, supra*, at 810-811 (noting that there is "not generally a realistic opportunity to adequately develop the record for appeal in post-trial motions" and that "[t]he time requirements for filing and presenting a motion for new trial would have made it virtually impossible for appellate counsel to adequately present an ineffective assistance claim to the trial court").

See also *Thompson v. State*, 9 S. W. 3d 808, 813-814, and n. 6 (Tex. Crim. App, 1999) ("[I]n the vast majority of cases, the undeveloped record on direct appeal will be insufficient for an appellant to satisfy the dual prongs of Strickland"; only "[r]arely will a reviewing court be provided the opportunity to make its determination on direct appeal with a record capable of providing a fair evaluation of the merits of the claim..."); *Goodspeed v. State*, 187 S. W. 3d 390, 392 (Tex. Crim. App. 2005) (similar); *Andrews v. State*, 159 S. W. 3d 98, 102-103 (Tex. Crim. App. 2005) (similar); *Ex parte Brown*, 158 S. W. 3d 449, 453 (Tex. Crim. App. 2005) (per curiam) (similar); *Jackson v. State*, 973 S. W. 2d 954, 957 (Tex. Crim. App. 1998) (per curiam) (similar). See also 42 G. Dix & J. Schmolesky, Texas Practice Series §29:76, pp. 844-845 (3d ed. 2011) (hereinafter Texas Practice) (explaining that "[o]ften" the requirement that a claim of ineffective assistance -of-trial-counsel be supported by a record containing direct evidence of why counsel acted as he did "will require that the claim...be raised in postconviction habeas proceedings where a full record on the matter can be raised").

This opinion considers whether, as a systematic matter, Texas affords meaningful review of a claim of ineffective assistance of trial counsel. The present capital case illustrates why it does not. The trial court appointed new counsel for Trevino eight days after sentencing. Counsel thus had 22 days to decide whether and on what grounds to make a motion for a new trial. She then may have had an additional 45 days to provide support for the motion but *without the help of a transcript* (which did not become available until much later – seven months after the trial). It would have been difficult, perhaps impossible, within that time frame to investigate Trevino's background, determine whether trial counsel had adequately done so, and then develop evidence about additional mitigating background circumstances. See *Reyes, supra*, at 816 ("[M]otions for new trial [must] be supported by affidavit … specifically showing the truth of the grounds of attack").

Second, were *Martinez* not to apply, the Texas procedural system would create significant unfairness. That is because Texas courts, in effect, have directed defendants to raise claims of ineffective assistance -of-trial-counsel on collateral, rather than on direct review. As noted, they have explained why direct review proceedings are likely inadequate. See *supra*, at 8-10. They have held that failure to raise the claim on direct review does not bar the defendant from raising the claim in collateral proceedings. See, *e.g.*, *Robinson*, 16 S. W. 3d, at 813; *Ex parte Duffy*, 607 S. W. 2d 507, 512-513 (Tex. Crim. App. 1980) (overruled on other grounds by *Hernandez v. State*, 988 S. W. 2d 770 (Tex. Crim. App. 1999)). They have held that the defendant's decision to raise the claim on direct review does not bar the defendant from also raising the claim in collateral proceedings. See, *e.g.*, *Lopez v. State*, 343 S. W. 3d 137, 143 (Tex. Crim. App. 2011); Torres, *supra*, at 475. They have suggested that appellate counsel's failure to raise the claim on direct review does not constitute "ineffective assistance of counsel." See *Sprouse v. State*, No. AP-74933, 2007 WL 283152, *7 (Tex. Crim. App., Jan. 31, 2007) (unpublished). And Texas' highest criminal court has explicitly stated that "[a]s a general rule" the defendant "should not raise an issue of ineffective assistance of counsel on direct appeal," but rather in collateral review proceedings. *Mata v. State*, 226 S. W. 3d 425, 430, n. 14 (2007) (internal quotation marks omitted). See *Robinson, supra*, at 810 ("[A] post-conviction writ proceeding, rather than a motion for new trial, is the preferred method for gathering the facts necessary to substantiate" an ineffective assistance -of-trial-counsel claim).

The criminal bar, not surprisingly, has taken this strong judicial advice seriously. See Guidelines and Standards for Texas Capital Counsel, 69 Tex. B. J. 966, 977, Guideline 12.2(B)(I)(d) (2006) ("[S]tate habeas corpus is the first opportunity for a capital client to raise challenges to the effectiveness of trial or direct appeal counsel"). Texas can now point to only a comparatively small number of cases in which a defendant has used the motion-for-a-new-trial mechanism to expand the record on appeal and then received a hearing on their ineffective assistance -of-trial-counsel claim on direct appeal. Brief for Respondent 35-36, and n. 6 (citing, inter alia, *State v. Morales*, 253 S. W. 3d 686, 689-691 (Tex. Crim. App. 2008); *Robertson v. State*, 187 S. W. 3d 475, 480-481 (Tex. Crim, App. 2006)). And, of those, precisely one case involves trial counsel's investigative failures of the kind at issue here. See *Armstrong v. State*, No. AP-75706, 2010 WL 359020 (Tex. Crim. App., Jan. 27, 2010) (unpublished). How could federal law deny defendants the benefit of *Martinez* solely because of the existence of a theoretically available procedural alternative, namely direct appellate review, that Texas procedures render so difficult, and in the typical case all but impossible, to use successfully, and which Texas courts so strongly discourage defendants from using?

Respondent argues that Texas courts enforce the relevant time limits more flexibly than we have suggested. Sometimes, for example, an appellate court can abate an appeal and remand the case for further record development in the trial court. See *Cooks v. State*, 240 S. W. 3d 906 (Tex. Crim. App. 2007). But the procedural possibilities to which Texas now points seem special, limited in their application, and, as far as we can tell, rarely used. See 43A Texas Practice §50:15, at 636-639; 43B id., §56:235, at 607-609. *Cooks*, for example, the case upon which respondent principally relies, involved a remand for further record development, but in circumstances where the lower court wrongly failed to give a defendant new counsel in time to make an ordinary new trial motion. 240 S. W. 3d, at 911. We do not believe that this, or other, special, rarely used procedural possibilities can overcome the Texas courts' own well-supported determination that collateral review normally constitutes the preferred-and indeed as a practical matter, the only-method for raising an ineffective assistance -of-trial-counsel claim.

Respondent further argues that there is no equitable problem to be solved in Texas because if counsel fails to bring a substantial claim of ineffective assistance -of-trial-counsel *on direct appeal*, the ineffectiveness of appellate counsel may constitute cause to excuse the procedural default. See *Murray v. Carrier*, 477 U. S. 478 (1986). But the respondent points to no case in which such a failure by appellate counsel has been deemed constitutionally ineffective. That lack of authority is not surprising given the fact that the Texas Court of Criminal Appeals has directed defendants to bring such claims on collateral review.

For the reasons just stated, we believe that the Texas procedural system a matter of its structure, design, and operation-does not offer most defendants a meaningful opportunity to present a claim of ineffective assistance -of-trial-counsel on direct appeal. What the Arizona law prohibited by explicit terms; Texas law precludes as a matter of course. And that being so, we can find no significant difference between this case and *Martinez*. The very factors that led this Court to create a narrow exception to *Coleman* in *Martinez* similarly argue for the application of that exception here.

The right involved – adequate assistance of counsel at trial – is similarly and critically important. In both instances, practical considerations, such as the need for a new lawyer, the need to expand the trial court record, and the need for sufficient time to develop the claim, argue strongly for initial consideration of the claim during collateral rather than on direct review. See *Martinez*, 566 U. S., at ___ (slip op., at 10); see also *Massaro v. United States*, 538 U. S. 500, 505 (2003). In both instances, failure to consider a lawyer's "ineffectiveness" during an initial review collateral proceeding as a potential "cause" for excusing a procedural default will deprive the defendant of any opportunity at all for review of an ineffective assistance -of-trial-counsel claim. See *Martinez, supra*, at ___ (slip op., at 7).

Thus, for present purposes, a distinction between (1) a State that denies permission to raise the claim on direct appeal and (2) a State that in theory, grants permission but, as a matter of procedural design and systemic operation, denies a meaningful opportunity to do so is a distinction without a difference. In saying this, we do not (any more than we did in *Martinez*) seek to encourage States to tailor direct appeals so that they provide a fuller opportunity to raise ineffective assistance -of-trial-counsel claims. That is a matter for the States to decide. And, as we have said, there are often good reasons for hearing the claim initially during collateral proceedings.

III

For these reasons, we conclude that where, as here, state procedural framework, by reason of its design and operation, makes it highly unlikely in a typical case that a defendant will have a meaningful opportunity to raise a claim of ineffective assistance -of-trial-counsel on direct appeal, our holding in *Martinez* applies:

> "[A] procedural default will not bar a federal habeas court from hearing a substantial claim of ineffective assistance at trial if, in the initial-review collateral proceeding, there was no counselor counsel in that proceeding was ineffective." 566 U. S., at ___ (slip op., at 15).

Given this holding, Texas submits that its courts should be permitted, in the first instance, to decide the merits of Trevino's ineffective assistance -of-trial-counsel claim. Brief for Respondent 58-60. We leave that matter to be determined on remand. Likewise, we do not decide here whether Trevino's claim of ineffective assistance -of-trial-counsel is substantial or whether Trevino's initial state habeas attorney was ineffective.

For these reasons we vacate the Fifth Circuit's judgment and remand the case for further proceedings consistent with this opinion.

It is so ordered.

Notes:

CHAPTER 6 ★★★

ADVANCING YOUR CLAIMS: GETTING RELIEF

Now that you are past all of the procedural defaults and your petition has moved past the state's Motion For Dismissal, you are ready to advance your claims. First, the court will order the state to file a response to your petition, where they will effectively deny everything you have raised and attempt to have your petition denied in totality.

Before you do anything else, you need to obtain your "Lodgment" from the district court. The attorney general is tasked with the responsibility to provide the district court with all of the records and documents that have been filed in your case as it moves through the state's court system, such as the trial, direct appeal, and the state habeas corpus proceedings.

The Lodgment itself consists of a detailed list of these things, accompanied by the actual documents and records themselves. Because it contains literally thousands of pages, the state does not provide you with a copy of the Lodgment. However, if you followed the instructions in my book *The Habeas Corpus Manual*, you should already have a copy of all these documents. If not, you should immediately request the Lodgment. This can be done by writing a simple letter to the court requesting it and asserting that you have never received the records and documents and require them to effectively advance and prove your claims.

Now that is done, let's get to what you can expect.

The State's Answer

After you have received the Court's order directing the state to respond to your petition, within a relatively short time, you will receive their "Answer" to your petition.

The Answer is basically a legal pleading – usually only just a few pages in length – containing a summary of the state's position in trying to have your petition denied relief. In effect, they are just trying to keep you in prison and uphold the "finality" of your case. It's their "defense" to your petition.

You shouldn't expect to see any case citations in the Answer. That will come in the way of their "Memorandum of Points and Authorities." It is usually around 25 pages long and contains the legal summary of your case in the state court, the court's finding of facts and conclusions of law, a discussion of the "standard of review" which the state wants the federal court to apply in your case, and the legal arguments and supporting cases that the attorney general is relying on to get you petition dismissed.

Basically, the Points and Authorities Memorandum gives the court the state's argument as to why your petition must be denied under the AEDPA, which is exactly what the court will do if you fail to file an aggressive and on-point Traverse (Response) to the state's arguments.

So, let's talk a little about that Traverse (Response).

Traverse (Petitioner's Response)

First, you aren't required to file a Traverse if you don't want to. But you are a damn fool if you choose not to. How else do you expect to argue your claims and defend against the state's Answer? I cannot tell you how many times I have seen petitions where the person chose not to file a Traverse. As expected, the denial was very fast in those cases.

So, let's take a look at what your Traverse should have, though I will provide you a copy to review at the end of the chapter. The Traverse itself is simply a short legal document that admits or denies the allegations set forth in the state's Answer. This is a "Traverse Pleading" to show the difference between other documents included in the Traverse.

Both the Traverse and the supporting Memorandum/Points and Authorities must have a case caption on the front page, and the title of the document should appear on the first page in the caption. The last page of each document must be the Proof of Service, which is a sworn declaration stating that a copy of the document was mailed to the State (Respondent) at the time you filed it.

The Traverse and the Memorandum/Points and Authorities must be filed in the district court within the time allowed by the scheduling order, or within any additional time to respond that you are granted by request (extension of time).

Supporting Exhibits

You are allowed to file exhibits in support of the Traverse if they are documents already in the state court records. If not, the attorney general will absolutely challenge any "new" exhibits as violating the exhaustion rules. If you want to include any "new" exhibits that are not in the state record, be sure to seek "leave" from the court to do so before you include them.

You will also need to explain to the court why they were not submitted in the state court proceedings, and how they rebut specific contentions relied upon by the attorney general. One very effective "trick" I've been successful with is to argue that the "new" exhibits are "rebuttals" of a point/argument that has been raised by the attorney general for the first time in the federal court. This works because usually, if you are sharp enough to catch it, the attorney general will, in fact, introduce an argument that is outside of the record.

Basically, the Traverse is your chance to let the court know, in a concise and direct way, what your response is to the state's Answer, contentions, and argument. I recommend that you simply use the state's Answer to respond by following the numbers in order and responding in order. For example, if the state addresses something in paragraph 1, then you should also respond to that something in paragraph 1.

I call it "tit-for-tat" responding, as I was trained.

You should not be afraid to agree with the state on anything that does not actually hurt you, such as if the attorney general says that you have exhausted your state remedies. You should respond in your Traverse that, "Agreed, the claims are exhausted."

Simple, right?

It really is at this stage.

On the other hand, if the attorney general makes a claim that you flat-out dispute, then do not hesitate to say so. You will not get another opportunity to do so. This is important where the attorney general agrees that you are in custody but denies that your custody is unlawful. There, you should respond that, "I agree as to custody, but that my confinement is unlawful and unconstitutional."

If the attorney general says you have failed to show that the state court's findings of fact of law were unreasonable, then say, "Petitioner has shown that the state court unreasonably found the facts, and unreasonably applied U.S. Supreme Court law in denying Petitioner's state habeas corpus claims."

Basically, what I am saying is to address every allegation used against you. And to do so in a fashion that refutes the state.

Memorandum/Points and Authorities Supporting Traverse

This is the most important document you will file next to the petition itself because it effectively proves your entire cause for obtaining relief. Thus, it must be done properly and effectively.

Typically, the attorney general's Answer will include:

(1) Statement of the Case: This provides a chronology of the history of the case from trial through direct appeal, state habeas corpus, and federal habeas corpus;
(2) Statement of Facts: This is a summary of the trial evidence that supports the verdict
(3) Argument: This section applies facts and law to have your whole petition thrown out and denied.

Here, I will give you some advice on how to compose your Points and Authorities Supporting Traverse.

Statement of the Case

Here, you will essentially create your own "Statement of the Case" while connecting it to any errors in the state's Answer. It is likely that the state will begin by citing dates, times, and events in the history of the case, starting with the indictment and leading through trial, verdict, and proceedings on direct appeal and state habeas corpus.

Though the state will likely relay all of these facts pretty correctly, they will, without doubt, downplay and deemphasize events that you want to point out to the court. If the state makes any errors, you need to point them out and correct them. To save time, if the state's account is accurate, you can simply admit that the state's version is, in fact, accurate, and the court can adopt it.

Statement of Facts

The attorney general's Statement of Facts will likely be only the facts from the trial of the case that support the case and conviction. Most likely, they will simply "copy and paste" the written opinion from the court of appeals related to your direct appeal or the state's brief filed in your direct appeal.

Again, these are usually accurate and don't require much disputing. The federal court will accept these facts as true unless they can be shown to be wrong by clear and convincing evidence in the record. You are better served here by arguing the facts in your Habeas Corpus Petition's Statement of Facts and not the facts from the trial record. The attorney general usually ignores this in its own Statement of Facts. That is beneficial to you.

Argument

First, I advise you to begin this section with a short summary of what you are trying to say, as briefly as possible. Do this so that a busy clerk or judge who is reading the Points and Authorities can get to the point of your petition without reading the entire thing. They will appreciate that.

The next section is the "Standard of Review," which reminds the court of the "recipe" that will assist them in their findings of fact and conclusions of law. The AEDPA places an immense and tough standard to overcome for you, and you can rest assured that the attorney general will pound home the AEDPA in their attempt to have your petition denied.

And so rather than arguing the AEDPA, which a losing fight for you, focus on telling the court that the attorney general has accurately stated the AEDPA, but has overlooked certain principles that favor you. The majority of which (which the attorney general will steer clear of and intentionally avoid) are the following:

- The state court made an unreasonable determination of the facts when it resolved disputed questions of fact against the petitioner (you) without affording you an evidentiary hearing.
- The attorney general can presume that the state court properly found the facts (presumption of correctness), but that presumption can be rebutted by clear and convincing evidence to the contrary.
- In deciding whether the state court has unreasonably applied U.S. Supreme Court law, the federal court, accepting as true the allegations of the petition that are backed up by trial records and/or the habeas record, cannot summarily (without a hearing) deny the petition where the petitioner has established a "prima facie case" for relief. See *Lafler v. Cooper*, 132 S.Ct. 1376 (2012).
- In an ineffective assistance of counsel case, the court cannot assume that trial counsel had a "tactical" reason for anything he didn't do unless there is support in the record for that determination.

After you have addressed the standard comes the "meat" of the Argument section, where you make your main points.

Conclusion

You will finish your argument section by saying this: "Based on the foregoing, this Court should grant an evidentiary hearing as a prelude to granting relief on the petition, and grant whatever other relief is just and proper."

After you have completed the Points and Authorities, go back and complete a Table of Contents and Table of Authorities to place at the front of the filing. The case law should be alphabetical.

Start to finish, the entire Points and Authorities should be no larger than 25 pages, which is a rule in most courts unless you have been granted "leave" to exceed that count. Excessively long arguments are not productive, and in most cases, will actually hurt your cause.

You need to keep reminding the court that the purpose of the Traverse is merely to determine whether an evidentiary hearing is necessary to resolve disputed questions of fact and not decide whether or not to grant relief on the petition. Normally, without an evidentiary hearing, petitions for habeas corpus are unsuccessful in the federal courts. Under the AEDPA, a hearing is *required* if: (1) the petitioner alleges facts which, if true, would entitle him to relief on the habeas corpus; (2) the state court has not, after a full hearing, reliably found the facts, *and* (3) the Petition does not consist solely of conclusionary, unsworn statements unsupported by any proof.

Looking at these requirements in reverse, number three is satisfied as long as the Petition you filed is supported by sworn declarations and/or admissible evidence. Number two is met when the petitioner has requested a hearing in state court, but the Petition was denied without one, which is usually always the case in Texas. Number one is the hardest of the requirements to meet. However, the court must accept as true the facts that the petitioner has alleged. So, where there is any factual dispute needing to be resolved, the court *must* accept the Petitioner's version of the facts and cannot reject them out of hand, no matter what the attorney general says and argues relating to a petitioner being "uncredible."

It is important, that you remind the court that the lower standard is the *only* one the petitioner needs to meet on the Traverse. There are plenty of instances where this can/should be done:

1. When the attorney general cites the "Standard of Review" at the start of the legal argument section of their brief, they will usually stress how hard it is to satisfy the AEDPA requirements but will often skip the entirely forgiving standard that relates to granting evidentiary hearings.
2. In the body of the legal argument section, when the attorney general has argued that you are not "credible," or that witnesses declarations supporting the petition are "not credible." There, you can respond that, "because credibility disputes can only be resolved at an Evidentiary Hearing, the attorney general's arguments attacking the "credibility" of the petition or the supporting witnesses, are, in fact, arguments *against* dismissing the petition."

Remember, in your Conclusion Section you want to be certain to request that the court hold an Evidentiary Hearing and then grant the petition for habeas corpus after that hearing.

Keep in mind when writing your Traverse, that you need to rebut every single argument made by the attorney general against you, as you will not get another opportunity to do so. It's much like the final two minutes of an NFL Football Game when your team is down. If they don't score in that last "opportunity" to do so, they will lose. In comparison, if you don't strike effectively the points and strong arguments of your claims and counter everything the attorney general has said in their Answer/Points and Authorities, you too will lose.

How do you do that?

By presenting the most on-point and favorable case law supporting your claims and attacking those provided by the attorney general against you, by showing that they are either non-applicable to your situation, or no longer "good law."

Objections (Magistrate)

After you have fully established your Traverse and filed it with the court, and after the Evidentiary Hearing (should you get one), the magistrate judge will issue the recommendation to the court, if you have selected that option. As I said previously, most district courts still appoint magistrate judges to handle preliminary findings and to submit recommendations upon those preliminary proceedings, etc.

Assuming then that the magistrate judge recommends dismissal of your petition (which is usually always the case), they will support those recommendations with written findings that are contained in the form of a "Report and Recommendation," also known as "R&R."

In most all instances, the R&R will be written in the form of an actual court decision, which will include procedural history, a short discussion of the applicable law and standards to your claims, the finding of facts and conclusions of law, and a recommended disposition or decision to the petition (dismissal or granting).

The R&R will be accompanied by a "Notice of Report and Recommendation," which will give you the deadline and procedure for filing your own Objections, which must be filed on time, or you will have waived your right to file it.

The district judge is not bound by the magistrate judge's written Findings or Recommendation's and has the authority to reject them based on your objections, though that is extremely rare in *pro se* cases (since pro se writers lack the know how to file a proper list of Objections, usually). And that is my purpose for writing this book.

Don't begin to worry! The formatting for the Objections is not as strict as the requirements for a Memorandum or Brief. Just simply list your objections and your reasons for them. The most important thing to object to are incorrect factual findings of the Magistrate by using the appellate record (habeas record).

You also need to challenge any and all incorrect legal theories and conclusions the Magistrate has gotten wrong, specifically if they have cited the wrong standard (which is common) under the AEDPA.

There aren't any page limits in the Objections but try to keep it brief and to the point, and under 25 pages where possible. Like a bullet, you need only one if it is used correctly and accurately. I therefore encourage you to choose your strongest objection's *first.*

Lastly, it is also common, unfortunately, for the magistrate judge to recommend that a Certificate of Appealability also be denied with your petition. If this happens, you need to fight it aggressively.

The next Chapter tells you how to do that.

Notes:

CHAPTER 7
GETTING A CERTIFICATE OF APPEALABILITY (COA)

After a 2009 Amendment to Rule II, a district judge must issue or deny a Certificate of Appealability (COA) when an order is entered denying the petition for habeas corpus, see 28 U.S.C. § 2253(c) (2). It is common for the district court, prior to issuing an order on the petition, to request that both parties submit their arguments for or against the issuance of a COA. (A COA grants permission for you to appeal to a circuit court).

Because a dismissal of a petition for habeas corpus by a *pro se* litigant is the most likely outcome, unfortunately, I recommend that you anticipate it. File an Application for COA *at the same time* you file your Objections. If that court denies the COA you may not appeal the denial itself, but you may seek a COA from the circuit court of appeals under the Federal Rules of Appellate Procedure, Rule 22. Filing a motion to reconsider a COA denial does not give you more time to appeal, so don't waste your time there.

Again, please don't start to worry and create anxiety for yourself. Most all *pro se* litigants seeking a petition for habeas corpus § 2254 that are or have been denied or dismissed, didn't have the tools and knowledge that you now have with this book. Though I have lost in many an effort on behalf of others, I have also been successful in the United States district courts, as well. Following proper procedure is a must, but that being said, it's the facts that win cases and not just procedure and case law. If your facts are strong and contained in the record, you have a very strong chance for relief.

As I said, there aren't any strict formatting requirements for a COA Application, and there aren't any page restrictions either. But, as I've taught over and over again in my books, keep it short. I'll give you a few recommendations and will also provide an example form at the back of the book for you to follow, along with others.

The first thing you should do is file and serve an original copy of your COA request separately from other pleadings, entitled:

"Petitioner's Application for Certificate of Appealability." Inside of the Application, you should have the following:

- A section entitled: "ISSUE(S) ON WHICH COA IS BEING SOUGHT" (Choose only your strongest claims and forget the rest.)
- A section entitled: "STANDARD OF REVIEW FOR COA" (I recommend the following standard, "A prisoner seeking a COA need only demonstrate a substantial showing of the denial of a constitutional right. A petitioner satisfies this standard by demonstrating that jurists of reason could disagree with the district court's resolution of his constitutional claims or that jurists could conclude the issues presented are adequate to deserve encouragement to proceed further." See *Miller-El v. Cockrell*, 537 U.S. 322 (2003)).
- A section entitled: "ARGUMENT" (Give your reasons why the court should grant a COA. I advise that you incorporate the Objections by reference here that you filed to the magistrate's or court's order. You can also use the arguments you raised in the Traverse.)
- A final section entitled: "CONCLUSION" (I'd advise simply saying: "Based on the foregoing, Petitioner respectfully submits that the Court's findings are subject to debate amongst jurists of

reason; and consequently, that a COA should be granted on one or more of the issues listed.")

Remember, even if the district court denies your COA, you can still proceed if you apply for and obtain a COA from the circuit court of appeals.

The Decision (Ruling)

At the conclusion of any Objections and Recommendations, and after some time has passed usually, the district court will reach a decision/ruling on your petition and your COA. If you are successful in obtaining an evidentiary hearing, the district court will appoint you an attorney to represent you there, and that hearing will proceed under the rules established by the court.

Because, however, the most likely and historically correct outcome of a *pro se* petition for § 2254 habeas corpus relief is a dismissal or denial, you need to be ready to take the steps necessary to obtain a COA. If the district court denies/dismisses your petition, you have 30 days from the "date of entry" (the date the Judgment is filed), to file a Notice of Appeal with the district court. (I will include an example at the end of this book.) This 30 day is applicable even if the district court has denied your COA or has not even ruled on the COA request yet.

Notice of Appeal

When you file your Notice of Appeal with the district court, you must either pay the filing fee or file to proceed *In forma pauperis* (as a poor person). The Notice of Appeal is a very simple filing that usually consists of only a single page.

This step is extremely important but does not provide you permission under AEDPA to file a brief for the appeal. You first have to apply for, and actually obtain, a COA. If you fail to file a Notice of Appeal on time, you will have waived your ability to do so.

U.S. Court of Appeals (Circuit Court)

In most cases you have 30 days from the date of your denial or dismissal to apply for a COA from the court of appeals. The actual procedure for doing this is different in each circuit, so you need to check with your appropriate circuit in writing for their rules. You can easily get more time by simply filing a Motion for Extension of Time in the circuit court before your time runs out. A simple letter in most cases, in place of a motion, will work just fine.

Here, when seeking a COA, you will use the exact same format as you used in the district court, with a few modifications. Such as:

- Title the document: "Motion for Certificate of Appealability and Statement of Reasons Why a Certificate Should Issue."
- File the original and one additional copy with the court of appeals (unless you've sought leave to exclude copies, since prisoners have no access to copy machines). Also serve a copy on the attorney general (unless again, you have been given permission to not do this, where the court of appeals will do so on your behalf).
- Include an introductory section since the court of appeals will not know anything about you or your case, entitled: "STATEMENT OF THE CASE," where you provide a step-by-step account of the steps leading up to your appeal for a COA.

Your COA application to the court of appeals will likely not face any fight from the attorney general, and the circuit court will rule without it. And so, state only the facts that are favorable to you.

Congratulations (If Your COA Was Granted)

In the rare event that the circuit court of appeals grants your COA, your case will then proceed under the court's briefing schedule. Importantly, if you can afford an attorney to represent you at this stage, you should immediately request one. Where granted, you will be appointed an attorney from a qualified panel of attorneys who specialize in this area.

You can either file a motion for appointment of counsel, or simply write the circuit court of appeals and request one. The circuit courts are obligated to construe anything you file or write in the most liberal light favoring you. And they usually do.

Do Not Give Up (If Your COA Was Denied)

In the usual event that your COA was denied by the circuit court of appeals, it means that both the district court and the circuit court have decided that your case is weak or unworthy and incapable of winning on appeal. You now have two choices:

1. Give up, and accept your situation; or
2. Keep fighting.

If you are guilty, the answer is quite simple: You shouldn't continue to bog down the system with frivolous and non-meritorious writs and pleadings, which makes it all that much harder for everyone else.

If, you are innocent or unjustly punished, the answer is also simple: *You keep on fighting!*

Rehearing

After losing in the circuit court, you have the right to seek a rehearing there, on the basis that the court reached its decision on the basis of some "mistake" of facts or laws when it made its decision.

To do this, you file a "Petition for Rehearing" within 14 days of the circuit court's judgment denying your COA. See Rule 40, Fed. R. App. Proc. There isn't any penalty for applying for a rehearing, so don't be afraid of anything. And, if the circuit court again denies your motion for rehearing … keep fighting!

Rehearing En Banc

Every circuit court of appeals is made up from several panels that have three judges. Every circuit court allows you, after losing before the panel in your case, to ask the circuit court to essentially rehear your case "en banc," or by all of the judges in the court.

This is done by filing a "Petition for Rehearing En Banc," where you tell the circuit court why your case should be one of the very few to be reheard *en banc*, since most are not. You must file your Petition for Rehearing En Banc within 14 days of the date of the circuit court's denial of your COA, unless you receive an extension of time.

Most circuit courts require that you provide 50 copies of your brief, so you will want to attempt to get the circuit court to waive or suspend that requirement, obviously, and unless you have a copy machine in your prison cell (I'm joking).

The Hail Mary (Writ of Certiorari)

If you have lost your bid in the circuit court of appeals to obtain a COA, you are left with the proverbial "Hail Mary" in all legal matters and proceedings: A Petition for Writ of Certiorari to the United States Supreme Court.

You have only 90 days after the circuit court of appeals issues a judgment affirming the district court's findings dismissing your habeas corpus to file the Petition for Writ of Certiorari. And, even if you didn't file for rehearing or rehearing *en banc*, you can still file the Writ of Certiorari.

I won't lie to you; the chances of succeeding here are pretty much nonexistent, since the Supreme Court of the United States (SCOTUS) only takes 100 cases per year, out of more than 10,000 requests for "Cert." Mathematically, that's less than a 1% chance of success. So it is 99% likely that the SCOTUS will simply deny your petition.

But if you've got the "balls" I commend you and encourage you to try, because there is still a chance! And you could be one of the few.

This brings me to the cost of the petition: $350. Before you freak out, you can get around that fee by filing an application to proceed *In forma pauperis* with the Supreme Court, if you in fact are indigent.

If you routinely have money deposited to your prison account, which you will be required to show a copy of when proceeding *In forma pauperis*, totaling more than $1,000 per year, your application will be denied by the SCOTUS.

The easiest way, which isn't easy at all, is to write to the Supreme Court and request their indigent booklet for a Writ of Certiorari. In my experience, however, it is far better than the traditional format. When you request the booklet, everything will come inside of it, to include the application for *In forma pauperis*.

As for the petition itself, it consists of the following:

- Reasons for Granting the Petition (Main section, where you explain the reason, your petition should be granted)
- Cover Sheet
- Questions presented
- List of Parties
- Table of Contents
- Index of Appendices
- Table of Authorities
- Opinions Below
- Jurisdictional Statement
- Statutory and Constitutional Provisions Involved
- Argument Summary
- Statement of the Case
- Statement of Pertinent Facts

- Reason for Granting Review
- Conclusion.

All of this is provided for and explained in the booklet you will request from the SCOTUS in writing called, "Guide for Prospective Indigent Petitioners for Writs of Certiorari." I will include the booklet at the end of this book, for your review, but have chosen not to "fill it out" since doing so would only serve to confuse. The contents of every Writ of Cert. are completely different.

What I will tell you, and the most important thing to remember, is that the United States Supreme Court does not care about your case individually. If you hope to succeed here, you must show the Supreme Court why the decision in your particular case is erroneous, and also how it affects the entire country. You can attempt to do this by showing that the decisions from another appellate circuit, or the Supreme Court itself, conflict with those in your case; that the issues in your case have consequences on everyone and not just you personally.

While you are waiting, you will want to start gathering the following documents you will need for the Writ of Certiorari:

- Direct Appeal Brief, and Opinion
- State Habeas Corpus Brief and Opinion
- Federal Habeas Corpus Brief and Opinion
- Circuit Court of Appeals Judgment and etc.

Now What?

I'm not going to sugarcoat it, if you have filed and lost in the Supreme Court it is checkmate. You are going to have to find some amount of peace in your situation and focus on making parole if that is an option for you.

Of course, you could always keep investigating and digging for a gold nugget of previously hidden evidence, DNA retesting or other, that prove you are innocent, or the Supreme Court could hand down a future decision that applies to you. I've also seen where an inmate received permission to file a subsequent state habeas based on a recantation by an expert witness (I filed that subsequent request and habeas corpus after having written it).

One thing is for sure: innocent people never give up and never stop fighting. Myself, more than most, advise you to continue to dig, investigate, educate yourself, and *fight*.

Notes:

CHAPTER 8

DEALING WITH DETAINERS AND EXTRADITION

More and more often, I am receiving letters and questions from inmates who are pressed with detainers and extradition issues. Since 90% of all inmates will be eligible for parole at some point, and both of these issues will prevent that, I have chosen to address them in this book.

Once a detainer is placed against you, release will only be to the custody of the agency holding the detainer. This can happen either during the current imprisonment or after. The Prison Records Office as well as the warden can access and determine if you have any detainers lodged against you. If it is possible that you have one (or more), I suggest that you get on top of them immediately. If not:

- You might lose the ability to have any future sentences related to the detainer run concurrently with the time you are now serving. See *Smith v. Hooey*, 393 U.S. at 379
- You might drive yourself crazy due to the added stress and anxiety associated with the detainer. See *Strunk v. United States*, 412 U.S. 434, 439, 37 L. Ed. 2d 56, 93 S. Ct. 2260 (1973).
- You may receive a higher prison security classification level due to the detainer and lose any trustee status you may be currently enjoying, etc.

The fastest way to deal with detainers and extradition is to start writing letters and filing motions in the court. To learn more about these topics, you should read the "Interstate Agreement on Detainers (IADA) and "The Uniform Criminal Extradition Act" (UCEA).

That being said, there are numerous ways to deal with these detainers, depending on the circumstances related to them. If the detainer is based on a probation violation or parole revocation, you will be best served by writing a letter seeking reinstatement of the probation, supervision, or parole you are accused of having violated. Another angle would be to agree to the revocation of the parole or probation and have its court ordered to run concurrent with your current term of incarceration. This is usually what happens in most cases.

If you are serving a long-time prison sentence, or have been in prison a long time already, and don't care about trustee status, you can simply ignore the detainer for a while. Then, later, file a motion to have it dismissed for failure to prosecute under the law.

If the pending detainer will likely result in you receiving a far greater prison term than you are currently serving, it is probably in your best interest to immediately file a motion requesting that an attorney be appointed to represent you.

I will now provide you with the correct method and forms to accomplish whatever avenue is best for your situation. Please consult the following inserts, "Interstate Agreement on Detainers Act" (IADA) and the "Uniform Criminal Extradition Act" (UCEA), and then evaluate the subsequent forms and modify whatever you need to fit your case.

Notes:

Interstate Agreement on Detainers Act

Pub. L. 91–538, Dec. 9, 1970, 84 Stat. 1397, as amended by Pub. L. 100–690, title VII, §7059, Nov. 18, 1988, 102 Stat. 4403

§ 1. Short title

This Act may be cited as the ''Interstate Agreement on Detainers Act.'' (Pub. L. 91–538, §1, Dec. 9, 1970, 84 Stat. 1397.)

§ 2. Enactment into law of Interstate Agreement on Detainers

The Interstate Agreement on Detainers is hereby enacted into law and entered into by the United States on its own behalf and on behalf of the District of Columbia with all jurisdictions legally joining in substantially the following form: ''The contracting States solemnly agree that:

Article I

"The party States find that charges outstanding against a prisoner, detainers based on untried indictments, information, or complaints and difficulties in securing speedy trial of persons already incarcerated in other jurisdictions, produce uncertainties which obstruct programs of prisoner treatment and rehabilitation. Accordingly, it is the policy of the party States and the purpose of this agreement to encourage the expeditious and orderly disposition of such charges and determination of the proper status of any and all detainers based on untried indictments, information, or complaints. The party States also find that proceedings with reference to such charges and detainers, when emanating from another jurisdiction, cannot properly be had in the absence of cooperative procedures. It is the further purpose of this agreement to provide such cooperative procedures.

Article II

''As used in this agreement:

(a) "'State' shall mean a State of the United States; the United States of America; a territory or possession of the United States; the District of Columbia; the Commonwealth of Puerto Rico.
(b) "'Sending State' shall mean a State in which a prisoner is incarcerated at the time that he initiates a request for final disposition pursuant to article III hereof or at the time that a request for custody or availability is initiated pursuant to article IV hereof.
(c) "'Receiving State' shall mean the State in which trial is to be had on an indictment, information, or complaint pursuant to article III or article IV hereof.

Article III

(a) "Whenever a person has entered upon a term of imprisonment in a penal or correctional institution of a party State, and whenever during the continuance of the term of imprisonment there is pending in any other party State any untried indictment, information, or complaint on the basis of which a detainer has been lodged against the prisoner, he shall be brought to trial within one hundred and eighty days after he shall have caused to be delivered to the prosecuting officer and the appropriate court of the prosecuting officer's jurisdiction written notice of the place of his imprisonment and his request for a final disposition to be made of the indictment, information, or complaint: Provided, That, for good cause shown in open court, the prisoner or his counsel being present, the court having jurisdiction of the matter may grant any necessary or reasonable continuance. The request of the prisoner shall be accompanied by a certificate of the appropriate official having custody of the prisoner, stating the term of commitment under which the prisoner is being held, the time already served, the time remaining to be served on the sentence, the amount of good time earned, the time of parole eligibility of the prisoner, and any decision of the State parole agency relating to the prisoner.

(b) "The written notice and request for final disposition referred to in paragraph (a) hereof shall be given or sent by the prisoner to the warden, commissioner of corrections, or other official having custody of him, who shall promptly forward it together with the certificate to the appropriate prosecuting official and court by registered or certified mail, return receipt requested.

(c) "The warden, commissioner of corrections, or other official having custody of the prisoner shall promptly inform him of the source and contents of any detainer lodged against him and shall also inform him of his right to make a request for final disposition of the indictment, information, or complaint on which the detainer is based.

(d) "Any request for final disposition made by a prisoner pursuant to paragraph (a) hereof shall operate as a request for final disposition of all untried indictments, information, or complaints on the basis of which detainers have been lodged against the prisoner from the State to whose prosecuting official the request for final disposition is specifically directed. The warden, commissioner of corrections, or other official having custody of the prisoner shall forthwith notify all appropriate prosecuting officers and courts in the several jurisdictions within the State to which the prisoner's request for final disposition is being sent of the proceeding being initiated by the prisoner. Any notification sent pursuant to this paragraph shall be accompanied by copies of the prisoner's written notice, request, and the certificate. If trial is not had on any indictment, information, or complaint contemplated hereby prior to the return of the prisoner to the original place of imprisonment, such indictment, information, or complaint shall not be of any further force or effect, and the court shall enter an order dismissing the same with prejudice.

(e) "Any request for final disposition made by a prisoner pursuant to paragraph (a) hereof shall also be deemed to be a waiver of extradition with respect to any charge or proceeding contemplated thereby or included therein by reason of paragraph (d) hereof, and a waiver of extradition to the receiving State to serve any sentence there imposed upon him, after completion of his term of imprisonment in the sending State. The request for final disposition shall also constitute a consent by the prisoner to the production of his body in any court where his presence may be required in order to effectuate the purposes of this agreement and a further consent voluntarily to be returned to the original place of imprisonment in accordance with the provisions of this agreement. Nothing in this paragraph shall prevent the imposition of a concurrent sentence if otherwise permitted by law.

(f) "Escape from custody by the prisoner subsequent to his execution of the request for final disposition referred to in paragraph (a) hereof shall void the request.

Article IV

(a) "The appropriate officer of the jurisdiction in which an untried indictment, information, or complaint is pending shall be entitled to have a prisoner against whom he has lodged a detainer and who is serving a term of imprisonment in any party State made available in accordance with article V(a) hereof upon presentation of a written request for temporary custody or availability to the appropriate authorities of the State in which the prisoner is incarcerated: Provided, That the court having jurisdiction of such indictment, information, or complaint shall have duly approved, recorded, and transmitted the request: And provided further, That there shall be a period of thirty days after receipt by the appropriate authorities before the request be honored, within which period the Governor of the sending State may disapprove the request for temporary custody or availability, either upon his own motion or upon motion of the prisoner.

(b) "Upon request of the officer's written request as provided in paragraph (a) hereof, the appropriate authorities having the prisoner in custody shall furnish the officer with a certificate stating the term of commitment under which the prisoner is being held, the time already served, the time remaining to be served on the sentence, the amount of good time earned, the time of parole eligibility of the prisoner, and any decisions of the State parole agency relating to the prisoner. Said authorities simultaneously shall furnish all other officers and appropriate courts in the receiving State who has lodged detainers against the prisoner with similar certificates and with notices informing them of the request for custody or availability and of the reasons therefor.

(c) "In respect of any proceeding made possible by this article, trial shall be commenced within one hundred and twenty days of the arrival of the prisoner in the receiving State, but for good cause shown in open court, the prisoner or his counsel being present, the court having jurisdiction of the matter may grant any necessary or reasonable continuance.

(d) "Nothing contained in this article shall be construed to deprive any prisoner of any right which he may have to contest the legality of his delivery as provided in paragraph (a) hereof, but such delivery may not be opposed or denied on the ground that the executive authority of the sending State has not affirmatively consented to or ordered such delivery.

(e) "If trial is not had on any indictment, information, or complaint contemplated hereby prior to the prisoner's being returned to the original place of imprisonment pursuant to article V(e) hereof, such indictment, information, or complaint shall not be of any further force or effect, and the court shall enter an order dismissing the same with prejudice.

Article V

(a) "In response to a request made under article III or article IV hereof, the appropriate authority in a sending State shall offer to deliver temporary custody of such prisoner to the appropriate authority in the State where such indictment, information, or complaint is pending against such person in order that speedy and efficient prosecution may be had. If the request for final disposition is made by the prisoner, the offer of temporary custody shall accompany the written notice provided for in article III of this agreement. In the case of a Federal prisoner, the appropriate authority in the receiving State shall be entitled to temporary custody as provided by this agreement or to the prisoner's presence in Federal custody at the place of trial, whichever custodial arrangement may be approved by the custodian.

(b) "The officer or other representative of a State accepting an offer of temporary custody shall present the following upon demand:

   (1) "Proper identification and evidence of his authority to act for the State into whose temporary custody this prisoner is to be given.

   (2) "A duly certified copy of the indictment, information, or complaint on the basis of which the detainer has been lodged and on the basis of which the request for temporary custody of the prisoner has been made.

(c) "If the appropriate authority shall refuse or fail to accept temporary custody of said person, or in the event that an action on the indictment, information, or complaint on the basis of which the detainer has been lodged is not brought to trial within the period provided in article III or article IV hereof, the appropriate court of the jurisdiction where the indictment, information, or complaint has been pending shall enter an order dismissing the same with prejudice, and any detainer based thereon shall cease to be of any force or effect.

(d) "The temporary custody referred to in this agreement shall be only for the purpose of permitting prosecution on the charge or charges contained in one or more untried indictments, information, or complaints which form the basis of the detainer or detainers or for prosecution on any other charge or charges arising out of the same transaction. Except for his attendance at court and while being transported to or from any place at which his presence may be required, the prisoner shall be held in a suitable jail or other facility regularly used for persons awaiting prosecution.

(e) "At the earliest practicable time consonant with the purposes of this agreement, the prisoner shall be returned to the sending State.

(f) "During the continuance of temporary custody or while the prisoner is otherwise being made available for trial as required by this agreement, time being served on the sentence shall continue to run but good time shall be earned by the prisoner only if, and to the extent that, the law and practice of the jurisdiction which imposed the sentence may allow.

(g) "For all purposes other than that for which temporary custody as provided in this agreement is exercised, the prisoner shall be deemed to remain in the custody of and subject to the jurisdiction of the sending State and any escape from temporary custody may be dealt with in the same manner as an escape from the original place of imprisonment or in any other manner permitted by law.

(h) "From the time that a party State receives custody of a prisoner pursuant to this agreement until such prisoner is returned to the territory and custody of the sending State, the State in which the one or more untried indictments, information, or complaints are pending or in which trial is being had shall be responsible for the prisoner and shall also pay all costs of transporting, caring for, keeping, and returning the prisoner. The provisions of this paragraph shall govern unless the States concerned shall have entered into a supplementary agreement providing for a different allocation of costs and responsibilities as between or among themselves. Nothing herein contained shall be construed to alter or affect any internal relationship among the departments, agencies, and officers of and in the government of a party State, or between a party State and its subdivisions, as to the payment of costs, or responsibilities therefor.

Article VI

(a) "In determining the duration and expiration dates of the time periods provided in articles III and IV of this agreement, the running of said time periods shall be tolled whenever and for as long as the prisoner is unable to stand trial, as determined by the court having jurisdiction of the matter.

(b) "No provision of this agreement, and no remedy made available by this agreement shall apply to any person who is adjudged to be mentally ill.

Article VII

"Each State party to this agreement shall designate an officer who, acting jointly with like officers of other party States, shall promulgate rules and regulations to carry out more effectively the terms and provisions of this agreement, and who shall provide, within and without the State, information necessary to the effective operation of this agreement.

Article VIII

"This agreement shall enter into full force and effect as to a party State when such State has enacted the same into law. A State party to this agreement may withdraw here from by enacting a statute repealing the same. However, the withdrawal of any State shall not affect the status of any proceedings already initiated by inmates or by State officers at the time such withdrawal takes effect, nor shall it affect their rights in respect thereof.

Article IX

''This agreement shall be liberally construed so as to effectuate its purposes. The provisions of this agreement shall be severable and if any phrase, clause, sentence, or provision of this agreement is declared to be contrary to the constitution of any party State or of the United States or the applicability thereof to any government, agency, person, or circumstance is held invalid, the validity of the remainder of this agreement and the applicability thereof to any government, agency, person, or circumstance shall not be affected thereby. If this agreement shall be held contrary to the constitution of any State party hereto, the agreement shall remain in full force and effect as to the remaining States and in full force and effect as to the State affected as to all severable matters.'' (Pub. L. 91–538, §2, Dec. 9, 1970, 84 Stat. 1397.)

§ 3. Definition of term "Governor" for purposes of United States and District of Columbia

The term ''Governor'' as used in the agreement on detainers shall mean with respect to the United States, the Attorney General, and with respect to the District of Columbia, the Mayor of the District of Columbia. (Pub. L. 91–538, §3, Dec. 9, 1970, 84 Stat. 1402.)

Transfer of Functions

''Mayor of the District of Columbia'' substituted in text for ''Commissioner of the District of Columbia'' pursuant to section 421 of Pub. L. 93–198. Office of Commissioner of District of Columbia, as established by Reorg. Plan No. 3, of 1967, abolished as of noon Jan. 2, 1975, by Pub. L. 93–198, title VII, §711, Dec. 24, 1973, 87 Stat. 818, and replaced by Office of Mayor of District of Columbia by section 421 of Pub. L. 93–198.

§ 4. Definition of term "appropriate court"

The term ''appropriate court'' as used in the agreement on detainers shall mean with respect to the United States, the courts of the United States, and with respect to the District of Columbia, the courts of the District of Columbia, in which indictments, information, or complaints, for which disposition is sought, are pending. (Pub. L. 91–538, §4, Dec. 9, 1970, 84 Stat. 1402.)

§ 5. Enforcement and cooperation by courts, departments, agencies, officers, and employees of United States and District of Columbia

All courts, departments, agencies, officers, and employees of the United States and of the District of Columbia are hereby directed to enforce the agreement on detainers and to cooperate with one another and with all party States in enforcing the agreement and effectuating its purpose. (Pub. L. 91–538, §5, Dec. 9, 1970, 84 Stat. 1402.)

§ 6. Regulations, forms, and instructions

For the United States, the Attorney General, and for the District of Columbia, the Mayor of the District of Columbia, shall establish such regulations, prescribe such forms, issue such instructions, and perform such other acts as he deems necessary for carrying out the provisions of this Act. (Pub. L. 91–538, §6,

Dec. 9, 1970, 84 Stat. 1403.) TRANSFER OF FUNCTIONS ''Mayor of the District of Columbia'' substituted in text for ''Commissioner of the District of Columbia'' pursuant to section 421 of Pub. L. 93–198. Office of Commissioner of District of Columbia, as established by Reorg. Plan No. 3 of 1967, abolished as of noon Jan. 2, 1975, by Pub. L. 93–198, title VII, §711, Dec. 24, 1973, 87 Stat. 818, and replaced by Office of Mayor of District of Columbia by section 421 of Pub. L. 93–198.

§ 7. Reservation of right to alter, amend, or repeal

The right to alter, amend, or repeal this Act is expressly reserved. (Pub. L. 91–538, §7, Dec. 9, 1970, 84 Stat. 1403.)

§ 8. Effective Date

This Act shall take effect on the ninetieth day after the date of its enactment. (Pub. L. 91–538, §8, Dec. 9, 1970, 84 Stat. 1403.)

References in Text

The date of its enactment, referred to in text, means Dec. 9, 1970.

§ 9. Special Provisions when United States is a Receiving State

Notwithstanding any provision of the agreement on detainers to the contrary, in a case in which the United States is a receiving State – (1) any order of a court dismissing any indictment, information, or complaint may be with or without prejudice. In determining whether to dismiss the case with or without prejudice, the court shall consider, among others, each of the following factors: The seriousness of the offense; the facts and circumstances of the case which led to the dismissal; and the impact of a reprosecution on the administration of the agreement on detainers and on the administration of justice; and (2) it shall not be a violation of the agreement on detainers if prior to trial the prisoner is returned to the custody of the sending State pursuant to an order of the appropriate court issued after reasonable notice to the prisoner and the United States and an opportunity for a hearing. (Pub. L. 91–538, §9, as added Pub. L. 100–690, title VII, §7059, Nov. 18, 1988, 102 Stat. 4403.)

Uniform Criminal Extradition Act

1) Where appearing in this section, the term "governor" includes any person performing the functions of governor by authority of the law of this state. The term "executive authority" includes the governor and any person performing the functions of governor in a state other than this state. The term "state", referring to a state other than this state, refers to any other state or territory, organized or unorganized, of the United States of America.
2) Subject to the qualifications of this section and the provisions of the Constitution of the United States controlling, and acts of congress in pursuance thereof, it is the duty of the governor of this state to have arrested and delivered up to the executive authority of any other state of the United States any person charged in that state with treason, a felony, or other crime who has filed from justice and is found in this state.
3) No demand for the extradition of a person charged with crime in another state shall be recognized by the governor unless in writing and accompanied by a copy of an indictment found or by an information supported by affidavit in the state having jurisdiction of the crime, or by a copy of an affidavit made before a magistrate there, together with a copy of any warrant which was issued thereon. The indictment, information, or affidavit made before the magistrate must substantially charge the person demanded with having committed a crime under the law of that state; and the copy must be authenticated by the executive authority making the demand, which shall be prima facie evidence of its truth.
4) When a demand shall be made upon the governor of this state by the executive authority of another state for the surrender of a person so charged with crime, the governor may call upon the attorney general or any prosecuting officer in this state to investigate or assist in investigating the demand, and to report to him the situation and circumstances of the person so demanded, and whether he ought to be surrendered.
5) A warrant of extradition shall not be issued unless the documents presented by the executive authority making the demand show that:
   a) except in cases arising under subsection 7 of this section, the accused was present in the demanding state at the time of the commission of the alleged crime, and thereafter filed from the state;
   b) the accused is now in this state; and
   c) he is lawfully charged by indictment found or by information filed by a prosecuting officer and supported by affidavit to the facts, or by affidavit made before a magistrate in that state, with having committed a crime under the laws of that state, or that he has been convicted of a crime in that state and has escaped from confinement or has broken the terms of his bail, probation, or parole, or that the sentence or some portion of it otherwise remains unexecuted and that the person claimed has not been discharged or otherwise released from the sentence.
6) When it is desired to have returned to this state a person charged in this state with a crime, and such person is imprisoned or is held under criminal proceedings then pending against him in another state, the governor of this state may agree with the executive authority of such other state for the extradition of such person before the conclusion of such proceedings or his term of sentence in such other state, upon condition that such person be returned to such other state at the expense of this state as soon as the prosecution in this state is terminated. The governor of this state may also surrender on demand of the executive authority of any other state any person in this state who is charged in the manner provided in subsection 24 of this section with having violated the laws of the state whose executive authority is making the demand, even though such person left the demanding state involuntarily.
7) The governor of this state may also surrender, on demand of the executive authority of any other

state, any person in this state charged in such other state in the manner provided in subsection 5 of this section with committing an act in this state, or in a third state, intentionally resulting in a crime in the state whose executive authority is making the demand; and the provisions of this section not otherwise inconsistent shall apply to such cases, notwithstanding that the accused was not in that state at the time of the commission of the crime and has not filed therefrom.

8) If the governor shall decide that the demand should be complied with, he shall sign a warrant of arrest, which shall be sealed with the state seal, and be directed to a sheriff, marshal, coroner, or other person whom he may think fit to entrust with the execution thereof; and the warrant must substantially recite the facts necessary to the validity of its issue.
9) Such warrant shall authorize the officer or other person to whom directed to arrest the accused at any place where he may be found within the state, to command the aid of all sheriffs and law enforcement officers in the execution of the warrant, and to deliver the accused subject to the provision of this section, to the duly authorized agent of the demanding state.
10) Every such officer or other person empowered to make the arrest shall have the same authority in arresting the accused to command assistance therein, as sheriffs and other officers have by law in the execution of any criminal process directed to them, with the like penalties against those who refuse their assistance.
11) No person arrested upon such warrant shall be delivered over to the agent whom the executive authority demanding him shall have appointed to receive him unless he has been informed of the demand made for his surrender, of the crime with which he is charged and that he has the right to demand legal counsel; and if the prisoner, his friends, or counsel shall state that he or they desire to test the legality of the arrest, the prisoner shall be taken forthwith before a judge of a court of record in this state who shall fix a reasonable time to be allowed him within which to apply for a writ of habeas corpus. And when such writ is applied for, notice thereof, and of the time and place of hearing thereon, shall be given to the public prosecuting officer of the county in which the arrest is made and in which the accused is in custody and to the said agent of the demanding state.
12) An officer who recklessly delivers to the agent for extradition of the demanding state a person in his custody under the governor's warrant in disobedience to subsection 11 of this section commits a Class B misdemeanor.
13) The officer or person executing the governor's warrant of arrest, or the agent of the demanding state to whom the prisoner may have been delivered, may, when necessary, confine the prisoner in the jail of any county or city through which he may pass; and the keeper of such jail must receive and safely keep the prisoner until the person having charge of him is ready to proceed on his route, such person being chargeable with the expense of keeping.
14) Whenever any person within this state shall be charged on the oath of any credible person before any judge of this state with the commission of a crime in any other state, and, except in cases arising under subsection 7 of this section, with having filed from justice, or whenever complaint shall have been made before any judge in this state setting forth on the affidavit of any credible person in another state that a treason or felony has been committed in such other state and that the accused has been charged in such state with the commission of the treason or felony, and, except in cases arising under subsection 7 of this section, has filed therefrom and is believed to have been found in this state, the judge shall issue a warrant directed to the sheriff of the county in which the oath or complaint is filed directing him to apprehend the person charged, wherever he may be found in this state, and bring him before the same or any other judge, who may be convenient of access to the place where the arrest may be made, to answer the charge or complaint and affidavit. A certified copy of the sworn charge or complaint and affidavit upon which the warrant is issued shall be

attached to the warrant.

15) The arrest of a person may be lawfully made also by an officer or a private citizen without a warrant upon reasonable information that the accused stands charged in the courts of another state with a crime punishable by death or imprisonment for a term exceeding one (1) year; but when so arrested the accused must be taken before a judge with all practicable speed, and complaint must be made against him under oath setting forth the ground for the arrest as in the last preceding subsection; and thereafter his answer shall be heard as if he has been arrested on warrant.
16) If from the examination before the judge, it appears that the person held is the person charged with having committed the crime alleged and that he probably committed the crime, and, except in cases arising under subsection 7 of this section, that he has filed from justice, the judge shall commit him to jail by a warrant reciting the accusation for such time specified in the warrant as will enable the arrest of the accused to be made under a warrant of the governor on a requisition of the executive authority of the state having jurisdiction of the offense, unless the accused gives bail as provided in subsection 17 of this section, or until he shall be legally discharged.
17) Unless the offense with which the prisoner is charged is shown to be an offense punishable by death or life imprisonment under the laws of the state in which it was committed, the judge must admit the person arrested to bail by bond or undertaking, with sufficient sureties, and in such sum as he deems proper, for his appearance before him at a time specified in such bond or undertaking, and for his surrender, to be arrested upon the warrant of the governor of this state. The prisoner shall not be admitted to bail after issuance of a warrant by the governor of this state.
18) If the accused is not yet arrested under warrant of the governor by the expiration of the time specified in the warrant, bond, or undertaking, the judge may discharge him or may recommit him to a further day, or may again take bail for his appearance and surrender, as provided in subsection 17 of this section; and at the expiration of the second period of commitment, or if he has been bailed and appeared according to the terms of his bond or undertaking, the judge may either discharge him, or may require him to enter into a new bond or undertaking, to appear and surrender himself at another day.
19) If the prisoner is admitted to bail and fails to appear and surrender himself according to the conditions of his bond, the court, by proper order, shall declare the bond forfeited; and recovery may be had thereon in the name of the state as in the case of other bonds or undertakings given by the accused in criminal proceedings within this state.
20) If a criminal prosecution has been instituted against such person under the laws of this state and is still pending, the governor at his discretion either may surrender him on the demand of the executive authority of another state or may hold him until he has been tried and discharged or convicted and punished in this state.
21) The guilt or innocence of the accused as to the crime of which he is charged may not be inquired into by the governor or in any proceedings after the demand for extradition accompanied by a charge of crime in legal form as above provided shall have been presented to the governor, except as it may be involved in identifying the person held as the person charged with the crime.
22) The governor may recall his warrant of arrest or may issue another warrant whenever he deems proper.
23) Whenever the governor of this state shall demand a person charged with a crime in this state from the chief executive of any other state or from the chief justice or an associate justice of the Supreme Court of the District of Columbia authorized to receive such demand under the laws of the United States, he shall issue a warrant under the seal of this state to some agent commanding him to receive the person so charged if delivered to him and convey him to the proper officer of the county

in this state in which the offense was committed.

24) When the return to this state of a person charged with a crime in this state is required, the prosecuting attorney of the county in which the offense is committed shall present to the governor his written application for a requisition for the return of the person charged, in which application shall be stated the name of the person so charged, the crime charged against him, the approximate time, place, and circumstances of its committal, the state in which he is believed to be, including the location of the accused therein at the time the application is made, and certifying that in the opinion of the said prosecuting attorney the ends of justice require the arrest and return of the accused to this state for trial, and that the proceeding is not instituted to enforce a private claim. The application shall be verified by affidavit, shall be executed in triplicate, and shall be accompanied by three (3) certified copies of the indictment returned, or information and affidavit filed, or of the complaint made to the magistrate, stating the offense with which the accused is charged. The prosecuting attorney may also attach such further affidavits and other documents in triplicate as he shall deem proper to be submitted with such application. One (1) copy of the application with the action of the governor indicated by the endorsement thereon and one (1) of the certified copies of the indictment or complaint or information and affidavit shall be filed in the office of the secretary of state to remain of record in that office. The other copies of all papers shall be forwarded with the governor's requisition.
25) The expenses shall be paid out of the general fund of the county treasury of the county wherein the crime is alleged to have been committed. The expenses shall be the fees paid to the officers of the state on whose governor the requisition is made, as now provided by law, for all necessary travel in returning such prisoner.
26) A person brought into this state on extradition based on a criminal charge shall not be subject to service of personal process in civil actions arising out of the same facts as the criminal proceeding to answer for which he is returned until he has been convicted in the criminal proceeding, or if acquitted, until he has had ample opportunity to return to the state from which he was extradited.
27) After a person has been brought back to this state upon extradition proceedings, he may be tried in this state for other crimes which he may be charged with having committed here, as well as that specified in the requisition for his extradition.
28) This section shall be so interpreted and construed as to effectuate its general purpose to make uniform the law of those states which enact it.
29) Nothing in this section contained shall be deemed to constitute a waiver by the state of its right, power, or privilege to regain custody of such person by extradition proceedings or otherwise for the purpose of trial, sentence, or punishment for any crime committed within this state, nor shall any proceedings had under this section which result in, or fail to result in, extradition be deemed a waiver by this state of any of its rights, privileges, or jurisdiction in any way whatsoever.
30) This section may be cited as the Uniform Criminal Extradition Act.

IC 35-33-10-3

As added by Acts 1981, P.L. 298, SEC.2. Amended by P.L. 178-1984, SEC.1.

Notes:

Inmate Request to Administration

01, January, 2020

Mr. John Doe
Senior Warden
[Address]

Re: Interstate Agreement on Detainers Act Request

Dear Warden Doe:

At this time I am officially requesting to invoke the Interstate Agreement on Detainers Act on the detainer that has been lodged against me from [name the state], through your office or the Records Office.

Your assistance in this matter is required under law, and also greatly appreciated.

Very respectfully,

[Sign here]

[Printed name and number]
[Address]

cc: p/file

Case No. __________

THE STATE OF TEXAS	§	
	§	
vs.	§	IN THE 100th JUDICIAL
	§	DISTRICT COURT OF
[Your Name]________,	§	DALLAS COUNTY, TEXAS
Defendant	§	
	§	

MOTION TO DISMISS FOR FAILURE TO PROSECUTE, VIOLATION OF THE SPEEDY TRIAL AND INTERSTATE AGREEMENT ON DETAINERS ACT

TO THE HONORABLE JUDGE OF SAID COURT:

COMES NOW [Your Name Here], the defendant, *pro se*, and moves this Honorable Court to dismiss the charges due to the state's failure to prosecute, and violation of the speedy trial and interstate agreement on detainers act. In support thereof, the defendant will show this Honorable Court as follows:

1. The County of ______, State of ______, has lodged a detainer against the defendant. See attached copy of the detainer.

2. The defendant has been in custody at ______, since ______ of 20_, and the State of ______, County of ______, has known of the defendant's whereabouts at all times.

3. On ______, 20_, defendant invoked the Interstate Agreement on Detainers Act at the Institution requesting the State of ______, County of ______, to prosecute the instant charges within 180 days. Alternatively, to dismiss the charges in totality. See attached copy of the Interstate Agreement of Detainers Act Request.

A memorandum brief in support of this motion is attached hereto and made part of this motion by reference herein.

Respectfully submitted on this ______ day of ______, 2021.

[Sign Here]

[Printed Name Here]
[Address]
[City, State, Zip Code]

Pro se

Case No. __________

THE STATE OF TEXAS	§	
	§	
	§	IN THE 100th JUDICIAL
vs.	§	DISTRICT COURT OF
	§	DALLAS COUNTY, TEXAS
	§	
[Your Name]________,	§	
Defendant	§	
	§	
	§	

MEMORANDUM IN SUPPORT OF MOTION TO DISMISS FOR FAILURE TO PROSECUTE, VIOLATION OF THE SPEEDY TRIAL AND INTERSTATE AGREEMENT ON DETAINERS ACT

COMES NOW [Your Name], the defendant, *pro se*, and files this memorandum supporting a motion to dismiss for failing to prosecute, violation of the speedy trial and interstate agreement on detainers act. See 18 U.S.C. Appx. Art. V (c).

Having filed the Interstate Agreement on Detainers Act, the State of ______, County of , had 180 days to bring the defendant to trial. See *United States v. Mauro*, 436 U.S. 340, 349-53, 98 S.Ct. 1834, 1841-44, 56 L.Ed. 2d 329 (1978). Once the request is made for trial, the prosecuting jurisdiction must bring the prisoner to trial within 180 days. 18 U.S.C. Appx. Art. III(a). A failure to do so, requires that the indictment against the prisoner be dismissed fully. See *Mauro, supra*.

Further, the prosecuting jurisdiction has a duty to provide to the defendant a speedy trial. See *Dickey v. Florida*, 398 U.S. 30, 37-38, 26 L.Ed.2d 26, 90 S.Ct. 1564 (1970). Indeed, "[T]he possibility that the defendant might receive a sentence at least partially concurrent with the one he is serving may be forever lost if trial of the pending charges is postponed." See *Smith v. Hooey*, 393 U.S. at 378 L.Ed. 607 (1969).

The State of ______, County of ______, has now failed to exercise due diligence in providing the defendant a prompt trial. Therefore, the defendant is entitled to immediate dismissal of the instant charges.

WHEREFORE, premises considered, the defendant respectfully urges this Honorable Court to issue an order to DISMISS the charges.

Respectfully submitted on this ______day of ______, 2021.

[Sign Here]

[Printed Name Here]
[Address]
[City, State, Zip Code]

Pro se

01, January, 2021

100th Judicial District Court Clerk of the Court
[Address]
[City, State, Zip Code]

Re: STATE OF TEXAS *v.*
Case No.

Dear Judge:

This letter is in reference to the above-entitled action. At this time, I hereby request a final disposition related to the pending charges. This case has been pending since ______ of 20_, and the prosecutor has taken no action whatsoever.

Thus, I am respectfully requesting final disposition at the earliest possible date.

Very respectfully,

[Sign Here]
[Print Name Here]
[Address]
[City, State, zip Code]

cc: District Attorney of ______ County

p/file.

Case No. __________

THE STATE OF TEXAS	§	
	§	
vs.	§	IN THE 100th JUDICIAL
	§	DISTRICT COURT OF
[Your Name]________,	§	DALLAS COUNTY, TEXAS
Defendant	§	

MOTION FOR SPEEDY TRIAL

TO THE HONORABLE JUDGE OF SAID COURT:

COMES NOW [Your Name], the defendant, *pro se*, and does respectfully move this Court for a fast and speedy trial pursuant to the Sixth and Fourteenth Amendments of the United States Constitution. In support thereof, defendant will show as follows:

1. The County of ______, State of Texas, has lodged a detainer against the defendant. See attached copy of the detainer.

2. Defendant hereby moves this Court for a fast and speedy trial entitled to him under the law, or alternatively, for the charges to be dismissed.

Respectfully submitted on this ______ day of ______, 2021.

[Sign Here]

[Printed Name Here]
[Address]
[City, State, Zip Code]

Pro Se

Case No. __________

THE STATE OF TEXAS	§	
	§	
	§	IN THE 100th JUDICIAL
vs.	§	DISTRICT COURT OF
	§	DALLAS COUNTY, TEXAS
	§	
[Your Name]________,	§	
Defendant	§	
	§	
	§	

MOTION TO REINSTATE PROBATION

TO THE HONORABLE JUDGE OF SAID COURT:

COMES NOW [Your Name], the defendant, *pro se*, and respectfully moves this Honorable Court to reinstate probation in this cause. The defendant will show this Court as follows:

1. On ______, 20_, this Court sentenced the defendant to: ______ (_) years of probation.

2. On ______, 20_, the State of Texas, County of ______, filed a Motion for revocation of probation for technical violation as follows:

[State the violation(s) here]

3. Defendant has now been in custody since ______ of 20, serving a sentence of ______ years/months. The State of Texas, County of ______ has known of the defendant's location.

4. The defendant respectfully moves this Honorable Court to reinstate probation and provide the opportunity for the defendant to complete his current sentence, as well as the probation related to this cause.

WHEREFORE, based upon the above, defendant respectfully urges this court to issue an order reinstating the probation and dismissing the warrant for arrest thus allowing the chance for defendant to complete the probation as ordered upon his release from custody.

Respectfully submitted on this ______ day of ______, 2021.

[Sign Here]

[Printed Name Here]
[Address]
[City, State, Zip Code]

Pro Se

Case No. __________

THE STATE OF TEXAS vs. [Your Name]________, Defendant	§ § § § § § § § § §	IN THE 100th JUDICIAL DISTRICT COURT OF DALLAS COUNTY, TEXAS

GUILTY PLEA IN ABSENTIA WITH WAIVER OF RIGHTS

TO THE HONORABLE JUDGE OF SAID COURT:

COMES NOW [Your Name], the defendant, *pro se*, and hereby respectfully enters a guilty plea in absentia to: "Failure to yield to right of way."

FACTUAL BASIS FOR PLEA

Defendant asserts the following in support of his plea: "On 3/1/2020, I was driving on Water Street. Upon approaching traffic, I failed to yield to another driver having the right

of way. I was subsequently arrested or issued a citation.

This Court has set the matter for a trial requiring the defendant's presence. Defendant is currently incarcerated at the ______ prison located at ______. Thus, the defendant requests to enter a Guilty Plea in Absentia with a Waiver of Rights to resolve this matter.

WAIVER OF RIGHT TO BE PRESENT

I, ______, hereby make this plea in absentia knowingly, willingly, voluntarily, and intelligently, and do hereby waive my right to be present and to have counsel to be appointed.

SENTENCE RECOMMENDATION

Defendant hereby moves this Honorable Court to impose a jail sentence of ______ to be served concurrently with defendant's current sentence. Alternatively, to impose a fine of $______, and a term of probation not to exceed two years.

WHEREFORE, based on the above, defendant urges this Court to grant this motion and allow the plea in Absentia in order to resolve this matter. As well, to accept the defendant's suggested sentence recommendation.

Respectfully submitted this ______ day of ______, 2021.

[Sign Here]

[Printed Name Here]
[Address]
[City, State, Zip Code]

Pro Se

Case No. __________

THE STATE OF TEXAS	§	
	§	IN THE 100th JUDICIAL
vs.	§	DISTRICT COURT OF
	§	DALLAS COUNTY, TEXAS
[Your Name]________,	§	
Defendant	§	

MOTION FOR APPOINTMENT OF COUNSEL

TO THE HONORABLE JUDGE OF SAID COURT:

COMES NOW [Your Name], defendant, *pro se*, and respectfully urges this Court pursuant to the Sixth and Fourteenth Amendments of the United States Constitution to appoint counsel to now represent him/her in the above-entitled and numbered cause. The defendant will show the Court as follows:

1. The State of Texas has charged defendant with ______ and with ______, and defendant faces a possible ______ term of incarceration or probation if convicted.

2. Defendant is already currently serving a ______ year term of incarceration and housed at . Currently, the State has lodged a detainer against the defendant for the charges.

3. Defendant does not have funds to hire counsel due to being incarcerated and unemployed. Therefore, defendant now requests counsel to be appointed to assist in this matter.

WHEREFORE, based on the above, defendant respectfully urges this Honorable Court to appoint counsel to represent him.

Respectfully submitted on this ______ day of ______, 2021.

[Sign Here]

[Printed Name Here]
[Address]
[City, State, Zip Code]

Pro Se

CHAPTER 9

FREEDOM OF INFORMATION ACT REQUEST

The Freedom of Information Act (FOIA), Title 5, United States Code, section 552, is probably the most overlooked and underestimated tool available to inmates in the post-conviction process.

The purpose of the act is to establish and provide the general philosophy of full disclosure of information, unless it is exempted under clearly delineated statutory language. And, because the act was structured to implore transparency, nearly every document and record held by the requested agency is available to the public, including you.

The Freedom of Information Act allows you a clear path to request documents and records that pertain to you, and if the records and documents are incorrect, *to correct them*. (Records and documents the state probably relied upon to convict and sentence you.)

Most states also have their own version of the Freedom of Information Act, which they tend to use to limit your access to records and documents, as is the case here in Texas. Here, Texas Government Code, Section 552.028(a) (1), provides that, "A government body is not required to accept or comply with a request from an individual for information who is imprisoned or confined in a correctional facility."

Most inmates accept that at face value and give up. That is the worst thing to do, since a further reading of the Section establishes that agencies are not prohibited from providing documents and records upon request by an inmate. In effect, if a state agency denies your request, you can appeal to the federal government for violation of the Freedom of Information Act.

In order to obtain such records and documents upon request to any agency, you must write a request letter to that agency and make a formal request for them. The same is true if you are denied access to the records and documents and have to file an appeal. You can find information about appealing denials by reading 28 CFR Part 16.9 Appeals. The appeals are governed by 5 U.S.C. §§552(a) (4) and 552(a) (6) (C).

When you appeal, you must mail it to: Freedom of Information Act Appeal, Office of Information and Privacy, U.S. Department of Justice, Flag Building, Suite 570, Washington, DC 20530-0001 (for appealing federal agencies only).

State appeals will be handled in the district court and a § 1983, if necessary, thereafter. You can also bring a civil suit under 28 U.S.C. § 1331 and 5 U.S.C. §552(a) (4) (B).

01, January, 2021

Texas Department of Public Safety
111 Main Street
Dallas, TX 75202

Re: Freedom of Information Act Request

Dear Department of Public Safety:

Under the Freedom of Information Act, 5 U.S.C. subsection 552(a), and the Privacy Act, 5 U.S.C. subsection 552(a), I am requesting access to all records related to: _________(State whatever specific records and documents you are seeking).

Pursuant to 5 U.S.C. §552(a) (6) (A) (i), I request that you make a determination regarding the release of this information within the 20-day statutory period.

I also request a fee waiver pursuant to 5 USCS §552(a) (4) (A) (111).

If you deny all or any part of this request, please cite each specific example of exception you think justifies your refusal to release under the law.

Very respectfully,

[Sign Here]
[Printed Name Here]
[Address]
[City, State, Zip Code]

01, January, 2021

Texas Department of Public Safety
111 Main Street
Dallas, TX 75202

Re: Freedom of Information Appeal

To the Administrator:

This in an appeal under the Freedom of Information Act, 5 U.S.C. §552.
On ______, 2021, I made an FOIA request to your agency for information and records related to: (State what you requested) that is in your agency's possession.
On ______, 2021, your agency denied my request because:_____________ (Cite reason given for denial).

The requested material is clearly releasable under the FOIA, and I consider your agency's denial to be arbitrary and greatly capricious.

Upon reconsideration, I expect that you will reverse the decision to deny my request. In the event that you do not grant my appeal, I intend to proceed with a lawsuit to compel your disclosure, which will incur great financial expense on your behalf.

Respectfully,

[Sign Here]
[Printed Name Here]
[Address]
[City, State, Zip Code]

The Freedom of Information Act, 5 U.S.C. § 552

Below is the full text of the Freedom of Information Act as amended by the "FOIA Improvement Act of 2016."

§ 552. Public information; agency rules, opinions, orders, records, and proceedings

(a) Each agency shall make available to the public information as follows:

(1) Each agency shall separately state and currently publish in the Federal Register for the guidance of the public –

(A) descriptions of its central and field organization and the established places at which, the employees (and in the case of a uniformed service, the members) from whom, and the methods whereby, the public may obtain information, make submittals or requests, or obtain decisions;

(B) statements of the general course and method by which its functions are channeled and determined, including the nature and requirements of all formal and informal procedures available;

(C) rules of procedure, descriptions of forms available or the places at which forms may be obtained, and instructions as to the scope and contents of all papers, reports, or examinations;

(D) substantive rules of general applicability adopted as authorized by law, and statements of general policy or interpretations of general applicability formulated and adopted by the agency; and

(E) each amendment, revision, or repeal of the foregoing.

Except to the extent that a person has actual and timely notice of the terms thereof, a person may not in any manner be required to resort to, or be adversely affected by, a matter required to be published in the Federal Register and not so published. For the purpose of this paragraph, matter reasonably available to the class of persons affected thereby is deemed published in the Federal Register when incorporated by reference therein with the approval of the Director of the Federal Register.

(2) Each agency, in accordance with published rules, shall make available for public inspection in an electronic format

(A) final opinions, including concurring and dissenting opinions, as well as orders, made in the adjudication of cases;

(B) those statements of policy and interpretations which have been adopted by the agency and are not published in the Federal Register;

(C) administrative staff manuals and instructions to staff that affect a member of the public;

(D) copies of all records, regardless of form or format –

(i) that have been released to any person under paragraph (3); and

(I) that because of the nature of their subject matter, the agency determines have become or are likely to become the subject of subsequent requests for substantially the same records; or

(II) that have been requested 3 or more times; and

(E) a general index of the records referred to under subparagraph (D);

unless the materials are promptly published, and copies offered for sale. For records created on or after November 1, 1996, within one year after such date, each agency shall make such records available, including by computer telecommunications or, if computer telecommunications means have not been established by the agency, by other electronic means. To the extent required to prevent a clearly unwarranted invasion of personal privacy, an agency may delete identifying details when it makes available or publishes an opinion, statement of policy, interpretation, staff manual, instruction, or copies of records referred to in subparagraph (D). However, in each case the justification for the deletion shall be explained fully in writing, and the extent of such deletion shall be indicated on the portion of the record, which is made available or published, unless including that indication would harm an interest protected by the exemption in subsection (b) under which the deletion is made. If technically feasible, the extent of the deletion shall be indicated at the place in the record where the deletion was made. Each agency shall also maintain and make available for public inspection in an electronic format current indexes providing identifying information for the public as to any matter issued, adopted, or promulgated after July 4, 1967, and required by this paragraph to be made available or published. Each agency shall promptly publish, quarterly or more frequently, and distribute (by sale or otherwise) copies of each index or supplements thereto unless it determines by order published in the Federal Register that the publication would be unnecessary and impracticable, in which case the agency shall nonetheless provide copies of an index on request at a cost not to exceed the direct cost of duplication. Each agency shall make the index referred to in subparagraph (E) available by computer telecommunications by December 31, 1999. A final order, opinion, statement of policy, interpretation, or staff manual or instruction that affects a member of the public may be relied on, used, or cited as precedent by an agency against a party other than an agency only if –

(i) it has been indexed and either made available or published as provided by this paragraph; or

(ii) the party has actual and timely notice of the terms thereof.

(3) (A) Except with respect to the records made available under paragraphs (1) and (2) of this subsection, and except as provided in subparagraph (E), each agency, upon any request for records which (i) reasonably describes such records and (ii) is made in accordance with published rules stating the time, place, fees (if any), and procedures to be followed, shall make the records promptly available to any person.

(B) In making any record available to a person under this paragraph, an agency shall provide the record in any form or format requested by the person if the record is readily reproducible by the agency in that form or format. Each agency shall make reasonable efforts to maintain its records in forms or formats that are reproducible for purposes of this section.

(C) In responding under this paragraph to a request for records, an agency shall make reasonable efforts to search for the records in electronic form or format, except when such efforts would significantly interfere with the operation of the agency's automated information system.

(D) For purposes of this paragraph, the term "search" means to review, manually or by automated means, agency records for the purpose of locating those records which are responsive to a request.

(E) An agency, or part of an agency, that is an element of the intelligence community (as that term is defined in section 3(4) of the National Security Act of 1947 (50 U.S.C. 401a (4))) shall not make any record available under this paragraph to –

(i) any government entity, other than a State, territory, commonwealth, or district of the United States, or any subdivision thereof; or

(ii) a representative of a government entity described in clause (i).

(4) (A)(i) In order to carry out the provisions of this section, each agency shall promulgate regulations, pursuant to notice and receipt of public comment, specifying the schedule of fees

applicable to the processing of requests under this section and establishing procedures and guidelines for determining when such fees should be waived or reduced. Such schedule shall conform to the guidelines which shall be promulgated, pursuant to notice and receipt of public comment, by the Director of the Office of Management and Budget and which shall provide for a uniform schedule of fees for all agencies.

(ii) Such agency regulations shall provide that –

(I) fees shall be limited to reasonable standard charges for document search, duplication, and review, when records are requested for commercial use;

(II) fees shall be limited to reasonable standard charges for document duplication when records are not sought for commercial use and the request is made by an educational or noncommercial scientific institution, whose purpose is scholarly or scientific research; or a representative of the news media; and

(III) for any request not described in (I) or (II), fees shall be limited to reasonable standard charges for document search and duplication.

In this clause, the term 'a representative of the news media' means any person or entity that gathers information of potential interest to a segment of the public, uses its editorial skills to turn the raw materials into a distinct work, and distributes that work to an audience. In this clause, the term 'news' means information that is about current events or that would be of current interest to the public. Examples of news-media entities are television or radio stations broadcasting to the public at large and publishers of periodicals (but only if such entities qualify as disseminators of 'news') who make their products available for purchase by or subscription by or free distribution to the general public. These examples are not all-inclusive. Moreover, as methods of news delivery evolve (for example, the adoption of the electronic dissemination of newspapers through telecommunications services), such alternative media shall be considered to be news-media entities. A freelance journalist shall be regarded as working for a news-media entity if the journalist can demonstrate a solid basis for expecting publication through that entity, whether or not the journalist is actually employed by the entity. A publication contract would present a solid basis for such an expectation; the Government may also consider the past publication record of the requester in making such a determination.

(iii) Documents shall be furnished without any charge or at a charge reduced below the fees established under clause (ii) if disclosure of the information is in the public interest because it is likely to contribute significantly to public understanding of the operations or activities of the government and is not primarily in the commercial interest of the requester.

(iv) Fee schedules shall provide for the recovery of only the direct costs of search, duplication, or review. Review costs shall include only the direct costs incurred during the initial examination of a document for the purposes of determining whether the documents must be disclosed under this section and for the purposes of withholding any portions exempt from disclosure under this section. Review costs may not include any costs incurred in resolving issues of law or policy that may be raised in the course of processing a request under this section. No fee may be charged by any agency under this section –

(I) if the costs of routine collection and processing of the fee are likely to equal or exceed the amount of the fee; or

(II) for any request described in clause (ii)(II) or (III) of this subparagraph for the first two hours of search time or for the first one hundred pages of duplication.

(v) No agency may require advance payment of any fee unless the requester has previously failed to pay fees in a timely fashion, or the agency has determined that the fee will exceed $250.

(vi) Nothing in this subparagraph shall supersede fees chargeable under a statute specifically providing for setting the level of fees for particular types of records.

(vii) In any action by a requester regarding the waiver of fees under this section, the court shall determine the matter de novo: Provided, That the court's review of the matter shall be limited to the record before the agency.

(viii) (I) Except as provided in subclause (II), an agency shall not assess any search fees (or in the case of a requester described under clause (ii)(II) of this subparagraph, duplication fees) under this subparagraph if the agency has failed to comply with any time limit under paragraph (6).

(II) (aa) If an agency has determined that unusual circumstances apply (as the term is defined in paragraph (6)(B)) and the agency provided a timely written notice to the requester in accordance with paragraph (6)(B), a failure described in subclause (I) is excused for an additional 10 days. If the agency fails to comply with the extended time limit, the agency may not assess any search fees (or in the case of a requester is described under clause (ii)(II) of this subparagraph, duplication fees).

(1) (bb) If an agency has determined that unusual circumstances apply and more than 5,000 pages are necessary to respond to the request, an agency may charge search fees (or in the case of a requester described under clause (ii) (II) of this subparagraph, duplication fees) if the agency has provided a timely written notice to the requester in accordance with paragraph 6(B) and the agency has discussed with the requester via written mail, electronic mail, or telephone (or made not less than 3 good-faith attempts to do so) how the requester could effectively limit the scope of the request in accordance with paragraph (6)(B)(ii).

(2) (cc) If a court has determined that exceptional circumstances exist (as that term is defined in paragraph (6)(C)), a failure described in subclause (I) shall be excused for the length of time provided by the court order.

(B) On complaint, the district court of the United States in the district in which the complainant resides, or has his principal place of business, or in which the agency records are situated, or in the District of Columbia, has jurisdiction to enjoin the agency from withholding agency records and to order the production of any agency records improperly withheld from the complainant. In such a case the court shall determine the matter de novo and may examine the contents of such agency records in camera to determine whether such records or any part thereof shall be withheld under any of the exemptions set forth in subsection (b) of this section, and the burden is on the agency to sustain its action. In addition to any other matters to which a court accords substantial weight, a court shall accord substantial weight to an affidavit of an agency concerning the agency's determination as to technical feasibility under paragraph (2)(C) and subsection (b) and reproducibility under paragraph (3)(B).

(C) Notwithstanding any other provision of law, the defendant shall serve an answer or otherwise plead to any complaint made under this subsection within thirty days after service upon the defendant of the pleading in which such complaint is made, unless the court otherwise directs for good cause is shown.

[(D) Repealed. Pub. L. 98-620, title IV, Sec. 402(2), Nov. 8, 1984, 98 Stat. 3357.]

(E) (i) The court may assess against the United States reasonable attorney fees and other litigation costs reasonably incurred in any case under this section in which the complainant has substantially prevailed.

(ii) For purposes of this subparagraph, a complainant has substantially prevailed if the complainant has obtained relief through either –

(I) a judicial order, or an enforceable written agreement or consent decree; or

(II) a voluntary or unilateral change in position by the agency, if the complainant's claim is not insubstantial.

(F) (i) Whenever the court orders the production of any agency records improperly withheld from the complainant and assesses against the United States reasonable attorney fees and other litigation costs, and the court additionally issues a written finding that the circumstances surrounding the withholding raise questions whether agency personnel acted arbitrarily or capriciously with respect to the withholding, the Special Counsel shall promptly initiate a proceeding to determine whether disciplinary action is warranted against the officer or employee who was primarily responsible for the withholding. The Special Counsel, after investigation and consideration of the evidence submitted, shall submit his findings and recommendations to the administrative authority of the agency concerned and shall send copies of the findings and recommendations to the officer or employee or his representative. The administrative authority shall take the corrective action that the Special Counsel recommends.

(ii) The Attorney General shall –

(I) notify the Special Counsel of each civil action described under the first sentence of clause (i); and

(II) annually submit a report to Congress on the number of such civil actions in the preceding year.

(iii) The Special Counsel shall annually submit a report to Congress on the actions taken by the Special Counsel under clause (i).

(G) In the event of noncompliance with the order of the court, the district court may punish for contempt the responsible employee, and in the case of a uniformed service, the responsible member.

(5) Each agency having more than one member shall maintain and make available for public inspection a record of the final votes of each member in every agency proceeding.

(6) (A) Each agency, upon any request for records made under paragraph (1), (2), or (3) of this subsection, shall –

(i) determine within 20 days (excepting Saturdays, Sundays, and legal public holidays) after the receipt of any such request whether to comply with such request and shall immediately notify the person making such a request of –

(I) such determination and the reasons therefore;

(II) the right of such person to seek assistance from the FOIA Public Liaison of the agency; and

(III) in the case of an adverse determination –

(3) (aa) the right of such person to appeal to the head of the agency, within a period determined by the head of the agency that is not less than 90 days after the date of such adverse determination; and

(4) (bb) the right of such person to seek dispute resolution services from the FOIA Public Liaison of the agency or the Office of Government Information Services; and

(ii) make a determination with respect to any appeal within twenty days (excepting Saturdays, Sundays, and legal public holidays) after the receipt of such appeal. If on appeal the denial of the request for records is in whole or in part upheld, the agency shall notify the person making such request of the provisions for judicial review of that determination under paragraph (4) of this subsection.

The 20-day period under clause (i) shall commence on the date on which the request is first received by the appropriate component of the agency, but in any event not later than ten days after the request is first received by any component of the agency that is designated in the agency's regulations under this section to receive requests under this section. The 20-day period shall not be tolled by the agency except –

(I) that the agency may make one request to the requester for information and toll the 20-day period while it is awaiting such information that it has reasonably requested from the requester under this section; or

(II) if necessary to clarify with the requester issues regarding fee assessment. In either case, the agency's receipt of the requester's response to the agency's request for information or clarification ends the tolling period.

(B) (i) In unusual circumstances as specified in this subparagraph, the time limits prescribed in either clause (i) or clause (ii) of subparagraph (A) may be extended by written notice to the person making such request setting forth the unusual circumstances for such extension and the date on which a determination is expected to be dispatched. No such notice shall specify a date that would result in an extension for more than ten working days, except as provided in clause (ii) of this subparagraph.

(ii) With respect to a request for which a written notice under clause (i) extends the time limits prescribed under clause (i) of subparagraph (A), the agency shall notify the person making the request if the request cannot be processed within the time limit specified in that clause and shall provide the person an opportunity to limit the scope of the request so that it may be processed within that time limit or an opportunity to arrange with the agency an alternative time frame for processing the request or a modified request. To aid the requester, each agency shall make available its FOIA Public Liaison, who shall assist in the resolution of any disputes between the requester and the agency and notify the requester of the right of the requester to seek dispute resolution services from the Office of Government Information Services. Refusal by the person to reasonably modify the request or arrange such an alternative time frame shall be considered as a factor in determining whether exceptional circumstances exist for purposes of subparagraph (C).

(iii) As used in this subparagraph, "unusual circumstances" means, but only to the extent reasonably necessary to the proper processing of the particular requests –

(I) the need to search for and collect the requested records from field facilities or other establishments that are separate from the office processing the request;

(II) the need to search for, collect, and appropriately examine a voluminous amount of separate and distinct records which are demanded in a single request; or

(III) the need for consultation, which shall be conducted with all practicable speed, with another agency having a substantial interest in the determination of the request or among two or more components of the agency having substantial subject-matter interest therein.

(iv) Each agency may promulgate regulations, pursuant to notice and receipt of public comment, providing for the aggregation of certain requests by the same requestor, or by a group of requestors acting in concert, if the agency reasonably believes that such requests actually constitute a single request, which would otherwise satisfy the unusual circumstances specified in this subparagraph, and the requests involve clearly related matters. Multiple requests involving unrelated matters shall not be aggregated.

(C) (i) Any person making a request to any agency for records under paragraph (1), (2), or (3) of this subsection shall be deemed to have exhausted his administrative remedies with respect to such request if the agency fails to comply with the applicable time limit provisions of this paragraph. If the Government can show exceptional circumstances exist and that the agency is exercising due diligence in responding to the request, the court may retain jurisdiction and allow the agency additional time to complete its review of the records. Upon any determination by an agency to comply with a request for records, the records shall be made promptly available to such person making such request. Any notification of denial of any request for records under this subsection shall set forth the names and titles or positions of each person responsible for the denial of such request.

(ii) For purposes of this subparagraph, the term "exceptional circumstances" does not include a delay that results from a predictable agency workload of requests under this section, unless the agency demonstrates reasonable progress in reducing its backlog of pending requests.

(iii) Refusal by a person to reasonably modify the scope of a request or arrange an alternative time frame for processing a request (or a modified request) under clause (ii) after being given an opportunity to do so by the agency to whom the person made the request shall be considered as a factor in determining whether exceptional circumstances exist for purposes of this subparagraph.

(D) (i) Each agency may promulgate regulations, pursuant to notice and receipt of public comment, providing for multitrack processing of requests for records based on the amount of work or time (or both) involved in processing requests.

(ii) Regulations under this subparagraph may provide a person making a request that does not qualify for the fastest multitrack processing an opportunity to limit the scope of the request in order to qualify for faster processing.

(iii) This subparagraph shall not be considered to affect the requirement under subparagraph (C) to exercise due diligence.

(E) (i) Each agency shall promulgate regulations, pursuant to notice and receipt of public comment, providing for expedited processing of requests for records –

(I) in cases in which the person requesting the records demonstrates a compelling need; and

(II) in other cases, determined by the agency.

(ii) Notwithstanding clause (i), regulations under this subparagraph must ensure –

(I) that a determination of whether to provide expedited processing shall be made, and notice of the determination shall be provided to the person making the request, within 10 days after the date of the request; and

(II) expeditious consideration of administrative appeals of such determinations of whether to provide expedited processing.

(iii) An agency shall process as soon as practicable any request for records to which the agency has granted expedited processing under this subparagraph. Agency action to deny or affirm denial of a request for expedited processing pursuant to this subparagraph, and failure by an agency to respond in a timely manner to such a request shall be subject to judicial review under paragraph (4), except that the judicial review shall be based on the record before the agency at the time of the determination.

(iv) A district court of the United States shall not have jurisdiction to review an agency denial of expedited processing of a request for records after the agency has provided a complete response to the request.

(v) For purposes of this subparagraph, the term "compelling need" means –

(I) that a failure to obtain requested records on an expedited basis under this paragraph could reasonably be expected to pose an imminent threat to the life or physical safety of an individual; or

(II) with respect to a request made by a person primarily engaged in disseminating information, urgency to inform the public concerning actual or alleged Federal Government activity.

(vi) A demonstration of a compelling need by a person making a request for expedited processing shall be made by a statement certified by such person to be true and correct to the best of such person's knowledge and belief.

(F) In denying a request for records, in whole or in part, an agency shall make a reasonable effort to estimate the volume of any requested matter the provision of which is denied and shall provide any such estimate to the person making the request, unless providing such estimate would harm an interest protected by the exemption in subsection (b) pursuant to which the denial is made.

(7) Each agency shall –

(A) establish a system to assign an individualized tracking number for each request received that will take longer than ten days to process and provide to each person making a request the tracking number assigned to the request; and

(B) establish a telephone line or Internet service that provides information about the status of a request to the person making the request using the assigned tracking number, including –

(i) the date on which the agency originally received the request; and

(ii) an estimated date on which the agency will complete action on the request.

(8) (A) An agency shall –

(i) withhold information under this section only if –

(I) the agency reasonably foresees that disclosure would harm an interest protected by an exemption described in subsection (b); or

(II) disclosure is prohibited by law; and

(ii) (I) consider whether partial disclosure of information is possible whenever the agency determines that a full disclosure of a requested record is not possible; and

(II) take reasonable steps necessary to segregate and release nonexempt information; and

(B) Nothing in this paragraph requires disclosure of information that is otherwise prohibited from disclosure by law, or otherwise exempted from disclosure under subsection (b)(3).

(b) This section does not apply to matters that are –

(1) (A) specifically authorized under criteria established by an Executive order to be kept secret in the interest of national defense or foreign policy and (B) are in fact properly classified pursuant to such Executive order;

(2) related solely to the internal personnel rules and practices of an agency;

(3) specifically exempted from disclosure by statute (other than section 552b of this title), if that statute –

(A) (i) requires that the matters be withheld from the public in such a manner as to leave no discretion on the issue; or

(ii) establishes particular criteria for withholding or refers to particular types of matters to be withheld; and

(B) if enacted after the date of enactment of the OPEN FOIA Act of 2009, specifically cites to this paragraph.

(4) trade secrets and commercial or financial information obtained from a person and privileged or confidential;

(5) inter-agency or intra-agency memorandums or letters that would not be available by law to a party other than an agency in litigation with the agency, provided that the deliberative process privilege shall not apply to records created 25 years or more before the date on which the records were requested;

(6) personnel and medical files and similar files the disclosure of which would constitute a clearly unwarranted invasion of personal privacy;

(7) records or information compiled for law enforcement purposes, but only to the extent that the production of such law enforcement records or information (A) could reasonably be expected to interfere with enforcement proceedings, (B) would deprive a person of a right to a fair trial or an impartial adjudication, (C) could reasonably be expected to constitute an unwarranted invasion of personal privacy, (D) could reasonably be expected to disclose the identity of a confidential source, including a State, local, or foreign agency or authority or any private institution which furnished information on a confidential basis, and, in the case of a record or information compiled by a criminal law enforcement authority in the course of a criminal investigation or by an agency conducting a lawful national security intelligence investigation, information furnished by a confidential source, (E) would disclose techniques and procedures for law enforcement investigations or prosecutions, or would disclose guidelines for law enforcement investigations or prosecutions if such disclosure could reasonably be expected to risk circumvention of the law, or (F) could reasonably be expected to endanger the life or physical safety of any individual;

(8) contained in or related to examination, operating, or condition reports prepared by, on behalf of, or for the use of an agency responsible for the regulation or supervision of financial institutions; or

(9) geological and geophysical information and data, including maps, concerning wells.

(5) Any reasonably segregable portion of a record shall be provided to any person requesting such record after deletion of the portions which are exempt under this subsection. The amount of information deleted, and the exemption under which the deletion is made, shall be indicated on the released portion of the record, unless including that indication would harm an interest protected by the exemption in this subsection under which the deletion is made. If technically feasible, the amount of the information deleted, and the exemption under which the deletion is made, shall be indicated at the place in the record where such deletion is made.

(c) (1) Whenever a request is made which involves access to records described in subsection (b)(7)(A) and –

(A) the investigation or proceeding involves a possible violation of criminal law; and

(B) there is reason to believe that (i) the subject of the investigation or proceeding is not aware of its pendency, and (ii) disclosure of the existence of the records could reasonably be expected to interfere with enforcement proceedings, the agency may, during only such time as that circumstance continues, treat the records as not subject to the requirements of this section.

(2) Whenever informant records maintained by a criminal law enforcement agency under an informant's name or personal identifier are requested by a third party according to the informant's name or personal identifier, the agency may treat the records as not subject to the requirements of this section unless the informant's status as an informant has been officially confirmed.

(3) Whenever a request is made which involves access to records maintained by the Federal Bureau of Investigation pertaining to foreign intelligence or counterintelligence, or international terrorism, and the existence of the records is classified information as provided in subsection (b)(1), the Bureau may, as long as the existence of the records remains classified information, treat the records as not subject to the requirements of this section.

(d) This section does not authorize the withholding of information or limit the availability of records to the public, except as specifically stated in this section. This section is not authority to withhold information from Congress.

(e) (1) On or before February 1 of each year, each agency shall submit to the Attorney General of the United States and to the Director of the Office of Government Information Services a report which shall cover the preceding fiscal year and which shall include –

(A) the number of determinations made by the agency not to comply with requests for records made to such agency under subsection (a) and the reasons for each such determination;

(B) (i) the number of appeals made by persons under subsection (a)(6), the result of such appeals, and the reason for the action upon each appeal that results in a denial of information; and

(ii) a complete list of all statutes that the agency relies upon to authorize the agency to withhold information under subsection (b)(3), the number of occasions on which each statute was relied upon, a description of whether a court has upheld the decision of the agency to withhold information under each such statute, and a concise description of the scope of any information withheld;

(C) the number of requests for records pending before the agency as of September 30 of the preceding year, and the median and average number of days that such requests had been pending before the agency as of that date;

(D) the number of requests for records received by the agency and the number of requests which the agency processed;

(E) the median number of days taken by the agency to process different types of requests, based on the date on which the requests were received by the agency;

(F) the average number of days for the agency to respond to a request beginning on the date on which the request was received by the agency, the median number of days for the agency to respond to such requests, and the range in number of days for the agency to respond to such requests;

(G) based on the number of business days that have elapsed since each request was originally received by the agency –

(i) the number of requests for records to which the agency has responded with a determination within a period up to and including 20 days, and in 20-day increments up to and including 200 days;

(ii) the number of requests for records to which the agency has responded with a determination within a period greater than 200 days and less than 301 days;

(iii) the number of requests for records to which the agency has responded with a determination within a period greater than 300 days and less than 401 days; and

(iv) the number of requests for records to which the agency has responded with a determination within a period greater than 400 days;

(H) the average number of days for the agency to provide the granted information beginning on the date on which the request was originally filed, the median number of days for the agency to provide the granted information, and the range in number of days for the agency to provide the granted information;

(I) the median and average number of days for the agency to respond to administrative appeals based on the date on which the appeals originally were received by the agency, the highest number of business days taken by the agency to respond to an administrative appeal, and the lowest number of business days taken by the agency to respond to an administrative appeal;

(J) data on the 10 active requests with the earliest filing dates pending at each agency, including the amount of time that has elapsed since each request was originally received by the agency;

(K) data on the 10 active administrative appeals with the earliest filing dates pending before the agency as of September 30 of the preceding year, including the number of business days that have elapsed since the requests were originally received by the agency;

(L) the number of expedited review requests that are granted and denied, the average and median number of days for adjudicating expedited review requests, and the number adjudicated within the required 10 days;

(M) the number of fee waiver requests that are granted and denied, and the average and median number of days for adjudicating fee waiver determinations;

(N) the total amount of fees collected by the agency for processing requests;

(O) the number of full-time staff of the agency devoted to processing requests for records under this section, and the total amount expended by the agency for processing such requests;

(P) the number of times the agency denied a request for records under subsection (c); and

(Q) the number of records that were made available for public inspection in an electronic format under subsection (a)(2).

(2) Information in each report submitted under paragraph (1) shall be expressed in terms of each principal component of the agency and for the agency overall.

(3) Each agency shall make each such report available for public inspection in an electronic format. In addition, each agency shall make the raw statistical data used in each report available in a timely manner for public inspection in an electronic format, which shall be available –

(A) without charge, license, or registration requirement;

(B) in an aggregated, searchable format; and

(C) in a format that may be downloaded in bulk.

(4) The Attorney General of the United States shall make each report which has been made available by electronic means available at a single electronic access point. The Attorney General of the United States shall notify the Chairman and ranking minority member of the Committee on Oversight and Government Reform of the House of Representatives and the Chairman and ranking minority member of the Committees on Homeland Security and Governmental Affairs and the Judiciary of the Senate, no later than March 1 of the year in which each such report is issued, that such reports are available by electronic means.

(5) The Attorney General of the United States, in consultation with the Director of the Office of Management and Budget, shall develop reporting and performance guidelines in connection with reports required by this subsection by October 1, 1997, and may establish additional requirements for such reports as the Attorney General determines may be useful.

(6) (A) The Attorney General of the United States shall submit to the Committee on Oversight and Government Reform of the House of Representatives, the Committee on the Judiciary of the Senate, and the President a report on or before March 1 of each calendar year, which shall include for the prior calendar year –

(i) a listing of the number of cases arising under this section;

(ii) a listing of –

(I) each subsection, and any exemption, if applicable, involved in each case arising under this section;

(II) the disposition of each case arising under this section; and

(III) the cost, fees, and penalties assessed under subparagraphs (E), (F), and (G) of subsection (a)(4); and

(iii) a description of the efforts undertaken by the Department of Justice to encourage agency compliance with this section.

(B) The Attorney General of the United States shall make –

(i) each report submitted under subparagraph (A) available for public inspection in an electronic format; and

(ii) the raw statistical data used in each report submitted under subparagraph (A) available for public inspection in an electronic format, which shall be made available –

(I) without charge, license, or registration requirement;

(II) in an aggregated, searchable format; and

(III) in a format that may be downloaded in bulk;

(f) For purposes of this section, the term –

(1) "agency" as defined in section 551(1) of this title includes any executive department, military department, Government corporation, Government controlled corporation, or other establishment in the executive branch of the Government (including the Executive Office of the President), or any independent regulatory agency; and

(2) 'record' and any other term used in this section in reference to information includes –

(A) any information that would be an agency record subject to the requirements of this section when maintained by an agency in any format, including an electronic format; and

(B) any information described under subparagraph (A) that is maintained for an agency by an entity under Government contract, for the purposes of records management.

(g) The head of each agency shall prepare and make available for public inspection in an electronic format, reference material or a guide for requesting records or information from the agency, subject to the exemptions in subsection (b), including –

(1) an index of all major information systems of the agency;

(2) a description of major information and record locator systems maintained by the agency; and

(3) a handbook for obtaining various types and categories of public information from the agency pursuant to chapter 35 of title 44, and under this section.

(h) (1) There is established the Office of Government Information Services within the National Archives and Records Administration. The head of the Office shall be the Director of the Office of Government Information Services.

(2) The Office of Government Information Services shall –

(A) review policies and procedures of administrative agencies under this section;

(B) review compliance with this section by administrative agencies; and

(C) identify procedures and methods for improving compliance under this section.

(3) The Office of Government Information Services shall offer mediation services to resolve

disputes between persons making requests under this section and administrative agencies as a nonexclusive alternative to litigation and may issue advisory opinions at the discretion of the Office or upon request of any party to a dispute.

(4) (A) Not less frequently than annually, the Director of the Office of Government Information Services shall submit to the Committee on Oversight and Government Reform of the House of Representatives, the Committee on the Judiciary of the Senate, and the President –

(i) A report on the findings of the information reviewed and identified under paragraph (2);

(ii) A summary of the activities of the Office of Government Information Services under paragraph (3), including –

(I) any advisory opinions issued; and

(II) the number of times each agency engaged in dispute resolution with the assistance of the Office of Government Information Services or the FOIA Public Liaison; and

(iii) Legislative and regulatory recommendations, if any, to improve the administration of this section.

(B) The Director of the Office of Government Information Services shall make each report submitted under subparagraph (A) available for public inspection in an electronic format.

(C) The Director of the Office of Government Information Services shall not be required to obtain the prior approval, comment, or review of any officer or agency of the United States, including the Department of Justice, the Archivist of the United States, or the Office of Management and Budget before submitting to Congress, or any committee or subcommittee thereof, any reports, recommendations, testimony, or comments, if such submissions include a statement indicating that the views expressed therein are those of the Director and do not necessarily represent the views of the President.

(5) The Director of the Office of Government Information Services may directly submit additional information to Congress and the President as the Director determines to be appropriate.

(6) Not less frequently than annually, the Office of Government Information Services shall conduct a meeting that is open to the public on the review and reports by the Office and shall allow interested persons to appear and present oral or written statements at the meeting.

(i) The Government Accountability Office shall conduct audits of administrative agencies on the implementation of this section and issue reports detailing the results of such audits.

(j) (1) Each agency shall designate a Chief FOIA Officer who shall be a senior official of such agency (at the Assistant Secretary or equivalent level).

(2) The Chief FOIA Officer of each agency shall, subject to the authority of the head of the agency –

(A) have agency-wide responsibility for efficient and appropriate compliance with this section;

(B) monitor implementation of this section throughout the agency and keep the head of the agency, the chief legal officer of the agency, and the Attorney General appropriately informed of the agency's performance in implementing this section;

(C) recommend to the head of the agency such adjustments to agency practices, policies, personnel, and funding as may be necessary to improve its implementation of this section;

(D) review and report to the Attorney General, through the head of the agency, at such times and in such formats as the Attorney General may direct, on the agency's performance in implementing this section;

(E) facilitate public understanding of the purposes of the statutory exemptions of this section by including concise descriptions of the exemptions in both the agency's handbook issued under subsection (g), and the agency's annual report on this section, and by providing an

overview, where appropriate, of certain general categories of agency records to which those exemptions apply;
(F) offer training to agency staff regarding their responsibilities under this section;
(G) serve as the primary agency liaison with the Office of Government Information Services and the Office of Information Policy; and
(H) designate 1 or more FOIA Public Liaisons.
(3) The Chief FOIA Officer of each agency shall review, not less frequently than annually, all aspects of the administration of this section by the agency to ensure compliance with the requirements of this section, including –
(A) agency regulations;
(B) disclosure of records required under paragraphs (2) and (8) of subsection (a);
(C) assessment of fees and determination of eligibility for fee waivers;
(D) the timely processing of requests for information under this section;
(E) the use of exemptions under subsection (b); and
(F) dispute resolution services with the assistance of the Office of Government Information Services or the FOIA Public Liaison.
(k) (1) There is established in the executive branch the Chief FOIA Officers Council (referred to in this subsection as the 'Council').
(2) The Council shall be comprised of the following members:
(A) The Deputy Director for Management of the Office of Management and Budget.
(B) The Director of the Office of Information Policy at the Department of Justice.
(C) The Director of the Office of Government Information Services.
(D) The Chief FOIA Officer of each agency.
(E) Any other officer or employee of the United States as designated by the Co-Chairs.
(3) The Director of the Office of Information Policy at the Department of Justice and the Director of the Office of Government Information Services shall be the Co-Chairs of the Council.
(4) The Administrator of General Services shall provide administrative and other support for the Council.
(5) (A) The duties of the Council shall include the following:
(i) Develop recommendations for increasing compliance and efficiency under this section.
(ii) Disseminate information about agency experiences, ideas, best practices, and innovative approaches related to this section.
(iii) Identify, develop, and coordinate initiatives to increase transparency and compliance with this section.
(iv) Promote the development and use of common performance measures for agency compliance with this section.
(B) In performing the duties described in subparagraph (A), the Council shall consult on a regular basis with members of the public who make requests under this section.
(6) (A) The Council shall meet regularly, and such meetings shall be open to the public unless the Council determines to close the meeting for reasons of national security or to discuss information exempt under subsection (b).
(B) Not less frequently than annually, the Council shall hold a meeting that shall be open to the public and permit interested persons to appear and present oral and written statements to the Council.
(C) Not later than 10 business days before a meeting of the Council, notice of such meeting shall be published in the Federal Register.

(D) Except as provided in subsection (b), the records, reports, transcripts, minutes, appendices, working papers, drafts, studies, agenda, or other documents that were made available to or prepared for or by the Council shall be made publicly available.

(E) Detailed minutes of each meeting of the Council shall be kept and shall contain a record of the persons present, a complete and accurate description of matters discussed, and conclusions reached, and copies of all reports received, issued, or approved by the Council. The minutes shall be redacted as necessary and made publicly available.

(l) FOIA Public Liaisons shall report to the agency Chief FOIA Officer and shall serve as supervisory officials to whom a requester under this section can raise concerns about the service the requester has received from the FOIA Requester Center, following an initial response from the FOIA Requester Center Staff. FOIA Public Liaisons shall be responsible for assisting in reducing delays, increasing transparency and understanding of the status of requests, and assisting in the resolution of disputes.

(m)(1) The Director of the Office of Management and Budget, in consultation with the Attorney General shall ensure the operation of a consolidated online request portal that allows a member of the public to submit a request for records under subsection (a) to any agency from a single website. The portal may include any additional tools the Director of the Office of Management and Budget finds will improve the implementation of this section.

(2) This subsection shall not be construed to alter the power of any other agency to create or maintain an independent online portal for the submission of a request for records under this section. The Director of the Office of Management and Budget shall establish standards for interoperability between the portal required under paragraph (1) and other request processing software used by agencies subject to this section.

CHAPTER 10

§ 2254 SAMPLE MOTIONS AND PLEADINGS

Here I have taken the liberty of providing some basic motions, forms, and pleadings designed to assist you in your habeas corpus efforts. You may add or subtract from them accordingly.

Since everyone's jurisdiction and facts are relatively different, you will need to use common sense and applicability when adopting these forms for your intended purpose. They are not "one size fits all" as written in the samples and require adaptation to your own specific facts. That being said, they all follow the Federal Civil Rules related to § 2254 and are usable in any federal court.

I have intentionally withheld a sample Points and Authorities Memorandum, since the Texas Department of Criminal Justice does not allow for me to provide one. I have contested this to exhaustion and have not prevailed in doing so. I recommend that you search your prison law library or obtain assistance from family or friends if you seek one to follow. In fact, a Points and Authorities Memorandum looks much like the state's response to your direct appeal, or state habeas corpus, a contention to your assertions and claims.

Lastly, I chose to include the sample forms you will more than likely require most, since there are literally hundreds of § 2254 motions and pleadings that can be utilized, which would create too large of a publication. My intent is to merely assist you, not to actually and literally write your appeal for you!

If you are still unable to comprehend or understand what needs to be done, then it's advisable that you do not handle the post-conviction matters yourself. Filing nothing is better than filing incorrectly or insufficiently, in all cases.

Author's Note: Remember to include a Certificate of Service at the end of all motions. I have intentionally not done so in most samples because each state has different rules and applications.

01, January, 2020

United States District Court
Northern District of Texas
111 S. Main Street
Anywhere, Texas, 75202

Dear Clerk:

At this time, I am requesting a packet for filing a petition for writ of habeas corpus § 2254. Please forward one to me at the address below.

I appreciate your assistance.

Respectfully,

[Sign Here]
[Print Name]
[Address]
[City, State, Zip]

IN THE UNITED STATES DISTRICT COURT
NORTHERN DISTRICT OF TEXAS
SHERMAN DIVISION

JOHN B. DOE Appellant, vs. NAME OF WARDEN Appellee.	§ § § § § § § § § §	Case No.__________________

MOTION FOR EXTENSION OF TIME TO FILE BRIEF

COMES NOW JOHN B. DOE, Appellant, *pro se*, and respectfully moves this Court to grant an extension of time to file brief or traverse in the above-styled action. In support thereof, appellant asserts as follows:

1. The current deadline for the filing is on ____________, ____________ 2021.

2. Appellant requests an additional 45 days from the date above.

3. Appellant requires additional time to research and prepare the brief/traverse because he/she has limited time and access to the law library.

[Cite all reasons here and continue numbering]

4. This is appellant's first request for additional time.

5. This motion is not intended to delay the proceedings.

WHEREFORE, the Appellant requests this Honorable Court to issue an order granting an additional 45 days from the cited deadline to file his/her brief/traverse.

Respectfully submitted this____________ day of ____________, 2021.

[Sign Here]
[Printed Name Here]
[Address]
[City, State, Zip Code]

Pro Se

IN THE UNITED STATES DISTRICT COURT
NORTHERN DISTRICT OF TEXAS
SHERMAN DIVISION

JOHN B. DOE Petitioner,	§ § § §	
vs.	§ §	Case No.__________________
NAME OF WARDEN Respondent.	§ § § §	

MOTION FOR EXPANSION OF RECORD

COMES NOW PETITIONER, *pro se*, and respectfully files this motion for expansion of the record pursuant to Rule 7(b) of 28 U.S.C. § 2254 proceedings.

Petitioner moves now to include all Exhibits and Affidavits attached to his petition and Memorandum/Brief in this cause. Under Rule 7(b), materials that may be required include letters predating the filing of this action, documents, exhibits, and answers under oath to written interrogatories propounded by the judge. Affidavits may also be submitted and considered as part of the record.

WHEREFORE, petitioner prays this Court grant this motion for expansion of the record.

Respectfully submitted this ____________ day of ____________, 2021.

[Sign Here]
[Printed Name Here]
[Address]
[City, State, Zip Code]
Pro Se

IN THE UNITED STATES DISTRICT COURT
NORTHERN DISTRICT OF TEXAS
SHERMAN DIVISION

JOHN B. DOE	§	
Petitioner,	§	
	§	
	§	
	§	Case No.__________________
vs.	§	
	§	
	§	
NAME OF WARDEN	§	
Respondent.	§	

MOTION FOR EVIDENTIARY HEARING

COMES NOW PETITIONER, *pro se*, and respectfully moves this Honorable Court for an Evidentiary Hearing pursuant to Rule 8, of 28 U.S.C. § 2254. Petitioner filed his § 2254 petition and moved for discovery material, the Respondent filed a response but failed to request an Evidentiary Hearing. In light of Rules 6 and 8 governing § 2254 proceedings, this Court should order an evidentiary hearing and appoint counsel to assist Petitioner.

WHEREFORE, premises considered, petitioner respectfully moves for an evidentiary hearing and appointment of counsel in these proceedings.

Respectfully submitted this ____________ day of_______________, 2021.

[Sign Here]
[Printed Name Here]
[Address]
[City, State, Zip Code]

Pro Se

IN THE UNITED STATES DISTRICT COURT
NORTHERN DISTRICT OF TEXAS
SHERMAN DIVISION

JOHN B. DOE	§	
Petitioner,	§	
	§	
	§	
	§	Case No.________________
vs.	§	
	§	
	§	
NAME OF WARDEN	§	
Respondent.	§	

NOTICE OF APPEAL

Notice is hereby issued that Petitioner, *pro se*, hereby appeals to the ____________ Circuit Court of Appeals from the final judgment denying ____________, and all of the pleadings thereto, entered for record in the above action on the __________ day of ____________, 2021.

Respectfully submitted,

[Sign Here]
[Printed Name Here]
[Address]
[City, State, Zip Code]

Pro Se

IN THE UNITED STATES DISTRICT COURT
NORTHERN DISTRICT OF TEXAS
SHERMAN DIVISION

JOHN B. DOE	§	
Petitioner,	§	
	§	
	§	
	§	Case No.__________________
vs.	§	
	§	
	§	
NAME OF WARDEN	§	
Respondent.	§	

MOTION FOR LEAVE TO PROCEED ON APPEAL *IN FORMA PAUPERIS*

COMES NOW PETITIONER, *pro se*, and respectfully moves this Honorable Court for leave to proceed on appeal through *in forma pauperis* from the judgement entered on _______ day of ____________, 2021, denying petitioner's § 2254 motion, and certificate of appealability, without prepayment of costs and fees or giving security.

Respectfully submitted on this ____________ day of ____________, 2021.

[Sign Here]
[Printed Name Here]
[Address]
[City, State, Zip Code]

Pro Se

IN THE UNITED STATES COURT OF APPEALS
FOR THE ___________ CIRCUIT
App. No. ___________

JOHN B. DOE
Appellant-Petitioner,

VS.

WARDEN NAME
Respondent-Appellee.

On Appeal from the United States District Court
For the Northern District of Texas
SHERMAN DIVISION

USDC No. ___________

MOTION FOR EXTENSION OF TIME TO FILE A REQUEST
FOR CERTIFICATE OF APPEALABILITY

TO THE HONORABLE JUDGES OF THE ___________ CIRCUIT COURT:

COMES NOW APPELLANT, *pro se*, and respectfully moves this Honorable court for an extension of time pursuant to Federal Rules of Appellate Procedure, Rule 26(b), to file his request for certificate of appealability. Appellant will show this Honorable Court the following in support:

1. This is Appellants first request for an extension of time.
2. Appellant needs time to research in perfecting a request for certificate of appealability due to his inexperience in the law.
3. This motion is made in the interest of justice and is not intended to delay the matter.
4. The Appellee will not be prejudiced by an extension of time.

WHEREFORE, premises considered, Appellant respectfully urges this Honorable Court to grant him an extension of time to file his request/motion for certificate of appealability.

Respectfully submitted on this ___________ day of ___________, 2021.

[Sign Here]
[Printed Name Here]
[Address]
[City, State, Zip Code]

Pro Se

IN THE UNITED STATES DISTRICT COURT
WESTERN DISTRICT OF TEXAS
WACO DIVISION

JOHN B. DOE	§	
Appellant,	§	
	§	
	§	
	§	Case No.__________________
vs.	§	
	§	
	§	
NAME OF WARDEN	§	
Appellee.	§	

MOTION FOR CERTIFICATE OF APPEALABILITY

TO THE HONORABLE JUDGE OF SAID COURT:

COMES NOW JOHN B. DOE, APPELLANT, *pro se*, and respectfully moves this Honorable Court pursuant to 28 U.S.C. § 2253(c) (2) to issue a Certificate of Appealability (COA) to appeal the denial of his/her 28 U.S.C. § 2254 motion to vacate, set aside, and correct his sentence. See *Slack v. McDaniel*, 529 U.S. 473, 484, 120 S.Ct. 1595, 146 L.Ed.2d 542 (2000); *Mille-El v. Cockrell*, 537 U.S. 322, 123 S.Ct. 1029, 1039, 154 L.Ed.2d 931 (2003).

I.
JURISDICTION

This Court has Jurisdiction to issue a COA under 28 U.S.C. §§ 2253(c) (2); and § 2254.

II.
STATEMENT OF CASE

[A Statement of the Case can be drafted using your direct appeal/habeas corpus brief, or your docket sheet]

III.

STATEMENT OF THE FACTS

[Cite the issues in your case that clearly establish the violation of your Constitutional rights]

A. Standard for Certificate of Appealability (COA)

Prior to obtaining an appeal from the district court's decision in a § 2254 action, the Antiterrorism and Death Penalty Act (AEDPA) requires that a petitioner must obtain a Certificate of Appealability. *Henry v. Cockrell*, 327 F.3d 429, 431 (5th Cir. 2003); 28 U.S.C. § 2253(c) (1). However, a COA will only be granted to a petitioner if they make "a substantial showing of the denial of a constitutional right." 28 U.S.C. § 2253 (c) (2). In order to make this showing, it must be demonstrated that a "reasonable juror could find the district court's decision debatable or wrong." *Slack v. McDaniel*, 529 U.S. 473, 484, 120 S.Ct. 1595, 146 L.Ed.2d 542 (2000). And, as the United States Supreme Court made clear, a COA is "jurisdictional prerequisite," and "until a COA has been issued, the federal court of appeals lacks any jurisdiction to rule on the merits of any appeal from a habeas petitioner." *Miller-El v. Cockrell*, 537 U.S. 322, 123 S.Ct. 1029, 1039,

154 L.Ed.2d 931 (2003).

ISSUE 1

[State the Issue here. Cite the constitutional error and how the district court committed error in the review of your § 2254 case. Make sure that they are Constitutional errors.]

ISSUE 2

[Continue to address your issues in order]

CONCLUSION

WHEREFORE, based on the foresaid, Appellant/Petitioner urges this Honorable Court to issue a Certificate of Appealability (COA) authorizing Appellant/Petitioner to now appeal the decision of the district court to deny him/her the claims of constitutional error as cited.

Respectfully submitted on this ___________ day of ___________, 2021.

[Sign Here]
[Printed Name Here]
[Address]
[City, State, Zip Code]

Pro Se

IN THE UNITED STATES COURT OF APPEALS
FOR THE ___________ CIRCUIT
App. No. ___________

JOHN B. DOE
Appellant-Petitioner,

VS.

WARDEN NAME
Respondent-Appellee.

On Appeal from the United States District Court
For the Northern District of Texas
SHERMAN DIVISION

MOTION FOR PERMISSION TO APPEAL *IN FORMA PAUPERIS*

TO THE HONORABLE JUDGES OF THE ___________ CIRCUIT COURT:

COMES NOW APPELLANT, *pro se*, and respectfully moves this Honorable Court for leave to proceed on appeal through *in forma pauperis* status from the judgment entered for record on ___________, 2021, denying Appellant's 28 U.S.C. § 2254 petition, without requiring prepayment of costs, fees, or giving security, therefore.

Respectfully submitted on this ___________ day of ___________, 2021.

[Sign Here]
[Printed Name Here]
[Address]
[City, State, Zip Code]

Pro Se

IN THE UNITED STATES COURT OF APPEALS
FOR THE FIFTH CIRCUIT

JOHN B. DOE	§	
Appellant,	§	Civil No.________________
	§	
vs.	§	
	§	
NAME OF WARDEN	§	
Appellee/Respondent	§	
	§	
______________________________	§	

CERTIFICATE OF INTERESTED PERSONS AND
CORPORATE DISCLOSURE STATEMENT

Pursuant to the Rules of Appellate Procedure, Appellant hereby informs this Honorable Court and Certifies that the following persons may have an active interest in the outcome of this case:

1. (Your Name), Appellant
2. District Court Judge (add name here)
3. Magistrate Judge (if applicable)
4. Attorney General (add name here)
5. Former Trial Attorney (add name here)
6. County District Attorney (add name here)

[Your Name Here]
Address

Pro se

IN THE UNITED STATES COURT OF APPEALS
FOR THE FIFTH CIRCUIT

Appeal No. 21-1111111

JOHN B. DOE

vs.

WARDEN OF PRISON

On appeal from the U.S. District Court for the Northern District of Texas, Sherman Division

Civil No. 6:20-CV-12345

PETITION FOR ISSUANCE OF CERTIFICATE OF APPEALABILITY

COMES NOW, JOHN B. DOE, Appellant in these proceedings, and respectfully moves this Honorable Court to issue a Certificate of Appealability. In support thereof, Appellant would show as follows:

I.

JURISDICTION

Pursuant to 28 U.S.C. §§ 2253(c) (2) and 2254, this Court of Appeals is granted with the authority and jurisdiction in this matter.

II.

STATEMENT OF THE CASE

[Here, you tell the Court all of the proceedings that have taken place in your case, including dates, such as direct appeal, post-conviction, rehearing, motions filed, etc.]

III.

STATEMENT OF THE FACTS

A. Standards for granting a certificate of appealability.

A petitioner is entitled to a certificate of appealability if he "makes a substantial showing of the denial of a constitutional right." 28 U.S.C. § 2253(c) (2). The United States Supreme Court in *Barefoot v. Estelle*, 463 U.S. 880, 893 (1983), held this to mean that the appellant need not show that he would prevail on the merits, but must "demonstrate that the issues are debatable among jurists of reason; that a court could resolve the issues [in a different manner]; or that the questions are 'adequate to deserve encouragement to proceed further.'" *Flieger v. Delo*, 16 F.3d 878, 883 (8th Cir. 1994).

What's more, the United States Supreme Court would later extend on this standard in saying,

> We do not require petitioner to prove … that some jurists would grant the petition for habeas corpus. Indeed, a claim can be debatable even though every jurist of reason might agree, after the COA has been granted and the case has received full consideration, that petitioner will not prevail. *Miller-El v. Cockrell*, 537 U.S. 322, 338 (2003).

Indeed, any doubts as to whether to issue a certificate of appealability should be resolved in favor of the appellant.

IV.

Issues as to which a certificate of appealability should be granted:

[Here, you want to argue against the district court's denial and present the issues that remain unresolved in your case]

V.

CONCLUSION

For the foregoing reasons, Mr. Doe prays this Court to issue a certificate of appealability as to each issue discussed in this application.

Respectfully submitted,

[Sign Here]
[Printed Name Here]
[Address]
[City, State, Zip Code]

Pro Se

CERTIFICATE OF SERVICE

I hereby certify that the foregoing was presented to:

[Name of attorney general]

[Address]

On this 15th day of January, 2021, by placing it in the United States Mail, postage prepaid.

[Sign Here]

IN THE UNITED STATES COURT OF APPEALS
FOR THE ___________ CIRCUIT

App. No. ___________

JOHN B. DOE
Appellant-Petitioner,

VS.

WARDEN NAME
Appellee-Respondent

MOTION FOR EXTENSION OF TIME TO FILE PETITION FOR REHEARING AND REHEARING EN BANC

TO THE HONORABLE JUSTICES OF THE ___________ CIRCUIT COURT:

COMES NOW APPELLANT, *pro se*, and respectfully moves this Honorable Court pursuant to Federal Rules of Appellate Procedure, Rule 26(b) and 27 for an order extending the time to file a Petition for Rehearing; Rehearing En Banc, or a writ of Certiorari, from the current date to 60 days extended.

This motion is not intended to delay the proceedings and is meant in the interest of justice only. Appellant requires additional time to research caselaw and procedures in the perfecting of such a motion, etc.

WHEREFORE, based on the above, appellant prays this Court will grant this motion in the interest of justice.

Respectfully submitted on this ____ day of ___________, 2020.

[Sign Here]
[Printed Name Here]
[Address]
[City, State, Zip Code]

Pro Se

IN THE UNITED STATES DISTRICT COURT
FOR THE NORTHERN DISTRICT OF TEXAS
SHERMAN DIVISION

JOHN B. DOE	§	
Petitioner,	§	No. 1:20-cv-123456
	§	
vs.	§	
	§	
	§	
NAME OF WARDEN	§	
Respondent.	§	
	§	

PETITIONER'S TRAVERSE IN RESPONSE TO ORDER TO SHOW CAUSE

1.

STANDARD FOR GRANTING RELIEF

Under 28 U.S.C. § 2254(d), relief should be granted when a state court adjudication "resulted in a decision that was contrary to, or involved an unreasonable application of, clearly established Federal law, as determined by the U.S. Supreme Court." In accordance, the U.S. Supreme Court in *Williams (Terry) v. Taylor*, 529 U.S. 362 (2000) held that § 2254(d)(1) "contrary to" clause required the rejection of state court decisions which were "substantially different from the relevant precedent of this Court." More so, in *Williams*, the Court opined that an incorrect application of the law is not the same as an unreasonable application of the law. In fact, the Court rejected the standard of the Fourth Circuit, which focused on whether "reasonable jurists" would find the state court determination to be reasonable. Id. at 409-410. In addition to where a state court's decision is "contrary to" or "an unreasonable application of clearly established federal law," 28 U.S.C. § 2254(d) (2) provides that a state court decision must be reversed, and relief must be granted if the state court proceeding "resulted in a decision that was based on an unreasonable determination of the facts in light of the evidence presented in the state court proceedings." This application was discussed in *Miller-El v. Cockrell*, 537 U.S. 322 (2003). In fact, the U.S. Supreme Court specifically directed its authority towards the Texas courts in *Miller-El*, Id, and discovered that the Texas court's determination of the facts in that case were unreasonable under 28 U.S.C. § 2254(d) (2). *Miller-El v. Dretke*, 525 U.S. 231, 266

(2005).

Lastly, and most importantly, where a legal issue has not been considered by the state court, this court must review it de novo. *Wiggins v. Smith*, 539 U.S. 510, 531 (2003).

II.

MERITS OF GROUNDS FOR RELIEF

The State has presented its views on the preservation of the issues in a separate section. Believing that this issue is somehow intertwined with the merits, Mr. Doe will address them separately.

1. Constitutional Violation when Doe was pulled over without any probable cause to do so.

First, the state contends that this Court cannot review this claim due to a pretext doctrine permitting law enforcement, upon probable cause and determination, to initiate a traffic stop. This contention in without any logical basis. The majority of Circuit Court's as well as the U.S. Supreme Court, have held that justification and probable cause to initiate a traffic stop is not subject to any procedural bar or determination after the fact. The same is true where trial counsel fails to suppress the fruits of that stop. *Sanders v. Cotton*, 398 F.3d 572, 579-580 (7th Cir. 2005), for an example, demonstrates the lead authority on procedural bar, the Seventh Circuit Court of Appeals.

Turning now to the merits, this Court should consider that there is a witness to corroborate Doe's contention that he in fact used his turning signal, as recorded on that witness's cellphone, that would destroy the arresting officer's testimony to the contrary. In fact, the testimony and cellphone would more so prove that the state's witness, the arresting officer, gave false and perjured testimony at Mr. Doe's trial. Indeed, this entire case revolves around whether or not there was probable cause to pull Mr. Doe over, search his car, and arrest him for a controlled substance. If there was not, then Mr. Doe's constitutional rights were violated, and his conviction and sentence are infirm.

2. Trial counsel was ineffective for failing to investigate and subpoena Judy Jackson.

As the records show, the state contends that trial counsel was not ineffective where he "had sound trial strategy for not calling this witness." But the state's contention fails miserably. At trial, the prosecution told the jury that Mr. Doe had "been drinking" on the day he was pulled over in a traffic stop for failing to use his turning signal. This wasn't even close to the truth, and there is nothing in the record anywhere to support it. And further, that Doe did not use his turning signal constituting probable cause.

In *Strickland v. Washington*, 466 U.S. 668, 690 (1984), the Court established that a reviewing court should analyze choices made by trial counsel with a bias towards the reasonableness of those choices. But nowhere did the Supreme Court require that the claimant establish direct evidence of an unreasonable choice. What's more, "even when trial counsel testifies as to his strategy, courts have regularly found their expressed "strategic" choices to be highly unreasonable, particularly where choices (like failing to interview and subpoena eyewitnesses) were based on inadequate investigation. *Williams (Terry), supra*; *Wiggins v. Smith*, 539 U.S. 510, 525-526 (2003); *Rompilla v. Beard*, 525 U.S. 374, 385-386 (2005). And, here again, these decisions held that trial counsel who failed to provide an adequate investigation into eyewitnesses, was not reasonable.

3. Cumulative Error and Prejudice.

Throughout the foregoing, Mr. Doe has shown how each individual instance of error has prejudiced him. However, that is not where it ends. It is long established that a Court must consider in totality and combination, all instances of ineffective assistance of counsel established cumulatively. And on-point with this case, is *White v. Roper*, 416 F.3d 728 (8th Cir. 2005), where the Court established prejudice from the counsel's failure to investigate and call a witness to testify. As to cumulative prejudice, the precedent is in continuity: *Kyles v. Whitley*, 514 U.S. 419 … 437 (1996); *Vincent v. Seabold*, 226 F.3d 681, 690 (6th Cir. 2000); *Jenkins v. Artuz*, 294 F.3d 284 (2nd Cir. 2002), respectively.

Thus, if even a single instance of ineffective assistance of counsel is determined to require relief, then all instances must be considered in accumulation.

III.

CONCLUSION

For the reasons presented in this Traverse, Mr. Doe prays this Court issue the writ of habeas corpus, and to vacate his conviction and sentence requiring a new trial within 60 days of this Court's order or be released from custody.

Respectfully submitted,

[Sign Here]
[Printed Name Here]
[Address]
[City, State, Zip Code]

Pro Se

CERTIFICATE OF SERVICE

I hereby declare under the penalty of perjury that the foregoing was presented to the following:
(Name of recipient)

(Address of recipient)

via U.S. Mail on this 13th day of May, 2021.

[Sign Here]

IN THE UNITED STATES DISTRICT COURT
NORTHERN DISTRICT OF TEXAS
SHERMAN DIVISION

JOHN B. DOE Petitioner, vs. NAME OF WARDEN Respondent.	§ § § § § § § § §	No. 1:20-cv-123456 PETITIONER'S OBJECTION TO REPORT AND RECOMMENDATION NOTED: January 1, 2021

I.
INTRODUCTION

John B. Doe objects to all adverse rulings in the Report and Recommendation (R&R) issued on December 22, 2020. Doe's position is set out primarily in Petitioner's Response to Respondent's Answer (Traverse) (Docket. 10), filed on October 5, 2020. Doe, hereby addresses the comments contained in the R&R.

II.
ARGUMENT

A. MR. DOE DID NOT RECEIVE EFFECTIVE ASSISTANCE OF COUNSEL AT TRIAL (CLAIM 1).

1. *Failure to Interview Judy Jackson*

At trial, Doe testified that prior to being pulled over by Officer Johnson, he had in fact turned his turn signal. To the contrary, Officer Johnson alleges that he had probable cause to initiate a traffic stop based on Doe's failure to use his turning signal. He claimed, this gave him probable cause to then initiate a search of Doe's vehicle. See Petitioner's Response at 4-9. Here, had trial counsel interviewed and issued a subpoena for Judy Jackson, who witnessed the entire event and recorded it on her cellphone, she could have offered crucial corroboration of Doe's trial testimony. Petitioner's Response 11-20. This testimony could have given Doe the credibility he needed to overcome the implied authority of the testifying Officer and changed the outcome of the entire trial.

2. *Failure to Object to Improper Argument*

Repeatedly, the prosecution argued that Doe "had been drinking" on the day of the traffic stop and subsequent arrest. *See* Petitioner's Response at 28-35. The prosecutor was completely wrong, and thus admitted into evidence false and perjured testimony that was far beyond improper. *U.S. v. Batman*, 123, U.S. 2020. Yet still, and in each incident, trial counsel failed to object. Indeed, Counsel's failure to Object to this improper and false testimony likely affected the results of the trial.

B. OTHER ACTS OF PROSECUTORIAL MISCONDUCT VIOLATED DOE's CONSTITUTIONAL RIGHTS (CLAIM 2).

The merits of these claims are discussed in Petitioner's Response at 35-40. In addition, the Court should consider the following case: *Johnson v. Smith*, 123 U.S. 500, 100 S.Ct. 2000, 123 L.Ed. 3d 3 (2020). The Texas Court of Criminal Appeals denied to consider these claims without a written order. Petitioner's Response at 45. The Court, therefore, cannot "adopt" a report that gives no basis for its conclusions.

C. CUMULATIVE ERROR (CLAIM 3)

The magistrate judge appears to have concluded that this claim fails because it is not based on clearly established U.S. Supreme Court law. As Doe explained in Petitioner's Response at 50-53, a petitioner must show only that his underlying constitutional claims are based on clearly established law of the U.S. Supreme Court. Cumulative error is not itself a ground for relief, but merely a process used by federal courts to evaluate the prejudice from several underlying constitutional violations.

As discussed throughout this Objection, this case pitted Doe's claims against the Officer's as to whether or not probable cause existed to initiate a protected stop and subsequent arrest. Counsel's ineffectiveness deprived Doe of a corroborating witness. The state's other improper arguments unfairly demeaned Doe's credibility. In the combination, at least, these errors deprived Doe of a fair trial.

III.

CONCLUSION

The Court should reject the Report and Recommendation and grant the writ of habeas corpus. In the alternative, it should grant an evidentiary hearing on the Claims.

DATED this 10th day of April, 2021.

Respectfully submitted:

[Sign Here]

[Printed Name and Address]

CHAPTER 11
BONUS MATERIAL

If I had a dollar for every time someone approached me wanting or needing a document, letter, form, etc., other than the typical pleadings associated with an appeal, I'd be the wealthiest man on the planet.

And so, right on time, and in answering the call, I will provide those most requested in this chapter. Again, they are not "one size fits all" and must be tailored to fit your unique needs, with the exception of general forms and materials that are, in fact, the same for everyone.

You are welcome.

Durable Power of Attorney

I, ____, my social security number being ______-____-________, do hereby appoint ____, who resides at ______________________________ in ______________________________, County of ___________________________ and the state of ____________________________, as my agent to act for me in my absence related to any and all of the following matters bearing my initials:

____________ (A) real property transactions

____________ (B) tangible personal property transactions;

____________ (C) stock and bond transactions;

____________ (D) commodity and options transactions;

____________ (E) estate, trust, and all beneficiary matters;

____________ (F) claims and litigations;

____________ (G) social security, Medicare, military, etc.;

____________ (H) 401k, retirement, banking, etc.;

____________ (I) IRS matters, tax matters, etc.;

____________ (J) any additional matters not named but intended and deemed necessary by the acting agent.

Special Instructions

____

____

____

*Unless indicated otherwise, this power of attorney remains in full effect and is not terminated by my disability or incapacity. *

In the event that the named agent should die, or becomes legally disabled or incapacitated, or resigns and refuses to act as my agent, I name the following to act alone, and in succession, in the other's place: ____, residing at

_______________________________, in the County of ______________________, in the State of _________________________________.

SIGNED THIS ____________ day of ________________, 20____.

State of ____________________________

County of ______________________________

Signed under oath before me on ____________________________,
by ____

I identified by his signature and documents presented at signing.

____

Notary Public

NOTARY SEAL

[Sign in front of notary]

[Printed name here]
[Address]

Last Will and Testament

I, ____________________________________, being of sound mind, body, and free will, and having full testamentary intent and capacity, do hereby voluntarily make, publish, and hereby execute this document as my Last Will and Testament.

1. My current residence is located at:

2. I hereby willingly and knowingly revoke any and all wills and codicils previously executed by me prior to this.

3. I hereby appoint ____ as the Executor of my estate. Further, I direct that no bond be required in any jurisdiction for the faithful exercise of his/her duties.

4. I hereby direct my Executor to pay all of my just and earned debts and other expenses of the administration of my estate.

5. I hereby give the following items:

6. The rest of my estate will be divided as follows:

7. Other

In Witness Whereof, I have signed this document as my Last Will and Testament on this ____________ day of ____________, 2021.

[Sign here]

[Printed name here]

The foregoing will of ______________________________________, dated ________________________________, was signed in our presence as a Last Will and Testament. We hereby declare that the maker is of sound mind and body, and of free will at the time of the signing of my name, in the presence of the maker.

[Witness sign here]

[Witness printed name here]

[Witness sign here]

[Witness printed name here]

Subscribed and sworn before me on this ____________ day of _____________, 2021.

____

Notary Public

Living Will

I, ____(Maker), being of sound mind, and body, hereby voluntarily declare that this directive is made this ____________ day of __________________, 2021, as my Living will in accordance with the laws of the state

of _________________________.

If I should have at any time an incurable condition caused by illness, disease, or injury certified to be terminal in condition by two licensed physicians, and where there is no reasonable expectation of recovery from said terminal condition, and where the application of life-sustaining methods and equipment would only prolong the moment of my imminent death, I hereby direct and request that said life-sustaining methods and equipment not be used, and that I be allowed to die naturally and not be kept alive by artificial or extraordinary means.

In the event that I am unable to give conscious direction regarding medical treatment or the use of said life-sustaining procedures, I hereby direct and request that this Living will be honored by my family, physicians and all other as the final and conclusive expression of my legal right to refuse medical treatment. I hereby appoint ___________________________ as my true and lawful attorney in fact to act for me and to make decisions concerning medical treatment, including the withdrawal or withholding of life support, in accordance with this Living Will. This power of attorney shall remain in the effect in the event that I should become or be declared to be disabled, incapacitated, or incompetent.

Until revoked by me, this Living Will shall remain active. My current residence is:

____

____ .

In witness Whereof I have signed this document as my declaration and Living Will.

[Makers signature

[Printed name]

The maker of this Living Will is personally known to me, is of sound mind, and has executed this document of his own free will.

[Witness signature]
[Witness printed name]
[Address]

[Witness sign here]
[Witness printed name]
[Address]

Subscribed and sworn before me on this ___________ day of ____________, 2021.

____
Notary Public

Case No. ____________________

Your Name Here Plaintiff, vs. Spouse's Name Here Defendant.	§ § § § § § § § § §	IN THE ___________________ JUDICIAL DISTRICT COURT OF ANYWHERE COUNTY, USA

COMPLAINT FOR DIVORCE

Plaintiff, ____________________________________, respectfully declares the following:

1. Plaintiff currently resides at: ____
____.

2. Plaintiff has been a resident of the State of ________________________________
for a period of ______________________________ years/months.

3. Defendant currently resides at the following: _______________________________
____.

4. Plaintiff and Defendant were married on the ________ day of _________________,
20____, and at the place of ____ (city)
___________________________ (county), ___________________________ (state).
A copy of the marriage license is attached where possible.

5. Plaintiff seeks a divorce from Defendant based on the following:

6. The marriage between the Plaintiff and Defendant is irretrievably broken and efforts at reconciliation have not been successful.

7. Plaintiff and Defendant do not own any property, and do not have any children together. The divorce is uncontested.

Wherefore, Plaintiff requests judgment dissolving the marriage between the parties and such further relief as the Plaintiff may have requested herein.

Verification

I, being of full age and mind, hereby certify that I am the Plaintiff in the foregoing Complaint for Divorce, that all declarations are true and correct, and that said Complaint is filed in good faith and without collusion.

[Signature]
[Printed name]
[Address]

Subscribed and sworn to before me on this day of ____________ day of ________________________, 20____

____
Notary Public

Case No. ____________________

Your Name Here Petitioner.	§ § § § §	IN THE 100th JUDICIAL DISTRICT COURT OF DALLAS COUNTY, TEXAS

MOTION TO CHANGE NAME

COMES NOW PETITIONER, and respectfully requests this Honorable Court allow him/her to change their name. In the support, Petitioner will show as follows:

1. Petitioner wishes to change his/her name from ______________________________,

to ______________________________________.

2. Petitioner resides at the following address: ________________________________

____.

3. Petitioner was born on the _______ day of ____________, 19__, at the place of

______________________________ (city), ____________________________ (county)

__________________________________ (state).

4. At birth, Petitioner was named ____,

and has always been known by that name, except for the following other names used:

____.

5. Petitioner's father is: ____

who resides at: ____?

6. Petitioner's mother is: ____

who resides at: ____?

7. Petitioner desires to change his/her name for the following reason(s): ___________

____.

WHEREFORE, Petitioner respectfully moves this Court to issue an order changing the petitioner's name.

Verification

I, ____, hereby certify that I am the petitioner in the foregoing Motion to Change Name and that all statements made herein are true and correct. I am aware that perjury and willful false statements will subject me to the punishments under the law.

[Sign Here]
[Printed Name Here]
[Address]
[City, State, Zip Code]

Pro Se

01, January, 2020

Name of Credit Reporting Agency
1234 Main St.
Anywhere, USA, 12345

Re: Request to Correct Errors in Credit Report

Dear Sir or Ma'am:

Please be advised that the following error(s) appear(s) in my credit report issued by your agency on the date of ________________________________, 2021.

1. (Describer the error(s); be specific)

Please correct my credit report as soon as possible to remove this incorrect information.

Sincerely,

[Sign Here]
[Printed Name Here]
[Address]
[City, State, Zip Code]

[Date of birth]
[Social Security number]

Major Credit Reporting Agencies

1. TransUnion: P.O. Box 6790
Fullerton, CA 92834
1-800-916-8800
transunion.com

2. Experian: 535 Anton Boulevard
Suite 100
Costa Mesa, CA 92626
1-888-397-3742
experian.com

3. Equifax: P.O. Box 740241
Atlanta, GA 30374
1-800-685-1111
equifax.com

* For a full copy of the Fair Credit Reporting Act, go to: https://www.ftc.gov/enforcement/rules/rulemaking-regulatory-reform-proceeding/fair-credit-reporting-act.

Or simply google search: "Fair Credit Reporting Act."

Registering Your Copyrights

A Copyright is granted under federal law to an author or creator of literary or artistic work(s). It creates the sole legal right of reproducing and selling your work as well as the right to prevent others from copying, stealing, and selling your work without your permission and compensation.

A Federal Copyright provides copyright protections under your state law, as well as under The Federal Copyright Act. This means simply that federal copyright protections is the only copyright protection available to protect your work(s).

- *Form TX* is used for registering nondramatic literary works
- *Form VA* is used for registering visual arts works.
- *Form PA* is used for registering performing arts.
- *Form SR* is used for registering sound recordings.

You can obtain the correct copyright form by going to: copyright.gov/forms. After filling out the correct form, you can file the form electronically or simply file it online at copyright.gov.

The fee for filing a copyright is around $35 currently if you apply online. If you choose to fill out the paper application, the fee is $85. Hiring an attorney to do either of these on your behalf will cost somewhere around $1,500.

If you choose to fill out the form yourself, you can then mail it the following address:

Register of Copyrights Library of Congress
101 Independence Ave, SE
Washington, DC 20559-6000

* I have included Forms TX, VA, PA, and SR for review.

Form TX

Detach and read these instructions before completing this form.
Make sure all applicable spaces have been filled in before you return this form.

BASIC INFORMATION

When to Use This Form: Use Form TX for registration of published or unpublished nondramatic literary works, excluding periodicals or serial issues. This class includes a wide variety of works: fiction, nonfiction, poetry, textbooks, reference works, directories, catalogs, advertising copy, compilations of information, and computer programs. For periodicals and serials, use Form SE.

Unpublished works: This form may be used to register one unpublished work. This form cannot be used to register a "collection" of two or more unpublished works. Any paper application submitted with more than one unpublished work may be refused. To register multiple unpublished works, you must use the online application for "A Group of Unpublished Works." For information about the online application, see *Multiple Works* (Circular 34).

Deposit to Accompany Application: An application for copyright registration must be accompanied by a deposit consisting of copies or phonorecords representing the entire work for which registration is to be made. The following are the general deposit requirements as set forth in the statute:

Unpublished Work: Deposit one complete copy (or phonorecord)

Published Work: Deposit two complete copies (or one phonorecord) of the best edition.

Work First Published Outside the United States: Deposit one complete copy (or phonorecord) of the first foreign edition.

Contribution to a Collective Work: Deposit one complete copy (or phonorecord) of the best edition of the collective work.

The Copyright Notice: Before March 1, 1989, the use of copyright notice was mandatory on all published works, and any work first published before that date should have carried a notice. For works first published on and after March 1, 1989, use of the copyright notice is optional. For more information about copyright notice, see *Copyright Notice* (Circular 3).

For Further Information: To speak to a Copyright Office staff member, call (202) 707-3000 or 1-877-476-0778 (toll free). Recorded information is available 24 hours a day. Order forms and other publications from the address in space 9 or call the Forms and Publications Hotline at (202) 707-9100. Access and download circulars, certain forms, and other information from the Copyright Office website at *www.copyright.gov*.

PRIVACY ACT ADVISORY STATEMENT Required by the Privacy Act of 1974 (P.L. 93-579)

The authority for requesting this information is title 17 U.S.C. §409 and §410. Furnishing the requested information is voluntary. But if the information is not furnished, it may be necessary to delay or refuse registration and you may not be entitled to certain relief, remedies, and benefits provided in chapters 4 and 5 of title 17 U.S.C.

The principal uses of the requested information are the establishment and maintenance of a public record and the examination of the application for compliance with the registration requirements of the copyright code.

Other routine uses include public inspection and copying, preparation of public indexes, preparation of public catalogs of copyright registrations, and preparation of search reports upon request.

NOTE: No other advisory statement will be given in connection with this application. Please keep this statement and refer to it if we communicate with you regarding this application.

LINE-BY-LINE INSTRUCTIONS

Please type or print using black ink. The form is used to produce the certificate.

1 SPACE 1: Title

Title of This Work: Every work submitted for copyright registration must be given a title to identify that particular work. If the copies or phonorecords of the work bear a title or an identifying phrase that could serve as a title, transcribe that wording *completely* and *exactly* on the application. Indexing of the registration and future identification of the work will depend on the information you give here.

Previous or Alternative Titles: Complete this space if there are any additional titles for the work under which someone searching for the registration might be likely to look or under which a document pertaining to the work might be recorded.

Publication as a Contribution: If the work being registered is a contribution to a periodical, serial, or collection, give the title of the contribution in the "Title of This Work" space. Then, in the line headed "Publication as a Contribution," give information about the collective work in which the contribution appeared.

2 SPACE 2: Author(s)

General Instructions: After reading these instructions, decide who are the "authors" of this work for copyright purposes. Then, unless the work is a "collective work," give the requested information about every "author" who contributed any appreciable amount of copyrightable matter to this version of the work. If you need further space, request Continuation Sheets. In the case of a collective work, such as an anthology, collection of essays, or encyclopedia, give information about the author of the collective work as a whole.

Name of Author: The fullest form of the author's name should be given. Unless the work was "made for hire," the individual who actually created the work is its "author." In the case of a work made for hire, the statute provides that "the employer or other person for whom the work was prepared is considered the author."

What Is a "Work Made for Hire"? A "work made for hire" is defined as (1) "a work prepared by an employee within the scope of his or her employment"; or (2) "a work specially ordered or commissioned for use as a contribution to a collective work, as a part of a motion picture or other audiovisual work, as a translation, as a supplementary work, as a compilation, as an instructional text, as a test, as answer material for a test, or as an atlas, if the parties expressly agree in a written instrument signed by them that the works shall be considered a work made for hire." If you have checked "Yes" to indicate that the work was "made for hire," you must give the full legal name of the employer (or other person for whom the work was prepared). You may also include the name of the employee along with the name of the employer (for example: "Elster Publishing Co., employer for hire of John Ferguson").

"Anonymous" or "Pseudonymous" Work: An author's contribution to a work is "anonymous" if that author is not identified on the copies or phonorecords of the work. An author's contribution to a work is "pseudonymous" if that author is identified on the copies or phonorecords under a fictitious name. If the work is "anonymous" you may: (1) leave the line blank; or (2) state "anonymous" on the line; or (3) reveal the author's identity. If the work is "pseudonymous" you may: (1) leave the line blank; or (2) give the pseudonym and identify it as such (for example: "Huntley Haverstock, pseudonym"); or (3) reveal the author's name, making clear which is the real name and which is the pseudonym (for example, "Judith Barton, whose pseudonym is Madeline Elster"). However, the citizenship or domicile of the author *must* be given in all cases.

Dates of Birth and Death: If the author is dead, the statute requires that the year of death be included in the application unless the work is anonymous or pseudonymous. The author's birth date is optional but is useful as a form of identification. Leave this space blank if the author's contribution was a "work made for hire."

Author's Nationality or Domicile: Give the country of which the author is a citizen or the country in which the author is domiciled. Nationality or domicile *must* be given in all cases.

Nature of Authorship: After the words "Nature of Authorship," give a brief general statement of the nature of this particular author's contribution to the work. Examples: "Entire text"; "Coauthor of entire text"; "Computer program"; "Editorial revisions"; "Compilation and English translation"; "New text."

3 SPACE 3: Creation and Publication

General Instructions: Do not confuse "creation" with "publication." Every application for copyright registration must state "the year in which creation of the work was completed." Give the date and nation of first publication only if the work has been published.

Creation: Under the statute, a work is "created" when it is fixed in a copy or phonorecord for the first time. Where a work has been prepared over a period of time, the part of the work existing in fixed form on a particular date constitutes the created work on that date. The date you give here should be the year in which the author completed the particular version for which registration is now being sought, even if other versions exist or if further changes or additions are planned.

Publication: The statute defines "publication" as "the distribution of copies or phonorecords of a work to the public by sale or other transfer of ownership, or by rental, lease, or lending." A work is also "published" if there has been an "offering to distribute copies or phonorecords to a group of persons for purposes of further distribution, public performance, or public display." Give the full date (month, day, year) when, and the country where, publication first occurred. If first publication took place simultaneously in the United States and other countries, it is sufficient to state "U.S.A."

4 SPACE 4: Claimant(s)

Name(s) and Address(es) of Copyright Claimant(s): Give the name(s) and address(es) of the copyright claimant(s) in this work even if the claimant is the same as the author. Copyright in a work belongs initially to the author of the work (including, in the case of a work made for hire, the employer or other person for whom the work was prepared). The copyright claimant is either the author of the work or a person or organization to whom the copyright initially belonging to the author has been transferred.

Transfer: The statute provides that, if the copyright claimant is not the author, the application for registration must contain "a brief statement of how the claimant obtained ownership of the copyright." If any copyright claimant named in space 4 is not an author named in space 2, give a brief statement explaining how the claimant(s) obtained ownership of the copyright. Examples: "By written contract"; "Transfer of all rights by author"; "Assignment"; "By will." Do not attach transfer documents or other attachments or riders.

5 SPACE 5: Previous Registration

General Instructions: The questions in space 5 are intended to show whether an earlier registration has been made for this work and, if so, whether there is any basis for a new registration. As a general rule, only one basic copyright registration can be made for the same version of a particular work.

Same Version: If this version is substantially the same as the work covered by a previous registration, a second registration is not generally possible unless: (1) the work has been registered in unpublished form and a second registration is now being sought to cover this first published edition; or (2) someone other than the author is identified as copyright claimant in the earlier registration, and the author is now seeking registration in his or her own name. If either of these two exceptions applies, check the appropriate box and give the earlier registration number and date. Otherwise, do not submit Form TX. Instead, write the Copyright Office for information about supplementary registration or recordation of transfers of copyright ownership.

Changed Version: If the work has been changed and you are now seeking registration to cover the additions or revisions, check the last box in space 5, give the earlier registration number and date, and complete both parts of space 6 in accordance with the instructions below.

Previous Registration Number and Date: If more than one previous registration has been made for the work, give the number and date of the latest registration.

6 SPACE 6: Derivative Work or Compilation

General Instructions: Complete space 6 if this work is a "changed version," "compilation," or "derivative work" and if it incorporates one or more earlier works that have already been published or registered for copyright or that have fallen into the public domain. A "compilation" is defined as "a work formed by the collection and assembling of preexisting materials or of data that are selected, coordinated, or arranged in such a way that the resulting work as a whole constitutes an original work of authorship." A "derivative work" is "a work based on one or more preexisting works." Examples of derivative works include translations, fictionalizations, abridgments, condensations, or "any other form in which a work may be recast, transformed, or adapted." Derivative works also include works "consisting of editorial revisions, annotations, or other modifications" if these changes, as a whole, represent an original work of authorship.

Preexisting Material (space 6a): For derivative works, complete this space *and* space 6b. In space 6a identify the preexisting work that has been recast, transformed, or adapted. The preexisting work may be material that has been previously published, previously registered, or that is in the public domain. An example of preexisting material might be: "Russian version of Goncharov's 'Oblomov.'"

Material Added to This Work (space 6b): Give a brief, general statement of the new material covered by the copyright claim for which registration is sought. *Derivative work* examples include: "Foreword, editing, critical annotations"; "Translation"; "Chapters 11–17." If the work is a *compilation*, describe both the compilation itself and the material that has been compiled. Example: "Compilation of certain 1917 speeches by Woodrow Wilson." A work may be both a derivative work and compilation, in which case a sample statement might be: "Compilation and additional new material."

7,8,9 SPACE 7,8,9: Fee, Correspondence, Certification, Return Address

Deposit Account: If you maintain a Deposit Account in the Copyright Office, identify it in space 7a. Otherwise leave the space blank and send the fee with your application and deposit.

Correspondence (space 7b): Give the name, address, area code, telephone number, fax number, and email address (if available) of the person to be consulted if correspondence about this application becomes necessary.

Certification (space 8): The application cannot be accepted unless it bears the date and the *signature* of the author or other copyright claimant, or the owner of exclusive right(s), or the duly authorized agent of author, claimant, or owner of exclusive right(s).

Address for Return of Certificate (space 9): The address box must be completed legibly because the certificate will be returned in a window envelope.

Copyright Office fees are subject to change. For current fees, check the Copyright Office website at www.copyright.gov, write the Copyright Office, or call (202) 707-3000.

Clear Form

Form TX

For a Nondramatic Literary Work
UNITED STATES COPYRIGHT OFFICE

REGISTRATION NUMBER

TX TXU

EFFECTIVE DATE OF REGISTRATION

Month Day Year

Privacy Act Notice: Sections 408-410 of title 17 of the *United States Code* authorize the Copyright Office to collect the personally identifying information requested on this form in order to process the application for copyright registration. By providing this information you are agreeing to routine uses of the information that include publication to give legal notice of your copyright claim as required by 17 U.S.C. §705. It will appear in the Office's online catalog. If you do not provide the information requested, registration may be refused or delayed, and you may not be entitled to certain relief, remedies, and benefits under the copyright law.

DO NOT WRITE ABOVE THIS LINE. IF YOU NEED MORE SPACE, USE A SEPARATE CONTINUATION SHEET.

1

TITLE OF THIS WORK ▼

PREVIOUS OR ALTERNATIVE TITLES ▼

PUBLICATION AS A CONTRIBUTION If this work was published as a contribution to a periodical, serial, or collection, give information about the collective work in which the contribution appeared. **Title of Collective Work ▼**

If published in a periodical or serial give: **Volume ▼** **Number ▼** **Issue Date ▼** **On Pages ▼**

2

a **NAME OF AUTHOR ▼**

DATES OF BIRTH AND DEATH Year Born ▼ Year Died ▼

Was this contribution to the work a "work made for hire"? ❑ Yes ❑ No

AUTHOR'S NATIONALITY OR DOMICILE Name of Country
OR { Citizen of ____ / Domiciled in ____

WAS THIS AUTHOR'S CONTRIBUTION TO THE WORK
Anonymous? ❑ Yes ❑ No
Pseudonymous? ❑ Yes ❑ No
If the answer to either of these questions is "Yes," see detailed instructions.

NATURE OF AUTHORSHIP Briefly describe nature of material created by this author in which copyright is claimed. ▼

b **NAME OF AUTHOR ▼**

DATES OF BIRTH AND DEATH Year Born ▼ Year Died ▼

Was this contribution to the work a "work made for hire"? ❑ Yes ❑ No

AUTHOR'S NATIONALITY OR DOMICILE Name of Country
OR { Citizen of ____ / Domiciled in ____

WAS THIS AUTHOR'S CONTRIBUTION TO THE WORK
Anonymous? ❑ Yes ❑ No
Pseudonymous? ❑ Yes ❑ No
If the answer to either of these questions is "Yes," see detailed instructions.

NATURE OF AUTHORSHIP Briefly describe nature of material created by this author in which copyright is claimed. ▼

c **NAME OF AUTHOR ▼**

DATES OF BIRTH AND DEATH Year Born ▼ Year Died ▼

Was this contribution to the work a "work made for hire"? ❑ Yes ❑ No

AUTHOR'S NATIONALITY OR DOMICILE Name of Country
OR { Citizen of ____ / Domiciled in ____

WAS THIS AUTHOR'S CONTRIBUTION TO THE WORK
Anonymous? ❑ Yes ❑ No
Pseudonymous? ❑ Yes ❑ No
If the answer to either of these questions is "Yes," see detailed instructions.

NATURE OF AUTHORSHIP Briefly describe nature of material created by this author in which copyright is claimed. ▼

NOTE

Under the law, the "author" of a "work made for hire" is generally the employer, not the employee (see instructions). For any part of this work that was "made for hire" check "Yes" in the space provided, give the employer (or other person for whom the work was prepared) as "Author" of that part, and leave the space for dates of birth and death blank.

3

a **YEAR IN WHICH CREATION OF THIS WORK WAS COMPLETED** **This information must be given in all cases.** Year

b **DATE AND NATION OF FIRST PUBLICATION OF THIS PARTICULAR WORK** **Complete this information ONLY if this work has been published.** Month ____ Day ____ Year ____ Nation

4

COPYRIGHT CLAIMANT(S) Name and address must be given even if the claimant is the same as the author given in space 2. ▼

See instructions before completing this space.

TRANSFER If the claimant(s) named here in space 4 is (are) different from the author(s) named in space 2, give a brief statement of how the claimant(s) obtained ownership of the copyright. ▼

DO NOT WRITE HERE OFFICE USE ONLY

APPLICATION RECEIVED

ONE DEPOSIT RECEIVED

TWO DEPOSITS RECEIVED

FUNDS RECEIVED

MORE ON BACK ▶ • Complete all applicable spaces (numbers 5-9) on the reverse side of this page. • See detailed instructions. • Sign the form at line 8.

DO NOT WRITE HERE

Page 1 of ____ pages

EXAMINED BY	FORM TX
CHECKED BY	
☐ CORRESPONDENCE Yes	FOR COPYRIGHT OFFICE USE ONLY

DO NOT WRITE ABOVE THIS LINE. IF YOU NEED MORE SPACE, USE A SEPARATE CONTINUATION SHEET.

5

PREVIOUS REGISTRATION Has registration for this work, or for an earlier version of this work, already been made in the Copyright Office?

❑ Yes ❑ No If your answer is "Yes," why is another registration being sought? (Check appropriate box.) ▼

a. ❑ This is the first published edition of a work previously registered in unpublished form.

b. ❑ This is the first application submitted by this author as copyright claimant.

c. ❑ This is a changed version of the work, as shown by space 6 on this application.

If your answer is "Yes," give: **Previous Registration Number** ▶ **Year of Registration** ▶

6

DERIVATIVE WORK OR COMPILATION

a **Preexisting Material** Identify any preexisting work or works that this work is based on or incorporates. ▼

See instructions before completing this space.

b **Material Added to This Work** Give a brief, general statement of the material that has been added to this work and in which copyright is claimed. ▼

7

a **DEPOSIT ACCOUNT** If the registration fee is to be charged to a deposit account established in the Copyright Office, give name and number of account.

Name ▼ Account Number ▼

b **CORRESPONDENCE** Give name and address to which correspondence about this application should be sent. Name / Address / Apt / City / State / Zip ▼

Area code and daytime telephone number ▶ Fax number ▶

Email ▶

8

CERTIFICATION* I, the undersigned, hereby certify that I am the

Check only one ▶
- ❑ author
- ❑ other copyright claimant
- ❑ owner of exclusive right(s)
- ❑ authorized agent of ______

Name of author or other copyright claimant, or owner of exclusive right(s) ▲

of the work identified in this application and that the statements made by me in this application are correct to the best of my knowledge.

Typed or printed name and date ▼ If this application gives a date of publication in space 3, do not sign and submit it before that date.

Date ▶

Signature ▼

9

Certificate will be mailed in window envelope to this address:

Name ▼

Number/Street/Apt ▼

City/State/Zip ▼

YOU MUST:
- Complete all necessary spaces
- Sign your application in space 8

SEND ALL 3 ELEMENTS IN THE SAME PACKAGE
1. Application form
2. Nonrefundable filing fee in check or money order payable to *U.S. Copyright Office*
3. Deposit material

MAIL TO:
Library of Congress
Copyright Office-TX
101 Independence Avenue SE
Washington, DC 20559-6000

*17 U.S.C. §506(e): Any person who knowingly makes a false representation of a material fact in the application for copyright registration provided for by section 409, or in any written statement filed in connection with the application, shall be fined not more than $2,500.

Form TX–Full Reviewed: 05/2019 Printed on recycled paper

Form VA

Detach and read these instructions before completing this form.
Make sure all applicable spaces have been filled in before you return this form.

BASIC INFORMATION

When to Use This Form: As a general rule, you may use Form VA for copyright registration of a published or unpublished work of the visual arts. This category includes "pictorial, graphic, or sculptural works," such as two-dimensional and three-dimensional works of fine, graphic, and applied art; photographs; prints and art reproductions; and maps, globes, charts, technical drawings, diagrams, and models.

Important note: This form may be used to register one published work or one unpublished work. This form cannot be used to register a "collection" of two or more works. Any paper application submitted with more than one work may be refused. To register multiple unpublished works, you must use the online application for "A Group of Unpublished Works." To register multiple photographs, you must use the online application for "Published Photographs" or "Unpublished Photographs." For information about these applications, see *Multiple Works* (Circular 34).

Likewise, this form cannot be used to register an architectural work, such as the design of a house, office building, church, museum, or other humanly habitable structure. To register a published or unpublished architectural work, you must submit the "Standard" online application through the electronic registration system. For information about this application, see *Copyright Registration of Architectural Works* (Circular 41).

What Does Copyright Protect? Copyright in a work of the visual arts protects those pictorial, graphic, or sculptural elements that, either alone or in combination, represent an "original work of authorship." The statute declares: "In no case does copyright protection for an original work of authorship extend to any idea, procedure, process, system, method of operation, concept, principle, or discovery, regardless of the form in which it is described, explained, illustrated, or embodied in such work."

Works of Artistic Craftsmanship and Designs: You may register "works of artistic craftsmanship" on Form VA, but the statute makes clear that protection extends to "their form" and not to "their mechanical or utilitarian aspects." The "design of a useful article" is considered copyrightable "only if, and only to the extent that, such design incorporates pictorial, graphic, or sculptural features that can be identified separately from, and are capable of existing independently of, the utilitarian aspects of the article."

Labels and Advertisements: Works prepared for use in connection with the sale or advertisement of goods and services may be registered if they contain "original work of authorship." Use Form VA if the copyrightable material in the work you are registering is mainly pictorial or graphic; use Form TX if it consists mainly of text. **Note:** Words and short phrases such as names, titles, and slogans cannot be protected by copyright, and the same is true of standard symbols, emblems, and other commonly used graphic designs that are in the public domain. When used commercially, material of that sort can sometimes be protected under state laws of unfair competition or under the federal trademark laws. For information about trademark registration, call the U.S. Patent and Trademark Office, at 1-800-786-9199 (toll free) or go to *www.uspto.gov*.

Deposit to Accompany Application: An application for copyright registration must be accompanied by a deposit consisting of copies representing the entire work for which registration is to be made.

Unpublished Work: Deposit one complete copy.

Published Work: Deposit two complete copies of the best edition.

Work First Published Outside the United States: Deposit one complete copy of the first foreign edition.

Contribution to a Collective Work: Deposit one complete copy of the best edition of the collective work.

The Copyright Notice: Before March 1, 1989, the use of copyright notice was mandatory on all published works, and any work first published before that date should have carried a notice. For works first published on and after March 1, 1989, use of the copyright notice is optional. For more information about copyright notice, see *Copyright Notice* (Circular 3).

For Further Information: To speak to a Copyright Office staff member, call (202) 707-3000 or 1-877-476-0778 (toll free). Recorded information is available 24 hours a day. Order forms and other publications from the address in space 9 or call (202) 707-9100 or 1-877-476-0778 (toll free). Access and download circulars, forms, and other information from the Copyright Office website at *www.copyright.gov*.

PRIVACY ACT ADVISORY STATEMENT Required by the Privacy Act of 1974 (P.L. 93-579)
The authority for requesting this information is title 17 U.S.C. §409 and §410. Furnishing the requested information is voluntary. But if the information is not furnished, it may be necessary to delay or refuse registration and you may not be entitled to certain relief, remedies, and benefits provided in chapters 4 and 5 of title 17 U.S.C.
The principal uses of the requested information are the establishment and maintenance of a public record and the examination of the application for compliance with the registration requirements of the copyright code.
Other routine uses include public inspection and copying, preparation of public indexes, preparation of public catalogs of copyright registrations, and preparation of search reports upon request.
NOTE: No other advisory statement will be given in connection with this application. Please keep this statement and refer to it if we communicate with you regarding this application.

LINE-BY-LINE INSTRUCTIONS

Please type or print using black ink. The form is used to produce the certificate.

1 SPACE 1: Title

Title of This Work: Every work submitted for copyright registration must be given a title to identify that particular work. If the copies of the work bear a title (or an identifying phrase that could serve as a title), transcribe that wording *completely* and *exactly* on the application. Indexing of the registration and future identification of the work will depend on the information you give here.

Publication as a Contribution: If the work being registered is a contribution to a periodical, serial, or collection, give the title of the contribution in the "Title of This Work" space. Then, in the line headed "Publication as a Contribution," give information about the collective work in which the contribution appeared.

Nature of This Work: Briefly describe the general nature or character of the pictorial, graphic, or sculptural work being registered for copyright. Examples: "Oil Painting"; "Charcoal Drawing"; "Etching"; "Sculpture"; "Map"; "Photograph"; "Scale Model"; "Lithographic Print"; "Jewelry Design"; "Fabric Design."

Previous or Alternative Titles: Complete this space if there are any additional titles for the work under which someone searching for the registration might be likely to look, or under which a document pertaining to the work might be recorded.

2 SPACE 2: Author(s)

General Instruction: After reading these instructions, decide who are the "authors" of this work for copyright purposes. Then, unless the work is a "collective work," give the requested information about every "author" who contributed any appreciable amount of copyrightable matter to this version of the work. If you need further space, request Continuation Sheets (Form CON). In the case of a collective work, such as a catalog of paintings or collection of cartoons by various authors, give information about the author of the collective work as a whole.

Name of Author: The fullest form of the author's name should be given. Unless the work was "made for hire," the individual who actually created the work is its "author." In the case of a work made for hire, the statute provides that "the employer or other person for whom the work was prepared is considered the author."

What Is a "Work Made for Hire"? A "work made for hire" is defined as: (1) "a work prepared by an employee within the scope of his or her employment"; or (2) "a work specially ordered or commissioned for use as a contribution to a collective work, as a part of a motion picture or other audiovisual work, as a translation, as a supplementary work, as a compilation, as an instructional text, as a test, as answer material for a test, or as an atlas, if the parties expressly agree in a written instrument signed by them that the work shall be considered a work made for hire." If you have checked "Yes" to indicate that the work was "made for hire," you must give the full legal name of the employer (or other person for whom the work was prepared). You may also include the name of the employee along with the name of the employer (for example: "Elster Publishing Co., employer for hire of John Ferguson").

"Anonymous" or "Pseudonymous" Work: An author's contribution to a work is "anonymous" if that author is not identified on the copies or phonorecords of the work. An author's contribution to a work is "pseudonymous" if that author is identified on the copies or phonorecords under a fictitious name. If the work is "anonymous" you may: (1) leave the line blank; or (2) state "anonymous" on the line; or (3) reveal the author's identity. If the work is "pseudonymous" you may: (1) leave the line blank; or (2) give the pseudonym and identify it as such (for example: "Huntley Haverstock, pseudonym"); or (3) reveal the author's name, making clear which is the real name and which is the pseudonym (for example: "Henry Leek, whose pseudonym is Priam Farrel"). However, the citizenship or domicile of the author *must* be given in all cases.

Dates of Birth and Death: If the author is dead, the statute requires that the year of death be included in the application unless the work is anonymous or pseudonymous. The author's birth date is optional but is useful as a form of identification. Leave this space blank if the author's contribution was a "work made for hire."

Author's Nationality or Domicile: Give the country of which the author is a citizen or the country in which the author is domiciled. Nationality or domicile *must* be given in all cases.

Nature of Authorship: Categories of pictorial, graphic, and sculptural authorship are listed below. Check the box(es) that best describe(s) each author's contribution to the work.

3-Dimensional sculptures: Fine art sculptures, toys, dolls, scale models, and sculptural designs applied to useful articles.

2-Dimensional artwork: Watercolor and oil paintings; pen and ink drawings; logo illustrations; greeting cards; collages; stencils; patterns; computer graphics; graphics appearing in screen displays; artwork appearing on posters, calendars, games, commercial prints and labels, and packaging; artwork applied to useful articles; designs reproduced on textiles, lace, and other fabrics and on wallpaper, carpeting, floor tile, wrapping paper, and clothing.

Reproductions of works of art: Reproductions of preexisting artwork made by, for example, lithography, photoengraving, or etching.

Maps: Cartographic representations of an area, such as state and county maps, atlases, marine charts, relief maps, and globes.

Photographs: Pictorial photographic prints and slides and holograms.

Jewelry designs: 3-dimensional designs applied to rings, pendants, earrings, necklaces, and the like.

Technical drawings: Diagrams illustrating scientific or technical information in linear form, such as blueprints or mechanical drawings.

Text: Textual material that accompanies pictorial, graphic, or sculptural works, such as comic strips, greeting cards, game rules, commercial prints or labels, and maps.

3 SPACE 3: Creation and Publication

General Instructions: Do not confuse "creation" with "publication." Every application for copyright registration must state "the year in which creation of the work was completed." Give the date and nation of first publication only if the work has been published.

Creation: Under the statute, a work is "created" when it is fixed in a copy or phonorecord for the first time. If a work has been prepared over a period of time, the part of the work existing in fixed form on a particular date constitutes the created work on that date. The date you give here should be the year in which the author completed the particular version for which registration is now being sought, even if other versions exist or if further changes or additions are planned.

Publication: The statute defines "publication" as "the distribution of copies or phonorecords of a work to the public by sale or other transfer of ownership, or by rental, lease, or lending"; a work is also "published" if there has been an "offering to distribute copies or phonorecords to a group of persons for purposes of further distribution, public performance, or public display." Give the full date (month, day, year) when, and the country where, publication first occurred. If first publication took place simultaneously in the United States and other countries, it is sufficient to state "U.S.A."

4 SPACE 4: Claimant(s)

Name(s) and Address(es) of Copyright Claimant(s): Give the name(s) and address(es) of the copyright claimant(s) in this work even if the claimant is the same as the author. Copyright in a work belongs initially to the author of the work, including, in the case of a work made for hire, the employer or other person for whom the work was prepared. The copyright claimant is either the author of the work or a person or organization to whom the copyright initially belonging to the author has been transferred.

Transfer: The statute provides that, if the copyright claimant is not the author, the application for registration must contain "a brief statement of how the claimant obtained ownership of the copyright." If any copyright claimant named in space 4 is not an author named in space 2, give a brief statement explaining how the claimant(s) obtained ownership of the copyright. Examples: "By written contract"; "Transfer of all rights by author"; "Assignment"; "By will." Do not attach transfer documents or other attachments or riders.

5 SPACE 5: Previous Registration

General Instructions: The questions in space 5 are intended to find out whether an earlier registration has been made for this work and, if so, whether there is any basis for a new registration. As a rule, only one basic copyright registration can be made for the same version of a particular work.

Same Version: If this version is substantially the same as the work covered by a previous registration, a second registration is not generally possible unless: (1) the work has been registered in unpublished form and a second registration is now being sought to cover this first published edition; or (2) someone other than the author is identified as a copyright claimant in the earlier registration, and the author is now seeking registration in his or her own name. If either of these two exceptions applies, check the appropriate box and give the earlier registration number and date. Otherwise, do not submit Form VA. Instead, write the Copyright Office for information about supplementary registration or recordation of transfers of copyright ownership.

Changed Version: If the work has been changed and you are now seeking registration to cover the additions or revisions, check the last box in space 5, give the earlier registration number and date, and complete both parts of space 6 in accordance with the instruction below.

Previous Registration Number and Date: If more than one previous registration has been made for the work, give the number and date of the latest registration.

6 SPACE 6: Derivative Work or Compilation

General Instructions: Complete space 6 if this work is a "changed version," "compilation," or "derivative work," and if it incorporates one or more earlier works that have already been published or registered for copyright, or that have fallen into the public domain. A "compilation" is defined as "a work formed by the collection and assembling of preexisting materials or of data that are selected, coordinated, or arranged in such a way that the resulting work as a whole constitutes an original work of authorship." A "derivative work" is "a work based on one or more preexisting works." Examples of derivative works include reproductions of works of art, sculptures based on drawings, lithographs based on paintings, maps based on previously published sources, or "any other form in which a work may be recast, transformed, or adapted." Derivative works also include works "consisting of editorial revisions, annotations, or other modifications" if these changes, as a whole, represent an original work of authorship.

Preexisting Material (space 6a): Complete this space *and* space 6b for derivative works. In this space identify the preexisting work that has been recast, transformed, or adapted. Examples of preexisting material might be "Grunewald Altarpiece" or "19th century quilt design." Do not complete this space for compilations.

Material Added to This Work (space 6b): Give a brief, general statement of the *additional* new material covered by the copyright claim for which registration is sought. In the case of a derivative work, identify this new material. Examples: "Adaptation of design and additional artistic work"; "Reproduction of painting by photolithography"; "Additional cartographic material"; "Compilation of photographs." If the work is a compilation, give a brief, general statement describing both the material that has been compiled *and* the compilation itself. Example: "Compilation of 19th century political cartoons."

7,8,9 SPACE 7, 8, 9: Fee, Correspondence, Certification, Return Address

Deposit Account: If you maintain a deposit account in the Copyright Office, identify it in space 7a. Otherwise, leave the space blank and send the fee with your application and deposit.

Correspondence (space 7b): Give the name, address, area code, telephone number, email address, and fax number (if available) of the person to be consulted if correspondence about this application becomes necessary.

Certification (space 8): The application cannot be accepted unless it bears the date and the *signature* of the author or other copyright claimant, or the owner of exclusive right(s), or the duly authorized agent of the author, claimant, or owner of exclusive right(s).

Address for Return of Certificate (space 9): The address box must be completed legibly since the certificate will be returned in a window envelope.

Copyright Office fees are subject to change. For current fees, check the Copyright Office website at www.copyright.gov, write the Copyright Office or call (202) 707-3000 or 1-877-476-0778 (toll free).

Clear Form

Form VA
For a Work of the Visual Arts
UNITED STATES COPYRIGHT OFFICE

REGISTRATION NUMBER

VA VAU

EFFECTIVE DATE OF REGISTRATION

Month Day Year

Privacy Act Notice: Sections 408-410 of title 17 of the *United States Code* authorize the Copyright Office to collect the personally identifying information requested on this form in order to process the application for copyright registration. By providing this information you are agreeing to routine uses of the information that include publication to give legal notice of your copyright claim as required by 17 U.S.C. §705. It will appear in the Office's online catalog. If you do not provide the information requested, registration may be refused or delayed, and you may not be entitled to certain relief, remedies, and benefits under the copyright law.

DO NOT WRITE ABOVE THIS LINE. IF YOU NEED MORE SPACE, USE A SEPARATE CONTINUATION SHEET.

1

TITLE OF THIS WORK ▼

NATURE OF THIS WORK ▼ See instructions

PREVIOUS OR ALTERNATIVE TITLES ▼

PUBLICATION AS A CONTRIBUTION If this work was published as a contribution to a periodical, serial, or collection, give information about the collective work in which the contribution appeared. **Title of Collective Work ▼**

If published in a periodical or serial give: **Volume ▼** **Number ▼** **Issue Date ▼** **On Pages ▼**

2

a **NAME OF AUTHOR ▼**

DATES OF BIRTH AND DEATH
Year Born ▼ Year Died ▼

WAS THIS CONTRIBUTION TO THE WORK A "WORK MADE FOR HIRE"?
❑ Yes
❑ No

AUTHOR'S NATIONALITY OR DOMICILE
Name of Country
OR { Citizen of / Domiciled in

WAS THIS AUTHOR'S CONTRIBUTION TO THE WORK
Anonymous? ❑ Yes ❑ No
Pseudonymous? ❑ Yes ❑ No
If the answer to either of these questions is "Yes," see detailed instructions.

NATURE OF AUTHORSHIP Check appropriate box(es). **See instructions**
❑ 3-Dimensional sculpture ❑ Map ❑ Technical drawing
❑ 2-Dimensional artwork ❑ Photograph ❑ Text
❑ Reproduction of work of art ❑ Jewelry design

NOTE
Under the law, the "author" of a "work made for hire" is generally the employer, not the employee (see instructions). For any part of this work that was "made for hire," check "Yes" in the space provided, give the employer (or other person for whom the work was prepared) as "Author" of that part, and leave the space for dates of birth and death blank.

b **NAME OF AUTHOR ▼**

DATES OF BIRTH AND DEATH
Year Born ▼ Year Died ▼

WAS THIS CONTRIBUTION TO THE WORK A "WORK MADE FOR HIRE"?
❑ Yes
❑ No

AUTHOR'S NATIONALITY OR DOMICILE
Name of Country
OR { Citizen of / Domiciled in

WAS THIS AUTHOR'S CONTRIBUTION TO THE WORK
Anonymous? ❑ Yes ❑ No
Pseudonymous? ❑ Yes ❑ No
If the answer to either of these questions is "Yes," see detailed instructions.

NATURE OF AUTHORSHIP Check appropriate box(es). **See instructions**
❑ 3-Dimensional sculpture ❑ Map ❑ Technical drawing
❑ 2-Dimensional artwork ❑ Photograph ❑ Text
❑ Reproduction of work of art ❑ Jewelry design

3

a **YEAR IN WHICH CREATION OF THIS WORK WAS COMPLETED**
Year ▶
This information must be given in all cases.

b **DATE AND NATION OF FIRST PUBLICATION OF THIS PARTICULAR WORK**
Complete this information ONLY if this work has been published.
Month ▶ Day ▶ Year ▶
Nation ▶

4

COPYRIGHT CLAIMANT(S) Name and address must be given even if the claimant is the same as the author given in space 2. ▼

See instructions before completing this space

TRANSFER If the claimant(s) named here in space 4 is (are) different from the author(s) named in space 2, give a brief statement of how the claimant(s) obtained ownership of the copyright. ▼

DO NOT WRITE HERE OFFICE USE ONLY
APPLICATION RECEIVED
ONE DEPOSIT RECEIVED
TWO DEPOSITS RECEIVED
FUNDS RECEIVED

MORE ON BACK ▶
• Complete all applicable spaces (numbers 5-9) on the reverse side of this page
• See detailed instructions • Sign the form at line 8

DO NOT WRITE HERE
Page 1 of ______ pages

EXAMINED BY

FORM VA

CHECKED BY

CORRESPONDENCE
❑ Yes

FOR COPYRIGHT OFFICE USE ONLY

DO NOT WRITE ABOVE THIS LINE. IF YOU NEED MORE SPACE, USE A SEPARATE CONTINUATION SHEET.

5

PREVIOUS REGISTRATION Has registration for this work, or for an earlier version of this work, already been made in the Copyright Office?
❑ **Yes** ❑ **No** If your answer is "Yes," why is another registration being sought? (Check appropriate box.) ▼
a. ❑ This is the first published edition of a work previously registered in unpublished form.
b. ❑ This is the first application submitted by this author as copyright claimant.
c. ❑ This is a changed version of the work, as shown by space 6 on this application.
If your answer is "Yes," give: **Previous Registration Number** ▼ **Year of Registration** ▼

6

DERIVATIVE WORK OR COMPILATION Complete both space 6a and 6b for a derivative work; complete only 6b for a compilation.
a. Preexisting Material Identify any preexisting work or works that this work is based on or incorporates. ▼

a

See instructions before completing this space

b. Material Added to This Work Give a brief, general statement of the material that has been added to this work and in which copyright is claimed. ▼

b

7

DEPOSIT ACCOUNT If the registration fee is to be charged to a Deposit Account established in the Copyright Office, give name and number of Account.
Name ▼ **Account Number** ▼

a

CORRESPONDENCE Give name and address to which correspondence about this application should be sent. Name/Address/Apt/City/State/Zip ▼

b

Area code and daytime telephone number ( ) Fax number ( )

Email

8

CERTIFICATION* I, the undersigned, hereby certify that I am the

check only one ▶
❑ author
❑ other copyright claimant
❑ owner of exclusive right(s)
❑ authorized agent of ____________
Name of author or other copyright claimant, or owner of exclusive right(s) ▲

of the work identified in this application and that the statements made by me in this application are correct to the best of my knowledge.

Typed or printed name and date ▼ If this application gives a date of publication in space 3, do not sign and submit it before that date.

Date ____________

Signature (X) ▼

X ____________

9

Certificate will be mailed in window envelope to this address:

Name ▼
Number/Street/Apt ▼
City/State/Zip ▼

YOU MUST:
- Complete all necessary spaces
- Sign your application in space 8

SEND ALL 3 ELEMENTS IN THE SAME PACKAGE:
1. Application form
2. Nonrefundable filing fee in check or money order payable to *U.S. Copyright Office*
3. Deposit material

MAIL TO:
Library of Congress
U.S. Copyright Office-VA
101 Independence Avenue SE
Washington, DC 20559-6000

*17 U.S.C. §506(e): Any person who knowingly makes a false representation of a material fact in the application for copyright registration provided for by section 409, or in any written statement filed in connection with the application, shall be fined not more than $2,500.

Form VA–Full Rev: 05/2019 Printed on recycled paper

Form PA

Detach and read these instructions before completing this form.
Make sure all applicable spaces have been filled in before you return this form.

BASIC INFORMATION

When to Use This Form: Use Form PA for registration of published or unpublished works of the performing arts. This class includes works prepared for the purpose of being "performed" directly before an audience or indirectly "by means of any device or process." Works of the performing arts include: (1) musical works, including any accompanying words; (2) dramatic works, including any accompanying music; (3) pantomimes and choreographic works; and (4) motion pictures and other audiovisual works.

Unpublished works: This form may be used to register one unpublished work. This form cannot be used to register a "collection" of two or more unpublished works. Any paper application submitted with more than one unpublished work may be refused. To register multiple unpublished works, you must use the online application for "A Group of Unpublished Works." For information about the online application, see *Multiple Works* (Circular 34).

Deposit to Accompany Application: An application for copyright registration must be accompanied by a deposit consisting of copies or phonorecords representing the entire work for which registration is made. The following are the general deposit requirements as set forth in the statute:

Unpublished Work: Deposit one complete copy (or phonorecord).

Published Work: Deposit two complete copies (or one phonorecord) of the best edition.

Work First Published Outside the United States: Deposit one complete copy (or phonorecord) of the first foreign edition.

Contribution to a Collective Work: Deposit one complete copy (or phonorecord) of the best edition of the collective work.

Motion Pictures: Deposit *both* of the following: (1) a separate written description of the contents of the motion picture; and (2) for a published work, one complete copy of the best edition of the motion picture; or, for an unpublished work, one complete copy of the motion picture or identifying material. Identifying material may be either an audiorecording of the entire soundtrack or one frame enlargement or similar visual print from each 10-minute segment.

The Copyright Notice: Before March 1, 1989, the use of copyright notice was mandatory on all published works, and any work first published before that date should have carried a notice. For works first published on and after March 1, 1989, use of the copyright notice is optional. For more information about copyright notice, see *Copyright Notice* (Circular 3).

For Further Information: To speak to a Copyright Office staff member, call (202) 707-3000 or 1-877-476-0778 (toll free). Recorded information is available 24 hours a day. Order forms and other publications from the address in space 9 or call (202) 707-9100 or 1-877-476-0778 (toll free). Access and download circulars, certain forms, and other information from the Copyright Office website at *www.copyright.gov*.

PRIVACY ACT ADVISORY STATEMENT Required by the Privacy Act of 1974 (P.L. 93-579)
The authority for requesting this information is title 17 U.S.C. §409 and §410. Furnishing the requested information is voluntary. But if the information is not furnished, it may be necessary to delay or refuse registration and you may not be entitled to certain relief, remedies, and benefits provided in chapters 4 and 5 of title 17 U.S.C.

The principal uses of the requested information are the establishment and maintenance of a public record and the examination of the application for compliance with the registration requirements of the copyright code.

Other routine uses include public inspection and copying, preparation of public indexes, preparation of public catalogs of copyright registrations, and preparation of search reports upon request.

NOTE: No other advisory statement will be given in connection with this application. Please keep this statement and refer to it if we communicate with you regarding this application.

LINE-BY-LINE INSTRUCTIONS

Please type or print using black ink. The form is used to produce the certificate.

1 SPACE 1: Title

Title of This Work: Every work submitted for copyright registration must be given a title to identify that particular work. If the copies or phonorecords of the work bear a title (or an identifying phrase that could serve as a title), transcribe that wording *completely* and *exactly* on the application. Indexing of the registration and future identification of the work will depend on the information you give here. If the work you are registering is an entire "collective work" (such as a collection of plays or songs), give the overall title of the collection. If you are registering one or more individual contributions to a collective work, give the title of each contribution, followed by the title of the collection. For an unpublished collection, you may give the titles of the individual works after the collection title.

Previous or Alternative Titles: Complete this space if there are any additional titles for the work under which someone searching for the registration might be likely to look, or under which a document pertaining to the work might be recorded. If you need a additional space, request a Continuation Sheet (Form CON).

Nature of This Work: Briefly describe the general nature or character of the work being registered for copyright. Examples: "Music"; "Song Lyrics"; "Words and Music"; "Drama"; "Musical Play"; "Choreography"; "Pantomime"; "Motion Picture"; "Audiovisual Work."

2 SPACE 2: Author(s)

General Instructions: After reading these instructions, decide who are the "authors" of this work for copyright purposes. Then, unless the work is a "collective work," give the requested information about every "author" who contributed any appreciable amount of copyrightable matter to this version of the work. If you need further space, request additional Continuation Sheets. In the case of a collective work such as a songbook or a collection of plays, give information about the author of the collective work as a whole.

Name of Author: The fullest form of the author's name should be given. Unless the work was "made for hire," the individual who actually created the work is its "author." In the case of a work made for hire, the statute provides that "the employer or other person for whom the work was prepared is considered the author."

What Is a "Work Made for Hire"? A "work made for hire" is defined as (1) "a work prepared by an employee within the scope of his or her employment"; or (2) "a work specially ordered or commissioned for use as a contribution to a collective work, as a part of a motion picture or other audiovisual work, as a translation, as a supplementary work, as a compilation, as an instructional text, as a test, as answer material for a test, or as an atlas, if the parties expressly agree in a written instrument signed by them that the work shall be considered a work made for hire." If you have checked "Yes" to indicate that the work was "made for hire," you must give the full legal name of the employer (or other person for whom the work was prepared). You may also include the name of the employee along with the name of the employer (for example: "Elster Music Co., employer for hire of John Ferguson").

"Anonymous" or "Pseudonymous" Work: An author's contribution to a work is "anonymous" if that author is not identified on the copies or phonorecords of the work. An author's contribution to a work is "pseudonymous" if that author is identified on the copies or phonorecords under a fictitious name. If the work is "anonymous" you may (1) leave the line blank; (2) state "anonymous" on the line; or (3) reveal the author's identity. If the work is "pseudonymous" you may (1) leave the line blank; (2) give the pseudonym and identify it as such (example: "Huntley Haverstock, pseudonym"); or (3) reveal the author's name, making clear which is the real name and which is the pseudonym (for example: "Judith Barton, whose pseudonym is Madeline Elster"). However, the citizenship or domicile of the author *must* be given in all cases.

Dates of Birth and Death: If the author is dead, the statute requires that the year of death be included in the application unless the work is anonymous or pseudonymous. The author's birth date is optional but is useful as a form of identification. Leave this space blank if the author's contribution was a "work made for hire."

Author's Nationality or Domicile: Give the country of which the author is a citizen, or the country in which the author is domiciled. Nationality or domicile *must* be given in all cases.

Nature of Authorship: Give a brief general statement of the nature of this particular author's contribution to the work. Examples: "Words"; "Coauthor of Music"; "Words and Music"; "Arrangement"; "Coauthor of Book and Lyrics"; "Dramatization"; "Screen Play"; "Compilation and English Translation"; "Editorial Revisions."

3 SPACE 3: Creation and Publication

General Instructions: Do not confuse "creation" with "publication." Every application for copyright registration must state "the year in which creation of the work was completed." Give the date and nation of first publication only if the work has been published.

Creation: Under the statute, a work is "created" when it is fixed in a copy or phonorecord for the first time. Where a work has been prepared over a period of time, the part of the work existing in fixed form on a particular date constitutes the created work on that date. The date you give here should be the year in which the author completed the particular version for which registration is now being sought, even if other versions exist or if further changes or additions are planned.

Publication: The statute defines "publication" as "the distribution of copies or phonorecords of a work to the public by sale or other transfer of ownership, or by rental, lease, or lending"; a work is also "published" if there has been an "offering to distribute copies or phonorecords to a group of persons for purposes of further distribution, public performance, or public display." Give the full date (month, day, year) when, and the country where, publication first occurred. If first publication took place simultaneously in the United States and other countries, it is sufficient to state "U.S.A."

4 SPACE 4: Claimant(s)

Name(s) and Address(es) of Copyright Claimant(s): Give the name(s) and address(es) of the copyright claimant(s) in this work even if the claimant is the same as the author. Copyright in a work belongs initially to the author of the work (including, in the case of a work made for hire, the employer or other person for whom the work was prepared). The copyright claimant is either the author of the work or a person or organization to whom the copyright initially belonging to the author has been transferred.

Transfer: The statute provides that, if the copyright claimant is not the author, the application for registration must contain "a brief statement of how the claimant obtained ownership of the copyright." If any copyright claimant named in space 4 is not an author named in space 2, give a brief statement explaining how the claimant(s) obtained ownership of the copyright. Examples: "By written contract"; "Transfer of all rights by author"; "Assignment"; "By will." Do not attach transfer documents or other attachments or riders.

5 SPACE 5: Previous Registration

General Instructions: The questions in space 5 are intended to show whether an earlier registration has been made for this work and, if so, whether there is any basis for a new registration. As a general rule, only one basic copyright registration can be made for the same version of a particular work.

Same Version: If this version is substantially the same as the work covered by a previous registration, a second registration is not generally possible unless (1) the work has been registered in unpublished form and a second registration is now being sought to cover this first published edition; or (2) someone other than the author is identified as copyright claimant in the earlier registration, and the author is now seeking registration in his or her own name. If either of these two exceptions applies, check the appropriate box and give the earlier registration number and date. Otherwise, do not submit Form PA; instead, contact the Copyright Office for information about supplementary registration or recordation of transfers of copyright ownership.

Changed Version: If the work has been changed and you are now seeking registration to cover the additions or revisions, check the last box in space 5, give the earlier registration number and date, and complete both parts of space 6 in accordance with the instructions below.

Previous Registration Number and Date: If more than one previous registration has been made for the work, give the number and date of the latest registration.

6 SPACE 6: Derivative Work or Compilation

General Instructions: Complete space 6 if this work is a "changed version," "compilation," or "derivative work," and if it incorporates one or more earlier works that have already been published or registered for copyright or that have fallen into the public domain. A "compilation" is defined as "a work formed by the collection and assembling of preexisting materials or of data that are selected, coordinated, or arranged in such a way that the resulting work as a whole constitutes an original work of authorship." A "derivative work" is "a work based on one or more preexisting works." Examples of derivative works include musical arrangements, dramatizations, translations, abridgments, condensations, motion picture versions, or "any other form in which a work may be recast, transformed, or adapted." Derivative works also include works "consisting of editorial revisions, annotations, or other modifications" if these changes, as a whole, represent an original work of authorship.

Preexisting Material (space 6a): Complete this space *and* space 6b for derivative works. In this space identify the preexisting work that has been recast, transformed, or adapted. For example, the preexisting material might be: "French version of Hugo's '*Le Roi s'amuse*'." Do not complete this space for compilations.

Material Added to This Work (space 6b): Give a brief general statement of the *additional* new material covered by the copyright claim for which registration is sought. In the case of a derivative work, identify this new material. Examples: "Arrangement for piano and orchestra"; "Dramatization for television"; "New film version"; "Revisions throughout; Act III completely new." If the work is a compilation, give a brief general statement describing both the material that has been compiled *and* the compilation itself. Example: "Compilation of 19th Century Military Songs."

7,8,9 SPACE 7, 8, 9: Fee, Correspondence, Certification, Return Address

Deposit Account: If you maintain a deposit account in the Copyright Office, identify it in space 7a. Otherwise, leave the space blank and send the fee with your application and deposit.

Correspondence (space 7b): Give the name, address, area code, telephone number, fax number, and email address of the person to be consulted if correspondence about this application becomes necessary.

Certification (space 8): The application cannot be accepted unless it bears the date and the *signature* of the author or other copyright claimant, the owner of exclusive right(s), or the duly authorized agent of the author, claimant, or owner of exclusive right(s).

Address for Return of Certificate (space 9): The address box must be completed legibly since the certificate will be returned in a window envelope.

MORE INFORMATION

How to Register a Recorded Work: If the musical or dramatic work that you are registering has been recorded (as a tape, disk, or cassette), you may choose either copyright application Form PA (Performing Arts) or Form SR (Sound Recordings), depending on the purpose of the registration.

Use Form PA to register the underlying musical composition or dramatic work. Form SR has been developed specifically to register a "sound recording" as defined by the Copyright Act—a work resulting from the "fixation of a series of sounds," separate and distinct from the underlying musical or dramatic work. Form SR should be used when the copyright claim is limited to the sound recording itself. (In one instance, Form SR may also be used to file for a copyright registration for both kinds of works—see (4) below.) Therefore:

(1) File Form PA if you are seeking to register the musical or dramatic work, not the "sound recording," even though what you deposit for copyright purposes may be in the form of a phonorecord.

(2) File Form PA if you are seeking to register the audio portion of an audiovisual work, such as a motion picture soundtrack; these are considered integral parts of the audiovisual work.

(3) File Form SR if you are seeking to register the "sound recording" itself, that is, the work that results from the fixation of a series of musical, spoken, or other sounds, but not the underlying musical or dramatic work.

(4) File Form SR if you are the copyright claimant for both the underlying musical or dramatic work and the sound recording, *and* you prefer to register both on the same form.

(5) File both forms PA and SR if the copyright claimant for the underlying work and sound recording differ, or you prefer to have separate registration for them.

"Copies" and "Phonorecords": To register for copyright, you are required to deposit "copies" or "phonorecords." These are defined as follows:

Musical compositions may be embodied (fixed) in "copies," objects from which a work can be read or visually perceived, directly or with the aid of a machine or device, such as manuscripts, books, sheet music, film, and videotape. They may also be fixed in "phonorecords," objects embodying fixations of sounds, such as tapes and phonograph disks, commonly known as phonograph records. For example, a song (the work to be registered) can be reproduced in sheet music ("copies") or phonograph records ("phonorecords"), or both.

Copyright Office fees are subject to change. For current fees, check the Copyright Office website at www.copyright.gov, write the Copyright Office, or call (202) 707-3000 or 1-877-476-0778 (toll free).

Clear Form

Form PA
For a Work of Performing Arts
UNITED STATES COPYRIGHT OFFICE

REGISTRATION NUMBER

PA PAU

EFFECTIVE DATE OF REGISTRATION

Month Day Year

Privacy Act Notice: Sections 408-410 of title 17 of the *United States Code* authorize the Copyright Office to collect the personally identifying information requested on this form in order to process the application for copyright registration. By providing this information you are agreeing to routine uses of the information that include publication to give legal notice of your copyright claim as required by 17 U.S.C. §705. It will appear in the Office's online catalog. If you do not provide the information requested, registration may be refused or delayed, and you may not be entitled to certain relief, remedies, and benefits under the copyright law.

DO NOT WRITE ABOVE THIS LINE. IF YOU NEED MORE SPACE, USE A SEPARATE CONTINUATION SHEET.

1

TITLE OF THIS WORK ▼

PREVIOUS OR ALTERNATIVE TITLES ▼

NATURE OF THIS WORK ▼ See instructions

2

a NAME OF AUTHOR ▼

DATES OF BIRTH AND DEATH
Year Born ▼ Year Died ▼

Was this contribution to the work a "work made for hire"?
❑ Yes
❑ No

AUTHOR'S NATIONALITY OR DOMICILE
Name of Country
OR { Citizen of
Domiciled in

WAS THIS AUTHOR'S CONTRIBUTION TO THE WORK
Anonymous? ❑ Yes ❑ No
Pseudonymous? ❑ Yes ❑ No
If the answer to either of these questions is "Yes," see detailed instructions

NATURE OF AUTHORSHIP Briefly describe nature of material created by this author in which copyright is claimed. ▼

b NAME OF AUTHOR ▼

DATES OF BIRTH AND DEATH
Year Born ▼ Year Died ▼

Was this contribution to the work a "work made for hire"?
❑ Yes
❑ No

AUTHOR'S NATIONALITY OR DOMICILE
Name of Country
OR { Citizen of
Domiciled in

WAS THIS AUTHOR'S CONTRIBUTION TO THE WORK
Anonymous? ❑ Yes ❑ No
Pseudonymous? ❑ Yes ❑ No
If the answer to either of these questions is "Yes," see detailed instructions

NATURE OF AUTHORSHIP Briefly describe nature of material created by this author in which copyright is claimed. ▼

c NAME OF AUTHOR ▼

DATES OF BIRTH AND DEATH
Year Born ▼ Year Died ▼

Was this contribution to the work a "work made for hire"?
❑ Yes
❑ No

AUTHOR'S NATIONALITY OR DOMICILE
Name of Country
OR { Citizen of
Domiciled in

WAS THIS AUTHOR'S CONTRIBUTION TO THE WORK
Anonymous? ❑ Yes ❑ No
Pseudonymous? ❑ Yes ❑ No
If the answer to either of these questions is "Yes," see detailed instructions

NATURE OF AUTHORSHIP Briefly describe nature of material created by this author in which copyright is claimed. ▼

NOTE

Under the law, the "author" of a "work made for hire" is generally the employer, not the employee (see instructions). For any part of this work that was "made for hire" check "Yes" in the space provided, give the employer (or other person for whom the work was prepared) as "Author" of that part, and leave the space for dates of birth and death blank.

3

a YEAR IN WHICH CREATION OF THIS WORK WAS COMPLETED **This information must be given in all cases.** Year

b DATE AND NATION OF FIRST PUBLICATION OF THIS PARTICULAR WORK **Complete this information ONLY if this work has been published.** Month Day Year Nation

4

COPYRIGHT CLAIMANT(S) Name and address must be given even if the claimant is the same as the author given in space 2. ▼

See instructions before completing this space.

TRANSFER If the claimant(s) named here in space 4 is (are) different from the author(s) named in space 2, give a brief statement of how the claimant(s) obtained ownership of the copyright. ▼

DO NOT WRITE HERE OFFICE USE ONLY

APPLICATION RECEIVED

ONE DEPOSIT RECEIVED

TWO DEPOSITS RECEIVED

FUNDS RECEIVED

MORE ON BACK ▶
• Complete all applicable spaces (numbers 5-9) on the reverse side of this page
• See detailed instructions • Sign the form at line 8

DO NOT WRITE HERE

Page 1 of pages

EXAMINED BY	FORM PA
CHECKED BY	
☐ CORRESPONDENCE Yes	FOR COPYRIGHT OFFICE USE ONLY

DO NOT WRITE ABOVE THIS LINE. IF YOU NEED MORE SPACE, USE A SEPARATE CONTINUATION SHEET.

5

PREVIOUS REGISTRATION Has registration for this work, or for an earlier version of this work, already been made in the Copyright Office?

❑ **Yes** ❑ **No** If your answer is "Yes," why is another registration being sought? (Check appropriate box.) ▼ If your answer is No, do **not** check box A, B, or C.

a. ❑ This is the first published edition of a work previously registered in unpublished form.

b. ❑ This is the first application submitted by this author as copyright claimant.

c. ❑ This is a changed version of the work, as shown by space 6 on this application.

If your answer is "Yes," give **Previous Registration Number ▼** **Year of Registration ▼**

6

DERIVATIVE WORK OR COMPILATION Complete both space 6a and 6b for a derivative work; complete only 6b for a compilation.

a **Preexisting Material** Identify any preexisting work or works that this work is based on or incorporates. ▼

See instructions before completing this space.

b **Material Added to This Work** Give a brief, general statement of the material that has been added to this work and in which copyright is claimed. ▼

7

a **DEPOSIT ACCOUNT** If the registration fee is to be charged to a Deposit Account established in the Copyright Office, give name and number of Account.
Name ▼ **Account Number ▼**

b **CORRESPONDENCE** Give name and address to which correspondence about this application should be sent. Name / Address / Apt / City / State / Zip ▼

Area code and daytime telephone number ( ) Fax number ( )

Email

8

CERTIFICATION* I, the undersigned, hereby certify that I am the

Check only one ▶
❑ author
❑ other copyright claimant
❑ owner of exclusive right(s)
❑ authorized agent of ______________
Name of author or other copyright claimant, or owner of exclusive right(s) ▲

of the work identified in this application and that the statements made by me in this application are correct to the best of my knowledge.

Typed or printed name and date ▼ If this application gives a date of publication in space 3, do not sign and submit it before that date.

______________ **Date** ______________

Signature (X) ▼

x ______________

9

Certificate will be mailed in window envelope to this address:

Name ▼
Number/Street/Apt ▼
City/State/Zip ▼

YOU MUST:
- Complete all necessary spaces
- Sign your application in space 8

SEND ALL 3 ELEMENTS IN THE SAME PACKAGE:
1. Application form
2. Nonrefundable filing fee in check or money order payable to *U.S. Copyright Office*
3. Deposit material

MAIL TO:
Library of Congress
Copyright Office-PA
101 Independence Avenue SE
Washington, DC 20559-6000

*17 U.S.C. §506(e): Any person who knowingly makes a false representation of a material fact in the application for copyright registration provided for by section 409, or in any written statement filed in connection with the application, shall be fined not more than $2,500.

Form PA–Full Printed: 05/2019 Printed on recycled paper

Form SR

Detach and read these instructions before completing this form.
Make sure all applicable spaces have been filled in before you return this form.

BASIC INFORMATION

When to Use This Form: Use Form SR for registration of published or unpublished sound recordings. Form SR should be used when the copyright claim is limited to the sound recording itself, and it may also be used where the same copyright claimant is seeking simultaneous registration of the underlying musical, dramatic, or literary work embodied in the phonorecord.

With one exception, "sound recordings" are works that result from the fixation of a series of musical, spoken, or other sounds. The exception is for the audio portions of audiovisual works, such as a motion picture soundtrack or an audio cassette accompanying a filmstrip. These are considered a part of the audiovisual work as a whole.

Unpublished works: This form may be used to register one unpublished work. This form cannot be used to register a "collection" of two or more unpublished works. Any paper application submitted with more than one unpublished work may be refused. To register multiple unpublished works, you must use the online application for "A Group of Unpublished Works." For information about the online application, see *Multiple Works* (Circular 34).

Deposit to Accompany Application: An application for copyright registration must be accompanied by a deposit consisting of phonorecords representing the entire work for which registration is to be made.

Unpublished Work: Deposit one complete phonorecord.

Published Work: Deposit two complete phonorecords of the best edition, together with "any printed or other visually perceptible material" published with the phonorecords.

Work First Published Outside the United States: Deposit one complete phonorecord of the first foreign edition.

Contribution to a Collective Work: Deposit one complete phonorecord of the best edition of the collective work.

The Copyright Notice: Before March 1, 1989, the use of copyright notice was mandatory on all published works, and any work first published before that date should have carried a notice. For works first published on and after March 1, 1989, use of the copyright notice is optional. For more information about copyright notice, see *Copyright Notice* (Circular 3).

For Further Information: To speak to a Copyright Office staff member, call (202) 707-3000 or 1-877-476-0778. Recorded information is available 24 hours a day. Order forms and other publications from Library of Congress, Copyright Office-COPUBS, 101 Independence Avenue SE, Washington, DC 20559 or call (202) 707-9100 or 1-877-476-0778 (toll free). Access and download circulars and other information from the Copyright Office website at *www.copyright.gov*.

PRIVACY ACT ADVISORY STATEMENT Required by the Privacy Act of 1974 (P.L. 93-579)
The authority for requesting this information is title 17 U S C §409 and §410 Furnishing the requested information is voluntary But if the information is not furnished, it may be necessary to delay or refuse registration and you may not be entitled to certain relief, remedies, and benefits provided in chapters 4 and 5 of title 17 U S C

The principal uses of the requested information are the establishment and maintenance of a public record and the examination of the application for compliance with the registration requirements of the copyright code

Other routine uses include public inspection and copying, preparation of public indexes, preparation of public catalogs of copyright registrations, and preparation of search reports upon request

NOTE No other advisory statement will be given in connection with this application Please keep this statement and refer to it if we communicate with you regarding this application

LINE-BY-LINE INSTRUCTIONS

Please type or print using black ink. The form is used to produce the certificate.

1 SPACE 1: Title

Title of This Work: Every work submitted for copyright registration must be given a title to identify that particular work. If the phonorecords or any accompanying printed material bears a title (or an identifying phrase that could serve as a title), transcribe that wording completely and exactly on the application. Indexing of the registration and future identification of the work may depend on the information you give here.

Previous, Alternative, or Contents Titles: Complete this space if there are any previous or alternative titles for the work under which someone searching for the registration might be likely to look, or under which a document pertaining to the work might be recorded. You may also give the individual contents titles, if any, in this space or you may use a Continuation Sheet (Form CON). Circle the term that describes the titles given.

2 SPACE 2: Author(s)

General Instructions: After reading these instructions, decide who are the "authors" of this work for copyright purposes. Then, unless the work is a "collective work," give the requested information about every "author" who contributed any appreciable amount of copyrightable matter to this version of the work. If you need further space, use additional Continuation Sheets. In the case of a collective work such as a collection of previously published or registered sound recordings, give information about the author of the collective work as a whole. If you are submitting this Form SR to cover the recorded musical, dramatic, or literary work as well as the sound recording itself, it is important for space 2 to include full information about the various authors of all of the material covered by the copyright claim, making clear the nature of each author's contribution.

Name of Author: The fullest form of the author's name should be given. Unless the work was "made for hire," the individual who actually created the work is its "author." In the case of a work made for hire, the statute provides that "the employer or other person for whom the work was prepared is considered the author."

What Is a "Work Made for Hire"? A "work made for hire" is defined as: (1) "a work prepared by an employee within the scope of his or her employment"; or (2) "a work specially ordered or commissioned for use as a contribution to a collective work, as a part of a motion picture or other audiovisual work, as a translation, as a supplementary work, as a compilation, as an instructional text, as a test, as answer material for a test, or as an atlas, if the parties expressly agree in a written instrument signed by them that the work shall be considered a work made for hire." If you have checked "Yes" to indicate that the work was "made for hire," you must give the full legal name of the employer (or other person for whom the work was prepared). You may also include the name of the employee along with the name of the employer (for example: "Elster Record Co., employer for hire of John Ferguson").

"Anonymous" or "Pseudonymous" Work: An author's contribution to a work is "anonymous" if that author is not identified on the copies or phonorecords of the work. An author's contribution to a work is "pseudonymous" if that author is identified on the copies or phonorecords under a fictitious name. If the work is "anonymous" you may: (1) leave the line blank; or (2) state "anonymous" on the line; or (3) reveal the author's identity. If the work is "pseudonymous" you may: (1) leave the line blank; or (2) give the pseudonym and identify it as such (for example: "Huntley Haverstock, pseudonym"); or (3) reveal the author's name, making clear which is the real name and which is the pseudonym (for example: "Judith Barton, whose pseudonym is Madeline Elster"). However, the citizenship or domicile of the author *must* be given in all cases.

Dates of Birth and Death: If the author is dead, the statute requires that the year of death be included in the application unless the work is anonymous or pseudonymous. The author's birth date is optional, but is useful as a form of identification. Leave this space blank if the author's contribution was a "work made for hire."

Author's Nationality or Domicile: Give the country in which the author is a citizen, or the country in which the author is domiciled. Nationality or domicile *must* be given in all cases.

Nature of Authorship: Sound recording authorship is the performance, sound production, or both, that is fixed in the recording deposited for registration. Describe this authorship in space 2 as "sound recording." If the claim also covers the underlying work(s), include the appropriate authorship terms for each author, for example, "words," "music," "arrangement of music," or "text."

Generally, for the claim to cover both the sound recording and the underlying work(s), every author should have contributed to both the sound recording *and* the underlying work(s). If the claim includes artwork or photographs, include the appropriate term in the statement of authorship.

3 SPACE 3: Creation and Publication

General Instructions: Do not confuse "creation" with "publication." Every application for copyright registration must state "the year in which creation of the work was completed." Give the date and nation of first publication only if the work has been published.

Creation: Under the statute, a work is "created" when it is fixed in a copy or phonorecord for the first time. If a work has been prepared over a period of time, the part of the work existing in fixed form on a particular date constitutes the created work on that date. The date you give here should be the year in which the author completed the particular version for which registration is now being sought, even if other versions exist or if further changes or additions are planned.

Publication: The statute defines "publication" as "the distribution of copies or phonorecords of a work to the public by sale or other transfer of ownership, or by rental, lease, or lending"; a work is also "published" if there has been an "offering to distribute copies or phonorecords to a group of persons for purposes of further distribution, public performance, or public display." Give the full date (month, date, year) when, and the country where, publication first occurred. If first publication took place simultaneously in the United States and other countries, it is sufficient to state "U.S.A."

4 SPACE 4: Claimant(s)

Name(s) and Address(es) of Copyright Claimant(s): Give the name(s) and address(es) of the copyright claimant(s) in the work even if the claimant is the same as the author. Copyright in a work belongs initially to the author of the work (including, in the case of a work made for hire, the employer or other person for whom the work was prepared). The copyright claimant is either the author of the work or a person or organization to whom the copyright initially belonging to the author has been transferred.

Transfer: The statute provides that, if the copyright claimant is not the author, the application for registration must contain "a brief statement of how the claimant obtained ownership of the copyright." If any copyright claimant named in space 4a is not an author named in space 2, give a brief statement explaining how the claimant(s) obtained ownership of the copyright. Examples: "By written contract"; "Transfer of all rights by author"; "Assignment"; "By will." Do not attach transfer documents or other attachments or riders.

5 SPACE 5: Previous Registration

General Instructions: The questions in space 5 are intended to show whether an earlier registration has been made for this work and, if so, whether there is any basis for a new registration. As a rule, only one basic copyright registration can be made for the same version of a particular work.

Same Version: If this version is substantially the same as the work covered by a previous registration, a second registration is not generally possible unless: (1) the work has been registered in unpublished form and a second registration is now being sought to cover this first published edition; or (2) someone other than the author is identified as copyright claimant in the earlier registration and the author is now seeking registration in his or her own name. If either of these two exceptions applies, check the appropriate box and give the earlier registration number and date. Otherwise, do not submit Form SR. Instead, write the Copyright Office for information about supplementary registration or recordation of transfers of copyright ownership.

Changed Version: If the work has been changed and you are now seeking registration to cover the additions or revisions, check the last box in space 5, give the earlier registration number and date, and complete both parts of space 6 in accordance with the instructions below.

Previous Registration Number and Date: If more than one previous registration has been made for the work, give the number and date of the latest registration.

6 SPACE 6: Derivative Work or Compilation

General Instructions: Complete space 6 if this work is a "changed version," "compilation," or "derivative work," and if it incorporates one or more earlier works that have already been published or registered for copyright, or that have fallen into the public domain, or sound recordings that were fixed before February 15, 1972. A "compilation" is defined as "a work formed by the collection and assembling of preexisting materials or of data that are selected, coordinated, or arranged in such a way that the resulting work as a whole constitutes an original work of authorship." A "derivative work" is "a work based on one or more preexisting works." Examples of derivative works include recordings reissued with substantial editorial revisions or abridgments of the recorded sounds, and recordings republished with new recorded material, or "any other form in which a work may be recast, transformed, or adapted." Derivative works also include works "consisting of editorial revisions, annotations, or other modifications" if these changes, as a whole, represent an original work of authorship.

Preexisting Material (space 6a): Complete this space *and* space 6b for derivative works. In this space identify the preexisting work that has been recast, transformed, or adapted. The preexisting work may be material that has been previously published, previously registered, or that is in the public domain. For example, the preexisting material might be: "1970 recording by Sperryville Symphony of Bach Double Concerto."

Material Added to This Work (space 6b): Give a brief, general statement of the *additional* new material covered by the copyright claim for which registration is sought. In the case of a derivative work, identify this new material. Examples: "Recorded performances on bands 1 and 3"; "Remixed sounds from original multitrack sound sources"; "New words, arrangement, and additional sounds." If the work is a compilation, give a brief, general statement describing both the material that has been compiled *and* the compilation itself. Example: "Compilation of 1938 recordings by various swing bands."

7,8,9 SPACE 7,8,9: Fee, Correspondence, Certification, Return Address

Deposit Account: If you maintain a deposit account in the Copyright Office, identify it in space 7a. Otherwise, leave the space blank and send the filing fee with your application and deposit. (See space 8 on form.) **Note:** Copyright Office fees are subject to change. For current fees, check the Copyright Office website at *www.copyright.gov*, write the Copyright Office, or call (202) 707-3000 or 1-877-476-0778 (toll free).

Correspondence (space 7b): Give the name, address, area code, telephone number, fax number, and email address (if available) of the person to be consulted if correspondence about this application becomes necessary.

Certification (space 8): This application cannot be accepted unless it bears the date and the *signature* of the author or other copyright claimant, or the owner of exclusive right(s), or the duly authorized agent of the author, claimant, or owner of exclusive right(s).

Address for Return of Certificate (space 9): The address box must be completed legibly since the certificate will be returned in a window envelope.

MORE INFORMATION

"Works": "Works" are the basic subject matter of copyright; they are what authors create and copyright protects. The statute draws a sharp distinction between the "work" and "any material object in which the work is embodied."

"Copies" and "Phonorecords": These are the two types of material objects in which "works" are embodied. In general, "copies" are objects from which a work can be read or visually perceived, directly or with the aid of a machine or device, such as manuscripts, books, sheet music, film, and videotape. "Phonorecords" are objects embodying fixations of sounds, such as audio tapes and phonograph disks. For example, a song (the "work") can be reproduced in sheet music ("copies") or phonograph disks ("phonorecords"), or both.

"Sound Recordings": These are "works," not "copies" or "phonorecords." "Sound recordings" are "works that result from the fixation of a series of musical, spoken, or other sounds, but not including the sounds accompanying a motion picture or other audiovisual work." Example: When a record company issues a new release, the release will typically involve two distinct "works": the "musical work" that has been recorded, and the "sound recording" as a separate work in itself. The material objects that the record company sends out are "phonorecords": physical reproductions of both the "musical work" and the "sound recording."

Should You File More Than One Application?

If your work consists of a recorded musical, dramatic, or literary work and if both that "work" and the sound recording as a separate "work" are eligible for registration, the application form you should file depends on the following:

File Only Form SR if: The copyright claimant is the same for both the musical, dramatic, or literary work and for the sound recording, and you are seeking a single registration to cover both of these "works."

File Only Form PA (or Form TX) if: You are seeking to register only the musical, dramatic, or literary work, not the sound recording. Form PA is appropriate for works of the performing arts; Form TX is for nondramatic literary works.

Separate Applications Should Be Filed on Form PA (or Form TX) and on Form SR if: (1) The copyright claimant for the musical, dramatic, or literary work is different from the copyright claimant for the sound recording; or (2) you prefer to have separate registrations for the musical, dramatic, or literary work and for the sound recording.

Copyright Office fees are subject to change. For current fees, check the Copyright Office website at www.copyright.gov, write the Copyright Office, or call (202) 707-3000 or 1-877-476-0778 (toll free).

Clear Form

Form SR
For a Sound Recording
UNITED STATES COPYRIGHT OFFICE

REGISTRATION NUMBER

SR SRU

EFFECTIVE DATE OF REGISTRATION

Month Day Year

Privacy Act Notice: Sections 408-410 of title 17 of the *United States Code* authorize the Copyright Office to collect the personally identifying information requested on this form in order to process the application for copyright registration. By providing this information you are agreeing to routine uses of the information that include publication to give legal notice of your copyright claim as required by 17 U.S.C. §705. It will appear in the Office's online catalog. If you do not provide the information requested, registration may be refused or delayed, and you may not be entitled to certain relief, remedies, and benefits under the copyright law.

DO NOT WRITE ABOVE THIS LINE. IF YOU NEED MORE SPACE, USE A SEPARATE CONTINUATION SHEET.

1

TITLE OF THIS WORK ▼

PREVIOUS, ALTERNATIVE, OR CONTENTS TITLES (CIRCLE ONE) ▼

2

a

NAME OF AUTHOR ▼

DATES OF BIRTH AND DEATH
Year Born ▼ Year Died ▼

Was this contribution to the work a "work made for hire"?
❑ Yes
❑ No

AUTHOR'S NATIONALITY OR DOMICILE
Name of Country
OR { Citizen of ▶
Domiciled in ▶

WAS THIS AUTHOR'S CONTRIBUTION TO THE WORK
Anonymous? ❑ Yes ❑ No
Pseudonymous? ❑ Yes ❑ No
If the answer to either of these questions is "Yes," see detailed instructions.

NATURE OF AUTHORSHIP Briefly describe nature of material created by this author in which copyright is claimed. ▼

NOTE

Under the law, the "author" of a "work made for hire" is generally the employer, not the employee (see instructions). For any part of this work that was "made for hire," check "Yes" in the space provided, give the employer (or other person for whom the work was prepared) as "Author" of that part, and leave the space for dates of birth and death blank.

b

NAME OF AUTHOR ▼

DATES OF BIRTH AND DEATH
Year Born ▼ Year Died ▼

Was this contribution to the work a "work made for hire"?
❑ Yes
❑ No

AUTHOR'S NATIONALITY OR DOMICILE
Name of Country
OR { Citizen of ▶
Domiciled in ▶

WAS THIS AUTHOR'S CONTRIBUTION TO THE WORK
Anonymous? ❑ Yes ❑ No
Pseudonymous? ❑ Yes ❑ No
If the answer to either of these questions is "Yes," see detailed instructions.

NATURE OF AUTHORSHIP Briefly describe nature of material created by this author in which copyright is claimed. ▼

c

NAME OF AUTHOR ▼

DATES OF BIRTH AND DEATH
Year Born ▼ Year Died ▼

Was this contribution to the work a "work made for hire"?
❑ Yes
❑ No

AUTHOR'S NATIONALITY OR DOMICILE
Name of Country
OR { Citizen of ▶
Domiciled in ▶

WAS THIS AUTHOR'S CONTRIBUTION TO THE WORK
Anonymous? ❑ Yes ❑ No
Pseudonymous? ❑ Yes ❑ No
If the answer to either of these questions is "Yes," see detailed instructions.

NATURE OF AUTHORSHIP Briefly describe nature of material created by this author in which copyright is claimed. ▼

3

a YEAR IN WHICH CREATION OF THIS WORK WAS COMPLETED
Year ▶
This information must be given in all cases.

b DATE AND NATION OF FIRST PUBLICATION OF THIS PARTICULAR WORK
Complete this information ONLY if this work has been published.
Month ▶ Day ▶ Year ▶
Nation ▶

4

a COPYRIGHT CLAIMANT(S) Name and address must be given even if the claimant is the same as the author given in space 2. ▼

See instructions before completing this space

b TRANSFER If the claimant(s) named here in space 4 is (are) different from the author(s) named in space 2, give a brief statement of how the claimant(s) obtained ownership of the copyright. ▼

DO NOT WRITE HERE
OFFICE USE ONLY

APPLICATION RECEIVED

ONE DEPOSIT RECEIVED

TWO DEPOSITS RECEIVED

FUNDS RECEIVED

MORE ON BACK ▶
• Complete all applicable spaces (numbers 5-9) on the reverse side of this page
• See detailed instructions
• Sign the form at line 8

DO NOT WRITE HERE
Page 1 of ____ pages

EXAMINED BY

FORM SR

CHECKED BY

CORRESPONDENCE
❑ Yes

FOR COPYRIGHT OFFICE USE ONLY

DO NOT WRITE ABOVE THIS LINE. IF YOU NEED MORE SPACE, USE A SEPARATE CONTINUATION SHEET.

5

PREVIOUS REGISTRATION Has registration for this work, or for an earlier version of this work, already been made in the Copyright Office?

❑ Yes ❑ No If your answer is "Yes," why is another registration being sought? (Check appropriate box) ▼

a. ❑ This work was previously registered in unpublished form and now has been published for the first time.

b. ❑ This is the first application submitted by this author as copyright claimant.

c. ❑ This is a changed version of the work, as shown by space 6 on this application.

If your answer is "Yes," give: **Previous Registration Number** ▼ **Year of Registration** ▼

6

DERIVATIVE WORK OR COMPILATION

Preexisting Material Identify any preexisting work or works that this work is based on or incorporates. ▼

a

See instructions before completing this space.

Material Added to This Work Give a brief, general statement of the material that has been added to this work and in which copyright is claimed. ▼

b

7

DEPOSIT ACCOUNT If the registration fee is to be charged to a deposit account established in the Copyright Office, give name and number of account.

a Name ▼ Account Number ▼

CORRESPONDENCE Give name and address to which correspondence about this application should be sent. Name/Address/Apt/City/State/Zip ▼

b

Area code and daytime telephone number ( ) Fax number ( )

Email

8

CERTIFICATION* I, the undersigned, hereby certify that I am the

Check only one ▼

❑ author ❑ owner of exclusive right(s)

❑ other copyright claimant ❑ authorized agent of

Name of author or other copyright claimant, or owner of exclusive right(s) ▲

of the work identified in this application and that the statements made by me in this application are correct to the best of my knowledge.

Typed or printed name and date ▼ If this application gives a date of publication in space 3, do not sign and submit it before that date.

Date

Signature ▼

9

Certificate will be mailed in window envelope to this address:

Name ▼

Number/Street/Apt ▼

City/State/Zip ▼

YOU MUST:
- Complete all necessary spaces
- Sign your application in space 8

SEND ALL 3 ELEMENTS IN THE SAME PACKAGE:
1. Application form
2. Nonrefundable filing fee in check or money order payable to *U.S. Copyright Office*
3. Deposit material

MAIL TO:
Library of Congress
U.S. Copyright Office-SR
101 Independence Avenue SE
Washington, DC 20559-6000

*17 U.S.C. §506(e): Any person who knowingly makes a false representation of a material fact in the application for copyright registration provided for by section 409, or in any written statement filed in connection with the application, shall be fined not more than $2,500.

Form SR-Full Rev: 05/2019 Printed on recycled paper

09, March, 2020

Office of the Clerk
Supreme Court of the United States
Washington, DC 20543-0001

Re: *Guide for Prospective Indigent Petitioners for Writs of Certiorari*

Dear Clerk:

I am hereby respectfully requesting a copy of your packet named above. I have requested it from the law library, however, they do not supply them.

I appreciate your assistance in these regards and thank you in advance.

Respectfully,

Raymond Lumsden
Hughes Unit
Rt 2 Box 4400
Gatesville, TX 76597

cc: p/file

July 2019

OFFICE OF THE CLERK
SUPREME COURT OF THE UNITED STATES
WASHINGTON, D. C. 20543

GUIDE FOR PROSPECTIVE INDIGENT PETITIONERS FOR WRITS OF CERTIORARI

I. Introduction

These instructions and forms are designed to assist petitioners who are proceeding *in forma pauperis* and without the assistance of counsel. A copy of the Rules of the Supreme Court, which establish the procedures that must be followed, is also enclosed. Be sure to read the following Rules carefully:

Rules 10-14 (Petitioning for certiorari)
Rule 29 (Filing and service on opposing party or counsel)
Rule 30 (Computation and extension of time)
Rules 33.2 and 34 (Preparing pleadings on 8.5 x 11-inch paper)
Rule 39 (Proceedings *in forma pauperis*)

II. Nature of Supreme Court Review

It is important to note that review in this Court by means of a writ of certiorari is not a matter of right, but of judicial discretion. The primary concern of the Supreme Court is not to correct errors in lower court decisions, but to decide cases presenting issues of importance beyond the particular facts and parties involved. The Court grants and hears argument in only about 1 of the cases that are filed each Term. The vast majority of petitions are simply denied by the Court without comment or explanation. The denial of a petition for a writ of certiorari signifies only that the Court has chosen not to accept the case for review and does not express the Court's view of the merits of the case.

Every petitioner for a writ of certiorari is advised to read carefully the Considerations Governing Review on Certiorari set forth in Rule 10. Important considerations for accepting a case for review include the existence of a conflict between the decision of which review is sought and a decision of another appellate court on the same issue. An important function of the Supreme Court is to resolve disagreements among lower courts about specific legal questions. Another consideration is the importance to the public of the issue.

III. The Time for Filing

You must file your petition for a writ of certiorari within 90 days from the date of the entry of the final judgment in the United States court of appeals or highest state appellate court or 90 days from the denial of a timely filed petition for rehearing. The issuance of a mandate or remittitur after judgment has been entered has no bearing on the computation of time and does not extend the time for filing. See Rules 13.1 and 13.3. Filing in the Supreme Court means the actual receipt of paper documents by the Clerk; or their deposit in the United States mail, with first-class postage prepaid, on or before the final date allowed for filing; or their delivery to a third-party commercial carrier, on or before the final date allowed for filing, for delivery to the Clerk within 3 calendar days. See Rule 29.2.

IV. What to File

Unless you are an inmate confined in an institution and not represented by counsel, file:

- An original and ten copies of a motion for leave to proceed *in forma pauperis* and an original and 10 copies of an affidavit or declaration in support thereof. See Rule 39.
- An original and 10 copies of a petition for a writ of certiorari with an appendix consisting of a copy of the judgment or decree you are asking this Court to review including any order on rehearing, and copies of any opinions or orders by any courts or administrative agencies that have previously considered your case. See Rule 14.1(i).
- One affidavit or declaration showing that all opposing parties or their counsel have been served with a copy of the papers filed in this Court. See Rule 29.

If you are an inmate confined in an institution and not represented by counsel, you need file only the original of the motion for leave to proceed *in forma pauperis*, affidavit or declaration when needed in support of the motion for leave to proceed *in forma pauperis*, the petition for a writ of certiorari, and proof of service.

If the court below appointed counsel in the current proceeding, no affidavit or declaration is required, but the motion should cite the provision of law under which counsel was appointed, or a copy of the order of appointment should be appended to the motion. See Rule 39.1.

The attached forms may be used for the original motion, affidavit or declaration, and petition, and should be stapled together in that order. The proof of service should be included as a detached sheet, and the form provided may be used.

The Court's practice is to scan and make available on its website most filings submitted by litigants representing themselves. The Court scans petitions, motions to proceed *in forma pauperis*, proofs of service, and the portion of an appendix that includes relevant lower court opinions and rulings. While the Court does not scan other portions of an appendix from a *pro se* litigant, the entire appendix is fully a part of the Court's record and is available to the Justices.

On the same page, list all cases in other courts that are directly related to the case in this Court. A case is directly related if it arises from the same trial court case as the case in this Court (including the proceedings directly on review in this case), or if it challenges the same criminal conviction or sentence as is challenged in this Court, whether on direct appeal or through state or federal collateral proceedings. Below is an example of the format that should be used for the list:

V. Page Limitation

The petition for a writ of certiorari may not exceed 40 pages excluding the pages that precede Page 1 of the form. The documents required to be contained in the appendix to the petition do not count toward the page limit. See Rule 33.2(b).

VI. Redaction of Personal Information

Pursuant to Rule 34.6, certain types of personal information should not be included in filings. For example, social security numbers and taxpayer identification numbers should be redacted so that only the last four digits of the number are included, and the names of minor children should be redacted so that only initials are included. In general, Rule 34.6 adopts the redaction practices that are applicable to cases in the lower federal courts. See, *e.g.*, Federal Rule of Civil Procedure 5.2.

VII. Method of Filing

All documents to be filed in this Court must be addressed to the Clerk, Supreme Court of the United States, Washington, D.C. 20543 and must be served on opposing parties or their counsel in accordance with Rule 29.

Instructions for Completing Forms

I. Motion for Leave to Proceed *In forma pauperis* – Rule 39

A. On the form provided for the motion for leave to proceed *in forma pauperis*, leave the case number blank. The number will be assigned by the Clerk when the case is docketed.

B. On the line in the case caption for "petitioner," type your name. As a *pro se* petitioner, you may represent only yourself. On the line for "respondent", type the name of the opposing party in the lower court. If there are multiple respondents, enter the first respondent, as the name appeared on the lower court decision, followed by "et al." to indicate that there are other respondents. The additional parties must be listed in the LIST OF PARTIES section of the petition.

C. If the lower courts in your case granted you leave to proceed *in forma pauperis*, check the appropriate space and indicate the court or courts that allowed you to proceed *in forma pauperis*. If none of the lower courts granted you leave to proceed *in forma pauperis*, check the block that so indicates.

D. Sign the motion on the signature line.

II. Affidavit or Declaration in Support of Motion for Leave to Proceed *In forma pauperis*

On the form provided, answer fully each of the questions. If the answer to a question is "0," "none," or "not applicable (N/A)," enter that response. If you need more space to answer a question or to explain your answer, attach a separate sheet of paper, identified with your name and the question number. Unless each question is fully answered, the Clerk will not accept the petition. The form must either be notarized or be in the form of a declaration. See 28 U.S.C. § 1746.

III. Cover Page – Rule 34

When you complete the form for the cover page:

A. Leave case number blank. The number will be assigned by the Clerk when the case is docketed.

B. Complete the case caption as you did on the motion for leave to proceed *in forma pauperis*.

C. List the court from which the action is brought on the line following the words "on petition for a writ of certiorari to." If your case is from a state court, enter the name of the court that last addressed the merits of the case. For example, if the highest state court denied discretionary review, and the state court of appeals affirmed the decision of the trial court, the state court of appeals should be listed. If your case is federal, the United States court of appeals that decided your case will always be listed here.

D. Enter your name, address, and telephone number in the appropriate spaces.

IV. Question(s) Presented

On the page provided, enter the question or questions that you wish the Court to review. The questions must be concise. Questions presented in cases accepted for review are usually no longer than two or three sentences. The purpose of the question presented is to assist the Court in selecting cases. State the issue you wish the Court to decide clearly and without unnecessary detail.

V. List of Parties and Related Cases

On the page provided, check either the box indicating that the names of all parties appear in the caption of the case on the cover page or the box indicating that there are additional parties. If there are additional parties, list them. Rule 12.6 states that all parties to the proceeding whose judgment is sought to be reviewed shall be deemed parties in this Court, and that all parties other than petitioner shall be respondents. The court whose judgment you seek to have this Court review is *not* a party.

On the same page, list all cases in other courts that are directly related to the case in this Court. A case is "directly related" if it arises from the same trial court case as the case in this Court (including the proceedings directly on review in this case), or if it challenges the same criminal conviction or sentence as is challenged in this Court, whether on direct appeal or through state or federal collateral proceedings. Below is an example of the format that should be used for this list:

- *Smith v. Jones*, No. 18-cv-200, U. S. District Court for the Western District of Pennsylvania. Judgment entered Oct. 1, 2018.
- Smith *v.* Jones, No. 18-1200, U. S. Court of Appeals for the Third Circuit. Judgment entered Apr. 15, 2019.

VI. Table of Contents

On the page provided, list the page numbers on which the required portions of the petition appear. Number the pages consecutively, beginning with the "Opinions Below" page as page 1.

VII. Index of Appendices

List the description of each document that is included in the appendix beside the appropriate appendix letter. Mark the bottom of the first page of each appendix with the appropriate designation, *e.g.*, "Appendix A." See Rule 14.1 pertaining to the items to be included in the appendix.

A. *Federal courts*: If you are asking the Court to review a decision of a federal court, the decision of the United States court of appeals should be designated Appendix A. Appendix A should be followed by the decision of the United States District court and the findings and recommendations of the United States magistrate judge, if there were any. If the United States court of appeals denied a timely filed petition for rehearing, a copy of that order should be appended next. If you are seeking review of a decision in a habeas corpus case, and the decision of either the United States District court or the United States Court of Appeals makes reference to a state court decision in which you were a party, a copy of the state court decision must be included in the appendix.

B. *State courts*: If you are asking the Court to review a decision of a state court, the decision of which review is sought should be designated Appendix A. Appendix A should be followed by the decision of the lower court or agency that was reviewed in the decision designated Appendix A. If the highest court of the state in which a decision could be had denied discretionary review, a copy of that order should follow. If an order denying a timely filed petition for rehearing starts the running of the time for filing a petition for a writ of certiorari pursuant to Rule 13.3, a copy of the order should be appended next.

As an example, if the state trial court ruled against you, the intermediate court of appeals affirmed the decision of the trial court, the state supreme court denied discretionary review and then denied a timely petition for rehearing, the appendices should appear in the following order:

Appendix A	Decision of State Court of Appeals
Appendix B	Decision of State Trial Court
Appendix C	Decision of State Supreme Court Denying Review
Appendix D	Order of State Supreme Court Denying Rehearing

VIII. Table of authorities

On the page provided, list the cases, statutes, treatises, and articles that you reference in your petition, and the page number of your petition where each authority appears.

IX. Opinions Below

In the space provided, indicate whether the opinions of the lower courts in your case have been published, and if so, the citation for the opinion below. For example, opinions of the United States courts of appeals are published in the Federal Reporter. If the opinion in your case appears at page 100 of volume 30 of the Federal Reporter, Third Series, indicate that the opinion is reported at 30 F. 3d 100. If the opinion has been designated for publication but has not yet been published, check the appropriate space. Also indicate where in the appendix each decision, reported or unreported, appears.

X. Jurisdiction

The purpose of the jurisdiction section of the petition is to establish the statutory source for the Court's jurisdiction and the dates that determine whether the petition is timely filed. The form sets out the pertinent statutes for federal and state cases. You need provide only the dates of the lower court decisions that establish the timeliness of the petition for a writ of certiorari. If an extension of time within which to file the petition for a writ of certiorari was granted, you must provide the requested information pertaining to the extension. If you seek to have the Court review a decision of a state court, you must provide the date the highest state court decided your case, either by ruling on the merits or denying discretionary review.

XI. Constitutional and Statutory Provisions Involved

Set out verbatim the constitutional provisions, treaties, statutes, ordinances and regulations involved in the case. If the provisions involved are lengthy, provide their citation and indicate where in the Appendix to the petition the text of the provisions appears.

XII. Statement of the Case

Provide a concise statement of the case containing the facts material to the consideration of the question(s) presented; you should summarize the relevant facts of the case and the proceedings that took place in the lower courts. You may need to attach additional pages, but the statement should be concise and limited to the relevant facts of the case.

XIII. Reasons for Granting the Petition

The purpose of this section of the petition is to explain to the Court why it should grant certiorari. It is important to read Rule 10 and address what compelling reasons exist for the exercise of the Court's discretionary jurisdiction. Try to show not only why the decision of the lower court may be erroneous, but the national importance of having the Supreme Court decide the question involved. It is important to show whether the decision of the court that decided your case is in conflict with the decisions of another appellate court; the importance of the case not only to you but to others similarly situated; and the ways the decision of the lower court in your case was erroneous. You will need to attach additional pages, but the reasons should be as concise as possible, consistent with the purpose of this section of the petition.

XIV. Conclusion

Enter your name and the date that you submit the petition.

XV. Proof of Service

You must serve a copy of your petition on counsel for respondent(s) as required by Rule 29. If you serve the petition by first-class mail or by third-party commercial carrier, you may use the enclosed proof of service form. If the United States or any department, office, agency, officer, or employee thereof is a party, you must serve the Solicitor General of the United States, Room 5614, Department of Justice, 950 Pennsylvania Ave., N.W., Washington, D. C. 20530-0001. The lower courts that ruled on your case are not parties and need not be served with a copy of the petition. The proof of service may be in the form of a declaration pursuant to 28 U.S.C. § 1746.

No. ____________________

____

IN THE

SUPREME COURT OF THE UNITED STATES

____

____________________ — PETITIONER
(Your Name)

VS.

____________________ — RESPONDENT(S)

MOTION FOR LEAVE TO PROCEED *IN FORMA PAUPERIS*

The petitioner asks leave to file the attached petition for a writ of certiorari without prepayment of costs and to proceed *in forma pauperis*.

Please check the appropriate boxes:

☐ Petitioner has previously been granted leave to proceed *in forma pauperis* in the following court(s):

____

____

☐ Petitioner has **not** previously been granted leave to proceed *in forma pauperis* in any other court.

☐ Petitioner's affidavit or declaration in support of this motion is attached hereto.

☐ Petitioner's affidavit or declaration is **not** attached because the court below appointed counsel in the current proceeding, and:

☐ The appointment was made under the following provision of law: __________
____, or

☐ a copy of the order of appointment is appended.

____
(Signature)

AFFIDAVIT OR DECLARATION
IN SUPPORT OF MOTION FOR LEAVE TO PROCEED *IN FORMA PAUPERIS*

I, ____________________, am the petitioner in the above-entitled case. In support of my motion to proceed *in forma pauperis*, I state that because of my poverty I am unable to pay the costs of this case or to give security therefor; and I believe I am entitled to redress.

1. For both you and your spouse estimate the average amount of money received from each of the following sources during the past 12 months. Adjust any amount that was received weekly, biweekly, quarterly, semiannually, or annually to show the monthly rate. Use gross amounts, that is, amounts before any deductions for taxes or otherwise.

Income source	**Average monthly amount during the past 12 months**		**Amount expected next month**	
	You	Spouse	You	Spouse
Employment	$	$	$	$
Self-employment	$	$	$	$
Income from real property (such as rental income)	$	$	$	$
Interest and dividends	$	$	$	$
Gifts	$	$	$	$
Alimony	$	$	$	$
Child Support	$	$	$	$
Retirement (such as social security, pensions, annuities, insurance)	$	$	$	$
Disability (such as social security, insurance payments)	$	$	$	$
Unemployment payments	$	$	$	$
Public-assistance (such as welfare)	$	$	$	$
Other (specify): ________	$	$	$	$
Total monthly income:	$	$	$	$

2. List your employment history for the past two years, most recent first. (Gross monthly pay is before taxes or other deductions.)

Employer	Address	Dates of Employment	Gross monthly pay
			$
			$
			$

3. List your spouse's employment history for the past two years, most recent employer first. (Gross monthly pay is before taxes or other deductions.)

Employer	Address	Dates of Employment	Gross monthly pay
			$
			$
			$

4. How much cash do you and your spouse have? $__________
Below, state any money you or your spouse have in bank accounts or in any other financial institution.

Financial institution	Type of account	Amount you have	Amount your spouse has
		$	$
		$	$
		$	$

5. List the assets, and their values, which you own or your spouse owns. Do not list clothing and ordinary household furnishings.

☐ Home
Value __________

☐ Other real estate
Value __________

☐ Motor Vehicle #1
Year, make & model __________
Value __________

☐ Motor Vehicle #2
Year, make & model __________
Value __________

☐ Other assets
Description __________
Value __________

6. State every person, business, or organization owing you or your spouse money, and the amount owed.

Person owing you or your spouse money	Amount owed to you	Amount owed to your spouse
__________	$__________	$__________
__________	$__________	$__________
__________	$__________	$__________

7. State the persons who rely on you or your spouse for support.

Name	Relationship	Age
__________	__________	__________
__________	__________	__________
__________	__________	__________

8. Estimate the average monthly expenses of you and your family. Show separately the amounts paid by your spouse. Adjust any payments that are made weekly, biweekly, quarterly, or annually to show the monthly rate.

	You	Your spouse
Rent or home-mortgage payment (include lot rented for mobile home) Are real estate taxes included? ☐ Yes ☐ No Is property insurance included? ☐ Yes ☐ No	$__________	$__________
Utilities (electricity, heating fuel, water, sewer, and telephone)	$__________	$__________
Home maintenance (repairs and upkeep)	$__________	$__________
Food	$__________	$__________
Clothing	$__________	$__________
Laundry and dry-cleaning	$__________	$__________
Medical and dental expenses	$__________	$__________

	You	Your spouse
Transportation (not including motor vehicle payments)	$________	$________
Recreation, entertainment, newspapers, magazines, etc.	$________	$________
Insurance (not deducted from wages or included in mortgage payments)		
Homeowner's or renter's	$________	$________
Life	$________	$________
Health	$________	$________
Motor Vehicle	$________	$________
Other: ____________	$________	$________
Taxes (not deducted from wages or included in mortgage payments)		
(specify): ____________	$________	$________
Installment payments		
Motor Vehicle	$________	$________
Credit card(s)	$________	$________
Department store(s)	$________	$________
Other: ____________	$________	$________
Alimony, maintenance, and support paid to others	$________	$________
Regular expenses for operation of business, profession, or farm (attach detailed statement)	$________	$________
Other (specify): ____________	$________	$________
Total monthly expenses:	$________	$________

9. Do you expect any major changes to your monthly income or expenses or in your assets or liabilities during the next 12 months?

☐ Yes ☐ No If yes, describe on an attached sheet.

10. Have you paid – or will you be paying – an attorney any money for services in connection with this case, including the completion of this form? ☐ Yes ☐ No

If yes, how much? ____________________

If yes, state the attorney's name, address, and telephone number:

11. Have you paid—or will you be paying—anyone other than an attorney (such as a paralegal or a typist) any money for services in connection with this case, including the completion of this form?

☐ Yes ☐ No

If yes, how much? ____________________

If yes, state the person's name, address, and telephone number:

12. Provide any other information that will help explain why you cannot pay the costs of this case.

I declare under penalty of perjury that the foregoing is true and correct.

Executed on: ____________________, 20____

____

(Signature)

No. ______________________

____

IN THE

SUPREME COURT OF THE UNITED STATES

____

______________________ — PETITIONER
(Your Name)

vs.

______________________ — RESPONDENT(S)

ON PETITION FOR A WRIT OF CERTIORARI TO

____
(NAME OF COURT THAT LAST RULED ON MERITS OF YOUR CASE)

PETITION FOR WRIT OF CERTIORARI

____
(Your Name)

____
(Address)

____
(City, State, Zip Code)

____
(Phone Number)

QUESTION(S) PRESENTED

LIST OF PARTIES

[ ] All parties appear in the caption of the case on the cover page.

[ ] All parties **do not** appear in the caption of the case on the cover page. A list of all parties to the proceeding in the court whose judgment is the subject of this petition is as follows:

TABLE OF CONTENTS

INDEX TO APPENDICES

APPENDIX A

APPENDIX B

APPENDIX C

APPENDIX D

APPENDIX E

APPENDIX F

TABLE OF AUTHORITIES CITED

CASES PAGE NUMBER

STATUTES AND RULES

OTHER

IN THE

SUPREME COURT OF THE UNITED STATES

PETITION FOR WRIT OF CERTIORARI

Petitioner respectfully prays that a writ of certiorari issue to review the judgment below.

OPINIONS BELOW

[ ] For cases from **federal courts**:

The opinion of the United States court of appeals appears at Appendix ______ to the petition and is

[ ] reported at ______________________________; or,
[ ] has been designated for publication but is not yet reported; or,
[ ] is unpublished.

The opinion of the United States district court appears at Appendix ______ to the petition and is

[ ] reported at ______________________________; or,
[ ] has been designated for publication but is not yet reported; or,
[ ] is unpublished.

[ ] For cases from **state courts**:

The opinion of the highest state court to review the merits appears at Appendix ______ to the petition and is

[ ] reported at ______________________________; or,
[ ] has been designated for publication but is not yet reported; or,
[ ] is unpublished.

The opinion of the ______________________________ court appears at Appendix ______ to the petition and is

[ ] reported at ______________________________; or,
[ ] has been designated for publication but is not yet reported; or,
[ ] is unpublished.

JURISDICTION

[ ] For cases from **federal courts**:

The date on which the United States Court of Appeals decided my case was ______________________.

[ ] No petition for rehearing was timely filed in my case.

[ ] A timely petition for rehearing was denied by the United States Court of Appeals on the following date: ______________________, and a copy of the order denying rehearing appears at Appendix ______.

[ ] An extension of time to file the petition for a writ of certiorari was granted to and including ________________ (date) on ________________ (date) in Application No. ___A______.

The jurisdiction of this Court is invoked under 28 U. S. C. § 1254(1).

[ ] For cases from **state courts**:

The date on which the highest state court decided my case was ____________. A copy of that decision appears at Appendix ______.

[ ] A timely petition for rehearing was thereafter denied on the following date: ______________________, and a copy of the order denying rehearing appears at Appendix ______.

[ ] An extension of time to file the petition for a writ of certiorari was granted to and including ________________ (date) on ________________ (date) in Application No. ___A______.

The jurisdiction of this Court is invoked under 28 U. S. C. § 1257(a).

CONSTITUTIONAL AND STATUTORY PROVISIONS INVOLVED

STATEMENT OF THE CASE

REASONS FOR GRANTING THE PETITION

CONCLUSION

The petition for a writ of certiorari should be granted.

Respectfully submitted,

____

Date: _________________________

No. ____________________

____

IN THE

SUPREME COURT OF THE UNITED STATES

____

________________________ — PETITIONER
(Your Name)

VS.

________________________ — RESPONDENT(S)

PROOF OF SERVICE

I, ________________________, do swear or declare that on this date, ________________, 20___, as required by Supreme Court Rule 29 I have served the enclosed MOTION FOR LEAVE TO PROCEED *IN FORMA PAUPERIS* and PETITION FOR A WRIT OF CERTIORARI on each party to the above proceeding or that party's counsel, and on every other person required to be served, by depositing an envelope containing the above documents in the United States mail properly addressed to each of them and with first-class postage prepaid, or by delivery to a third-party commercial carrier for delivery within 3 calendar days.

The names and addresses of those served are as follows:

____

____

____

I declare under penalty of perjury that the foregoing is true and correct.

Executed on ________________________, 20___

____
(Signature)

RULES OF THE SUPREME COURT OF THE UNITED STATES

Adopted April 18, 2019

Effective July 1, 2019

SUPREME COURT OF THE UNITED STATES

1 First Street, N. E. Washington, DC 20543

Clerk of the Court	(202) 479-3011
Reporter of Decisions	(202) 479-3390
Marshal of the Court	(202) 479-3333
Librarian	(202) 479-3175
Telephone Operator	(202) 479-3000

Visit the U.S. Supreme Court Website http://www.supremecourt.gov

Mailing Address of the Solicitor General of the United States (see Rule 29.4)

Room 5616 Department of Justice
950 Pennsylvania Avenue, N. W.
Washington, DC 20530-0001

PART I. The Court

Rule 1. Clerk

1. The Clerk receives documents for filing with the Court and has authority to reject any submitted filing that does not comply with these Rules.
2. The Clerk maintains the Court's records and will not permit any of them to be removed from the Court building except as authorized by the Court. Any document filed with the Clerk and made a part of the Court's records may not thereafter be withdrawn from the official Court files. After the conclusion of proceedings in this Court, original records and documents transmitted to this Court by any other court will be returned to the court from which they were received.

3. Unless the Court or the Chief Justice orders otherwise, the Clerk's office is open from 9 a.m. to 5 p.m., Monday through Friday, except on federal legal holidays listed in 5 U.S.C. § 6103.

Rule 2. Library

1. The Court's library is available for use by appropriate personnel of this Court, members of the Bar of this Court, Members of Congress and their legal staffs, and attorneys for the United States and for federal departments and agencies.
2. The library's hours are governed by regulations made by the Librarian with the approval of the Chief Justice or the Court.
3. Library books may not be removed from the Court building, except by a Justice or a member of a Justice's staff.

Rule 3. Term

The Court holds a continuous annual Term commencing on the first Monday in October and ending on the day before the first Monday in October of the following year. See 28 U.S.C. § 2. At the end of each Term, all cases pending on the docket are continued to the next Term.

Rule 4. Sessions and Quorum

1. Open sessions of the Court are held beginning at 10 a.m. on the first Monday in October of each year and thereafter as announced by the Court. Unless it orders otherwise, the Court sits to hear arguments from 10 a.m. until noon and from 1 p.m. until 3 p.m.
2. Six Members of the Court constitute a quorum. See 28 U.S.C. § 1. In the absence of a quorum on any day appointed for holding a session of the Court, the Justices attending – or if no Justice is present, the Clerk or a Deputy Clerk – may announce that the Court will not meet until there is a quorum.
3. When appropriate, the Court will direct the Clerk or the Marshal to announce recesses.

PART II. Attorneys and Counselors

Rule 5. Admission to the Bar

1. To qualify for admission to the Bar of this Court, an applicant must have been admitted to practice in the highest court of a State, Commonwealth, Territory or Possession, or the District of Columbia for a period of at least three years immediately before the date of application; must not have been the subject of any adverse disciplinary action pronounced or in effect during that 3-year period; and must appear to the Court to be of good moral and professional character.
2. Each applicant shall file with the Clerk (1) a certificate from the presiding judge, clerk, or other authorized official of that court evidencing the applicant's admission to practice there and the applicant's current good standing, and (2) a completely executed copy of the form approved by this Court and furnished by the Clerk containing (a) the applicant's personal statement, and (b) the statement of two sponsors endorsing the correctness of the applicant's statement, stating that the applicant possesses all the qualifications required for admission, and affirming that the applicant is of good moral and professional character. Both sponsors must be members of the Bar of this Court who personally know, but are not related to, the applicant.
3. If the documents submitted demonstrate that the applicant possesses the necessary

qualifications, and if the applicant has signed the oath or affirmation and paid the required fee, the Clerk will notify the applicant of acceptance by the Court as a member of the Bar and issue a certificate of admission. An applicant who so wishes may be admitted in open court on oral motion by a member of the Bar of this Court, provided that all other requirements for admission have been satisfied.

4. Each applicant shall sign the following oath or affirmation: I, ..., do solemnly swear (or affirm) that as an attorney and as a counselor of this Court, I will conduct myself uprightly and according to law, and that I will support the Constitution of the United States.
5. The fee for admission to the Bar and a certificate bearing the seal of the Court is $200, payable to the United States Supreme Court. The Marshal will deposit such fees in a separate fund to be disbursed by the Marshal at the direction of the Chief Justice for the costs of admissions, for the benefit of the Court and its Bar, and for related purposes.
6. The fee for a duplicate certificate of admission to the Bar bearing the seal of the Court is $15, and the fee for a certificate of good standing is $10, payable to the United States Supreme Court. The proceeds will be maintained by the Marshal as provided in paragraph 5 of this Rule.

Rule 6. Argument *Pro hac vice*

1. An attorney not admitted to practice in the highest court of a State, Commonwealth, Territory or Possession, or the District of Columbia for the requisite three years, but otherwise eligible for admission to practice in this Court under Rule 5.1, may be permitted to argue *pro hac vice*.
2. An attorney qualified to practice in the courts of a foreign state may be permitted to argue *pro hac vice*.
3. Oral argument *pro hac vice* is allowed only on motion of the counsel of record for the party on whose behalf leave is requested. The motion shall state concisely the qualifications of the attorney who is to argue *pro hac vice*. It shall be filed with the Clerk, in the form required by Rule 21, no later than the date on which the respondent's or appellee's brief on the merits is due to be filed, and it shall be accompanied by proof of service as required by Rule 29.

Rule 7. Prohibition Against Practice

No employee of this Court shall practice as an attorney or counselor in any court or before any agency of government while employed by the Court; nor shall any person after leaving such employment participate in any professional capacity in any case pending before this Court or in any case being considered for filing in this Court, until two years have elapsed after separation; nor shall a former employee ever participate in any professional capacity in any case that was pending in this Court during the employee's tenure.

Rule 8. Disbarment and Disciplinary Action

1. Whenever a member of the Bar of this Court has been disbarred or suspended from practice in any court of record or has engaged in conduct unbecoming a member of the Bar of this Court, the Court will enter an order suspending that member from practice before this Court and affording the member an opportunity to show cause, within 40 days, why a disbarment order should not be entered. Upon response, or if no response is timely filed, the Court will enter an appropriate order.
2. After reasonable notice and an opportunity to show cause why disciplinary action should not be

taken, and after a hearing, if material facts are in dispute, the Court may take any appropriate disciplinary action against any attorney who is admitted to practice before it for conduct unbecoming a member of the Bar or for failure to comply with these Rules or any Rule or order of the Court.

Rule 9. Appearance of Counsel

1. An attorney seeking to file a document in this Court in a representative capacity must first be admitted to practice before this Court as provided in Rule 5, except that admission to the Bar of this Court is not required for an attorney appointed under the Criminal Justice Act of 1964, see 18 U.S.C. § 3006A(d)(7), or under any other applicable federal statute. The attorney whose name, address, and telephone number appear on the cover of a document presented for filing is considered counsel of record. If the name of more than one attorney is shown on the cover of the document, the attorney who is counsel of record shall be clearly identified. See Rule 34.1(f).
2. An attorney representing a party who will not be filing a document shall enter a separate notice of appearance as counsel of record indicating the name of the party represented. A separate notice of appearance shall also be entered whenever an attorney is substituted as counsel of record in a particular case.

PART III. Jurisdiction on Writ of Certiorari

Rule 10. Considerations Governing Review on Certiorari

Review on a writ of certiorari is not a matter of right but of judicial discretion. A petition for a writ of certiorari will be granted only for compelling reasons. The following, although neither controlling nor fully measuring the Court's discretion, indicate the character of the reasons the Court considers:

(a) a United States court of appeals has entered a decision in conflict with the decision of another United States court of appeals on the same important matter; has decided an important federal question in a way that conflicts with a decision by a state court of last resort; or has so far departed from the accepted and usual course of judicial proceedings, or sanctioned such a departure by a lower court, as to call for an exercise of this Court's supervisory power;

(b) a state court of last resort has decided an important federal question in a way that conflicts with the decision of another state court of last resort or of a United States court of appeals;

(c) a state court or a United States court of appeals has decided an important question of federal law that has not been, but should be, settled by this Court, or has decided an important federal question in a way that conflicts with relevant decisions of this Court.

A petition for a writ of certiorari is rarely granted when the asserted error consists of erroneous factual findings or the misapplication of a properly stated rule of law.

Rule 11. Certiorari to a United States Court of Appeals Before Judgment

A petition for a writ of certiorari to review a case pending in a United States court of appeals, before judgment is entered in that court, will be granted only upon a showing that the case is of such imperative public importance as to justify deviation from normal appellate practice and to require immediate determination in this Court. See 28 U.S.C.§ 2101(e).

Rule 12. Review on Certiorari: How Sought; Parties

1. Except as provided in paragraph 2 of this Rule, the petitioner shall file 40 copies of a petition for a writ of certiorari, prepared as required by Rule 33.1, and shall pay the Rule 38(a) docket fee.
2. A petitioner proceeding *in forma pauperis* under Rule 39 shall file an original and 10 copies of a petition for a writ of certiorari prepared as required by Rule 33.2, together with an original and 10 copies of the motion for leave to proceed *in forma pauperis*. A copy of the motion shall precede and be attached to each copy of the petition. An inmate confined in an institution, if proceeding *in forma pauperis* and not represented by counsel, need file only an original petition and motion.
3. Whether prepared under Rule 33.1 or Rule 33.2, the petition shall comply in all respects with Rule 14 and shall be submitted with proof of service as required by Rule 29. The case then will be placed on the docket. It is the petitioner's duty to notify all respondents promptly, on a form supplied by the Clerk, of the date of filing, the date the case was placed on the docket, and the docket number of the case. The notice shall be served as required by Rule 29.
4. Parties interested jointly, severally, or otherwise in a judgment may petition separately for a writ of certiorari; or any two or more may join in a petition. A party not shown on the petition as joined therein at the time the petition is filed may not later join in that petition. When two or more judgments are sought to be reviewed on a writ of certiorari to the same court and involve identical or closely related questions, a single petition for a writ of certiorari covering all the judgments suffices. A petition for a writ of certiorari may not be joined with any other pleading, except that any motion for leave to proceed *in forma pauperis* shall be attached.
5. No more than 30 days after a case has been placed on the docket, a respondent seeking to file a conditional cross-petition (*i. e.*, a cross-petition that otherwise would be untimely) shall file, with proof of service as required by Rule 29, 40 copies of the cross-petition prepared as required by Rule 33.1, except that a cross-petitioner proceeding *in forma pauperis* under Rule 39 shall comply with Rule 12.2. The cross-petition shall comply in all respects with this Rule and Rule 14, except that material already reproduced in the appendix to the opening petition need not be reproduced again. A cross-petitioning respondent shall pay the Rule 38(a) docket fee or submit a motion for leave to proceed *in forma pauperis*. The cover of the cross-petition shall indicate clearly that it is a conditional cross-petition. The cross-petition then will be placed on the docket, subject to the provisions of Rule 13.4. It is the cross-petitioner's duty to notify all cross-respondents promptly, on a form supplied by the Clerk, of the date of filing, the date the cross-petition was placed on the docket, and the docket number of the cross-petition. The notice shall be served as required by Rule 29. A cross-petition for a writ of certiorari may not be joined with any other pleading, except that any motion for leave to proceed *in forma pauperis*

shall be attached. The time to file a conditional cross-petition will not be extended.

6. All parties to the proceeding in the court whose judgment is sought to be reviewed are deemed parties entitled to file documents in this Court, unless the petitioner notifies the Clerk of this Court in writing of the petitioner's belief that one or more of the parties below have no interest in the outcome of the petition. A copy of such notice shall be served as required by Rule 29 on all parties to the proceeding below. A party noted as no longer interested may remain a party by notifying the Clerk promptly, with service on the other parties, of an intention to remain a party. All parties other than the petitioner are considered respondents, but any respondent who supports the position of a petitioner shall meet the petitioner's time schedule for filing documents, with the following exception: A response of a party aligned with petitioner below who supports granting the petition shall be filed within 30 days after the case is placed on the docket, and that time will not be extended. Counsel for such respondent shall ensure that counsel of record for all parties receive notice of its intention to file a brief in support within 20 days after the case is placed on the docket. A respondent not aligned with petitioner below who supports granting the petition, or a respondent aligned with petitioner below who takes the position that the petition should be denied, is not subject to the notice requirement and may file a response within the time otherwise provided by Rule 15.3. Parties who file no document will not qualify for any relief from this Court.
7. The clerk of the court having possession of the record shall keep it until notifies by the Clerk of this Court to certify and transmit it. In any document filed with this Court, a party may cite or quote from the record, even if it has not been transmitted to this Court. When requested by the Clerk of this Court to certify and transmit the record, or any part of it, the clerk of the court having possession of the record shall number the documents to be certified and shall transmit therewith a numbered list specifically identifying each document transmitted. If the record, or stipulated portions, have been printed for the use of the court below, that printed record, plus the proceedings in the court below, may be certified as the record unless one of the parties or the Clerk of this Court requests otherwise. The record may consist of certified copies, but if the lower court is of the view that original documents of any kind should be seen by this Court, that court may provide by order for the transport, safekeeping, and return of such originals.

Rule 13. Review on Certiorari: Time for Petitioning

1. Unless otherwise provided by law, a petition for a writ of certiorari to review a judgment in any case, civil or criminal, entered by a state court of last resort or a United States court of appeals (including the United States Court of Appeals for the Armed Forces) is timely when it is filed with the Clerk of this Court within 90 days after entry of the judgment. A petition for a writ of certiorari seeking review of a judgment of a lower state court that is subject to discretionary review by the state court of last resort is timely when it is filed with the Clerk within 90 days after entry of the order denying discretionary review.
2. The Clerk will not file any petition for a writ of certiorari that is jurisdictionally out of time. See, *e. g.*, 28 U.S.C. § 2101(c).
3. The time to file a petition for a writ of certiorari runs from the date of entry of the judgment or order sought to be reviewed, and not from the issuance date of the mandate (or its equivalent under local practice). But if a petition for rehearing is timely filed in the lower

court by any party, or if the lower court appropriately entertains an untimely petition for rehearing or *sua sponte* considers rehearing, the time to file the petition for a writ of certiorari for all parties (whether or not they requested rehearing or joined in the petition for rehearing) runs from the date of the denial of rehearing or, if rehearing is granted, the subsequent entry of judgment.

4. A cross-petition for a writ of certiorari is timely when it is filed with the Clerk as provided in paragraphs 1, 3, and 5 of this Rule, or in Rule 12.5. However, a conditional cross-petition (which except for Rule 12.5 would be untimely) will not be granted unless another party's timely petition for a writ of certiorari is granted.
5. For good cause, a Justice may extend the time to file a petition for a writ of certiorari for a period not exceeding 60 days. An application to extend the time to file shall set out the basis for jurisdiction in this Court, identify the judgment sought to be reviewed, include a copy of the opinion and any order respecting rehearing, and set out specific reasons why an extension of time is justified. The application must be filed with the Clerk at least 10 days before the date the petition is due, except in extraordinary circumstances. The application must clearly identify each party for whom an extension is being sought, as any extension that might be granted would apply solely to the party or parties named in the application. For the time and manner of presenting the application, see Rules 21, 22, 30, and 33.2. An application to extend the time to file a petition for a writ of certiorari is not favored.

Rule 14. Content of a Petition for a Writ of Certiorari

1. A petition for a writ of certiorari shall contain, in the order indicated:

(a) The questions presented for review, expressed concisely in relation to the circumstances of the case, without unnecessary detail. The questions should be short and should not be argumentative or repetitive. If the petitioner or respondent is under a death sentence that may be affected by the disposition of the petition, the notation "capital case" shall precede the questions presented. The questions shall be set out on the first page following the cover, and no other information may appear on that page. The statement of any question presented is deemed to comprise every subsidiary question fairly included therein. Only the questions set out in the petition, or fairly included therein, will be considered by the Court.

(b) (i) A list of all parties to the proceeding in the court whose judgment is sought to be reviewed (unless the caption of the case contains the names of all the parties);

(ii) a corporate disclosure statement as required by Rule 29.6; and

(iii) a list of all proceedings in state and federal trial and appellate courts, including proceedings in this Court, that are directly related to the case in this Court. For each such proceeding, the list should include the court in question, the docket number and case caption for the proceeding, and the date of entry of the judgment. For the purposes of this rule, a case is "directly related" if it arises from the same trial court case as the case in this Court (including the proceedings directly on review in this case), or if it challenges the same criminal conviction or sentence as is challenged in this Court, whether on direct appeal or through state or federal collateral proceedings.

(c) If the petition prepared under Rule 33.1 exceeds 1,500 words or exceeds fve pages if prepared under Rule 33.2, a table of contents and a table of cited authorities. The table of contents shall include the items contained in the appendix.

(d) Citations of the official and unofficial reports of the opinions and orders entered in the case by courts or administrative agencies.

(e) A concise statement of the basis for jurisdiction in this Court, showing:

(i) the date the judgment or order sought to be reviewed was entered (and, if applicable, a statement that the petition is filed under this Court's Rule 11);

(ii) the date of any order respecting rehearing, and the date and terms of any order granting an extension of time to file the petition for a writ of certiorari;

(iii) express reliance on Rule 12.5, when a cross-petition for a writ of certiorari is filed under that Rule, and the date of docketing of the petition for a writ of certiorari in connection with which the cross-petition is filed;

(iv) the statutory provision believed to confer on this Court jurisdiction to review on a writ of certiorari the judgment or order in question; and

(v) if applicable, a statement that the notifications required by Rule 29.4(b) or (c) have been made.

(f) The constitutional provisions, treaties, statutes, ordinances, and regulations involved in the case, set out verbatim with appropriate citation. If the provisions involved are lengthy, their citation alone suffices at this point, and their pertinent text shall be set out in the appendix referred to in subparagraph 1(i).

(g) A concise statement of the case setting out the facts' material to consideration of the questions presented, and also containing the following:

(i) If review of a state-court judgment is sought, specification of the stage in the proceedings, both in the court of first instance and in the appellate courts, when the federal questions sought to be reviewed were raised; the method or manner of raising them and the way in which they were passed on by those courts; and pertinent quotations of specific portions of the record or summary thereof, with specific reference to the places in the record where the matter appears (*e. g.*, court opinion, ruling on exception, portion of court's charge and exception thereto, assignment of error), so as to show that the federal question was timely and properly raised and that this Court has jurisdiction to review the judgment on a writ of certiorari. When the portions of the record relied on under this subparagraph are voluminous, they shall be included in the appendix referred to in subparagraph 1(i).

(ii) If review of a judgment of a United States court of appeals is sought, the basis for federal jurisdiction in the court of first instance.

(h) A direct and concise argument amplifying the reasons relied on for allowance of the writ. See Rule 10.

(i) An appendix containing, in the order indicated:

(i) the opinions, orders, findings of fact, and conclusions of law, whether written or orally given and transcribed, entered in conjunction with the judgment sought to be reviewed;

(ii) any other relevant opinions, orders, findings of fact, and conclusions of law entered in the case by courts or administrative agencies, and, if reference thereto is necessary to ascertain the grounds of the judgment, of those in companion cases (each document shall include the caption showing the name of the issuing court or agency, the title and number of the case, and the date of entry);

(iii) any order on rehearing, including the caption showing the name of the issuing

court, the title and number of the case, and the date of entry;
(iv) the judgment sought to be reviewed if the date of its entry is different from the date of the opinion or order required in sub-subparagraph (i) of this subparagraph;
(v) material required by subparagraphs 1(f) or 1(g)(i); and
(vi) any other material the petitioner believes essential to understand the petition.

(6) If the material required by this subparagraph is voluminous, it may be presented in a separate volume or volumes with appropriate covers.

2. All contentions in support of a petition for a writ of certiorari shall be set out in the body of the petition, as provided in subparagraph 1(h) of this Rule. No separate brief in support of a petition for a writ of certiorari may be filed, and the Clerk will not file any petition for a writ of certiorari to which any supporting brief is annexed or appended.
3. A petition for a writ of certiorari should be stated briefly and in plain terms and may not exceed the word or page limitations specified in Rule 33.
4. The failure of a petitioner to present with accuracy, brevity, and clarity whatever is essential to ready and adequate understanding of the points requiring consideration is sufficient reason for the Court to deny a petition.
5. If the Clerk determines that a petition submitted timely and in good faith is in a form that does not comply with this Rule or with Rule 33 or Rule 34, the Clerk will return it with a letter indicating the deficiency. A corrected petition submitted in accordance with Rule 29.2 no more than 60 days after the date of the Clerk's letter will be deemed timely.

Rule 15. Briefs in Opposition; Reply Briefs; Supplemental Briefs

1. A brief in opposition to a petition for a writ of certiorari may be filed by the respondent in any case, but is not mandatory except in a capital case, see Rule 14.1(a), or when ordered by the Court.
2. A brief in opposition should be stated briefly and in plain terms and may not exceed the word or page limitations specified in Rule 33. In addition to presenting other arguments for denying the petition, the brief in opposition should address any perceived misstatement of fact or law in the petition that bears on what issues properly would be before the Court if certiorari were granted. Counsel is admonished that they have an obligation to the Court to point out in the brief in opposition, and not later, any perceived misstatement made in the petition. Any objection to consideration of a question presented based on what occurred in the proceedings below, if the objection does not go to jurisdiction, may be deemed waived unless called to the Court's attention in the brief in opposition. A brief in opposition should identify any directly related cases that were not identified in the petition under Rule 14.1(b)(iii), including for each such case the information called for by Rule 14.1(b)(iii).
3. Any brief in opposition shall be filed within 30 days after the case is placed on the docket, unless the time is extended by the Court or a Justice, or by the Clerk under Rule 30.4. Forty copies shall be filed, except that a respondent proceeding *in forma pauperis* under Rule 39, including an inmate of an institution, shall file the number of copies required for a petition by such a person under Rule 12.2, together with a motion for leave to proceed *in forma pauperis*, a copy of which shall precede and be attached to each copy of the brief in opposition. If the petitioner is proceeding *in forma pauperis*, the respondent shall prepare its brief in opposition, if any, as required by Rule 33.2, and shall file an original and 10 copies of that brief. Whether prepared under Rule 33.1 or Rule 33.2, the brief in opposition shall comply with the requirements of Rule 24 governing a respondent's brief, except that

no summary of the argument is required. A brief in opposition may not be joined with any other pleading, except that any motion for leave to proceed *in forma pauperis* shall be attached. The brief in opposition shall be served as required by Rule 29.

4. No motion by a respondent to dismiss a petition for a writ of certiorari may be filed. Any objections to the jurisdiction of the Court to grant a petition for a writ of certiorari shall be included in the brief in opposition.
5. The Clerk will distribute the petition to the Court for its consideration upon receiving an express waiver of the right to file a brief in opposition, or, if no waiver or brief in opposition is filed, upon the expiration of the time allowed for filing. If a brief in opposition is timely filed, the Clerk will distribute the petition, brief in opposition, and any reply brief to the Court for its consideration no less than 14 days after the brief in opposition is filed, unless the petitioner expressly waives the 14-day waiting period.
6. Any petitioner may file a reply brief addressed to new points raised in the brief in opposition, but distribution and consideration by the Court under paragraph 5 of this Rule will not be deferred pending its receipt. Forty copies shall be filed, except that a petitioner proceeding *in forma pauperis* under Rule 39, including an inmate of an institution, shall file the number of copies required for a petition by such a person under Rule 12.2. The reply brief shall be served as required by Rule 29.
7. If a cross-petition for a writ of certiorari has been docketed, distribution of both petitions will be deferred until the cross-petition is due for distribution under this Rule.
8. Any party may file a supplemental brief at any time while a petition for a writ of certiorari is pending, calling attention to new cases, new legislation, or other intervening matter not available at the time of the party's last filing. A supplemental brief shall be restricted to new matter and shall follow, insofar as applicable, the form for a brief in opposition prescribed by this Rule. Forty copies shall be filed, except that a party proceeding *in forma pauperis* under Rule 39, including an inmate of an institution, shall file the number of copies required for a petition by such a person under Rule 12.2. The supplemental brief shall be served as required by Rule 29.

Rule 16. Disposition of a Petition for a Writ of Certiorari

1. After considering the documents distributed under Rule 15, the Court will enter an appropriate order. The order may be a summary disposition on the merits.
2. Whenever the Court grants a petition for a writ of certiorari, the Clerk will prepare, sign, and enter an order to that effect and will notify forthwith counsel of record and the court whose judgment is to be reviewed. The case then will be scheduled for briefing and oral argument. If the record has not previously been filed in this Court, the Clerk will request the clerk of the court having possession of the record to certify and transmit it. A formal writ will not issue unless specially directed.
3. Whenever the Court denies a petition for a writ of certiorari, the Clerk will prepare, sign, and enter an order to that effect and will notify forthwith counsel of record and the court whose judgment was sought to be reviewed. The order of denial will not be suspended pending disposition of a petition for rehearing except by order of the Court or a Justice.

PART IV. Other Jurisdiction

Rule 17. Procedure in an Original Action

1. This Rule applies only to an action invoking the Court's original jurisdiction under Article III of the Constitution of the United States. See also 28 U.S.C. § 1251 and U. S. Constitution, Amendment. 11. A petition for an extraordinary writ in aid of the Court's appellate jurisdiction shall be filed as provided in Rule 20.
2. The form of pleadings and motions prescribed by the Federal Rules of Civil Procedure is followed. In other respects, those Rules and the Federal Rules of Evidence may be taken as guides.
3. The initial pleading shall be preceded by a motion for leave to file and may be accompanied by a brief in support of the motion. Forty copies of each document shall be filed, with proof of service. Service shall be as required by Rule 29, except that when an adverse party is a State, service shall be made on both the Governor and the Attorney General of that State.
4. The case will be placed on the docket when the motion for leave to file and the initial pleading are filed with the Clerk. The Rule 38(a) docket fee shall be paid at that time.
5. No more than 60 days after receiving the motion for leave to file and the initial pleading, an adverse party shall file 40 copies of any brief in opposition to the motion, with proof of service as required by Rule 29. The Clerk will distribute the filed documents to the Court for its consideration upon receiving an express waiver of the right to file a brief in opposition, or, if no waiver or brief is filed, upon the expiration of the time allowed for filing. If a brief in opposition is timely filed, the Clerk will distribute the filed documents to the Court for its consideration no less than 10 days after the brief in opposition is filed. A reply brief may be filed, but consideration of the case will not be deferred pending its receipt. The Court thereafter may grant or deny the motion, set it for oral argument, direct that additional documents be filed, or require that other proceedings be conducted.
6. A summons issued out of this Court shall be served on the defendant 60 days before the return day specified therein. If the defendant does not respond by the return day, the plaintiff may proceed *ex parte*.
7. Process against a State issued out of this Court shall be served on both the Governor and the Attorney General of that State.

Rule 18. Appeal from a United States District Court

1. When a direct appeal from a decision of a United States district court is authorized by law, the appeal is commenced by filing a notice of appeal with the clerk of the district court within the time provided by law after entry of the judgment sought to be reviewed. The time to file may not be extended. The notice of appeal shall specify the parties taking the appeal, designate the judgment, or part thereof, appealed from and the date of its entry, and specify the statute or statutes under which the appeal is taken. A copy of the notice of appeal shall be served on all parties to the proceeding as required by Rule 29, and proof of service shall be filed in the district court together with the notice of appeal.
2. All parties to the proceeding in the district court are deemed parties entitled to file documents in this Court, but a party having no interest in the outcome of the appeal may so notify the Clerk of this Court and shall serve a copy of the notice on all other parties. Parties interested jointly, severally, or otherwise in the judgment may appeal separately, or

any two or more may join in an appeal. When two or more judgments involving identical or closely related questions are sought to be reviewed on appeal from the same court, a notice of appeal for each judgment shall be filed with the clerk of the district court, but a single jurisdictional statement covering all the judgments suffices. Parties who file no document will not qualify for any relief from this Court.

3. No more than 60 days after filing the notice of appeal in the district court, the appellant shall file 40 copies of a jurisdictional statement and shall pay the Rule 38 docket fee, except that an appellant proceeding *in forma pauperis* under Rule 39, including an inmate of an institution, shall file the number of copies required for a petition by such a person under Rule 12.2, together with a motion for leave to proceed *in forma pauperis*, a copy of which shall precede and be attached to each copy of the jurisdictional statement. The jurisdictional statement shall follow, insofar as applicable, the form for a petition for a writ of certiorari prescribed by Rule 14 and shall be served as required by Rule 29. The case will then be placed on the docket. It is the appellant's duty to notify all appellees promptly, on a form supplied by the Clerk, of the date of filing, the date the case was placed on the docket, and the docket number of the case. The notice shall be served as required by Rule 29. The appendix shall include a copy of the notice of appeal showing the date it was filed in the district court. For good cause, a Justice may extend the time to file a jurisdictional statement for a period not exceeding 60 days. An application to extend the time to file a jurisdictional statement shall set out the basis for jurisdiction in this Court; identify the judgment sought to be reviewed; include a copy of the opinion, any order respecting rehearing, and the notice of appeal; and set out specific reasons why an extension of time is justified. For the time and manner of presenting the application, see Rules 21, 22, and 30. An application to extend the time to file a jurisdictional statement is not favored.
4. No more than 30 days after a case has been placed on the docket, an appellee seeking to file a conditional cross-appeal (*i. e.*, a cross-appeal that otherwise would be untimely) shall file, with proof of service as required by Rule 29, a jurisdictional statement that complies in all respects (including number of copies filed) with paragraph 3 of this Rule, except that material already reproduced in the appendix to the opening jurisdictional statement need not be reproduced again. A cross-appealing appellee shall pay the Rule 38 docket fee or submit a motion for leave to proceed *in forma pauperis*. The cover of the cross-appeal shall indicate clearly that it is a conditional cross-appeal. The cross-appeal then will be placed on the docket. It is the cross-appellant's duty to notify all cross-appellees promptly, on a form supplied by the Clerk, of the date of filing, the date the cross-appeal was placed on the docket, and the docket number of the cross-appeal. The notice shall be served as required by Rule 29. A cross-appeal may not be joined with any other pleading, except that any motion for leave to proceed *in forma pauperis* shall be attached. The time to file a cross-appeal will not be extended.
5. After a notice of appeal has been filed in the district court, but before the case is placed on this Court's docket, the parties may dismiss the appeal by stipulation filed in the district court, or the district court may dismiss the appeal on the appellant's motion, with notice to all parties. If a notice of appeal has been filed, but the case has not been placed on this Court's docket within the time prescribed for docketing, the district court may dismiss the appeal on the appellee's motion, with notice to all parties, and may make any just order with respect to costs. If the district court has denied the appellee's motion to dismiss the appeal, the appellee may move this Court to docket and dismiss the appeal by filing an

original and 10 copies of a motion presented in conformity with Rules 21 and 33.2. The motion shall be accompanied by proof of service as required by Rule 29, and by a certificate from the clerk of the district court, certifying that a notice of appeal was filed and that the appellee's motion to dismiss was denied. The appellant may not thereafter file a jurisdictional statement without special leave of the Court, and the Court may allow costs against the appellant.

6. Within 30 days after the case is placed on this Court's docket, the appellee may file a motion to dismiss, to affirm, or in the alternative to affirm or dismiss. Forty copies of the motion shall be filed, except that an appellee proceeding *in forma pauperis* under Rule 39, including an inmate of an institution, shall file the number of copies required for a petition by such a person under Rule 12.2, together with a motion for leave to proceed *in forma pauperis*, a copy of which shall precede and be attached to each copy of the motion to dismiss, to affirm, or in the alternative to affirm or dismiss. The motion shall follow, insofar as applicable, the form for a brief in opposition prescribed by Rule 15 and shall comply in all respects with Rule 21.
7. The Clerk will distribute the jurisdictional statement to the Court for its consideration upon receiving an express waiver of the right to file a motion to dismiss or to affirm or, if no waiver or motion is filed, upon the expiration of the time allowed for filing. If a motion to dismiss or to affirm is timely filed, the Clerk will distribute the jurisdictional statement, motion, and any brief opposing the motion to the Court for its consideration no less than 14 days after the motion is filed, unless the appellant expressly waives the 14-day waiting period.
8. Any appellant may file a brief opposing a motion to dismiss or to affirm, but distribution and consideration by the Court under paragraph 7 of this Rule will not be deferred pending its receipt. Forty copies shall be filed, except that an appellant proceeding *in forma pauperis* under Rule 39, including an inmate of an institution, shall file the number of copies required for a petition by such a person under Rule 12.2. The brief shall be served as required by Rule 29.
9. If a cross-appeal has been docketed, distribution of both jurisdictional statements will be deferred until the cross-appeal is due for distribution under this Rule.
10. Any party may file a supplemental brief at any time while a jurisdictional statement is pending, calling attention to new cases, new legislation, or other intervening matter not available at the time of the party's last filing. A supplemental brief shall be restricted to new matter and shall follow, insofar as applicable, the form for a brief in opposition prescribed by Rule 15. Forty copies shall be filed, except that a party proceeding *in forma pauperis* under Rule 39, including an inmate of an institution, shall file the number of copies required for a petition by such a person under Rule 12.2. The supplemental brief shall be served as required by Rule 29.
11. The clerk of the district court shall retain possession of the record until notified by the Clerk of this Court to certify and transmit it. See Rule 12.7.
12. After considering the documents distributed under this Rule, the Court may dispose summarily of the appeal on the merits, note probable jurisdiction, or postpone consideration of jurisdiction until a hearing of the case on the merits. If not disposed of summarily, the case stands for briefing and oral argument on the merits. If consideration of jurisdiction is postponed, counsel, at the outset of their briefs and at oral argument, shall address the question of jurisdiction. If the record has not previously been filed in this Court, the Clerk

of this Court will request the clerk of the court in possession of the record to certify and transmit it.

13. If the Clerk determines that a jurisdictional statement submitted timely and in good faith is in a form that does not comply with this Rule or with Rule 33 or Rule 34, the Clerk will return it with a letter indicating the deficiency. If a corrected jurisdictional statement is submitted in accordance with Rule 29.2 no more than 60 days after the date of the Clerk's letter it will be deemed timely.

Rule 19. Procedure on a Certified Question

1. A United States court of appeals may certify to this Court a question or proposition of law on which it seeks instruction for the proper decision of a case. The certificate shall contain a statement of the nature of the case and the facts on which the question or proposition of law arises. Only questions or propositions of law may be certified, and they shall be stated separately and with precision. The certificate shall be prepared as required by Rule 33.2 and shall be signed by the clerk of the court of appeals.
2. When a question is certified by a United States court of appeals, this Court, on its own motion or that of a party, may consider and decide the entire matter in controversy. See 28 U.S.C. § 1254(2).
3. When a question is certified, the Clerk will notify the parties and docket the case. Counsel shall then enter their appearances. After docketing, the Clerk will submit the certificate to the Court for a preliminary examination to determine whether the case should be briefed, set for argument, or dismissed. No brief may be filed until the preliminary examination of the certificate is completed.
4. If the Court orders the case briefed or set for argument, the parties will be notified and permitted to file briefs. The Clerk of this Court then will request the clerk of the court in possession of the record to certify and transmit it. Any portion of the record to which the parties wish to direct the Court's particular attention should be printed in a joint appendix, prepared in conformity with Rule 26 by the appellant or petitioner in the court of appeals, but the fact that any part of the record has not been printed does not prevent the parties or the Court from relying on it.
5. A brief on the merits in a case involving a certified question shall comply with Rules 24, 25, and 33.1, except that the brief for the party who the appellant or petitioner is below shall be filed within 45 days of the order requiring briefs or setting the case for argument.

Rule 20. Procedure on a Petition for an Extraordinary Writ

1. Issuance by the Court of an extraordinary writ authorized by 28 U.S.C. § 1651(a) is not a matter of right, but of discretion sparingly exercised. To justify the granting of any such writ, the petition must show that the writ will be in aid of the Court's appellate jurisdiction, that exceptional circumstances warrant the exercise of the Court's discretionary powers, and that adequate relief cannot be obtained in any other form or from any other court.
2. A petition seeking a writ authorized by 28 U.S.C. § 1651(a), § 2241, or § 2254(a) shall be prepared in all respects as required by Rules 33 and 34. The petition shall be captioned "In re [name of petitioner]" and shall follow, insofar as applicable, the form of a petition for a writ of certiorari prescribed by Rule 14. All contentions in support of the petition shall be included in the petition. The case will be placed on the docket when 40 copies of the

petition are filed with the Clerk and the docket fee is paid, except that a petitioner proceeding *in forma pauperis* under Rule 39, including an inmate of an institution, shall file the number of copies required for a petition by such a person under Rule 12.2, together with a motion for leave to proceed *in forma pauperis*, a copy of which shall precede and be attached to each copy of the petition. The petition shall be served as required by Rule 29 (subject to subparagraph 4(b) of this Rule).

3. (a) A petition seeking a writ of prohibition, a writ of mandamus, or both in the alternative shall state the name and office or function of every person against whom relief is sought and shall set out with particularity why the relief sought is not available in any other court. A copy of the judgment with respect to which the writ is sought, including any related opinion, shall be appended to the petition together with any other document essential to understanding the petition.
   (b) The petition shall be served on every party to the proceeding with respect to which relief is sought. Within 30 days after the petition is placed on the docket, a party shall file 40 copies of any brief or briefs in opposition thereto, which shall comply fully with Rule 15. If a party named as a respondent does not wish to respond to the petition, that party may so advise the Clerk and all other parties by letter. All persons served are deemed respondents for all purposes in the proceedings in this Court.
4. (a) A petition seeking a writ of habeas corpus shall comply with the requirements of 28 U.S.C. §§ 2241 and 2242, and in particular with the provision in the last paragraph of § 2242, which requires a statement of the "reasons for not making application to the district court of the district in which the applicant is held." If the relief sought is from the judgment of a state court, the petition shall set out specifically how and where the petitioner has exhausted available remedies in the state courts or otherwise comes within the provisions of 28 U.S.C. § 2254(b). To justify the granting of a writ of habeas corpus, the petitioner must show that exceptional circumstances warrant the exercise of the Court's discretionary powers, and that adequate relief cannot be obtained in any other form or from any other court. This writ is rarely granted.
   (b) Habeas corpus proceedings, except in capital cases, are *ex parte*, unless the Court requires the respondent to show cause why the petition for a writ of habeas corpus should not be granted. A response, if ordered, or in a capital case, shall comply fully with Rule 15. Neither the denial of the petition, without more, nor an order of transfer to a district court under the authority of 28 U.S.C. § 2241(b), is an adjudication on the merits, and therefore does not preclude further application to another court for the relief sought.
5. The Clerk will distribute the documents to the Court for its consideration when a brief in opposition under subparagraph 3(b) of this Rule has been filed, when a response under subparagraph 4(b) has been ordered and filed, when the time to file has expired, or when the right to file has been expressly waived.
6. If the Court orders the case set for argument, the Clerk will notify the parties whether additional briefs are required, when they shall be filed, and, if the case involves a petition for a common-law writ of certiorari, that the parties shall prepare a joint appendix in accordance with Rule 26.

PART V. Motions and Applications

Rule 21. Motions to the Court

1. Every motion to the Court shall clearly state its purpose and the facts on which it is based and may present legal argument in support thereof. No separate brief may be filed. A motion should be concise and shall comply with any applicable page limits. Non-dispositive motions and applications in cases in which certiorari has been granted, probable jurisdiction noted, or consideration of jurisdiction postponed shall state the position on the disposition of the motion or application of the other party or parties to the case. Rule 22 governs an application addressed to a single Justice.
2. (a) A motion in any action within the Court's original jurisdiction shall comply with Rule 17.3.
   (b) A motion to dismiss as moot (or a suggestion of mootness), a motion for leave to file a brief as *amicus curiae*, and any motion the granting of which would dispose of the entire case or would affect the final judgment to be entered (other than a motion to docket and dismiss under Rule 18.5 or a motion for voluntary dismissal under Rule 46) shall be prepared as required by Rule 33.1, and 40 copies shall be filed, except that a movant proceeding *in forma pauperis* under Rule 39, including an inmate of an institution, shall file a motion prepared as required by Rule 33.2, and shall file the number of copies required for a petition by such a person under Rule 12.2. The motion shall be served as required by Rule 29.
   (c) Any other motion to the Court shall be prepared as required by Rule 33.2; the moving party shall file an original and 10 copies. The Court subsequently may order the moving party to prepare the motion as required by Rule 33.1; in that event, the party shall file 40 copies.
3. A motion to the Court shall be filed with the Clerk and shall be accompanied by proof of service as required by Rule 29. No motion may be presented in open Court, other than a motion for admission to the Bar, except when the proceeding to which it refers is being argued. Oral argument on a motion will not be permitted unless the Court so directs.
4. Any response to a motion shall be filed as promptly as possible considering the nature of the relief sought and any asserted need for emergency action, and, in any event, within 10 days of receipt, unless the Court or a Justice, or the Clerk under Rule 30.4, orders otherwise. A response to a motion prepared as required by Rule 33.1, except a response to a motion for leave to file an *amicus curiae* brief (see Rule 37.5), shall be prepared in the same manner if time permits. In an appropriate case, the Court may act on a motion without waiting for a response.

Rule 22. Applications to Individual Justices

1. An application addressed to an individual Justice shall be filed with the Clerk, who will transmit it promptly to the Justice concerned if an individual Justice has authority to grant the sought relief.
2. The original and two copies of any application addressed to an individual Justice shall be prepared as required by Rule 33.2 and shall be accompanied by proof of service as required by Rule 29.
3. An application shall be addressed to the Justice allotted to the Circuit from which the case

arises. An application arising from the United States Court of Appeals for the Armed Forces shall be addressed to the Chief Justice. When the Circuit Justice is unavailable for any reason, the application addressed to that Justice will be distributed to the Justice then available who is next junior to the Circuit Justice; the turn of the Chief Justice follows that of the most junior Justice.

4. A Justice denying an application will note the denial thereon. Thereafter, unless action thereon is restricted by law to the Circuit Justice or is untimely under Rule 30.2, the party making an application, except in the case of an application for an extension of time, may renew it to any other Justice, subject to the provisions of this Rule. Except when the denial is without prejudice, a renewed application is not favored. Renewed application is made by a letter to the Clerk, designating the Justice to whom the application is to be directed, and accompanied by 10 copies of the original application and proof of service as required by Rule 29.
5. A Justice to whom an application for a stay or for bail is submitted may refer it to the Court for determination.
6. The Clerk will advise all parties concerned, by appropriately speedy means, of the disposition made of an application.

Rule 23. Stays

1. A stay may be granted by a Justice as permitted by law.
2. A party to a judgment sought to be reviewed may present to a Justice an application to stay the enforcement of that judgment. See 28 U.S.C. § 2101(f).
3. An application for a stay shall set out with particularity why the relief sought is not available from any other court or judge. Except in the most extraordinary circumstances, an application for a stay will not be entertained unless the relief requested was first sought in the appropriate court or courts below or from a judge or judges thereof. An application for a stay shall identify the judgment sought to be reviewed and have appended thereto a copy of the order and opinion, if any, and a copy of the order, if any, of the court or judge below denying the relief sought and shall set out specific reasons why a stay is justified. The form and content of an application for a stay are governed by Rules 22 and 33.2.
4. A judge, court, or Justice granting an application for a stay pending review by this Court may condition the stay on the filing of a supersedeas bond having an approved surety or sureties. The bond will be conditioned on the satisfaction of the judgment in full, together with any costs, interest, and damages for delay that may be awarded. If a part of the judgment sought to be reviewed has already been satisfied, or is otherwise secured, the bond may be conditioned on the satisfaction of the part of the judgment not otherwise secured or satisfied, together with costs, interest, and damages.

PART VI. Briefs on the Merits and Oral Argument

Rule 24. Briefs on the Merits: In General

1. A brief on the merits for a petitioner or an appellant shall comply in all respects with Rules 33.1 and 34 and shall contain in the order here indicated:
   (a) The questions presented for review under Rule 14.1(a). The questions shall be set out on the first page following the cover, and no other information may appear on that page.

The phrasing of the questions presented need not be identical with that in the petition for a writ of certiorari or the jurisdictional statement, but the brief may not raise additional questions or change the substance of the questions already presented in those documents. At its option, however, the Court may consider a plain error not among the questions presented but evident from the record and otherwise within its jurisdiction to decide.

(b) A list of all parties to the proceeding in the court whose judgment is under review (unless the caption of the case in this Court contains the names of all parties). Any amended corporate disclosure statement as required by Rule 29.6 shall be placed here.

(c) If the brief exceeds 1,500 words, a table of contents and a table of cited authorities.

(d) Citations of the official and unofficial reports of the opinions and orders entered in the case by courts and administrative agencies.

(e) A concise statement of the basis for jurisdiction in this Court, including the statutory provisions and time factors on which jurisdiction rests.

(f) The constitutional provisions, treaties, statutes, ordinances, and regulations involved in the case, set out verbatim with appropriate citation. If the provisions involved are lengthy, their citation alone suffices at this point, and their pertinent text, if not already set out in the petition for a writ of certiorari, jurisdictional statement, or an appendix to either document, shall be set out in an appendix to the brief.

(g) A concise statement of the case, setting out the fact's material to the consideration of the questions presented, with appropriate references to the joint appendix, *e. g.*, App. 12, or to the record, *e. g.*, Record 12.

(h) A summary of the argument, suitably paragraphed. The summary should be a clear and concise condensation of the argument made in the body of the brief; mere repetition of the headings under which the argument is arranged is not sufficient.

(i) The argument, exhibiting clearly the points of fact and of law presented and citing the authorities and statutes relied on.

(j) A conclusion specifying with particularity the relief the party seeks.

2. A brief on the merits for a respondent or an appellee shall conform to the foregoing requirements, except those items required by subparagraphs 1(a), (b), (d), (e), (f), and (g) of this Rule need not be included unless the respondent or appellee is dissatisfied with their presentation by the opposing party.
3. A brief on the merits may not exceed the word limitations specified in Rule 33.1(g). An appendix to a brief may include only relevant material, and counsel are cautioned not to include in an appendix arguments or citations that properly belong in the body of the brief.
4. A reply brief shall conform to those portions of this Rule applicable to the brief for a respondent or an appellee, but, if appropriately divided by topical headings, need not contain a summary of the argument.
5. A reference to the joint appendix or to the record set out in any brief shall indicate the appropriate page number. If the reference is to an exhibit, the page numbers at which the exhibit appears, at which it was offered in evidence, and at which it was ruled on by the judge shall be indicated, *e. g.*, Pl. Exh. 14, Record 199, 2134.
6. A brief shall be concise, logically arranged with proper headings, and free of irrelevant, immaterial, or scandalous matter. The Court may disregard or strike a brief that does not comply with this paragraph.

Rule 25. Briefs on the Merits: Number of Copies and Time to File

1. The petitioner or appellant shall file 40 copies of the brief on the merits within 45 days of the order granting the writ of certiorari, noting probable jurisdiction, or postponing consideration of jurisdiction. Any respondent or appellee who supports the petitioner or appellant shall meet the petitioner's or appellant's time schedule for filing documents.
2. The respondent or appellee shall file 40 copies of the brief on the merits within 30 days after the brief for the petitioner or appellant is filed.
3. The petitioner or appellant shall file 40 copies of the reply brief, if any, within 30 days after the brief for the respondent or appellee is filed, but any reply brief must actually be received by the Clerk not later than 2 p.m. 10 days before the date of oral argument. Any respondent or appellee supporting the petitioner or appellant may file a reply brief.
4. If cross-petitions or cross-appeals have been consolidated for argument, the Clerk, upon request of the parties, may designate one of the parties to file an initial brief and reply brief as provided in paragraphs 1 and 3 of this Rule (as if the party were petitioner or appellant), and may designate the other party to file an initial brief as provided in paragraph 2 of this Rule and, to the extent appropriate, a supplemental brief following the submission of the reply brief. In such a case, the Clerk may establish the time for the submission of the briefs and alter the otherwise applicable word limits. Except as approved by the Court or a Justice, the total number of words permitted for the briefs of the parties cumulatively shall not exceed the maximum that would have been allowed in the absence of an order under this paragraph.
5. The time periods stated in paragraphs 1, 2, and 3 of this Rule may be extended as provided in Rule 30. An application to extend the time to file a brief on the merits is not favored. If a case is advanced for hearing, the time to file briefs on the merits may be abridged as circumstances require pursuant to an order of the Court on its own motion or that of a party.
6. A party wishing to present late authorities, newly enacted legislation, or other intervening matter that was not available in time to be included in a brief may file 40 copies of a supplemental brief, restricted to such new matter and otherwise presented in conformity with these Rules, up to the time the case is called for oral argument or by leave of the Court thereafter.
7. After a case has been argued or submitted, the Clerk will not file any brief, except that of a party filed by leave of the Court.
8. The Clerk will not file any brief that is not accompanied by proof of service as required by Rule 29.

Rule 26. Joint Appendix

1. Unless the Clerk has allowed the parties to use the deferred method described in paragraph 4 of this Rule, the petitioner or appellant, within 45 days after entry of the order granting the writ of certiorari, noting probable jurisdiction, or postponing consideration of jurisdiction, shall file 40 copies of a joint appendix, prepared as required by Rule 33.1. The joint appendix shall contain: (1) the relevant docket entries in all the courts below; (2) any relevant pleadings, jury instructions, findings, conclusions, or opinions; (3) the judgment, order, or decision under review; and (4) any other parts of the record that the parties particularly wish to bring to the Court's attention. Any of the foregoing items already reproduced in a petition for a writ of certiorari, jurisdictional statement, brief in opposition

to a petition for a writ of certiorari, motion to dismiss or affirm, or any appendix to the foregoing, that was prepared as required by Rule 33.1, need not be reproduced again in the joint appendix. The petitioner or appellant shall serve three copies of the joint appendix on each of the other parties to the proceeding as required by Rule 29.

2. The parties are encouraged to agree on the contents of the joint appendix. In the absence of agreement, the petitioner or appellant, within 10 days after entry of the order granting the writ of certiorari, noting probable jurisdiction, or postponing consideration of jurisdiction, shall serve on the respondent or appellee a designation of parts of the record to be included in the joint appendix. Within 10 days after receiving the designation, a respondent or appellee who considers the parts of the record so designated insufficient shall serve on the petitioner or appellant a designation of additional parts to be included in the joint appendix, and the petitioner or appellant shall include the parts so designated. If the Court has permitted the respondent or appellee to proceed *in forma pauperis*, the petitioner or appellant may seek by motion to be excused from printing portions of the record the petitioner or appellant considers unnecessary. In making these designations, counsel should include only those materials the Court should examine; unnecessary designations should be avoided. The record is on file with the Clerk and available to the Justices, and counsel may refer in briefs and in oral argument to relevant portions of the record not included in the joint appendix.
3. When the joint appendix is filed, the petitioner or appellant immediately shall file with the Clerk a statement of the cost of printing 50 copies and shall serve a copy of the statement on each of the other parties as required by Rule 29. Unless the parties agree otherwise, the cost of producing the joint appendix shall be paid initially by the petitioner or appellant; but a petitioner or appellant who considers that parts of the record designated by the respondent or appellee are unnecessary for the determination of the issues presented may so advise the respondent or appellee, who then shall advance the cost of printing the additional parts, unless the Court or a Justice otherwise fixes the initial allocation of the costs. The cost of printing the joint appendix is taxed as a cost in the case, but if a party unnecessarily causes matter to be included in the joint appendix or prints excessive copies, the Court may impose these costs on that party.
4. (a) On the parties' request, the Clerk may allow preparation of the joint appendix to be deferred until after the briefs have been filed. In that event, the petitioner or appellant shall file the joint appendix no more than 14 days after receiving the brief for the respondent or appellee. The provisions of paragraphs 1, 2, and 3 of this Rule shall be followed, except that the designations referred to therein shall be made by each party when that party's brief is served. Deferral of the joint appendix is not favored.

   (b) If the deferred method is used, the briefs on the merits may refer to the pages of the record. In that event, the joint appendix shall include in brackets on each page thereof the page number of the record where that material may be found. A party wishing to refer directly to the pages of the joint appendix may serve and file copies of its brief prepared as required by Rule 33.2 within the time provided by Rule 25, with appropriate references to the pages of the record. In that event, within 10 days after the joint appendix is filed, copies of the brief prepared as required by Rule 33.1 containing references to the pages of the joint appendix in place of, or in addition to, the initial references to the pages of the record, shall be served and filed. No other change may be made in the brief as initially served and filed, except those typographical errors may be corrected.

5. The joint appendix shall be prefaced by a table of contents showing the parts of the record that it contains, in the order in which the parts are set out, with references to the pages of the joint appendix at which each part begins. The relevant docket entries shall be set out after the table of contents, followed by the other parts of the record in chronological order. When testimony contained in the reporter's transcript of proceedings is set out in the joint appendix, the page of the transcript at which the testimony appears shall be indicated in brackets immediately before the statement that is set out. Omissions in the transcript or in any other document printed in the joint appendix shall be indicated by asterisks. Immaterial formal matters (*e. g.*, captions, subscriptions, acknowledgments) shall be omitted. A question and its answer may be contained in a single paragraph.
6. Two lines must appear at the bottom of the cover of the joint appendix: (1) The first line must indicate the date the petition for the writ of certiorari was filed or the date the appeal was docketed; (2) the second line must indicate the date certiorari was granted or the date jurisdiction of the appeal was noted or postponed.
7. Exhibits designated for inclusion in the joint appendix may be contained in a separate volume or volumes suitably indexed. The transcript of a proceeding before an administrative agency, board, commission, or officer used in an action in a district court or court of appeals is regarded as an exhibit for the purposes of this paragraph.
8. The Court, on its own motion or that of a party, may dispense with the requirement of a joint appendix and may permit a case to be heard on the original record (with such copies of the record, or relevant parts thereof, as the Court may require) or on the appendix used in the court below, if it conforms to the requirements of this Rule.
9. For good cause, the time limits specified in this Rule may be shortened or extended by the Court or a Justice, or by the Clerk under Rule 30.4.

Rule 27. Calendar

1. From time to time, the Clerk will prepare a calendar of cases ready for argument. A case ordinarily will not be called for argument less than two weeks after the brief on the merits for the respondent or appellee is due.
2. The Clerk will advise counsel when they are required to appear for oral argument and will publish a hearing list in advance of each argument session for the convenience of counsel and the information of the public.
3. The Court, on its own motion or that of a party, may order those two or more cases involving the same or related questions be argued together as one case or on such other terms as the Court may prescribe.

Rule 28. Oral Argument

1. Oral argument should emphasize and clarify the written arguments in the briefs on the merits. Counsel should assume that all Justices have read the briefs before oral argument. Oral argument read from a prepared text is not favored.
2. The petitioner or appellant shall open and may conclude the argument. A cross-writ of certiorari or cross-appeal will be argued with the initial writ of certiorari or appeal as one case in the time allowed for that one case, and the Court will advise the parties who shall open and close.

3. Unless the Court directs otherwise, each side is allowed one-half hour for argument. Counsel is not required to use all the allotted time. Any request for additional time to argue shall be presented by motion under Rule 21 in time to be considered at a scheduled Conference prior to the date of oral argument and no later than 7 days after the respondent's or appellee's brief on the merits is filed and shall set out specifically and concisely why the case cannot be presented within the half-hour limitation. Additional time is rarely accorded.
4. Only one attorney will be heard for each side, except by leave of the Court on motion filed in time to be considered at a scheduled Conference prior to the date of oral argument and no later than 7 days after the respondent's or appellee's brief on the merits is filed. Any request for divided argument shall be presented by motion under Rule 21 and shall set out specifically and concisely why more than one attorney should be allowed to argue. Divided argument is not favored.
5. Regardless of the number of counsels participating in oral argument, counsel making the opening argument shall present the case fairly and completely and not reserve points of substance for rebuttal.
6. Oral argument will not be allowed on behalf of any party for whom a brief has not been filed.
7. By leave of the Court, and subject to paragraph 4 of this Rule, counsel for an *amicus curiae* whose brief has been filed as provided in Rule 37 may argue orally on the side of a party, with the consent of that party. In the absence of consent, counsel for an *amicus curiae* may seek leave of the Court to argue orally by a motion setting out specifically and concisely why oral argument would provide assistance to the Court not otherwise available. Such a motion will be granted only in the most extraordinary circumstances.
8. Oral arguments may be presented only by members of the Bar of this Court. Attorneys who are not members of the Bar of this Court may make a motion to argue *pro hac vice* under the provisions of Rule 6.

PART VII. Practice and Procedure

Rule 29. Filing and Service of Documents; Special Notifications; Corporate Listing

1. Any document required or permitted to be presented to the Court or to a Justice shall be filed with the Clerk in paper form.
2. A document is timely filed if it is received by the Clerk in paper form within the time specified for filing; or if it is sent to the Clerk through the United States Postal Service by first-class mail (including express or priority mail), postage prepaid, and bears a postmark, other than a commercial postage meter label, showing that the document was mailed on or before the last day for filing; or if it is delivered on or before the last day for filing to a third-party commercial carrier for delivery to the Clerk within 3 calendar days. If submitted by an inmate confined in an institution, a document is timely filed if it is deposited in the institution's internal mail system on or before the last day for filing and is accompanied by a notarized statement or declaration in compliance with 28 U.S.C. § 1746 setting out the date of deposit and stating that first-class postage has been prepaid. If the postmark is missing or not legible, or if the third-party commercial carrier does not provide the date the document was received by the carrier, the Clerk will require the person who sent the document to submit a notarized statement or declaration in compliance with 28 U.S.C. §

1746 setting out the details of the filing and stating that the filing took place on a particular date within the permitted time.

3. Any document required by these Rules to be served may be served personally, by mail, or by third-party commercial carrier for delivery within 3 calendar days on each party to the proceeding at or before the time of filing. If the document has been prepared as required by Rule 33.1, three copies shall be served on each other party separately represented in the proceeding. If the document has been prepared as required by Rule 33.2, service of a single copy on each other separately represented party suffices. If personal service is made, it shall consist of delivery at the office of the counsel of record, either to counsel or to an employee therein. If service is by mail or third-party commercial carrier, it shall consist of depositing the document with the United States Postal Service, with no less than first-class postage prepaid, or delivery to the carrier for delivery within 3 calendar days, addressed to counsel of record at the proper address. When a party is not represented by counsel, service shall be made on the party, personally, by mail, or by commercial carrier. Ordinarily, service on a party must be by a manner at least as expeditious as the manner used to file the document with the Court. An electronic version of the document shall also be transmitted to all other parties at the time of filing or reasonably contemporaneous therewith, unless the party filing the document is proceeding pro se and *in forma pauperis* or the electronic service address of the party being served is unknown and not identifiable through reasonable efforts.

4. (a) If the United States or any federal department, office, agency, officer, or employee is a party to be served, service shall be made on the Solicitor General of the United States, Room 5616, Department of Justice, 950 Pennsylvania Ave., N. W., Washington, DC 20530-0001. When an agency of the United States that is a party is authorized by law to appear before this Court on its own behalf, or when an officer or employee of the United States is a party, the agency, officer, or employee shall be served in addition to the Solicitor General.

   (b) In any proceeding in this Court in which the constitutionality of an Act of Congress is drawn into question, and neither the United States nor any federal department, office, agency, officer, or employee is a party, the initial document filed in this Court shall recite that 28 U.S.C. § 2403(a) may apply and shall be served on the Solicitor General of the United States, Room 5616, Department of Justice, 950 Pennsylvania Ave., N. W., Washington, DC 20530-0001. In such a proceeding from any court of the United States, as defined by 28 U.S.C. § 451, the initial document also shall state whether that court, pursuant to 28 U.S.C. § 2403(a), certified to the Attorney General the fact that the constitutionality of an Act of Congress was drawn into question. See Rule 14.1(e)(v).

   (c) In any proceeding in this Court in which the constitutionality of any statute of a State is drawn into question, and neither the State nor any agency, officer, or employee thereof is a party, the initial document filed in this Court shall recite that 28 U.S.C. § 2403(b) may apply and shall be served on the Attorney General of that State. In such a proceeding from any court of the United States, as defined by 28 U.S.C. § 451, the initial document also shall state whether that court, pursuant to 28 U.S.C. § 2403(b), certified to the State Attorney General the fact that the constitutionality of a statute of that State was drawn into question. See Rule 14.1(e)(v).

5. Proof of service, when required by these Rules, shall accompany the document when it is presented to the Clerk for filing and shall be separate from it. Proof of service shall contain,

or be accompanied by, a statement that all parties required to be served have been served, together with a list of the names, addresses, and telephone numbers of counsel indicating the name of the party or parties each counsel represents. It is not necessary that service on each party required to be served be made in the same manner or evidenced by the same proof. Proof of service may consist of any one of the following:

(a) an acknowledgment of service, signed by counsel of record for the party served, and bearing the address and telephone number of such counsel;

(b) a certificate of service, reciting the facts and circumstances of service in compliance with the appropriate paragraph or paragraphs of this Rule, and signed by a member of the Bar of this Court representing the party on whose behalf service is made or by an attorney appointed to represent that party under the Criminal Justice Act of 1964, see 18 U.S.C. § 3006A(d)(7), or under any other applicable federal statute; or

(c) a notarized affidavit or declaration in compliance with 28 U.S.C. § 1746, reciting the facts and circumstances of service in accordance with the appropriate paragraph or paragraphs of this Rule, whenever service is made by any person not a member of the Bar of this Court and not an attorney appointed to represent a party under the Criminal Justice Act of 1964, see 18 U.S.C. § 3006A(d)(7), or under any other applicable federal statute.

6. Every document, except a joint appendix or *amicus curiae* brief, filed by or on behalf of a nongovernmental corporation shall contain a corporate disclosure statement identifying the parent corporations and listing any publicly held company that owns 10% or more of the corporation's stock. If there is no parent or publicly held company owning 10% or more of the corporation's stock, a notation to this effect shall be included in the document. If a statement has been included in a document filed earlier in the case, reference may be made to the earlier document (except when the earlier statement appeared in a document prepared under Rule 33.2), and only amendments to the statement to make it current need be included in the document being filed. In addition, whenever there is a material change in the identity of the parent corporation or publicly held companies that own 10% or more of the corporation's stock, counsel shall promptly inform the Clerk by letter and include, within that letter, any amendment needed to make the statement current.
7. In addition to the filing requirements set forth in this Rule, all filers who are represented by counsel must submit documents to the Court's electronic filing system in conformity with the ''Guidelines for the Submission of Documents to the Supreme Court's Electronic Filing System'' issued by the Clerk.

Rule 30. Computation and Extension of Time

1. In the computation of any period of time prescribed or allowed by these Rules, by order of the Court, or by an applicable statute, the day of the act, event, or default from which the designated period begins to run is not included. The last day of the period shall be included, unless it is a Saturday, Sunday, federal legal holiday listed in 5 U.S.C. § 6103, or day on which the Court building is closed by order of the Court or the Chief Justice, in which event the period shall extend until the end of the next day that is not a Saturday, Sunday, federal legal holiday, or day on which the Court building is closed.
2. Whenever a Justice or the Clerk is empowered by law or these Rules to extend the time to file any document, an application or motion seeking an extension shall be filed within the

period sought to be extended. An application to extend the time to file a petition for a writ of certiorari or to file a jurisdictional statement must be filed at least 10 days before the specified final filing date as computed under these Rules; if filed less than 10 days before the final filing date, such application will not be granted except in the most extraordinary circumstances.

3. An application to extend the time to file a petition for a writ of certiorari, to file a jurisdictional statement, to file a reply brief on the merits, or to file a petition for rehearing of any judgment or decision of the Court on the merits shall be made to an individual Justice and presented and served on all other parties as provided by Rule 22. Once denied, such an application may not be renewed.
4. A motion to extend the time to file any document or paper other than those specified in paragraph 3 of this Rule may be presented in the form of a letter to the Clerk setting out specific reasons why an extension of time is justified. The letter shall be served on all other parties as required by Rule 29. The motion may be acted on by the Clerk in the first instance, and any party aggrieved by the Clerk's action may request that the motion be submitted to a Justice or to the Court. The Clerk will report action under this paragraph to the Court as instructed.

Rule 31. Translations

Whenever any record to be transmitted to this Court contains material written in a foreign language without a translation made under the authority of the lower court, or admitted being correct, the clerk of the court transmitting the record shall advise the Clerk of this Court immediately so that this Court may order that a translation be supplied and, if necessary, printed as part of the joint appendix.

Rule 32. Models, Diagrams, Exhibits, and Lodgings

1. Models, diagrams, and exhibits of material forming part of the evidence taken in a case and brought to this Court for its inspection shall be placed in the custody of the Clerk at least two weeks before the case is to be heard or submitted.
2. All models, diagrams, exhibits, and other items placed in the custody of the Clerk shall be removed by the parties no more than 40 days after the case is decided. If this is not done, the Clerk will notify counsel to remove the articles forthwith. If they are not removed within a reasonable time thereafter, the Clerk will destroy them or dispose of them in any other appropriate way.
3. Any party or *amicus curiae* desiring to lodge non-record material with the Clerk must set out in a letter, served on all parties, a description of the material proposed for lodging and the reasons why the non-record material may properly be considered by the Court. The material proposed for lodging may not be submitted until and unless requested by the Clerk.

Rule 33. Document Preparation: Booklet Format; 81/2by 11-Inch Paper Format

1. *Booklet Format*: (a) Except for a document expressly permitted by these Rules to be submitted on 8-1/2 by 11-inch paper, see, *e. g.*, Rules 21, 22, and 39, every document filed with the Court shall be prepared in a 61/8by 91/4-inch booklet format using a standard typesetting process (*e. g.*, hot metal, photocomposition, or computer typesetting) to produce

text printed in typographic (as opposed to typewriter) characters. The process used must produce a clear, black image on white paper. The text must be reproduced with a clarity that equals or exceeds the output of a laser printer.

(b) The text of every booklet-format document, including any appendix thereto, shall be typeset in a Century family (*e. g.*, Century Expanded, New Century Schoolbook, or Century Schoolbook) 12-point type with 2-point or more leading between lines. Quotations in excess of 50 words shall be indented. The typeface of footnotes shall be 10-point type with 2-point or more leading between lines. The text of the document must appear on both sides of the page.

(c) Every booklet-format document shall be produced on paper that is opaque, unglazed, and not less than 60 pounds in weight, and shall have margins of at least three-fourths of an inch on all sides. The text field, including footnotes, may not exceed 41/8 by 71/8 inches. The document shall be bound firmly in at least two places along the left margin (saddle stitch or perfect binding preferred) so as to permit easy opening, and no part of the text should be obscured by the binding. Spiral, plastic, metal, or string bindings may not be used. Copies of patent documents, except opinions, may be duplicated in such size as is necessary in a separate appendix.

(d) Every booklet-format document shall comply with the word limits shown on the chart in subparagraph 1(g) of this Rule. The word limits do not include the questions presented, the list of parties and the corporate disclosure statement, the table of contents, the table of cited authorities, the listing of counsel at the end of the document, or any appendix. The word limits include footnotes. Verbatim quotations required under Rule 14.1(f) and Rule 24.1(f), if set out in the text of a brief rather than in the appendix, are also excluded. For good cause, the Court or a Justice may grant leave to file a document in excess of the word limits, but application for such leave is not favored. An application to exceed word limits shall comply with Rule 22 and must be received by the Clerk at least 15 days before the filing date of the document in question, except in the most extraordinary circumstances.

(e) Every booklet-format document shall have a suitable cover consisting of 65-pound weight paper in the color indicated on the chart in subparagraph 1(g) of this Rule. If a separate appendix to any document is filed, the color of its cover shall be the same as that of the cover of the document it supports. The Clerk will furnish a color chart upon request. Counsel shall ensure that there is adequate contrast between the printing and the color of the cover. A document filed by the United States, or by any other federal party represented by the Solicitor General, shall have a gray cover. A joint appendix, answer to a bill of complaint, motion for leave to intervene, and any other document not listed in subparagraph 1(g) of this Rule shall have a tan cover.

(f) Forty copies of a booklet-format document shall be filed, and one unbound copy of the document on 8 ½- by 11-inch paper shall also be submitted.

(g) Word limits and cover colors for booklet-format documents are as follows:

Type of Document	**Word Limits**	**Color of Cover**
(i) Petition for a Writ of Certiorari (Rule 14); Motion for Leave to File a Bill of Complaint and Brief in Support (Rule 17.3); Jurisdictional Statement (Rule 18.3); Petition for an Extraordinary Writ (Rule 20.2)	9,000	white

(ii) Brief in Opposition (Rule 15.3); Brief in Opposition to Motion for Leave to File an Original Action (Rule 17.5); Motion to Dismiss or Affirm (Rule 18.6); Brief in Opposition to Mandamus or Prohibition (Rule 20.3(b)); Response to a Petition for Habeas Corpus (Rule 20.4); Respondent's Brief in Support of Certiorari (Rule 12.6)	9,000	orange
(iii) Reply to Brief in Opposition (Rules 15.6 and 17.5); Brief Opposing a Motion to Dismiss or Affirm (Rule 18.8)	3,000	tan
(iv) Supplemental Brief (Rules 15.8, 17, 18.10, and 25.6)	3,000	tan
(v) Brief on the Merits for Petitioner or Appellant (Rule 24); Exceptions by Plaintiff to Report of Special Master (Rule 17)	13,000	light blue
(vi) Brief on the Merits for Respondent or Appellee (Rule 24.2); Brief on the Merits for Respondent or Appellee Supporting Petitioner or Appellant (Rule 12.6); Exceptions by Party Other Than Plaintiff to Report of Special Master (Rule 17)	13,000	light red
(vii) Reply Brief on the Merits (Rule 24.4)	6,000	yellow
(viii) Reply to Plaintiff's Exceptions to Report of Special Master (Rule 17)	13,000	orange
(ix) Reply to Exceptions by Party Other Than Plaintiff to Report of Special Master (Rule 17)	13,000	yellow
(x) Brief for an *amicus curiae* at the Petition Stage or pertaining to a Motion for Leave to file a Bill of Complaint (Rule 37.2)	6,000	cream
(xi) Brief for an *amicus curiae* Identified in Rule 37.4 in Support of the Plaintiff, Petitioner, or Appellant, or in Support of Neither Party, on the Merits or in an Original Action at the Exceptions Stage (Rule 37.3)	9,000	light green
(xii) Brief for any Other *amicus curiae* in Support of the Plaintiff, Petitioner, or Appellant, or in Support of Neither Party, on the Merits or in an Original Action at the Exceptions Stage (Rule 37.3)	8,000	light green
(xiii) Brief for an *amicus curiae* Identified in Rule 37.4 in Support of the Defendant, Respondent, or Appellee, on the Merits or in an Original Action at the Exceptions Stage (Rule 37.3)	9,000	dark green
(xiv) Brief for any Other *amicus curiae* in Support of the Defendant, Respondent, or Appellee, on the Merits or in an Original Action at the Exceptions Stage (Rule 37.3)	8,000	dark green
(xv) Petition for Rehearing (Rule 44)	3,000	tan

(h) A document prepared under Rule 33.1 must be accompanied by a certificate signed by the attorney, the unrepresented party, or the preparer of the document stating that the brief complies with the word limitations. The person preparing the certificate may rely on the word count of the word-processing system used to prepare the document. The word-processing system must be set to include footnotes in the word count. The certificate must state the number of words in the document. The certificate shall accompany the document when it is presented to the Clerk for filing and shall be separate from it. If the certificate is signed by a person other than a member of the Bar of this Court, the counsel of record, or the unrepresented party, it must contain a notarized affidavit or declaration in compliance with 28 U.S.C. § 1746.

2. *8 ½- by 11-Inch Paper Format:* (a) The text of every document, including any appendix thereto, expressly permitted by these Rules to be presented to the Court on 8 ½- by 11-inch paper shall appear double spaced, except for indented quotations, which shall be single

spaced, on opaque, unglazed, white paper. The document shall be stapled or bound at the upper left-hand corner. Copies, if required, shall be produced on the same type of paper and shall be legible. The original of any such document (except a motion to dismiss or affirm under Rule 18.6) shall be signed by the party proceeding pro se or by counsel of record who must be a member of the Bar of this Court, or an attorney appointed under the Criminal Justice Act of 1964, see 18 U.S.C.§ 3006A(d)(7), or under any other applicable federal statute. Subparagraph 1(g) of this Rule does not apply to documents prepared under this paragraph.

(b) Page limits for documents presented on 8 ½- by 11-inch paper are: 40 pages for a petition for a writ of certiorari, jurisdictional statement, petition for an extraordinary writ, brief in opposition, or motion to dismiss or affirm; and 15 pages for a reply to a brief in opposition, brief opposing a motion to dismiss or affirm, supplemental brief, or petition for rehearing. The exclusions specified in subparagraph 1(d) of this Rule apply.

Rule 34. Document Preparation: General Requirements

Every document, whether prepared under Rule 33.1 or Rule 33.2, shall comply with the following provisions:

1. Each document shall bear on its cover, in the order indicated, from the top of the page:
   (a) the docket number of the case or, if there is none, a space for one;
   (b) the name of this Court;
   (c) the caption of the case as appropriate in this Court;
   (d) the nature of the proceeding and the name of the court from which the action is brought (*e. g.*, "On Petition for Writ of Certiorari to the United States Court of Appeals for the Fifth Circuit"; or, for a merits brief, "On Writ of Certiorari to the United States Court of Appeals for the Fifth Circuit");
   (e) the title of the document (*e. g.*, "Petition for Writ of Certiorari," "Brief for Respondent," "Joint Appendix");
   (f) the name of the attorney who is counsel of record for the party concerned (who must be a member of the Bar of this Court except as provided in Rule 9.1) and on whom service is to be made, with a notation directly thereunder identifying the attorney as counsel of record and setting out counsel's office address, e-mail address, and telephone number. Only one counsel of record may be noted on a single document, except that counsel of record for each party must be listed on the cover of a joint appendix. The names of other members of the Bar of this Court or of the bar of the highest court of State acting as counsel, and, if desired, their addresses, may be added, but counsel of record shall be clearly identified. Names of persons other than attorneys admitted to a state bar may not be listed, unless the party is appearing pro se, in which case the party's name, address, and telephone number shall appear.
   (g) The foregoing shall be displayed in an appropriate typographical manner and, except for identification of counsel, may not be set in type smaller than standard 11-point, if the document is prepared as required by Rule 33.1.
2. Every document (other than a joint appendix), that exceeds 1,500 words when prepared under Rule 33.1, or that exceeds five pages when prepared under Rule 33.2, shall contain a

table of contents and a table of cited authorities (*i. e.*, cases alphabetically arranged, constitutional provisions, statutes, treatises, and other materials) with references to the pages in the document where such authorities are cited.

3. The body of every document shall bear at its close the name of counsel of record and such other counsel, identified on the cover of the document in conformity with subparagraph 1(f) of this Rule, as may be desired.
4. Every appendix to a document must be preceded by a table of contents that provides a description of each document in the appendix.
5. All references to a provision of federal statutory law should ordinarily be cited to the United States Code, if the provision has been codified therein. In the event the provision has not been classified to the United States Code, citation should be to the Statutes at Large. Additional or alternative citations should be provided only if there is a particular reason why those citations are relevant or necessary to the argument.
6. A case in which privacy protection was governed by Federal Rule of Appellate Procedure 25(a)(5), Federal Rule of Bankruptcy Procedure 9037, Federal Rule of Civil Procedure 5.2, or Federal Rule of Criminal Procedure 49.1 is governed by the same Rule in this Court. In any other case, privacy protection is governed by Federal Rule of Civil Procedure 5.2, except that Federal Rule of Criminal Procedure governs when an extraordinary writ is sought in a criminal case. If the Court schedules briefing and oral argument in a case that was governed by Federal Rule of Civil Procedure 5.2(c) or Federal Rule of Criminal Procedure 49.1(c), the parties shall submit electronic versions of all prior and subsequent flings with this Court in the case, subject to the redaction Rules set forth above.

Rule 35. Death, Substitution, and Revivor; Public Officers

1. If a party dies after the filing of a petition for a writ of certiorari to this Court, or after the filing of a notice of appeal, the authorized representative of the deceased party may appear and, on motion, be substituted as a party. If the representative does not voluntarily become a party, any other party may suggest the death on the record and, on motion, seek an order requiring the representative to become a party within a designated time. If the representative then fails to become a party, the party so moving, if a respondent or appellee, is entitled to have the petition for a writ of certiorari or the appeal dismissed, and if a petitioner or appellant, is entitled to proceed as in any other case of nonappearance by a respondent or appellee. If the substitution of a representative of the deceased is not made within six months after the death of the party, the case shall abate.
2. Whenever a case cannot be revived in the court whose judgment is sought to be reviewed, because the deceased party's authorized representative is not subject to that court's jurisdiction, proceedings will be conducted as this Court may direct.
3. When a public officer who is a party to a proceeding in this Court in an official capacity die, resigns, or otherwise ceases to hold office, the action does not abate and any successor in office is automatically substituted as a party. The parties shall notify the Clerk in writing of any such successions. Proceedings following the substitution shall be in the name of the substituted party, but any misnomer not affecting substantial rights of the parties will be disregarded.
4. A public officer who is a party to a proceeding in this Court in an official capacity may be described as a party by the officer's official title rather than by name, but the Court may

require the name to be added.

Rule 36. Custody of Prisoners in Habeas Corpus Proceedings

1. Pending review in this Court of a decision in a habeas corpus proceeding commenced before a court, Justice, or judge of the United States, the person having custody of the prisoner may not transfer custody to another person unless the transfer is authorized under this Rule.
2. Upon application by a custodian, the court, Justice, or judge who entered the decision under review may authorize transfer and the substitution of a successor custodian as a party.
3. (a) Pending review of a decision failing or refusing to release a prisoner, the prisoner may be detained in the custody from which release is sought or in other appropriate custody or may be enlarged on personal recognizance or bail, as may appear appropriate to the court, Justice, or judge who entered the decision, or to the court of appeals, this Court, or a judge or Justice of either court.
   (b) Pending review of a decision ordering release, the prisoner shall be enlarged on personal recognizance or bail, unless the court, Justice, or judge who entered the decision, or the court of appeals, this Court, or a judge or Justice of either court, orders otherwise.
4. An initial order respecting the custody or enlargement of the prisoner, and any recognizance or surety taken, shall continue in effect pending review in the court of appeals and in this Court unless for reasons shown to the court of appeals, this Court, or a judge or Justice of either court, the order is modified or an independent order respecting custody, enlargement, or surety is entered.

Rule 37. Brief for an *Amicus Curiae*

1. An *amicus curiae* brief that brings to the attention of the Court relevant matter not already brought to its attention by the parties may be of considerable help to the Court. An *amicus curiae* brief that does not serve this purpose burdens the Court, and its filing is not favored. An *amicus curiae* brief may be filed only by an attorney admitted to practice before this Court as provided in Rule 5.
2. (a) An *amicus curiae* brief submitted before the Court's consideration of a petition for a writ of certiorari, motion for leave to file a bill of complaint, jurisdictional statement, or petition for an extraordinary writ may be filed if it reflects that written consent of all parties has been provided, or if the Court grants leave to file under subparagraph 2(b) of this Rule. An *amicus curiae* brief in support of a petitioner or appellant shall be filed within 30 days after the case is placed on the docket or a response is called for by the Court, whichever is later, and that time will not be extended. An *amicus curiae* brief in support of a motion of a plaintiff for leave to file a bill of complaint in an original action shall be filed within 60 days after the case is placed on the docket, and that time will not be extended. An *amicus curiae* brief in support of a respondent, an appellee, or a defendant shall be submitted within the time allowed for filing a brief in opposition or a motion to dismiss or affirm. An *amicus curiae* filing a brief under this subparagraph shall ensure that the counsel of record for all parties receive notice of its intention to file an *amicus curiae* brief at least 10 days prior to the due date for the *amicus curiae* brief, unless the *amicus curiae* brief is filed earlier than 10 days before the due date. Only one signatory to any *amicus curiae* brief filed

jointly by more than one *amicus curiae* must timely notify the parties of its intent to file that brief. The *amicus curiae* brief shall indicate that counsel of record received timely notice of the intent to file the brief under this Rule and shall specify whether consent was granted, and its cover shall identify the party supported. Only one signatory to an *amicus curiae* brief filed jointly by more than one *amicus curiae* must obtain consent of the parties to file that brief. A petitioner or respondent may submit to the Clerk a letter granting blanket consent to *amicus curiae* briefs, stating that the party consents to the filing of *amicus curiae* briefs in support of either or of neither party. The Clerk will note all notices of blanket consent on the docket.

(b) When a party to the case has withheld consent, a motion for leave to file an *amicus curiae* brief before the Court's consideration of a petition for a writ of certiorari, motion for leave to file a bill of complaint, jurisdictional statement, or petition for an extraordinary writ may be presented to the Court. The motion, prepared as required by Rule 33.1 and as one document with the brief sought to be filed, shall be submitted within the time allowed for filing an *amicus curiae* brief, and shall indicate the party or parties who have withheld consent and state the nature of the movant's interest. Such a motion is not favored.

3. (a) An *amicus curiae* brief in a case before the Court for oral argument may be filed if it reflects that written consent of all parties has been provided, or if the Court grants leave to file under subparagraph 3(b) of this Rule. The brief shall be submitted within 7 days after the brief for the party supported is filed, or if in support of neither party, within 7 days after the time allowed for filing the petitioner's or appellant's brief. Motions to extend the time for filing an *amicus curiae* brief will not be entertained. The 10-day notice requirement of subparagraph 2(a) of this Rule does not apply to an *amicus curiae* brief in a case before the Court for oral argument. The *amicus curiae* brief shall specify whether consent was granted, and its cover shall identify the party supported or indicate whether it suggests affirmance or reversal. The Clerk will not file a reply brief for an *amicus curiae*, or a brief for an *amicus curiae* in support of, or in opposition to, a petition for rehearing. Only one signatory to an *amicus curiae* brief filed jointly by more than one *amicus curiae* must obtain consent of the parties to file that brief. A petitioner or respondent may submit to the Clerk a letter granting blanket consent to *amicus curiae* briefs, stating that the party consents to the filing of *amicus curiae* briefs in support of either or of neither party. The Clerk will note all notices of blanket consent on the docket.

(b) When a party to a case before the Court for oral argument has withheld consent, a motion for leave to file an *amicus curiae* brief may be presented to the Court. The motion, prepared as required by Rule 33.1 and as one document with the brief sought to be filed, shall be submitted within the time allowed for filing an *amicus curiae* brief, and shall indicate the party or parties who have withheld consent and state the nature of the movant's interest.

4. No motion for leave to file an *amicus curiae* brief is necessary if the brief is presented on behalf of the United States by the Solicitor General; on behalf of any agency of the United States allowed by law to appear before this Court when submitted by the agency's authorized legal representative; on behalf of a State, Commonwealth, Territory, or Possession when submitted by its Attorney General; or on behalf of a city, county, town, or similar entity when submitted by its authorized law officer.
5. A brief or motion filed under this Rule shall be accompanied by proof of service as required

by Rule 29 and shall comply with the applicable provisions of Rules 21, 24, and 33.1 (except that it suffices to set out in the brief the interest of the *amicus curiae*, the summary of the argument, the argument, and the conclusion). A motion for leave to file may not exceed 1,500 words. A party served with the motion may file an objection thereto, stating concisely the reasons for withholding consent; the objection shall be prepared as required by Rule 33.2.

6. Except for briefs presented on behalf of *amicus curiae* listed in Rule 37.4, a brief filed under this Rule shall indicate whether counsel for a party authored the brief in whole or in part and whether such counsel or a party made a monetary contribution intended to fund the preparation or submission of the brief and shall identify every person other than the *amicus curiae*, its members, or its counsel, who made such a monetary contribution. The disclosure shall be made in the first footnote on the first page of text.

Rule 38. Fees

Under 28 U.S.C. § 1911, the fees charged by the Clerk are:

(a) for docketing a case on a petition for a writ of certiorari or on appeal or for docketing any other proceeding, except a certified question or a motion to docket and dismiss an appeal under Rule 18.5, $300;
(b) for filing a petition for rehearing or a motion for leave to file a petition for rehearing, $200;
(c) for reproducing and certifying any record or paper, $1 per page; and for comparing with the original thereof any photographic reproduction of any record or paper, when furnished by the person requesting its certification, $.50 per page;
(d) for a certificate bearing the seal of the Court, $10; and
(e) for a check paid to the Court, Clerk, or Marshal that is returned for lack of funds, $35.

Rule 39. Proceedings *In Forma Pauperis*

1. A party seeking to proceed *in forma pauperis* shall file a motion for leave to do so, together with the party's notarized affidavit or declaration (in compliance with 28 U.S.C. § 1746) in the form prescribed by the Federal Rules of Appellate Procedure, Form 4. The motion shall state whether leave to proceed *in forma pauperis* was sought in any other court and, if so, whether leave was granted. If the court below appointed counsel for an indigent party, no affidavit or declaration is required, but the motion shall cite the provision of law under which counsel was appointed, or a copy of the order of appointment shall be appended to the motion.
2. If leave to proceed *in forma pauperis* is sought for the purpose of filing a document, the motion, and an affidavit or declaration if required, shall be filed together with that document and shall comply in every respect with Rule 21. As provided in that Rule, it suffices to file an original and 10 copies, unless the party is an inmate confined in an institution and is not represented by counsel, in which case the original, alone, suffices. A copy of the motion, and affidavit or declaration if required, shall precede and be attached to each copy of the accompanying document.
3. Except when these Rules expressly provide that a document shall be prepared as required by Rule 33.1, every document presented by a party proceeding under this Rule shall be prepared as required by Rule 33.2 (unless such preparation is impossible). Every document

shall be legible. While making do allowance for any case presented under this Rule by a person appearing pro se, the Clerk will not file any document if it does not comply with the substance of these Rules or is jurisdictionally out of time.

4. When the documents required by paragraphs 1 and 2 of this Rule are presented to the Clerk, accompanied by proof of service as required by Rule 29, they will be placed on the docket without the payment of a docket fee or any other fee.
5. The respondent or appellee in a case filed *in forma pauperis* shall respond in the same manner and within the same time as in any other case of the same nature, except that the filing of an original and 10 copies of a response prepared as required by Rule 33.2, with proof of service as required by Rule 29, suffices. The respondent or appellee may challenge the grounds for the motion for leave to proceed *in forma pauperis* in a separate document or in the response itself.
6. Whenever the Court appoints counsel for an indigent party in a case set for oral argument, the briefs on the merits submitted by that counsel, unless otherwise requested, shall be prepared under the Clerk's supervision. The Clerk also will reimburse appointed counsel for any necessary travel expenses to Washington, D. C., and return in connection with the argument.
7. In a case in which certiorari has been granted, probable jurisdiction noted, or consideration of jurisdiction postponed, this Court may appoint counsel to represent a party financially unable to afford an attorney to the extent authorized by the Criminal Justice Act of 1964, 18 U.S.C. § 3006A, or by any other applicable federal statute.
8. If satisfied that a petition for a writ of certiorari, jurisdictional statement, or petition for an extraordinary writ is frivolous or malicious, the Court may deny leave to proceed *in forma pauperis*.

Rule 40. Veterans, Seamen, and Military Cases

1. A veteran suing under any provision of law exempting veterans from the payment of fees or court costs, may proceed without prepayment of fees or costs or furnishing security therefore and may file a motion for leave to proceed on papers prepared as required by Rule 33.2. The motion shall ask leave to proceed as a veteran and be accompanied by an affidavit or declaration setting out the moving party's veteran status. A copy of the motion shall precede and be attached to each copy of the petition for a writ of certiorari or other substantive document filed by the veteran.
2. A seaman suing under 28 U.S.C. § 1916 may proceed without prepayment of fees or costs or furnishing security therefore and may file a motion for leave to proceed on papers prepared as required by Rule 33.2. The motion shall ask leave to proceed as a seaman and be accompanied by an affidavit or declaration setting out the moving party's seaman status. A copy of the motion shall precede and be attached to each copy of the petition for a writ of certiorari or other substantive document filed by the seaman.
3. An accused person petitioning for a writ of certiorari to review a decision of the United States Court of Appeals for the Armed Forces under 28 U.S.C. § 1259 may proceed without prepayment of fees or costs or furnishing security therefore and without filing an affidavit of indigency but is not entitled to proceed on papers prepared as required by Rule 33.2, except as authorized by the Court on separate motion under Rule 39.

PART VIII. Disposition of Cases

Rule 41. Opinions of the Court

Opinions of the Court will be released by the Clerk immediately upon their announcement from the bench, or as the Court otherwise directs. Thereafter, the Clerk will cause the opinions to be issued in slip form, and the Reporter of Decisions will prepare them for publication in the preliminary prints and bound volumes of the United States Reports.

Rule 42. Interest and Damages

1. If a judgment for money in a civil case is affirmed, any interest allowed by law is payable from the date the judgment under review was entered. If a judgment is modified or reversed with a direction that a judgment for money be entered below, the courts below may award interest to the extent permitted by law. Interest in cases arising in a state court is allowed at the same rate that similar judgments bear interest in the courts of the State in which judgment is directed to be entered. Interest in cases arising in a court of the United States is allowed at the interest rate authorized by law.
2. When a petition for a writ of certiorari, an appeal, or an application for other relief is frivolous, the Court may award the respondent or appellee just damages, and single or double costs under Rule 43. Damages or costs may be awarded against the petitioner, appellant, or applicant, against the party's counsel, or against both party and counsel.

Rule 43. Costs

2. If the Court affirms a judgment, the petitioner or appellant shall pay costs unless the Court otherwise orders.
3. If the Court reverses or vacates a judgment, the respondent or appellee shall pay costs unless the Court otherwise orders.
4. The Clerk's fees and the cost of printing the joint appendix are the only taxable items in this Court. The cost of the transcript of the record from the court below is also a taxable item but shall be taxable in that court as costs in the case. The expenses of printing briefs, motions, petitions, or jurisdictional statements are not taxable.
5. In a case involving a certified question, costs are equally divided unless the Court otherwise orders, except that if the Court decides the whole matter in controversy, as permitted by Rule 19.2, costs are allowed as provided in paragraphs 1 and 2 of this Rule.
6. To the extent permitted by 28 U.S.C. § 2412, costs under this Rule are allowed for or against the United States or an officer or agent thereof, unless expressly waived or unless the Court otherwise orders.
7. When costs are allowed in this Court, the Clerk will insert an itemization of the costs in the body of the mandate or judgment sent to the court below. The prevailing side may not submit a bill of costs.
8. In extraordinary circumstances the Court may adjudge double costs.

Rule 44. Rehearing

1. Any petition for the rehearing of any judgment or decision of the Court on the merits shall be filed within 25 days after entry of the judgment or decision, unless the Court or a Justice

shortens or extends the time. The petitioner shall file 40 copies of the rehearing petition and shall pay the filing fee prescribed by Rule 38(b), except that a petitioner proceeding *in forma pauperis* under Rule 39, including an inmate of an institution, shall file the number of copies required for a petition by such a person under Rule 12.2. The petition shall state its grounds briefly and distinctly and shall be served as required by Rule 29. The petition shall be presented together with certification of counsel (or of a party unrepresented by counsel) that it is presented in good faith and not for delay; one copy of the certificate shall bear the signature of counsel (or of a party unrepresented by counsel). A copy of the certificate shall follow and be attached to each copy of the petition. A petition for rehearing is not subject to oral argument and will not be granted except by a majority of the Court, at the instance of a Justice who concurred in the judgment or decision.

2. Any petition for the rehearing of an order denying a petition for a writ of certiorari or extraordinary writ shall be filed within 25 days after the date of the order of denial and shall comply with all the form and filing requirements of paragraph 1 of this Rule, including the payment of the filing fee if required, but its grounds shall be limited to intervening circumstances of a substantial or controlling effect or to other substantial grounds not previously presented. The time for filing a petition for the rehearing of an order denying a petition for a writ of certiorari or extraordinary writ will not be extended. The petition shall be presented together with certification of counsel (or of a party unrepresented by counsel) that it is restricted to the grounds specified in this paragraph and that it is presented in good faith and not for delay; one copy of the certificate shall bear the signature of counsel (or of a party unrepresented by counsel). The certificate shall be bound with each copy of the petition. The Clerk will not file a petition without a certificate. The petition is not subject to oral argument.
3. The Clerk will not file any response to a petition for rehearing unless the Court requests a response. In the absence of extraordinary circumstances, the Court will not grant a petition for rehearing without first requesting a response.
4. The Clerk will not file consecutive petitions and petitions that are out of time under this Rule.
5. The Clerk will not file any brief for an *amicus curiae* in support of, or in opposition to, a petition for rehearing.
6. If the Clerk determines that a petition for rehearing submitted timely and in good faith is in a form that does not comply with this Rule or with Rule 33 or Rule 34, the Clerk will return it with a letter indicating the deficiency. A corrected petition for rehearing submitted in accordance with Rule 29.2 no more than 15 days after the date of the Clerk's letter will be deemed timely.

Rule 45. Process; Mandates

1. All process of this Court issues in the name of the President of the United States.
2. In a case on review from a state court, the mandate issues 25 days after entry of the judgment, unless the Court or a Justice shortens or extends the time, or unless the parties stipulate that it issue sooner. The filing of a petition for rehearing stays the mandate until disposition of the petition, unless the Court orders otherwise. If the petition is denied, the mandate issues forthwith.
3. In a case on review from any court of the United States, as defined by 28 U.S.C. § 451, a formal mandate does not issue unless specially directed; instead, the Clerk of this Court will

send the clerk of the lower court a copy of the opinion or order of this Court and a certified copy of the judgment. The certified copy of the judgment, prepared and signed by this Court's Clerk, will provide for costs if any are awarded. In all other respects, the provisions of paragraph 2 of this Rule apply.

Rule 46. Dismissing Cases

1. At any stage of the proceedings, whenever all parties file with the Clerk an agreement in writing that a case be dismissed, specifying the terms for payment of costs, and pay to the Clerk any fees then due, the Clerk, without further reference to the Court, will enter an order of dismissal.
2. (a) A petitioner or appellant may file a motion to dismiss the case, with proof of service as required by Rule 29, tendering to the Clerk any fees due and costs payable. No more than 15 days after service thereof, an adverse party may file an objection, limited to the amount of damages and costs in this Court alleged to be payable or to showing that the moving party does not represent all petitioners or appellants. The Clerk will not file any objection not so limited.
   (b) When the objection asserts that the moving party does not represent all the petitioners or appellants, the party moving for dismissal may file a reply within 10 days, after which time the matter will be submitted to the Court for its determination.
   (c) If no objection is filed – or if upon objection going only to the amount of damages and costs in this Court, the party moving for dismissal tenders the additional damages and costs in full within 10 days of the demand therefore – the Clerk, without further reference to the Court, will enter an order of dismissal. If, after objection as to the amount of damages and costs in this Court, the moving party does not respond by a tender within 10 days, the Clerk will report the matter to the Court for its determination.
3. No mandate or other process will issue on a dismissal under this Rule without an order of the Court.

PART IX. Definitions and Effective Date

Rule 47. Reference to "State Court" and "State Law"

The term "state court," when used in these Rules, includes the District of Columbia Court of Appeals, the Supreme Court of the Commonwealth of Puerto Rico, the courts of the Northern Mariana Islands, the local courts of Guam, and the Supreme Court of the Virgin Islands. References in these Rules to the statutes of a State include the statutes of the District of Columbia, the Commonwealth of Puerto Rico, the Commonwealth of the Northern Mariana Islands, the Territory of Guam, and the Territory of the Virgin Islands.

Rule 48. Effective Date of Rules

1. These Rules, adopted April 18, 2019, will be effective July 1, 2019.
2. The Rules govern all proceedings after their effective date except that the amendments to Rules 25.3 and 33.1(g) will apply only to cases in which certiorari was granted, or a direct appeal or original action was set for argument, after the effective date.

Notes:

Index to Rules

FEDERAL DISTRICT COURT DIRECTORY

Note: Some Federal websites give specific addresses for mailings, others do not. Most often the first address listed is the main courthouse for the given district. Filings should be addressed to "Office of the Clerk" at the appropriate address below.

Middle District of Alabama

Frank M. Johnson Jr
U.S. Courthouse Complex
One Church Street
Montgomery, AL 36104
(334) 954-3600

Northern District of Alabama

Hugo L. Black
United States Courthouse
1729 5th Avenue North
Birmingham, AL 35203
(205) 278-1700

United States District Court
101 Holmes Avenue
Huntsville, AL 35801
(256) 534-6495

Southern District of Alabama

United States District Court
Southern District of Alabama
155 St. Joseph Street
Mobile, AL 36602
(251) 690-2371

District of Alaska

U.S. District Court
3609 Tongass Avenue #5822
Ketchikan, AK 99901
(907) 586-7458

District of Arizona

Sandra Day O'Connor
United States Courthouse
401 W. Washington St., Suite 130, SPC 1
Phoenix, AZ 85003-2118
(602) 322-7200

Evo A. DeConcini
United States Courthouse
405 W. Congress Street, Suite 1500
Tucson, AZ 85701-5010
(520) 205-4200

John M. Roll
United States Courthouse
98 West 1st Street
Yuma, AZ 85364
(928) 329-4766

AWD Building
123 N. San Francisco Street, Suite 200
Flagstaff, AZ 86001
(928) 774-2566

Eastern District of Arkansas

United States Courthouse
500 West Capitol Avenue
Little Rock, AR 72201
(501) 604-5351

United States Courthouse
617 Walnut
Helena, AR 72342

United States Courthouse
615 South Main Street
Room 312
Jonesboro, AR 72401

Western District of Arkansas

Judge Isaac C. Parker

Federal Building
30 South 6th Street, Room 1038
Fort Smith, Arkansas 72901-2437
(479) 783-6833

Central District of California

First Street U.S. Courthouse
350 W 1st Street, Suite 4311
Los Angeles, CA 90012-4565
(213) 894-1565

Edward R. Roybal Federal Building and United States Courthouse
255 East Temple Street
Los Angeles, CA 90012-3332

George E. Brown, Jr. Federal Building
and United States Courthouse
3470 Twelfth Street Riverside, CA 92501-3801
(951) 328-4450

Ronald Reagan Federal Building
and U.S. Courthouse
411 West 4th Street, Room 1053
Santa Ana, CA 92701-4516
(714) 338-4750

Eastern District of California

Robert T. Matsui Federal Courthouse
501 I Street, Room 4-200
Sacramento, CA 95814
(916) 930-4000

Robert E. Coyle Federal Courthouse
2500 Tulare Street, Room 1501
Fresno, CA 93721
(559) 499-5600

Northern District of California

United States District Court
450 Golden Gate Avenue
San Francisco, CA 94102
(415) 522-2000

Southern District of California

United States District Court
Southern District of California
333 West Broadway, Suite 420
San Diego, CA 92101
(619) 557-5600

District of Colorado

Alfred A. Arraj United States Courthouse, Room A105901
19th Street Denver, CO 80294-3589
(303) 844-3433

District of Connecticut

Richard C. Lee U.S. Courthouse
141 Church Street
New Haven, CT 06510
(203) 773-2140

Abraham Ribicoff Federal Building
450 Main Street
Suite A012
Hartford, CT 06103
(860) 240-3200

Brien McMahon Federal Building
915 Lafayette Boulevard
Bridgeport, CT 06604
(203) 579-5861

District of Delaware

United States District Court
844 North King St Unit 18
Wilmington, DE 19801-3570
(302) 573-6170

District of Columbia

United States District Court
333 Constitution Avenue N.W.
Washington D.C. 20001
Room 1225
(202) 354-3000

Middle District of Florida

United States District Court
2110 First Street
Fort Myers, Florida 33901
(239) 461-2000

United States District Court
300 North Hogan Street
Jacksonville, Florida 32202
(904) 549-1900

United States District Court
207 Northwest Second Street
Ocala, Florida 34475
(352) 369-4860

United States District Court
401 West Central Boulevard
Orlando, Florida 32801
(407) 835-4200

United States District Court
801 North Florida Avenue
Tampa, Florida 33602
(813) 301-5400

Northern District of Florida

United States Courthouse
401 SE First Avenue
Gainesville, FL 3260
(352) 380-2400

Southern District of Florida

Wilkie D. Ferguson, Jr. U.S. Courthouse
400 North Miami Avenue
Miami, FL 33128
(305) 523-5100

Middle District of Georgia

United States Courthouse
475 Mulberry Street
Macon, GA 31201
(478) 752-3497

United States Courthouse
201 West Broad Avenue
Albany, Georgia 31701
(229) 430-8432

United States Courthouse
115 East Hancock Avenue
Athens, Georgia 30601
(706) 227-1094

United States Courthouse
120 12th Street
Columbus, GA 31902
(706) 649-7816

United States Courthouse
401 North Patterson Street
Valdosta, GA 31601
(229) 242-3616

Northern District of Georgia

Richard B. Russell Federal Building
2211 United States Courthouse
75 Ted Turner Drive, SW
Atlanta, GA 30303-3309
(404) 215-1600

Southern District of Georgia

United States Courthouse
600 James Brown Blvd.
Augusta, GA 30901
(706) 849-4400

United States Courthouse
801 Gloucester Street
Brunswick, GA 31520
(912) 280-1330

United States Courthouse
125 Bull Street
Savannah, GA 31401
912-650-4020

United States Courthouse,
Dublin
PO Box 1130
Augusta, GA 30903

United States Courthouse,
Waycross
PO Box 1636

Brunswick, GA 31521
(912) 283-2870

United States Courthouse,
Statesboro
PO Box 8286
Savannah, GA 31412
(912) 764-3276

District of Guam

United States Courthouse
520 W Soledad Ave FL 4
Hagatna, Guam 96910
(671) 969-4500

District of Hawaii

United States Courthouse
300 Ala Moana Blvd., Room C338
Honolulu, HI 96850
(808) 541-1300

District of Idaho

United States Courthouse
550 W. Fort Street
Suite 400
Boise ID 83724
(208) 334-1361

Central District of Illinois

305 U.S. Courthouse
100 N.E. Monroe Street
Peoria, IL 61602
(309) 671-7117

218 U.S. Courthouse
201 S. Vine Street
Urbana, IL 61802
(217) 373-5830

151 U.S. Courthouse
600 E. Monroe Street
Springfield, IL 62701
(217) 492-4020

Clerk's Office (for filings)
322 16th Street
Suite 200 A
Rock Island, IL 61201

United States Courthouse
131 E. 4th Street
Davenport, IA 52801
(309) 793-5778

Northern District of Illinois

Everett McKinley Dirksen United States Courthouse
219 South Dearborn Street
Chicago, IL 60604
(312) 435-5670

Stanley J. Roszkowski United States Courthouse
327 South Church Street
Rockford, IL 61101
(815) 987-4354

Southern District of Illinois

United States Courthouse
301 West Main Street
Benton, IL 62812
(618) 439-7760

United States Courthouse
750 Missouri Avenue
East St. Louis, IL 62201
(618) 482-9371

Northern District of Indiana

United States District Court
1300 S. Harrison St.
Fort Wayne, IN 46802
(260) 423-3000

United States District Court
5400 Federal Plaza Suite 2300
Hammond, IN 46320
(219) 852-6500

United States District Court
Charles A. Halleck Federal Building
230 North Fourth St., Room 105
Lafayette, IN 47901-1322
(765) 420-6250

United States District Court
102 Federal Building
204 S Main St
South Bend, IN 46601
(574) 246-8000

Southern District of Indiana

Birch Bayh Federal Building & U.S. Courthouse
46 East Ohio Street
Indianapolis, IN 46204
(317) 229-3700

U.S. Courthouse
921 Ohio Street
Terre Haute, IN 47807
(812) 231-1840

Winfield K. Denton Federal Building & U.S. Courthouse
101 Northwest Martin Luther King Boulevard
Evansville, IN 47708
(812) 434-6410

Lee H. Hamilton Federal Building and U.S. Courthouse
121 West Spring Street
New Albany, IN 47150
(812) 542-4510

Northern District of Iowa

U.S. District Court
111 Seventh Avenue SE
Cedar Rapids, IA 52401-2101
(319) 286-2300

U.S. District Court
320 6th Street
Sioux City, IA 51101
(712) 233-3900

Southern District of Iowa

U.S. District Courthouse
123 East Walnut Street
Des Moines, IA 50309
(515) 284-6248

U.S. District Courthouse
131 East 4th Street
Davenport, IA 52801
(563) 884-7607

U.S. District Courthouse
8 South 6th Street
Council Bluffs, IA 51501
(712) 328-0283

District of Kansas

U.S. District Courthouse
500 State Ave
Kansas City, KS 66101
(913) 735-2200

U.S. District Courthouse
444 S.E. Quincy
Topeka, KS 66683
(785) 338-5400

U.S. District Courthouse
401 N. Market
Wichita, KS 67202
(316) 315-4200

Eastern District of Kentucky

U.S. District Courthouse
101 Barr Street
Lexington, KY 40507
(859) 233-2503

U.S. District Courthouse
1405 Greenup Avenue
Ashland, KY 41101
(606) 329-2465

U.S. District Courthouse
35 W. 5th Street
Covington, KY 41011
(859) 392-7925

U.S. District Courthouse
330 West Broadway
Frankfort, KY 40601
(502) 223-5225

U.S. District Courthouse
310 South Main Street

London, KY 40741
(606) 877-7910

U.S. District Courthouse
110 Main Street
Pikeville, KY 41501
(606) 437-6160

Western District of Kentucky

U.S. District Courthouse
241 East Main Street, Suite 120
Bowling Green, KY 42101-2175
(502) 625-3509

Eastern District of Louisiana

U.S. District Court
Eastern District of Louisiana
Room C-151
500 Poydras Street
New Orleans, LA 70130
(504) 589-7751

Middle District of Louisiana

Russell B. Long Federal Building and United States Courthouse
777 Florida Street
Suite 139
Baton Rouge, LA 70801
(225) 389-3500

Western District of Louisiana

United States Courthouse
515 Murray Street, Suite 105
Alexandria, LA 71301
(318) 473-7415

United States Courthouse
800 Lafayette Street, Suite 2100
Lafayette LA 70501
(337) 593-5000

United States Courthouse
800 Lafayette Street, Suite 2100
Lafayette LA70501
(337) 593-5000

United States Courthouse
201 Jackson Street, Suite 215
Monroe, LA 71201
(318) 322-6740

United States Courthouse
300 Fannin Street, Suite 1167
Shreveport, LA 71101
(318) 676-4273

District of Maine

Edward T. Gignoux U.S. Courthouse
156 Federal Street
Portland, ME 04101
(207) 780-3356

Margaret Chase Smith Federal Building & Courthouse
202 Harlow Street
Bangor, ME 04401
(207) 945-0575

District of Maryland

United States Courthouse
101 West Lombard Street
Baltimore, MD 21201
(410) 962-2600

United States Courthouse
6500 Cherrywood Lane
Greenbelt, MD 20770
(301) 344-0660

United States Courthouse
129 E. Main Street, Rm. 104
Salisbury, MD 21803
(410) 962-2600

District of Massachusetts

United States Courthouse
1 Courthouse Way
Boston, MA 02210
(617) 748-9152

United States Courthouse
595 Main Street

Worcester, MA 01608
(508) 929-9900

United States Courthouse
300 State Street
Springfield, MA 01105
(413) 785-6800

Eastern District of Michigan

Theodore Levin U.S. Courthouse
231 W. Lafayette Blvd., Room 599
Detroit, MI 48226
(313) 234-5000

United States Courthouse
P.O. Box 913
Bay City, MI 48707

Federal Building and U.S. Courthouse
600 Church Street, Room 140
Flint, MI 48502

Western District of Michigan

399 Federal Bldg.
110 Michigan St NW
Grand Rapids MI 49503
(616) 456-2381

113 Federal Bldg.
315 W Allegan St
Lansing MI 48933
(517) 377-1559

107 Federal Bldg.
410 W Michigan Ave
Kalamazoo MI 49007
(269) 337-5706

330 Federal Bldg.
202 W Washington St
PO Box 698
Marquette MI 49855
(906) 226-202

District of Minnesota

Diana E. Murphy United States Courthouse
300 South Fourth Street - Suite 202
Minneapolis, MN 55415
(612) 664-5000

Warren E. Burger Federal Building and U.S. Courthouse
316 North Robert Street - Suite 100
St. Paul, MN 55101

Gerald W. Heaney Federal Building and U.S. Courthouse and Customhouse
515 West First Street - Suite 417
Duluth, MN 55802-1397

Edward J. Devitt United States Courthouse and Federal Building
118 South Mill Street
212 USPO Building
Fergus Falls, MN 56537

Northern District of Mississippi

United States District Court
203 Gilmore Drive
Amory, MS 38821
(662) 369-4952

Post Office and Federal Building
305 Main Street
Greenville, MS 38701
(662) 234-1971

Federal Building
911 Jackson Avenue East
Oxford, MS 38655
(662) 234-1971

Southern District of Mississippi

Thad Cochran United States Courthouse
501 E. Court Street
Suite 2.500
Jackson, MS 39201
(601) 608-4000

William M. Colmer Federal Building & United States Courthouse
701 North Main Street, Suite 200
Hattiesburg, MS 39401
(601) 255-6400

Dan M. Russell, Jr., United States Courthouse
2012 15th Street, Suite 403
Gulfport, MS 39501
(228) 563-1700

United States Courthouse
109 South Pearl Street, 2nd Floor
Natchez, MS 39120

Eastern District of Missouri

United States Courthouse
111 South 10th Street
St. Louis, MO 63102
(314) 244-7900

Western District of Missouri

Charles Evans Whittaker U.S. Courthouse
400 E. 9th Street
Kansas City, MO 64106
(816) 512-5000

Christopher S. Bond Court House
80 Lafayette Street
Jefferson City, MO 65101
(573) 636-4015

United States Courthouse
222 N. John Q. Hammons Parkway
Springfield, MO 65806
(417) 865-3869

District of Montana

James F. Battin Federal Courthouse
2601 2nd Avenue North Billings, MT 59101
(406) 247-7000

Mike Mansfield Federal Courthouse
400 N. Main Butte, MT 59701
(406) 497-1279

Missouri River Federal Courthouse
125 Central Avenue West Great Falls, MT 59404
(406) 727-1922

Russell Smith Federal Courthouse
201 E. Broadway
Missoula, MT 59802
(406) 542-7260

District of Nebraska

Roman L. Hruska Federal Courthouse
111 South 18th Plaza
Suite 1152
Omaha, NE 68102
(402) 661-7350
(866) 220-4381

District of Nevada

Bruce R. Thompson Federal Courthouse
400 S. Virginia St.
Reno, NV 89501
(775) 686-5800

Lloyd D. George Federal Courthouse
333 Las Vegas Blvd. South
Las Vegas, NV 89101
(702) 464-5400

District of New Hampshire

U.S. District Court
55 Pleasant Street, Room 110
Concord, NH 03301
(603) 225-1423

District of New Jersey

Mitchell H. Cohen Building and U.S. Courthouse
4th & Cooper Streets
Camden, NJ 08101
(856) 757-5021

Martin Luther King Building and U.S. Courthouse
50 Walnut Street
Newark, NJ 07102
(973) 645-3730

Clarkson S. Fisher Building and U.S. Courthouse
402 East State Street
Trenton, NJ 08608
(609) 989-2065

District of New Mexico

Pete V. Domenici U.S. Courthouse
333 Lomas Blvd NW, Suite 270

Albuquerque, NM 87102
(505) 348-2000

U.S. District Court
100 N. Church Street, Suite 280
Las Cruces, NM, 88001
(575) 528-1400

Santiago E. Campos U.S. Courthouse
106 S. Federal Place
Santa Fe, NM, 87501
(505) 988-6481

U.S. Courthouse
500 N. Richardson
Roswell, NM 88201
(575) 637-7960

Eastern District of New York

U.S. Courthouse
225 Cadman Plaza East
Brooklyn, NY 11201
(718) 613-2665

U.S. Courthouse
100 Federal Plaza
Central Islip, NY 11722
(631) 712-6060

Northern District of New York

James T. Foley U.S. Courthouse
Suite 509
445 Broadway
Albany, NY 12207
(518) 257-1800

Binghamton U.S. Courthouse
15 Henry St.
Binghamton, NY 13901
(607) 773-2893

U.S. District Court
The Gateway Building
14 Durkee St.
Plattsburgh, NY 12901
(518) 247-4501

U.S. District Court
PO Box 7367
Syracuse, NY 13261
(315) 234-8500

Alexander Pirnie Federal Building & U.S. Courthouse
10 Broad St.
Utica, NY 13501
(315) 793-8151

Southern District of New York

Daniel Patrick Moynihan
United States Courthouse
500 Pearl Street
New York, NY 10007 – 1312
(212) 805-0136

Hon. Charles L. Brieant Jr.
Federal Building and Courthouse
300 Quarropas Street
White Plains, NY 10601
(914) 390-4100

Thurgood Marshall
United States Courthouse
40 Foley Square
New York, NY 10007
(212) 805-0175

United States Courthouse
355 Main Street
Poughkeepsie, NY 12601

Western District of New York

United States District Court
2 Niagara Square
Buffalo, NY 14202
(716) 551-1700

United States District Court
100 State Street
Rochester, NY 14614
(585) 613-4000

Eastern District of North Carolina

U.S. District Court
PO Box 25670

Raleigh, NC 27611
(919) 645-1700

United States Courthouse
201 South Evans St., Rm 209
Greenville, NC 27858
(252) 830.6009

United States Courthouse
413 Middle Street
New Bern, NC 28560
(252) 638.8534

United States Courthouse
1003 South 17th Street
Wilmington, NC 28401
(910) 815.4663

Middle District of North Carolina

U.S. District Court
L. Richardson Preyer Courthouse
324 W. Market Street
Greensboro, NC 27401-2544
(336) 332-6000

Western District of North Carolina

United States Courthouse
Charles R. Jonas Federal Building
401 West Trade Street, Room 1301
Charlotte, NC 28202
(704) 350-7400

United States Courthouse
100 Otis Street, Room 309
Asheville, NC 28801
(828) 771-7200

United States Courthouse
200 West Broad Street, Room 304
Statesville, NC 28677
(704) 883-1000

District of North Dakota

U.S. District Court
PO Box 1193
Bismarck ND 58502-1193
(701) 530-2300

Quentin N. Burdick
U.S. Courthouse
655 1st Ave. North, #130
Fargo, ND 58102-4932
(701) 297-7000

District of Northern Mariana Islands

United States District Court
P.O. Box 500687
Saipan, MP 96950
(670) 237-1200

Northern District of Ohio

John F. Seiberling Federal Building & U.S. Courthouse
2 South Main Street
Akron, Ohio 44308
(330) 252-6000

Carl B. Stokes U.S. Court House
801 West Superior Avenue
Cleveland, Ohio 44113
(216) 357-7000

James M. Ashley and Thomas W. L. Ashley U.S. Courthouse
1716 Spielbusch Avenue
Toledo, Ohio 43604
(419) 213-5500

Thomas D. Lambros Federal Building & U.S. Courthouse
125 Market Street
Youngstown, Ohio 44503
(330) 884-7400

Southern District of Ohio

Potter Stewart U.S. Courthouse, Room 103
100 East Fifth Street
Cincinnati, Ohio 45202
(513) 564-7500

Joseph P. Kinneary U.S. Courthouse, Room 121
85 Marconi Boulevard

Columbus, Ohio 43215
(614) 719-3000

Walter H. Rice Federal Building and U.S.
Courthouse, Room 712
200 W. Second Street
Dayton, Ohio 45402
(937) 512-1400

Eastern District of Oklahoma

U.S. District Court
PO Box 607
Muskogee, OK 74402
(918) 684-7920

Northern District of Oklahoma

Page Belcher Federal Building
333 W. 4th Street, Room 411
Tulsa, OK 74103
(918) 699-4700

Boulder Building
224 S. Boulder Ave.
Tulsa, OK 74103
(918) 699-4700

Western District of Oklahoma

William J. Holloway, Jr. United States
Courthouse
200 NW 4th Street
Oklahoma City, OK 73102
(405) 609-5000

District of Oregon

Mark O. Hatfield U.S. Courthouse
1000 S.W. Third Ave.
Portland, OR 97204
(503) 326-8000

Wayne L. Morse U.S. Courthouse
405 East Eighth Ave.
Eugene, OR 97401
(541) 431-4100

James A. Redden U.S. Courthouse
310 West Sixth St.
Medford, OR 97501
(541) 608-8777

Eastern District of Pennsylvania

James A. Byrne U.S. Courthouse
601 Market Street
Philadelphia, PA 19106
(215) 597-7704

Edward N. Cahn U.S. Courthouse & Federal
Bldg.
504 W. Hamilton Street
Allentown, PA 18101

The Gateway Building
201 Penn Street
Reading, PA 19601

Holmes Building, 4th Floor
101 Larry Holmes Drive
Easton, PA 18042-7722

Middle District of Pennsylvania

U.S. District Court
PO Box 1148
235 N. Washington Avenue
Scranton, PA 18501-1148
(570) 207-5600

U.S. District Court
228 Walnut Street,
P.O. Box 983
Harrisburg, PA 17108
(717) 221-3920

U.S. Courthouse and Federal Office Building
240 West Third Street, Suite 218
Williamsport, PA 17701
(570) 323-6380

Max Rosenn U.S. Courthouse
197 South Main Street
Wilkes-Barre, PA 18701

Western District of Pennsylvania

U.S. Courthouse
17 South Park Row

Erie, PA 16501
(814) 464-9600

U.S. Courthouse
208 Penn Traffic Building
319 Washington Street
Johnstown, PA 15901
(814) 533-4504

Joseph F. Weis, Jr.
U.S. Courthouse
700 Grant Street
Pittsburgh, PA 15219
(412) 208-7500

District of Puerto Rico

United States District Court
150 Ave. Carlos Chardon Ste. 150
San Juan, PR 00918-1767
(787) 772-3000

District of Rhode Island

One Exchange Terrace
Federal Building and Courthouse
Providence, RI 02903
(401) 752-7200

District of South Carolina

Charleston Federal Courthouse
85 Broad Street
Charleston, South Carolina 29401
(843) 579-1401

J. Waties Waring Judicial Center
83 Meeting Street
Charleston, South Carolina 29401

Matthew J. Perry, Jr. Courthouse
901 Richland Street
Columbia, South Carolina 29201
(803) 765-5816

McMillan Federal Building
401 West Evans Street
Florence, South Carolina 29501
(843) 676-3820

Clement F. Haynsworth Federal Building and
U.S. Courthouse
300 East Washington Street
Greenville, South Carolina 29601
(864) 241-2700

District of South Dakota

U.S. Courthouse
400 S Phillips Ave
Sioux Falls, SD 57104
(605) 330-6600

Andrew W. Bogue Federal Building and U.S.
Courthouse
515 Ninth Street
Rapid City, SD 57701
(605) 399-6000

PO Box 7147
U.S. Post Office and Courthouse
225 South Pierre Street
Pierre, SD 57501
(605) 945-4600

U.S. District Court
102 Fourth Avenue S.E., Room 408
Aberdeen, SD 57401
(605) 945-4600

Eastern District of Tennessee

U.S. District Court
900 Georgia Avenue, Suite 309
Chattanooga, TN 37402
(423) 752-5200

U.S. District Court
220 West Depot Street, Suite 200
Greeneville, TN 37743
(423) 639-3105

U.S. District Court
800 Market Street, Suite 130
Knoxville, TN 37902
(865) 545-4228

U.S. District Court
200 South Jefferson Street

Winchester, TN 37398
(931) 967-1444

Middle District of Tennessee

U.S. District Court
801 Broadway, Room 800
Nashville, TN 37203
(615) 736-5498

Western District of Tennessee

U.S. District Court
167 N. Main Street
Room 242
Memphis, TN 38103
(901) 495-1200

U.S. District Court
111 South Highland Avenue
Room 262
Jackson, TN 38301
(731) 421-9200

Eastern District of Texas

Jack Brooks Federal Building and United States Courthouse
300 Willow Street, Suite 104
Beaumont, TX 77701
(409) 654-7000

Ward R. Burke United States Courthouse
104 North Third Street
Lufkin, TX 75901
(936) 632-2739

Sam B. Hall Jr. Federal Building and United States Courthouse
100 East Houston Street Room 125
Marshall, TX 75670
(903) 935-2912

United States Courthouse
7940 Preston Road Room 101
Plano, TX 75024
(214) 872-4800

Paul Brown United States Courthouse
101 East Pecan Street Room 216
Sherman, TX 75090
(903) 892-2921

United States Courthouse and Post Office
500 North State Line Avenue, Room 301
Texarkana, TX 75501
(903) 794-8561

William M. Steger Federal Building and United States Courthouse
211 West Ferguson Street Room 106
Tyler, TX 75702
(903) 590-1000

Northern District of Texas

United States District Court
341 Pine Street, Room 2008
Abilene, TX 79601
(325) 677-6311

United States District Court
205 SE 5th Avenue, Room 133
Amarillo, TX 79101-1559
(806) 468-3800

United States District Court
1100 Commerce Street, Room 1452
Dallas, TX 75242
(214) 753-2200

United States District Court
501 West 10th Street, Room 310
Fort Worth, TX 76102-3673
(817) 850-6600

United States District Court
1205 Texas Avenue, Room 209
Lubbock, TX 79401-4091
(806) 472-1900

United States District Court
33 E. Twohig Avenue, Room 202
San Angelo, TX 76903-6451
(325) 655-4506

United States District Court
1000 Lamar Street, Room 203
Wichita Falls, TX 76301
(940) 767-1902

Southern District of Texas

United States District Court
600 E. Harrison St.
Brownsville, TX 78520
(956) 548-2500

United States District Court
1133 N. Shoreline Blvd.
Corpus Christi, TX 78401
(361) 888-3142

United States District Court
601 Rosenberg
Galveston, TX 77550
(409) 766-3530

United States District Court
515 Rusk Street
Houston, TX 77002
(713) 250-5500

United States District Court
1300 Victoria St.
Laredo, TX 78040
(956) 723-3542

United States District Court
1701 W. Business Hwy 83
McAllen, TX 78501
(956) 618-8065

United States District Court
312 S. Main, Room 406
Victoria, TX 77901
(361) 788-5000

Western District of Texas

U.S. District Court
2450 State Hwy. 118
Alpine, TX79830
(432) 837-7323

U.S. District Clerk's Office
501 West Fifth Street, Suite 1100
Austin, TX 78701
(512) 916-5896

U.S. District Clerk's Office
111 East Broadway, Room L100
Del Rio, TX 78840
(830) 703-2054

U.S. District Clerk's Office
525 Magoffin Avenue, Suite 105
El Paso, TX 79901
(915) 534-6725

MG Williams Judicial Center
P. O. Box 5507
Fort Hood, TX 76544-0507
(254) 287-5158

U.S. District Clerk's Office
200 East Wall, Room 222
Midland, TX 79701
(432) 686-4001

U.S. District Clerk's Office
410 South Cedar
Pecos, TX 79772
(432) 445-4228

U.S. District Clerk's Office
655 E. Cesar E. Chavez Blvd., Room G65
San Antonio, TX 78206
(210) 472-6550

U.S. District Clerk's Office
800 Franklin Ave., Room 380
Waco, TX 76701
(254) 750-1501

District of Utah

U.S. District Court
351 South West Temple
Salt Lake City, UT 84101
(801) 524-6100

District of Vermont

United States District Court
11 Elmwood Avenue, Room 200
Burlington, VT 05401
(802) 951-6301

District of Virgin Islands

Ron de Lugo Federal Building
5500 Veterans Drive, Rm 310
St. Thomas, VI 00802

Almeric L. Christian Federal Building
3013 Estate Golden Rock, Suite 219
St. Croix, VI 00820
(340) 718-1130

Eastern District of Virginia

United States District Court
600 Granby Street
Norfolk, VA 23510
(757) 222-7499

United States District Court
401 Courthouse Square
Alexandria, VA 22314

United States District Court
701 East Broad Street
Richmond, VA 23219

United States District Court
2400 West Avenue
Newport News, VA 23607
(757) 247-0785

Western District of Virginia

United States District Court
180 W. Main Street
Room 104
Abingdon, VA 24210
(276) 628-5116

United States District Court
180 W. Main Street, Room 104
Abingdon, VA 24210
(276) 523-3557

United States District Court
255 W. Main Street, Room 304
Charlottesville, VA 22902
(434) 296-9284

United States District Court
P.O. Box 1400
Danville, VA 24543
(434) 793-7147

United States District Court
116 N. Main Street, Room 314
Harrisonburg, VA 22802
(540) 434-3181

United States District Court
1101 Court Street, Suite A66
Lynchburg, VA 24504
(434) 847-5722

United States District Court
210 Franklin Road S.W., Suite 540
Roanoke, VA 24011-2208
(540) 857-5100

Eastern District of Washington

U.S. District Court
P.O. Box 1493
Spokane, WA 99210-1493
(509) 458-3400

U.S. District Court
PO Box 2706
Yakima, WA 98907
(509) 573-6600

U.S. District Court
825 Jadwin Avenue, Room 174
Richland, WA 99352
(509) 943-8170

Western District of Washington

U.S. District Court
700 Stewart Street, Suite 2310
Seattle, WA 98101
(206) 370-8400

U.S. Courthouse
1717 Pacific Avenue, Room 3100
Tacoma, WA 98402-3200
(253) 882-3800

Northern District of West Virginia

U.S. Courthouse
500 West Pike Street, Room 301
P.O. Box 2857
Clarksburg, WV 26302
(304) 622-8513

The Jennings Randolph Federal Center
P.O. Box 1518
300 Third Street
Elkins, WV 26241
(304) 636-1445

Southern District of West Virginia

U.S. Courthouse
601 Federal Street, Room 1000
Bluefield, WV 24701
(304) 327-9798

U.S. Courthouse
P. O. Box 2546
Charleston, WV 25329
(304) 347-3000

Sidney L. Christie Federal Building
845 Fifth Avenue, Room 101
Huntington, WV 25701
(304) 529-5588

U.S. Courthouse
110 North Heber Street, Room 119
Beckley, WV 25801
(304) 253-7481

Eastern District of Wisconsin

United States Federal Building and Courthouse
517 E. Wisconsin Ave. Rm. 362
Milwaukee, WI 53202
(414) 297-3372

Jefferson Court Building
125 S. Jefferson St., Rm. 102
Green Bay, WI 54301-4541
(920) 884-3720

Western District of Wisconsin

U.S. District Court
Western District of Wisconsin
120 North Henry Street, Room 320
Madison, WI 53703
(608) 264-5156

District of Wyoming

United States District Court
2120 Capitol Avenue, Room 2131
Cheyenne, WY 82001-3658
(307) 433-2120

United States District Court
111 South Wolcott, Room 121
Casper, WY 82601-2534
(307) 232-2620

Yellowstone Justice Center
P.O. Box 387
Yellowstone National Park, WY 82190
(307) 344-2569

FEDERAL COURT OF APPEALS DIRECTORY

U.S. Court of Appeals for the First Circuit

John Joseph Moakley U.S. Courthouse
1 Courthouse Way
Boston, MA 02210
(617) 748-9057

U.S. Court of Appeals for the Second Circuit

Thurgood Marshall United States Courthouse
40 Foley Square
New York, New York 10007
(212) 857-8500

U.S. Court of Appeals for the Third Circuit

James A. Byrne United States Courthouse
601 Market Street
Philadelphia, PA 19106
(215) 597-2995

U.S. Court of Appeals for the Fourth Circuit

Lewis F. Powell Jr. Courthouse and Annex
1100 East Main Street, Suite 501
Richmond, VA 23219
(804) 916-2700

U.S. Court of Appeals for the Fifth Circuit

600 S. Maestri Place, Suite 115
New Orleans, LA 70130
(504) 310-7700

U.S. Court of Appeals for the Sixth Circuit

Potter Stewart U.S. Courthouse
100 East Fifth Street
Cincinnati, Ohio 45202
(513) 564-7000

U.S. Court of Appeals for the Seventh Circuit

Everett McKinley Dirksen United States Courthouse
219 S. Dearborn Street, Room 2722
Chicago, IL 60604
(312) 435-5850

U.S. Court of Appeals for the Eighth Circuit

Thomas F. Eagleton Courthouse
111 South 10th Street
Room 24.329
St. Louis, MO. 63102
(314) 244-2400

U.S. Court of Appeals for the Ninth Circuit

The James R. Browning Courthouse
95 7th Street
San Francisco, CA 94103
(415) 355-8000

U.S. Court of Appeals for the Tenth Circuit

Byron White Court House
1823 Stout Street
Denver, CO 80257
(303) 844-3157

U.S. Court of Appeals for the Eleventh Circuit

Elbert P. Tuttle Courthouse
56 Forsyth Street, N.W.
Atlanta, GA 30303
(404) 335-6100

U.S. Court of Appeals for the District of Columbia Circuit

E. Barrett Prettyman U.S. Courthouse and
William B. Bryant Annex
333 Constitution Ave., NW, Room 5205
Washington, DC 20001
(202) 216-7000

U.S. Court of Appeals for the Federal Circuit

717 Madison Place, N.W., Room 401
Washington D.C. 20439
(202) 275-8000

GLOSSARY OF LEGAL TERMS ★★★

A

Acquittal: A jury verdict that a criminal defendant is not guilty or the finding of a judge that the evidence is insufficient to support a conviction.

Active judge: A judge in the full-time service of the court. Compared to senior judge.

Administrative Office of the United States Courts (AO): The federal agency responsible for collecting court statistics, administering the federal courts' budget, and performing many other administrative and programmatic functions under the direction and supervision of the Judicial Conference of the United States.

Admissible: A term used to describe evidence that may be considered by a jury or judge in civil and criminal cases.

Adversary proceeding: A lawsuit arising in or related to a bankruptcy case that begins by filing a complaint with the court, that is, a "trial" that takes place within the context of a bankruptcy case.

Affidavit: A written or printed statement made under oath.

Affirmed; In the practice of the court of appeals, it means that the court of appeals has concluded that the lower court decision is correct and will stand as rendered by the lower court.

Alternate juror: A juror selected in the same manner as a regular juror who hears all the evidence but does not help decide the case unless called on to replace a regular juror.

Alternative dispute resolution (ADR): A procedure for settling a dispute outside the courtroom. Most forms of ADR are not binding and involve the referral of the case to a neutral party such as an arbitrator or mediator.

Amicus curiae: Latin for "friend of the court." It is advice formally offered to the court in a brief filed by an entity interested in, but not a party to, the case.

Answer: The formal written statement by a defendant in a civil case that responds to a complaint, articulating the grounds for defense.

Appeal: A request made after a trial by a party that has lost on one or more issues, asking a higher court to review the decision to determine if it was correct. To make such a request is "to appeal" or "to take an appeal." One who appeals is called the "appellant;" the other party is the "appellee."

Appellant: The party who appeals a district court's decision, usually seeking reversal of that decision.

Appellate: About appeals, an appellate court has the power to review the judgment of a lower court (trial court) or tribunal. For example, the U.S. Circuit Courts of Appeals review the decisions of the U.S. District Courts.

Appellee: The party who opposes an appellant's appeal and who seeks to persuade the appeals court to affirm the district court's decision.

Arraignment: A proceeding in which a criminal defendant is brought into court, told of the charges in an indictment or information, and asked to plead guilty or not guilty.

Article III judge: A federal judge who is appointed for life, during "good behavior," under Article III of the Constitution. Article III judges are nominated by the President and confirmed by the Senate.

Assets: Property of all kinds, including real and personal, tangible and intangible.

Assume: An agreement to continue performing duties under a contract or lease.

Automatic stay: An injunction that automatically stops lawsuits, foreclosures, garnishments, and most collection activities against the debtor the moment a bankruptcy petition is filed.

B

Bail: The release, prior to trial, of a person accused of a crime under specified conditions designed to assure that person's appearance in court when required. Also, it can refer to the amount of bond money posted as a financial condition of pretrial release.

Bench trial: A trial without a jury, in which the judge serves as the factfinder.

Brief: A written statement submitted in a trial or appellate proceeding that explains one side's legal and factual arguments.

Burden of proof: The duty to prove disputed facts. In civil cases, a plaintiff generally has the burden of proving his or her case. In criminal cases, the government has the burden of proving the defendant's guilt. (See standard of proof.)

C

Capital offense: A crime punishable by death.

Case file: A complete collection of every document filed in court in a case.

Case law: The law as established in previous court decisions. A synonym for legal precedent. Akin to common law, which springs from tradition and judicial decisions.

Caseload: The number of cases handled by a judge or a court.

Cause of action: A legal claim.

Chambers: The offices of a judge and his or her staff.

Chief judge: The judge who has primary responsibility for the administration of a court; chief judges are determined by seniority

Clerk of court: The court officer who oversees administrative functions, especially managing the flow of cases through the court. The clerk's office is often called a court's central nervous system.

Common law: The legal system that originated in England and is now in use in the United States, which relies on the articulation of legal principles in a historical succession of judicial decisions. Common law principles can be changed by legislation.

Community service: A special condition the court imposes that requires an individual to work – without pay – for a civic or nonprofit organization.

Complaint: A written statement that begins a civil lawsuit in which the plaintiff details the claims against the defendant.

Concurrent sentence: Prison terms for two or more offenses to be served at the same time, rather than one after the other. Example: Two five-year sentences and one three-year sentence, if served concurrently, result in a maximum of five years behind bars.

Consecutive sentence: Prison terms for two or more offenses to be served one after the other. Example: Two five-year sentences and one three-year sentence, if served consecutively, result in a maximum sentence of 13 years in prison.

Contract: An agreement between two or more people that creates an obligation to do or not to do a particular thing.

Conviction: A judgment of guilt against a criminal defendant.

Counsel: Legal advice: a term also used to refer to the lawyers in a case.

Count: An allegation in an indictment or information, charging a defendant with a crime. An indictment or information may contain allegations that the defendant committed more than one crime. Each allegation is referred to as a count.

Court: Government entity authorized to resolve legal disputes. Judges sometimes use "court" to refer to themselves in the third person, as in "the court has read the briefs."

Court reporter: A person who makes a word-for-word record of what is said in court, generally by using a stenographic machine, shorthand, or audio recording, and then produces a transcript of the proceedings upon request.

D

Damages: Money that a defendant pays a plaintiff in a civil case if the plaintiff has won. Damages may be compensatory (for loss or injury) or punitive (to punish and deter future misconduct).

De facto: Latin, meaning "in fact" or "actually." Something that exists in fact but not as a matter of law.

De jure: Latin, meaning "in law." Something that exists by operation of law.

De novo: Latin, meaning "anew." A trial de novo is a completely new trial. Appellate review de novo implies no deference to the trial judge's ruling.

Declaratory judgment: A judge's statement about someone's rights. For example, a plaintiff may seek a declaratory judgment that a particular statute, as written, violates some constitutional right.

Default judgment: A judgment awarding a plaintiff the relief sought in the complaint because the defendant has failed to appear in court or otherwise respond to the complaint.

Defendant: An individual (or business) against whom a lawsuit is filed.

Defendant: In a civil case, the person or organization against whom the plaintiff brings suit; in a criminal case, the person accused of the crime.

Deposition: An oral statement made before an officer authorized by law to administer oaths. Such statements are often taken to examine potential witnesses, to obtain discovery, or to be used later in trial. See discovery.

Discovery: Procedures used to obtain disclosure of evidence before trial.

Dismissal with prejudice: Court action that prevents an identical lawsuit from being filed later.

Dismissal without prejudice: Court action that allows the later filing.

Docket: A log containing the complete history of each case in the form of brief chronological entries summarizing the court proceedings.

Due process: In criminal law, the constitutional guarantee that a defendant will receive a fair and impartial trial. In civil law, the legal rights of someone who confronts an adverse action threatening liberty or property.

E

En banc: French, meaning "on the bench." All judges of an appellate court sitting together to hear a case, as opposed to the routine disposition by panels of three judges. In the Ninth Circuit, an en banc panel consists of 11 randomly selected judges.

Evidence: Information presented in testimony or in documents that is used to persuade the fact finder (judge or jury) to decide the case in favor of one side or the other.

Ex parte: A proceeding brought before a court by one party only, without notice to or challenge by the other side.

Exclusionary rule: Doctrine that says evidence obtained in violation of a criminal defendant's constitutional or statutory rights is not admissible at trial.

Exculpatory evidence: Evidence indicating that a defendant did not commit the crime.

F

Federal Public Defender: An attorney employed by the federal courts on a full-time basis to provide legal defense to defendants who are unable to afford counsel. The judiciary administers the federal defender program pursuant to the Criminal Justice Act.

Federal Public Defender Organization: As provided for in the Criminal Justice Act, an organization established within a federal judicial circuit to represent criminal defendants who cannot afford an adequate defense. Each organization is supervised by a federal public defender appointed by the court of appeals for the circuit.

Federal question jurisdiction refers to the jurisdiction granted to federal courts in cases involving the interpretation and application of the U.S. Constitution, acts of Congress, and treaties.

Felony: A serious crime, usually punishable by at least one year in prison.

File: To place a paper in the official custody of the clerk of court to enter into the files or records of a case.

G

Grand jury: A body of 16-23 citizens who listen to evidence of criminal allegations, which is presented by the prosecutors, and determine whether there is probable cause to believe an individual committed an offense. See also indictment and U.S. attorney.

H

Habeas corpus: Latin, meaning "you have the body." A writ of habeas corpus generally is a judicial order forcing law enforcement authorities to produce a prisoner they are holding and to justify the prisoner's continued confinement. Federal judges receive petitions for a writ of habeas corpus from state prison inmates who say their state prosecutions violated federally protected rights in some way.

Hearsay: Evidence presented by a witness who did not see or hear the incident in question but heard about it from someone else. With some exceptions, hearsay generally is not admissible as evidence at trial.

Home confinement: A special condition the court imposes that requires an individual to remain at home except for certain approved activities such as work and medical appointments. Home confinement may include the use of electronic monitoring equipment, such as a transmitter attached to the wrist or ankle, to help ensure that the person stays at home as required.

I

Impeachment: 1. The process of calling a witness's testimony into doubt. For example, if the attorney can show that the witness may have fabricated portions of his testimony, the witness is said to be "impeached;" 2. The constitutional process whereby the House of Representatives may "impeach" (accuse of misconduct) high officers of the federal government, who are then tried by the Senate.

In camera: Latin, meaning in a judge's chambers. Often means outside the presence of a jury and the public, in private.

In forma pauperis: "In the manner of a pauper." Permission is given by the court to a person to file a case without payment of the required court fees because the person cannot pay them.

Inculpatory evidence: Evidence indicating that a defendant did commit the crime.

Indictment: The formal charge issued by a grand jury stating that there is enough evidence that the defendant committed the crime to justify having a trial; it is used primarily for felonies. See also information.

Information: A formal accusation by a government attorney that the defendant committed a misdemeanor. See also indictment.

Injunction: A court order preventing one or more named parties from taking some action. A preliminary injunction is often issued to allow fact-finding so a judge can determine whether a permanent injunction is justified.

Interrogatories: A form of discovery consisting of written questions to be answered in writing and under oath.

Issue 1. The disputed point between parties in a lawsuit; 2. To send out officially, as in a court issuing an order.

J

Judge: An official of the Judicial branch with authority to decide lawsuits brought before courts. Used generically, the term judge may also refer to all judicial officers, including Supreme Court justices.

Judgeship: The position of judge. By statute, Congress authorizes the number of judgeships for each district and appellate court.

Judgment: The official decision of a court to finally resolve the dispute between the parties to the lawsuit.

Judicial Conference of the United States The policy-making entity for the federal court system. A 27-judge body whose presiding officer is the Chief Justice of the United States.

Jurisdiction: The legal authority of a court to hear and decide a certain type of case. It is also used as a synonym for venue, meaning the geographic area over which the court has territorial jurisdiction to decide cases.

Jurisprudence: The study of law and the structure of the legal system

Jury: The group of persons selected to hear the evidence in a trial and render a verdict on matters of fact. See also grand jury.

Jury instructions: A judge's directions to the jury before it begins deliberations regarding the factual questions it must answer and the legal rules that it must apply.

L

Lawsuit: A legal action started by a plaintiff against a defendant based on a complaint that the defendant failed to perform a legal duty, which resulted in harm to the plaintiff.

Litigation A case, controversy, or lawsuit. Participants (plaintiffs and defendants) in lawsuits are called litigants.

M

Magistrate Judge: A judicial officer of a district court who conducts initial proceedings in criminal cases, decides criminal misdemeanor cases, conducts many pretrial civil and criminal matters on behalf of district judges, and decides civil cases with the consent of the parties.

Mental health treatment: A special condition the court imposes to require an individual to undergo evaluation and treatment for a mental disorder. Treatment may include psychiatric, psychological, and sex offense-specific evaluations, inpatient or outpatient counseling, and medication.

Misdemeanor: An offense punishable by one year of imprisonment or less. See also felony.

Mistrial: An invalid trial caused by fundamental error. When a mistrial is declared, the trial must start again with the selection of a new jury.

Moot: Not subject to a court ruling because the controversy has not actually arisen or has ended

Motion: A request by a litigant to a judge for a decision on an issue relating to the case.

Motion in Limine A pretrial motion requesting the court to prohibit the other side from presenting, or even referring to, evidence on matters said to be so highly prejudicial that no steps taken by the judge can prevent the jury from being unduly influenced.

N

Nolo contenderé: No contest. A plea of nolo contendere has the same effect as a plea of guilty, as far as the criminal sentence is concerned, but may not be considered as an admission of guilt for any other purpose.

O

Opinion: A judge's written explanation of the decision of the court. Because a case may be heard by three or more judges in the Court of Appeals, the opinion in appellate decisions can take several forms. If all the judges completely agree on the result, one judge will write the opinion for all. If all the judges do not agree, the formal decision will be based upon the view of the majority, and one member of the majority will write the opinion. The judges who did not agree with the majority may write separately in dissenting or concurring opinions to present their views. A dissenting opinion disagrees with the majority opinion because of the reasoning and/or the principles of law the majority used to decide the case. A concurring opinion agrees with the decision of the majority opinion but offers further comment or clarification or even an entirely different reason for reaching the same result. Only the majority opinion can serve as a binding precedent in future cases. See also precedent.

Oral argument: An opportunity for lawyers to summarize their position before the court and also to answer the judges' questions.

P

Panel: 1. In appellate cases, a group of judges (usually three) is assigned to decide the case; 2. In the jury selection process, the group of potential jurors; 3. The list of attorneys who are both available and qualified to serve as court-appointed counsel for criminal defendants who cannot afford their own counsel.

Parole: The release of a prison inmate – granted by the U.S. Parole Commission – after the inmate has completed part of his or her sentence in a federal prison. When the parolee is released to the community, he or she is placed under the supervision of a U.S. probation officer.

The Sentencing Reform Act of 1984 abolished parole in favor of a determinate sentencing system in which the sentence is set by sentencing guidelines. Now, without the option of parole, the term of imprisonment the court imposes is the actual time the person spends in prison.

Per curiam Latin, meaning "for the court." In appellate courts, often refers to an unsigned opinion.

Peremptory challenge A district court may grant each side in a civil or criminal trial the right to exclude a certain number of prospective jurors without cause or giving a reason.

Petit jury (or trial jury): A group of citizens who hear the evidence presented by both sides at trial and determine the facts in dispute. Federal criminal juries consist of 12 persons. Federal civil juries consist of at least six persons.

Petty offense: A federal misdemeanor punishable by six months or less in prison.

Plaintiff: A person or business that files a formal complaint with the court.

Plea: In a criminal case, the defendant's statement pleading "guilty" or "not guilty" in answer to the charges. See also nolo contendere.

Pleadings: Written statements filed with the court that describe a party's legal or factual assertions about the case.

Precedent: A court decision in an earlier case with facts and legal issues similar to a dispute currently before a court. Judges will generally "follow precedent," - meaning that they use the principles established in earlier cases to decide new cases that have similar facts and raise similar legal issues. A judge will disregard precedent if a party can show that the earlier case was wrongly decided, or that it differed in some significant way from the current case.

Presentence report: A report prepared by a court's probation officer after a person has been convicted of an offense, summarizing for the court the background information needed to determine the appropriate sentence.

Pretrial conference: A meeting of the judge and lawyers to plan the trial, discuss which matters should be presented to the jury, review proposed evidence and witnesses, and set a trial schedule. Typically, the judge and the parties also discuss the possibility of settlement of the case.

Pretrial service: A function of the federal courts that takes place at the very start of the criminal justice process – after a person has been arrested and charged with a federal crime and before he or she goes to trial. Pretrial services officers focus on investigating the backgrounds of these persons to help the court determine whether to release or detain them while they await trial. The decision is based on whether these individuals are likely to flee or pose a threat to the community. If the court orders release, a pretrial services officer supervises the person in the community until he or she returns to court.

Pro per: A slang expression sometimes used to refer to a pro se litigant. It is a corruption of the Latin phrase "in propria persona."

Pro se Representing oneself. Serving as one's own lawyer.

Pro tem: Temporary.

Probation Sentencing option in the federal courts. With probation, instead of sending an individual to prison, the court releases the person to the community and orders him or her to complete a period of supervision monitored by a U.S. probation officer and to abide by certain conditions.

Probation officer Officers of the probation office of a court. Probation officer duties include conducting presentence investigations, preparing presentence reports on convicted defendants, and supervising released defendants.

Procedure: The rules for conducting a lawsuit; there are rules of civil procedure, criminal procedure, evidence, bankruptcy, and appellate procedure.

Prosecute: To charge someone with a crime. A prosecutor tries a criminal case on behalf of the government

R

Record A written account of the proceedings in a case, including all pleadings, evidence, and exhibits submitted in the course of the case.

Remand: Send back.

Reverse: The act of a court setting aside the decision of a lower court. A reversal is often accompanied by a remand to the lower court for further proceedings.

S

Sanction: A penalty or other type of enforcement used to bring about compliance with the law or with rules and regulations.

Senior judge: A federal judge who, after attaining the requisite age and length of judicial experience, takes senior status, thus creating a vacancy among a court's active judges. A senior judge retains the judicial office and may cut back his or her workload by as much as 75 percent, but many opt to keep a larger caseload.

Sentence: The punishment ordered by a court for a defendant convicted of a crime.

Sentencing guidelines: A set of rules and principles established by the United States Sentencing Commission that trial judges use to determine the sentence for a convicted defendant.

Sequester To separate. Sometimes, juries are sequestered from outside influences during their deliberations.

Service of process The delivery of writs or summonses to the appropriate party.

Standard of Proof: Degree of Proof Required. In criminal cases, prosecutors must prove a defendant's guilt "beyond a reasonable doubt." The majority of civil lawsuits require proof "by a preponderance of the evidence" (50 percent plus), but in some the standard is higher and requires "clear and convincing" proof.

Statute: A law passed by a legislature.

Statute of limitations: The time within which a lawsuit must be filed or a criminal prosecution must begin. The deadline can vary, depending on the type of civil case or the crime charged.

Sua sponte Latin, meaning "of its own will." Often refers to a court taking an action in a case without being asked to do so by either side.

Subordination: The act or process by which a person's rights or claims are ranked below those of others.

Subpoena: A command issued under a court's authority to a witness to appear and give testimony.

Subpoena duces tecum A command to a witness to appear and produce documents.

T

Temporary restraining order Akin to a preliminary injunction, it is a judge's short-term order forbidding certain actions until a full hearing can be conducted. Often referred to as a TRO.

Testimony Evidence presented orally by witnesses during trials or before grand juries.

Toll: See statute of limitations.

Tort: A civil, not criminal, wrong. A negligent or intentional injury against a person or property, with the exception of breach of contract.

Transcript: A written, word-for-word record of what was said, either in a proceeding such as a trial, or during some other formal conversation, such as a hearing or oral deposition

U

U.S. Attorney: A lawyer appointed by the President in each judicial district to prosecute and defend cases for the federal government. The U.S. Attorney employs a staff of Assistant U.S. Attorneys who appear as the government's attorneys in individual cases.

Uphold The appellate court agrees with the lower court decision and allows it to stand. See affirmed.

V

Venue: The geographic area in which a court has jurisdiction. A change of venue is a change or transfer of a case from one judicial district to another.

Verdict: The decision of a trial jury or a judge that determines the guilt or innocence of a criminal defendant or that determines the final outcome of a civil case.

Voir dire: Jury selection process of questioning prospective jurors, to ascertain their qualifications and determine any basis for challenge.

W

Warrant Court authorization, most often for law enforcement officers, to conduct a search or make an arrest.

Witness: A person called upon by either side in a lawsuit to give testimony before the court or jury.

Writ: A written court order directing a person to take, or refrain from taking, a certain act.

Writ of certiorari: An order issued by the U.S. Supreme Court directing the lower court to transmit records for a case which it will hear on appeal.

A MOMENT WITH THE AUTHOR

Often, more than I can count actually, I have been asked by fellow prisoners and correctional officers where I stand politically. Up until now it has been my policy not to discuss politics or religion, so I have usually declined to answer questions related to either. But recently I've been thinking that since so many prisoners *automatically* identify as "Democrat," without having any relative understanding of what being a Democrat can mean, I would give my opinions and thoughts, finally.

The number one reason given by most prisoners when asked their political stance, that of being a Democrat, is: "I want better prison laws and to be released." This answer has always perplexed me, since, well, Democrats have traditionally, and historically passed the most restrictive laws relative to prisons, those that negatively affect prisoners. For instance, the AEDPA and PLRA, written and pushed through in 1996 under Democratic President Bill Clinton and supported by current President Joe Biden.

The AEDPA and PLRA are two laws that worsened, and in many cases completely eliminate a prisoner's ability to challenge their convictions and sentences, as well as to file lawsuits to protect their rights while in prison. After having a Congress controlled by Democrats, as well as a Democratic President in Obama, those laws were never repealed or amended. Simply stated, Democrats have not done a damn thing for prisoners.

So why do ninety-nine percent of prisoners stand as Democrats? The simple answer is, ego.

Even considering all of the negative effects and consequences of a socialist society, we prisoners tend to think only of ourselves and what benefits "us" – earlier release, better prison conditions, etc. – all of which, as I've explained, is simply untrue and unlikely under Democrat leadership. But, even if it were possible, consider the effects it would have on, for instance … your children.

Democrats spend without regards to inflation, Gross Domestic Product, or considerations related to consumption. Democrats pass laws that allow transgenders to share a bathroom with your daughter and to compete against her in sporting events (see Biden's Executive Order: EO 13988). Democrats pass laws that allow our country to be invaded by foreign entities through immigration, which have committed atrocities against the United States (see Biden's Executive Order: EO 10141).

Democrats pass laws that allow for your earnings and hard work to be "split equally" amongst those who have no motivation to succeed, and simply live off of your hard work and achievements. This is what a "Socialist Society" means and does. Democrats allow our southern border to be overrun by Mexican Nationals to the extent we cannot effectively operate our customs, traditions, and agendas that have made our country elite for 300 years.

I have nothing against Mexican Nationals whatsoever, and I appreciate their heritage, customs, and work ethic. But why do you think they want to leave Mexico so badly and seek refuge here in America in the first place? It is because of our institutions and infrastructure – the most sought in the entire world … far better than those of Mexico are.

We are educated, wealthy by measure, healthy, militarily elite, and we have values and principles – all of which have been made and measured by conservative means over the past 200 years. By conservative, I mean Republican. By Republican, I mean God-fearing and Bible-following Christians.

When Democrats look at others, their ego evokes envy and hate, a desire to control. They truly don't wish everyone well, at least not more so than themselves. They might want to see you successful, but not more successful than they are. Need proof? Well, think back to all of the wars America has fought over the long history of our country. Who were the Presidents at the times of those wars? Woodrow Wilson, Franklin Roosevelt, Lyndon B. Johnson, Harry S. Truman … far more Democrats than Republicans, indeed.

Republicans wage war when it becomes necessary to advance the safety and security of our nation, and only if it cannot be avoided. Republicans build strength and security in our elite military, so other nations do not even think about trying to push us around. Have Republican Presidents gone to war? Yes. But did they do so of their own initiative and choice, or because we were attacked in some sort of way? Ahhhhhhhh … the truth now emerges.

Are you a conspiracy theorist, like most prisoners? Then think of this: Pearl Harbor, the Kennedy Assassination, World War II, 9/11, etc., are all believed to have been carried out by the CIA, if you follow conspiracy logic. The CIA is most funded by Democrats. And we only went to World War I and II because leaders of those other countries, like Winston Churchill, begged Democratic Presidents to help them fight.

And so here we are again, back to the ego.

Ego is the will and desire to receive and to enjoy by yourself, for yourself, even when it is at the expense of other people … like your mother, father, grandparents, and children … people you love, adore, and swear to protect in every way.

So, while Democrats *might* eventually pass laws that will help *you*, those same laws will effectively hurt and harm those you claim to love and protect. Imagine walking out of prison only to find your loved ones being killed in war or working endless hours to pay the bills because they have to share their income with freeloaders.

You learn your first day out that at school your daughter is forced to use the bathroom where boys can walk in and see her without any consequences; you find your mother has contracted a disease brought into our country by sick immigrants who have not been vaccinated and are dying. Or you learn your dad has been killed in terrorist attack here in the U.S., because foreigners were allowed to immigrate here in spite of their open hatred for America. Your aunt and uncle are dying at home because someone broke in to rob them, and there were not enough police officers to respond to their calls for help because Democrats defunded them.

Even now your children are receiving far less of an education than you were offered, because schools are no longer allowed to effectively teach them due to the beliefs, customs, and religions of foreign or immigrant children. Today children are not even taught cursive writing. And American History is out because "it offends others," so we are limited to Black History, Asian History, and Spanish Cultures in our American schools. Democrats have made this the policy, even though mixed culture *is* American History.

Are you willing to make those you love sacrifice and suffer, just because you want to get out of prison early? Really? Because that is what being a Democrat means. Or are you willing to suffer for them in order for them to have a good, safe, and prosperous life in your absence? Me personally, I will stay here forever if it means that my loved ones have the best life available for them in my absence, without hesitation.

True love is all about personal sacrifice and suffering.

Our ego is like a software program in a computer that immerses us from within. It draws all of our attention to ourselves and makes us focus only on ourselves, at the expense of everyone else … at the expense of those that love us and whom we claim to love in return.

True love means to regard others as we do ourselves, to know their wishes and desires, to sense their needs and dreams, and to do whatever we can to protect, nourish, and guarantee their success and happiness.

Do you believe it a coincidence that the majority if COVID deaths are black, Hispanic, and dark-complected people, people who are traditionally Democrat? Or that COVID exploded just before a presidential election? Do you believe it is just coincidence that the country responsible for the release of COVID is China, who has a long history and financial connection to the man who was running for President on the Democratic ticket, Joe Biden? I'm talking to my conspiracy theorists here.

Fear invokes action faster than any other force. Fear of getting COVID sent 170 Million Democrats, many of them African Americans and Hispanics, to the election polls for the first time in American History. Without COVID, Joe Biden could never have defeated Donald Trump, and he knew it.

Still don't agree? Then take a look at the retirement homes in America that house our elderly relatives. We have the greatest number of retirement and nursing homes in the entire world. Why? Because the family members of those elderly people simply don't want to carry the burdens associated with caring for someone who is old or disabled. They don't want to have their own lives and freedoms hindered by the issues associated with caring for an elderly person. Why else would someone abandon their elderly loved one to be cared for (or not) by complete strangers, people who do not love them at all? This is morally forbidden in most every other country in the world – including China, North Korea, Russia, and even Iran.

The answer is ego.

It's no more complicated than that.

Recently, someone told me that "I'm Democrat because Jesus was." I stood in complete amazement, as he truly believed that. As I wrote in my book, *Ask. Believe. Receive. Our Power to Control Our Own Destiny*, Jesus was certainly not a Democrat, nor was He poor, and He did not have an ego.

His parents were traveling to Bethlehem to pay their taxes; something poor people did not do. Joseph and Mary only stayed in the "manger" because there wasn't any more room at the inn – not because they couldn't afford it. Further, Jesus had a large estate and surrounded himself with large groups that he was responsible for feeding, clothing, etc. He went to school to learn how to be a carpenter, which poor folks did not do in those times or even today. All of these things are common today in Republican households and systems: affluence, education, and accountability.

And so, in closing out my thoughts, I ask you … are you a true Democrat? Do you want prison reform and change at the expense of those you love and hold dear? Are you enjoying your stimulus money or hoping for it, in spite of it meaning that your children and grandchildren will have to work harder and longer to repay it all? Do you care that your children and grandchildren will not have Social Security or Retirement Fund when they are older, because inflation has crippled the value of the dollar? Are you comfortable with the fact that they will have to work well into their 70s and 80s just to survive, all so *you* can have a few "benefits" today?

If you are willing to push that responsibility and hardships on those that you truly love and hold dear, then I say, yes, you are certainly a Democrat.

However, if you appreciate discipline, accountability, faith, education, health, wealth, business, free-trade, freedom, safety, and long-term advancements and increases … then no, you are not a Democrat.

So, in answer to all of those questions concerning my political leaning, I identify (to borrow a leftist term) as a Libertarian Republican. I hold value to the ways we were raised in this country "back in the day," as well as the independence, freedom, and liberty associated with a smaller government, absent in our private lives and choices.

I believe in military, police, and infrastructure. I believe in family, values, and tradition. I believe in education, faith, and freedom. I believe in our Constitution, in its original meaning. I believe in prisons, jails, and accountability, although I also believe in reform and humanity during incarceration. I believe in a "higher power" regardless of its name. I believe in love, a soul, and eternity.

I believe in immigration, but only a controlled immigration. I believe in police, emergency response, and law enforcement, just as much as I believe in our military. Defunding any endangers us all.

I believe that mothers should lead our countries and guide us in all things. Imagine a United Nations, Congressional Hearing, or Senate Hearing where the mothers of our leaders could attend. Put Putin, Biden, Trump, or any world leader in a room with their mother and watch them turn to putty. Mothers would make the entire world better.

I believe that every race, ethnicity, culture, and creed is only responsible for ensuring its own success and continuance. Nature weeds out the weak in all things: plants, animals, sea creatures, and entire cultures. If one culture ensures the survival of another by "leveling the playing field" it is counteracting nature's way of ending the weakest link. It should not be so. Nature and higher powers intended all things to stand on their own. Nobody owes anything to the other, and only the strong and capable should conquer and advance.

I believe a state should be limited in its punishment to that of the United States government. No state should be able to punish an individual more severely than the federal government itself would allow.

I believe in life after death, and I believe the purpose of life is to train our soul and prepare it for the ever after – whatever and wherever that might be.

I believe we all have a single soulmate and no matter what or who else we spend time with, we eventually return to that person who never leaves our thoughts and heart.

Finally, I believe that our children are our most precious natural resource. They are God's way of showing us that He hasn't yet given up on us; His way of rewarding us for our struggles and hardships.

And now you know.

– R.

ABOUT THE AUTHOR

Raymond E. Lumsden continues to fight his wrongful conviction and sentence from within the Texas Department of Criminal Justice. In addition, he continues the fight for prison reform through impact civil rights litigation(s) in the federal courts of Texas, Fifth Circuit Court of Appeals, and the United States Supreme Court.

This is his fourth book in a *pro se* legal series, which is dedicated to educating and assisting *pro se* litigants in their post-conviction, civil rights, criminal law, and legal research & writing pursuits. Raymond is extensively educated, trained, and certified in all areas of law. Currently, he is completing his Juris Doctorate Program, and also recently graduated from a three-year Astrology Program with Honors. Like a true Sagittarian, Raymond's thirst for knowledge and education is unquenchable. Soon, he will begin a two-year correspondence program, in Advanced Forensic DNA Study.

Raymond is a Minnesota raised Native, and a diehard Chicago Bears Fan.

More importantly, Raymond is the proud father of Anthony, Alyssa, Joshua, and Rylee. He has two grandchildren, Rysen and Aniyah.

FREEBIRD PUBLISHERS

Thanks for your interest in Freebird Publishers!

We value our customers and would love to hear from you! Reviews are an important part in bringing you quality publications. We love hearing from our readers-rather it's good or bad (though we strive for the best)!

If you could take the time to review/rate any publication you've purchased with Freebird Publishers we would appreciate it!

If your loved one uses Amazon, have them post your review on the books you've read. This will help us tremendously, in providing future publications that are even more useful to our readers and growing our business.

Amazon works off of a 5 star rating system. When having your loved one rate us be sure to give them your chosen star number as well as a written review. Though written reviews aren't required, we truly appreciate hearing from you.

Sample Review Received on Inmate Shopper

poeticsunshine

Truly a guide

Reviewed in the United States on June 29, 2023

Verified Purchase

This book is a powerhouse of information. My son had to calm/ground himself to prioritize where to start.

Made in United States
Cleveland, OH
05 November 2026

47670551R00220